Fort Worth Then

Fort Worth Then

The Art of Samuel P. Ziegler

Scott Grant Barker and Gregory H. Dow

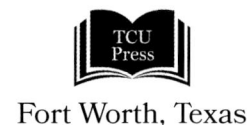

TCU
Press

Fort Worth, Texas

Library of Congress Cataloging-in-Publication Data

Names: Barker, Scott Grant, author. | Ziegler, Samuel P., 1882-1967,
  artist. | Dow, Gregory H., 1955- author. | Tyler, Ronnie C., 1941-
  writer of preface.
Title: Fort Worth then : the art of Samuel P. Ziegler / Scott Grant Barker
  and Gregory H. Dow.
Description: Fort Worth : TCU Press, [2023] | Includes bibliographical
  references.
Identifiers: LCCN 2023007068 | ISBN 9780875658506 (hardcover)
Subjects: LCSH: Ziegler, Samuel P., 1882-1967–Themes, motives. | Landscape
  painting–Texas–Fort Worth. | Art, American–Texas–Fort Worth. | Fort
  Worth (Tex.)–In art. | Fort Worth (Tex.)–Economic conditions–20th
  century. | Fort Worth (Tex.)–In art.
Classification: LCC N6537.Z544 B37 2023 | DDC
  709.764/531–dc23/eng/20230227
LC record available at https://lccn.loc.gov/2023007068

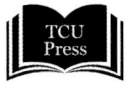

TCU Box 298300
Fort Worth, Texas 76129
www.tcupress.com

Design by Bill Brammer

Contents

About the Artist

Selected Works of Art

Foreword

Ron Tyler

Texas entered the twentieth century with "all hands busy, all wheels humming," according to the Navasota *Daily Examiner*.[1] Its most important seaport, Galveston, had been virtually destroyed by a hurricane in September 1900, but railroads had linked the remotest parts of the then-largest state in the Union, and in January 1901 the unprecedented geyser that erupted from the Spindletop salt dome near Beaumont marked the beginning of the modern petroleum industry. Its cities grew substantially as immigrants from the Old South and Europe made it the second-most populous state west of the Mississippi River (behind Missouri) and "the only Southern State which is fully imbued with the spirit of Northern enterprise," according to a correspondent for the trade journal the *American Stationer*.[2] Another traveling salesman candidly remarked that "Texas is an empire in itself."[3]

Yet Texas was still largely a rural state in 1900, with agriculture dominating the economy. Windmills and barbed wire had opened West Texas cattle country to cotton growing, where the "rough men with wild, staring eyes" that President Chester A. Arthur had condemned in 1881 still herded livestock.[4] As their image evolved, cowboys became prominent subjects for novelists such as Owen Wister and artists Frederic Remington and Charles M. Russell—and, in one instance, even Samuel P. Ziegler.

Ziegler was a thirty-five-year-old skilled musician and trained artist when he arrived in the growing city of Fort Worth in the fall of 1917. He immediately employed his talents, teaching music at Texas Christian University and, in his spare time, exploring and documenting his new community. He soon produced landscape paintings and drawings of the TCU campus; the stately Carnegie Public Library; the construction of the Sanguinet & Staats–designed W. T. Waggoner Building, one of the tallest buildings in the Southwest; and the ornate Majestic Theatre, where he sometimes played in the orchestra. "Samuel P. Ziegler . . . has caught all the light and color . . . in his canvas," according to a *Fort Worth Star-Telegram* critic.[5] He became president of the Fort Worth Painters Club in 1931.[6]

Observant of his new home, Ziegler watched as Fort Worth transitioned from a regional agricultural, railroad, and meat packing center to the state's fourth largest city: in rapid succession General Motors built a new Chevrolet factory in 1916; Camp Bowie, established in 1917, trained more than one hundred thousand soldiers in World War I; and major oil strikes in West Texas—Breckenridge, Ranger, and Desdemona—brought rapid social and economic change, oil-related jobs, and ancillary businesses while creating several local millionaires. The city's population reached 106,482 by 1920.

Ziegler took up etching and lithography in the late 1920s and 1930s, several years before the founding of such print-related organizations as the Associated American Artists, the Dallas Print and Drawing Collectors Society, and the Lone Star Printmakers, and before the artists of the Fort Worth Circle became prominent. Like many of his contemporaries—printmakers John Sloan, Martin Lewis, and Louis Lozowick in New York and Robert Riggs in Philadelphia, for examples— his subjects were hometown views: the TCU campus, churches, the new Post Office and Texas & Pacific Railway station, the farmer's market, Bewley Mills, Forest Park, scenes of the Ranger oil-fields, and the nearby cowboys and ranches. He sketched in West Texas, the Davis Mountains, and New Mexico.[7]

Meanwhile, Ziegler taught hundreds of students at TCU, especially after World War II, when the GI Bill enabled many veterans to attend college. Among them were the modernist painter Jack Boynton and Melvin C. Warren, who became a noted western artist and sculptor. In 1948, Ziegler presented an exhibition in celebration of TCU's seventy-fifth anniversary, prompting a *Star-Telegram* reporter to observe that "every painting has a story."[8]

Artist and *Star-Telegram* columnist Sallie Blyth Mummert noted that Ziegler's "accurate renderings of some of the architectural history of our city . . . added greatly to the cultural life of Fort Worth." She even found his picture of "an automobile, aloft on a greasing stand[,]" an "everyday modern activity in an amusing composition," concluding that, as with all good art, Ziegler's work "makes one realize that all life is very entertaining if only we have time to pause and eyes to see."[9] Unfortunately, Ziegler printed few copies of his images, making them almost as rare as his paintings and drawings. But they provide a fascinating and unique document of the city's explosive growth between World Wars I and II.

[1]"'Tis a Brand-New Year," *Daily Examiner* (Navasota, TX), Jan. 1, 1900, 1.

[2]George W. Knott, "Texas," *American Stationer*, 26 (Aug. 15, 1889), 400.

[3]"Signs of the Times," *Stoves and Hardware Reporter*, 29 (July 22, 1897), 11.

[4]Chester A. Arthur, First Annual Message, Dec. 6, 1881, http://www.presidency.ucsb.edu/ws/index.php?pid=29522. Accessed June 8, 2022.

[5]Sallie Blyth Mummert, "Growth of Texas Art Seen in New Exhibit," *Fort Worth Star-Telegram*, May 30, 1922.

[6]"Painters' Club Hears Talk by Prof. Gaines," *Fort Worth Star-Telegram*, Feb. 8, 1931.

[7]Sallie Blyth Mummert, "Local Artists Anticipate Fiesta Show," *Fort Worth Star-Telegram*, June 13, 1937.

[8]"Paintings by S. P. Ziegler Depict Growth of TCU," *Fort Worth Star-Telegram*, June 6, 1948.

[9]"Ziegler Exhibit of Unusual Interest," *Fort Worth Star-Telegram*, Jan. 15, 1933.

The Art of Samuel P. Ziegler
Through the Eyes of a Collector

Gregory H. Dow

Samuel P. Ziegler was born on January 4, 1882, the oldest of nine siblings. His father, Christian Ziegler, was a Pennsylvania farmer by trade and married to Mary Rebecca Peters. The Ziegler family immigrated to Lancaster County, Pennsylvania, from Württemberg, Germany. Samuel left the family farm to attend the Pennsylvania Academy of the Fine Arts in Philadelphia, where he studied under William Merritt Chase, Thomas P. Anschutz, and Hugh H. Breckenridge. All three of these artists were accomplished portrait painters, but their real interest was impressionism. These three teachers had a profound influence on Ziegler and his painting style.

Ziegler painted his first small landscape in June of 1905. The landscape's loose brushwork presaged the impressionistic style that his later paintings would feature. He was among a select group to win the Pennsylvania Academy's top award, a William Emlen Cresson Memorial Traveling Scholarship in 1912, a cash award that allowed him to travel to European art centers that year. He returned to Philadelphia and the academy by 1914. He spent most of his time in 1915 sketching the Pennsylvania countryside and working as a contract musician in the resort town of Beach Haven, New Jersey, where he painted a number of small impressionist beach scenes.

Samuel Ziegler moved to Fort Worth, Texas, in September 1917 to take a position with the music faculty of Texas Christian University. Two events happened in Fort Worth about the same time: the U. S. Army training camp called Camp Bowie officially opened August 24, 1917, in Arlington Heights, and oil was discovered on the McCleskey farm near Ranger, Texas, in October 1917, leading to a rapid expansion of Fort Worth's economy. Over 100,000 men were trained at Camp Bowie before they left for the European front and the largest war the world had seen up to that time. The oil boom was on in Fort Worth as many oil companies moved their offices to town. Ziegler later produced an etching of the J. H. McCleskey No. 1 well, a historically significant image among the several oil well etchings that he made. His broken-stroke painting style had matured by 1922, when he produced a large oil painting of the Fort Worth Carnegie Public Library at night. This painting of the library hung in the University Club at the Metropolitan Hotel in downtown Fort Worth for many years.

Ziegler's favorite landscape subject was the Trinity River, the focus of a series he liked to call "creek bank" paintings. He produced numerous oil paintings and even an etching of the river during the years between his arrival in Texas up to about 1935. Some of his best impressionist paintings were painted in the period of 1928 to 1932. This is when he produced many works using the broken color technique that he had mastered.

He painted some portraiture, but his main interests, in addition to the Trinity River, were Fort Worth scenery and the changing downtown skyline. As the cut stone buildings of the late nineteenth century were being razed to make way for the new art deco / PWA-style buildings, he was there to record the transition. His usual approach to an artistic idea was an on-site sketch, which might be turned into an etching at a later time. If he liked the subject enough, it could also become a lithograph or a competently rendered oil painting. When he was away from his TCU classroom, he spent almost all of his time making art. He produced more artworks featuring Fort Worth subject matter than any other fine artist of his day.

During the 1940s and WWII, many of Ziegler's paintings were somber and toned down in color. From 1941 to 1945, he created a series of war-related paintings. After the war, the climate of the local art scene began to change. The Fort Worth Circle painters, who served as the city's artistic avant-garde, were becoming established and winning most of the awards at the Local Artists Show, a popular event held annually at the Fort Worth Public Library. Mr. Ziegler attempted to embrace this new style of abstract painting and produced paintings in this manner but with only moderate success, even though many of his abstracts were well conceived. He retired from TCU in 1953 and thereafter continued painting in his studio in the Administration Building on campus.

As the 1950s drew to a close, his health was somewhat affected by advancing age. He had had an outstanding career at Texas Christian University, where he taught many hundreds of students over a period of twenty-seven years. Some of those students became prominent Fort Worth artists in the postwar period.

Ziegler passed away on April 7, 1967, at eighty-five years of age. He had a profound effect on the art scene in Fort Worth through the many images of the downtown business district that he left behind, along with the alluring Trinity River scenery that he so much loved to paint.

Samuel P. Ziegler and Fort Worth

Scott Grant Barker

Few things fascinated artist Samuel P. Ziegler (1882-1967) more than the rapidly evolving land-scape of his adopted hometown of Fort Worth, Texas. Ziegler came to Fort Worth in 1917 after living in Philadelphia, Pennsylvania, for fifteen years, so perhaps it was the newness of the Texas environment that caused him to look at his surroundings with fresh eyes and a heightened sense of curiosity. Once settled, Ziegler wasted no time keeping a visual diary of the city he came to know. First using paint and pencil and then printer's ink, in 1918 he began a long-running series of artworks that depicted views of the Trinity River, major buildings on the Texas Christian University campus, prominent churches, and important buildings in downtown Fort Worth and the surround-ing area. He was particularly attracted to buildings under construction and older buildings facing demolition, a tendency fueled by an acute awareness of the temporal nature of manmade struc-tures. He also became intensely interested in the oil fields of West Texas and the rural ranches that coexisted with the drillers.

Ziegler's paintings were typically loose and impressionistic. His skillful drawings, etchings, and lithographs were conceived with a desire for visual accuracy. Collectively, his paintings and graphic works formed a visual record of Fort Worth in the 1920s and 1930s that stood markedly apart from the efforts of every other artist working in the city. Ziegler's surviving prints and drawings, most of them published here for the first time, can now be seen as valuable additions to both Texas art history and Fort Worth's recorded past.

The first fifteen years of Ziegler's career were largely spent in Philadelphia, where he worked as a painter and professional musician. A child of farmers in Lancaster County, Pennsylvania, he left the family farm at age twenty-one, worked as a hotel clerk, and then, in 1904, enrolled in the Pennsylvania Academy of the Fine Arts, where he studied easel painting, on and off, for ten years. Concurrent with his art studies, he trained as a classical musician and cellist at the Philadelphia Musical Academy, where he successfully transitioned from student to faculty member.[1] As a student, and later as a professional, his income was mainly derived from performing as a string musician and giving private lessons to younger players. William Merritt Chase, one of Ziegler's most storied art teachers at the Pennsylvania Academy of the Fine Arts, once tried to get Ziegler to choose between art and music as his primary focus, but Ziegler was unable to do so. If not for major disruptions in Philadelphia's cultural life brought on by the onset of World War I, his career may have remained status quo; but in 1917, the year of America's entry into the war, Ziegler could no longer find work as a musician and, needing employment, answered the call from a little-known denominational college in Fort Worth, Texas, looking for a music teacher.

Ziegler was hired in 1917 as an instructor of music and music theory at Texas Christian University and, at age thirty-five, went there to create a new life for himself, his wife, and their children. He moved to Texas on an offer to teach music, but his years of schooling at the Pennsylvania Academy of the Fine Arts made him one of the most highly trained painters ever to immigrate to Fort Worth, a circumstance that would prove to be the key to his future.

Texas Christian University, upon Ziegler's arrival, was entering its eighth academic year since relocating to Fort Worth from Waco. The university was housed in a cluster of new buildings sitting on a Johnson grass prairie southwest of town.[2] At the time, the new campus was linked to greater Fort Worth only by a streetcar line and a two-lane road. Fort Worth was a young city by most measures, with a population just under one hundred thousand.[3] The community was experiencing rapid growth fueled by the meat packing industry and was poised to reap the economic benefits of a huge new U. S. Army training base called Camp Bowie and soon-to-be discovered oil deposits in nearby counties.

In the 1920s and 1930s, local scenery was often depicted by artists who were attracted by the intrinsic appeal of urban life and nature's place in it. Ziegler too was quickly spellbound by the intermingling of Fort Worth's buildings, parks, and waterways. The Fort Worth Painters Club, a group of professional artists that Ziegler cofounded in 1920, mounted an exhibit filled with paintings of Fort Worth scenery in 1922.[4] These artworks carried titles such as *Misty Morning on the Trinity*, *Trinity Park*, *Beyond Arlington Heights*, *Fort Worth at Sunset*, *North Fort Worth*, and *Fort Worth in Trinity Flats*, each image conveying an artist's interpretation of a physical place somewhere in the city.

Ziegler, like his peers, was always guided by artistic considerations when it came to choosing subject matter for sketches and paintings, but he was also influenced by an unusual sensitivity to the city's pace of growth, an awareness that prompted him to systematically select city views representative of that growth from among a long list of possible choices. The only other local artist who seemed to share a kindred view was Nelson M. Davidson, a staff artist with the *Fort Worth Star-Telegram*. Davidson produced numerous pencil sketches of Fort Worth street scenes in the mid-1930s for use as newspaper illustrations, thus enhancing the reading experience for *Star-Telegram* subscribers.[5] But for the most part, pleasing scenes of Trinity Park, Forest Park, and Lake Worth were the ever-popular motifs for many Fort Worth painters before and during the Great Depression.

In an article that appeared in 1943, Ziegler spoke about Fort Worth from a visual artist's point of view. "There is a wealth of paintable material in Fort Worth," he said. "The city is free of smoke; the buildings are clean looking and colorful, and when seen against the clear bright Texas skies there is a picture ready to be recorded, no matter in what direction one looks." He went on, "The artist will also find sympathetic material in our landmarks, the buildings of yesteryear. These pioneer buildings retire graciously into an antique atmosphere and seem to reflect the greatness of their day. Sometimes we find them among modern office buildings vainly clinging to the past, an example of waste according to the industrial viewpoint, but a source of rich material for the painter."[6]

At first, Ziegler was attracted to sights on or near the Texas Christian University campus. His first attempt at depicting local scenery was made in 1918, when he produced a painting of campus buildings as seen from the second floor of Brite College of the Bible. The heavily wooded banks of the Trinity River were just a short walk from his home, and his earliest Trinity River paintings also date to 1918. Needing additional income, Ziegler landed a part-time job as a Vaudevillian musician and used his vantage point from the orchestra pit of the Majestic Theatre to sketch scenes of the ornate auditorium in which performances were held. In pencil drawings he recorded the rise of the W. T. Waggoner Building (constructed 1919-1920), the city's tallest skyscraper at the time. Ziegler left Texas Christian University in 1919, lured by an invitation to head the art department at Texas Woman's College (now Texas Wesleyan University) in east Fort Worth. However, he maintained his family's home next to the TCU campus and returned to Texas Christian University in 1925 as head of the visual art program there.[7]

Other paintings that Ziegler produced during these early years in Fort Worth included *A Texas Acropolis* (1920), a view of Texas Christian University's main buildings isolated against the western sky. *Building the Memorial Arch* (1923) captured construction of a monument to those who fought and died in World War I. Surrounded by scaffolding at the time he painted it, the impressive cast-stone arch was a gift to TCU from the Class of 1923. *Building the Foundation for the Library* (1924) documented construction of the Mary Couts Burnett Library, the first permanent TCU building located on the east side of University Drive. *Campus Panorama* recorded the view from the steps of the new Mary Couts Burnett Library as the artist looked westward at campus buildings across the street. Downtown Fort Worth as seen from the windows of his new TCU art classrooms was the subject of a painting called *Skyline Over Campus Tree Tops* (1925).

Ziegler loved to paint outdoors. In a personal note, he recalled his fondness for painting the landscape *en plein air*: "In 1925, I started on a program of landscape that continued through ten years (perhaps the happiest years of my art career), which consisted in going direct to nature and painting a finished canvas each time I went out."[8]

Samuel Ziegler's zest for printmaking grew out of one of the more unusual episodes of his career, when a casual remark made to a *Fort Worth Star-Telegram* reporter made its way into the newspaper.[9] His comment, made in the spring of 1927, referred to tentative plans to visit the West Texas oil fields that summer in order to see them for himself. Only two months before, in the pages of that same newspaper, nationally-known printmaker Bernhardt Wall had extolled the artistic possibilities of just such a trip.[10] Ziegler's musings about a sketching trip out west were published as fact and quickly led to a formal invitation from the Eastland Chamber of Commerce to "come among them and paint the very interesting oil activities thereabouts."[11] Thus obligated, he accepted the chamber's offer of hospitality and in the summer of 1927 undertook the first of several annual forays to Eastland County and points west. Unlike Dallas artist Frank Reaugh, whose summer sketching trips to far West Texas were group affairs, Ziegler traveled alone. His stated purpose was to make a visual record of the sights and techniques in use in the Texas oil industry at the time. Oil paintings were the primary means of compiling this visual record, but he also looked to prints as an alternate way to capture and disseminate representative images. Stone lithography was the first form of printmaking that he explored, followed soon after by a serious interest in etching.

Stone lithography was a fine art printmaking technique that many of Ziegler's peers at the Pennsylvania Academy of the Fine Arts had mastered. It was practiced by Texas artists as nearby as Dallas; however, in the 1920s and 1930s, the technique had not been adopted by any fine artist in Fort Worth. The likely reason for this was economic. Specialized presses on which lithographs were printed, and lithograph stones on which images were first drawn, were expensive. No fine artist in Fort Worth had yet made an investment in such equipment. In order to produce fine art lithographic prints, an artist in Fort Worth had to either purchase such equipment or contract with a vendor in another city who provided the service. Records related to Ziegler's printmaking activities are scarce; however, one surviving letter from the Philadelphia firm of Ketterlinus Lithographic Manufacturing Company points to this firm as Ziegler's choice for reproducing West Texas oil field drawings and Fort Worth sketches in the lithographic medium.[12]

This letter, dated August 17, 1927, was written to Ziegler by Robert G. Leinroth, manager of the art department of the Ketterlinus Lithographic Manufacturing Company in Philadelphia. The date of the letter coincides with Ziegler's first trip to Eastland County. The tone of the letter and much of its content make it clear that Leinroth and Ziegler knew each other from Ziegler's time in Philadelphia. Leinroth refers to shared experiences in Beach Haven (New Jersey) and says, "I hope your family endures in good health and are all happy in their present abode. My regards to all of them . . . " An earlier paragraph contains Leinroth's instructions on how to prepare a lithographic crayon drawing on paper for transfer to a lithograph stone using a scraper. He referred to a previous communication by writing, "I note what you say about your lithographs and if you will send one of the subjects, I will be better able to size the matter up and transfer it and let you see the results." This method of transferring a drawing from paper to a lithograph stone would have been easier and cheaper to accomplish than another available method, which involved mail-ordering an actual lithograph stone, drawing directly on the stone, and then shipping it back to the printer for proofs to be pulled. Ziegler apparently opted for drawing on sheets of clean, hard paper and then mailing the drawn images to Ketterlinus, where proofs were made.

How many Ziegler drawings were reproduced as lithographs is unknown; however, combining the number of surviving lithographs with other litho prints known only by their titles in exhibit catalogues and other sources, the number is between forty and fifty. Oil field scenery and the urban landscape of Fort Worth were the exclusive subject matter of this particular print series. Except for a select few that are signed in the stone, most surviving Ziegler lithographs are unsigned. They are not found in multiples and are typically printed on lightweight, low rag content paper measuring twelve and a half by eighteen inches per sheet. These facts suggest that surviving lithographs are proof copies supplied by Ketterlinus. The puzzling scarcity of these lithographs and the fragility of existing examples make it appear that Ziegler, probably for financial reasons, did not order even modest runs, say twenty-five to fifty copies, of each image on rag paper. Each lithograph reproduced in this book is the only known example, preserved through the efforts of Ziegler's late daughter, Samye Ziegler Hunt, and collector Gregory H. Dow of Fort Worth.

The second form of printmaking that Samuel Ziegler adopted, and over which he had more control, was etching, a technique that he practiced for approximately ten years. Etching was well-suited to Ziegler's situation because the equipment took up little space, the process used chemicals that were readily available, and resulting prints could be reproduced in any number at a low cost. Ziegler used this process to depict Texas oil field scenes, TCU campus buildings, and interesting views in the downtown Fort Worth area. Unlike his lithographs, whose origins are vague, Ziegler's etchings are more thoroughly documented with regard to titles and quantities printed.[13] Most of the etchings reproduced in this book are represented by multiple examples printed on rag paper. Most surviving etchings are in good condition, and many are signed in pencil by the artist.

For making prints, Ziegler acquired a hand-operated etching press manufactured by Model Specialty Company of New York City. The press weighed about seventy-five pounds and occupied a tabletop in a spare bedroom in his home. The 24 x 12–inch bed limited the size of any single printing plate to approximately 9 x 7 inches or smaller. Consequently, Ziegler's etchings were printed on modest-sized pieces of rag paper that he would sometimes mat for exhibition. He typically etched on copper plates but was known to use zinc plates also. By 1929, two years after his initial foray into West Texas, Ziegler had begun a correspondence with master etcher Bernhardt Wall of Lime Rock, Connecticut.[14] Mr. Wall, who had visited Fort Worth and was friendly with Fort Worth etcher Blanche McVeigh, supplied Ziegler with detailed instructions and supply lists for producing etched images on metal plates. Whether Ziegler received any formal training in the technique or learned strictly by trial and error is not clear. Ziegler's efforts at lithography began in 1927, but by 1929 his embrace of etching as a serious activity had emerged and, going forward, he repeatedly relied on etching to depict images of West Texas and the city he most admired.

An interesting assessment of Ziegler's early printmaking efforts appeared in 1928, when Frances Battaile Fisk profiled him in her book, *A History of Texas Artists and Sculptors*. Fisk wrote, "In connection with his painting, Mr. Ziegler is making a series of lithographs of Fort Worth, its industries and improvements, as well as the general activities. He is trying to set forth the aesthetic possibilities in our present-day life and surroundings. He plans to make a series of etchings, as he prefers the more refined (pictorial) treatment of this medium, using similar subjects as he found in the oil fields which are especially fine for the graphic arts. He hopes to someday specialize in some phase of Texas life suited to his particular temperament and to the medium itself."[15]

Ziegler's enthusiasm for recording Fort Worth scenery was likely fueled, at least in part, by a significant building boom that placed the city in a constant state of expansion and renewal. To see evidence of the changes going on around him, Ziegler had to look no further than out the front window of his home, which faced the construction site for TCU's new Mary Couts Burnett Library (opened 1925). In the downtown business district no fewer than thirteen office buildings were constructed between 1920 and 1930, ranging in height from eleven to twenty-four stories.[16] The introduction of so many high-rise buildings, all within a few blocks of each other, drastically altered the skyline that Ziegler first saw in 1917. Numerous other smaller construction projects dotted the downtown streets as well. On the south end of the downtown area, and just to the west, a second transformation took place. This spate of new construction, fueled largely by federal money, resulted in a new United States Post Office (1933), new United States Federal Courthouse (1933), the Will Rogers Memorial Center complex (1936), a new Fort Worth City Hall (1938), and new Fort Worth Public Library (1939).

One of the most ambitious Fort Worth renewal projects of the time involved the creation of grade separation between the railway tracks of the Texas & Pacific Railroad and the city streets that bisected the Texas & Pacific Railroad Reservation on the southern edge of the downtown area. Long a hazardous transit for private automobiles, Fort Worthians traveling through the T&P Reservation along South Main Street, Jennings Avenue, and South Henderson Street were forced to wait for passing trains and risk collisions with trains as they drove across multiple sets of high-use tracks. The massive construction project to build the South Main Street and Jennings Avenue underpasses, along with the South Henderson Street underpass, began in 1930. As part of the project, Fort Worth's nineteenth-century Texas & Pacific Passenger Station was replaced by a new passenger terminal (opened 1931), and the original Texas & Pacific Freight Depot was supplanted by a massive new warehouse complex. Taken together, these transformative projects, along with others, remade the character of Fort Worth in a span of just twenty years. Samuel Ziegler, in the mold of a true artist, took note of virtually every change.

Ziegler's heyday as a printmaker lasted about ten years, although to the end of his life he periodically exhibited his lithographs and etchings, usually in settings where they were shown in tandem with paintings from his Fort Worth series. One early success as a printmaker came in April 1929, when he received a cash prize from the Southern States Art League Exhibition in San Antonio for an impressive lithograph of the Eastland discovery field.[17] He exhibited a strong mix of etchings and lithographs in January 1933 at the Collins Art Company gallery in Fort Worth.[18] Four lithographs, including *First Methodist Church* and *W. I. Cook Memorial Hospital*, and fifteen etchings were displayed, along with several paintings of local subjects. Etchings included *Wrecking the Old T&P Station, Monroe Street Doorway at Post Office, Sinclair Building at Night, Sky — Lake Worth, Perkins Gusher,* and *McCloud No. 1.* Etchings of several Fort Worth churches were also shown in this 1933 exhibition.

He again combined paintings and prints in a 1936 exhibition in Abilene, Texas, sponsored by the Art Unit of the Abilene Women's Forum.[19] Several West Texas etchings were part of this exhibit, including *The Last of the Herd, West Texas Ranch, Lone Yucca, West Texas Sky,* and *Burning the Slush Pit.* Etchings of Fort Worth subjects included *Building the New T&P Station*, *A Grain Elevator, On the Grease Rack,* and *Oil Refinery.* Lithograph titles in this exhibit included *Dairy Farm, Modern Gothic* (First Methodist Church), *W. I. Cook Memorial Hospital,* and *Southern Cottage.*

Mr. Ziegler's records do not reveal when he drew his last lithograph or pulled his last etching. During the 1940s he aggressively exhibited paintings of the Texas oil fields, achieving particular success in June 1943 when the Philbrook Art Center (now Philbrook Museum of Art) in Tulsa, Oklahoma, offered him a solo exhibition of these works.[20] There were no prints exhibited in the Tulsa venue. Ziegler also took pride in his long-running series of scenes from the Texas Christian University campus and organized exhibits of these paintings in 1942 and 1948.[21] He also offered an exhibit of thirty-five paintings from the historic Fort Worth series in 1943.[22] He put forty-six historic

TCU and Fort Worth canvases on public view in October 1949. Ziegler's etchings and lithographs were not included in exhibitions of the 1940s until the October 1949 show, which was held at Texas Christian University.[23] Tellingly, the checklist for this 1949 exhibit named thirteen lithographs and nine etchings, each one a familiar image produced during Mr. Ziegler's printmaking sessions ten to twenty years before. It seems likely, based on the exhibition record, that by 1939, or possibly earlier, his experimentation with printmaking had ended.

All artists create because they must, and some do so with great clarity of purpose. Samuel P. Ziegler was a keen observer of Fort Worth's changing landscape and possessed an unusual sensitivity to the city's pace of growth. He viewed himself as a recorder of history, and this awareness set him apart from almost all of his contemporaries. On his own initiative, Ziegler unleashed a full range of artistic media to capture the look and feel of Fort Worth as he knew it, and the prints, drawings, and paintings presented here are evidence of that concerted effort. It is not possible to find and record every image that once comprised Samuel Ziegler's body of work. Since his death in 1967, many of his paintings, prints, and drawings have been dispersed, while many others have been lost to water damage or fire. A significant number, however, do remain available for study. Much of what remains is gathered in this book, standing in testament to Samuel Ziegler's singular fascination with his adopted home, the city *Where the West Begins*.

[1]*47th Annual Prospectus: Philadelphia Musical Academy, 1915-1916* (Philadelphia: Yearbook of the Philadelphia Musical Academy, 1915), 3. At the PMA Ziegler worked as a teacher of violoncello.

[2]Colby D. Hall, *History of Texas Christian University: A College of the Cattle Frontier* (Fort Worth: Texas Christian University Press, 1947), 145-46.

[3]*City of Fort Worth, Texas Municipal Life, 1931-1937* (Fort Worth: Publication of the Bureau of Municipal Research, City of Fort Worth, Texas, Series I, No. 1, August 1937), 40. Fort Worth's population grew from 73,312 to 106,482 between 1910 and 1920.

[4]"Scenes Around Fort Worth Theme of Most "Landscapes" at Painters' Club Exhibit," *Fort Worth Star-Telegram*, 26 November 1922, 13. The Fort Worth Painters Club was cofounded by Samuel Ziegler and Sallie Blyth Mummert in 1920.

[5]In addition to his newspaper work, Davidson published several booklets of illustrations between 1936 and 1939. One of them, *Pencil Trails: Fort Worth Frontier Centennial*, was entirely devoted to sketches of the 1936 Fort Worth Frontier Centennial grounds. Another published Davidson booklet documented major buildings on the 1936 Texas Centennial Exposition fairgrounds in Dallas.

[6]*Fort Worth Provides Art Inspiration* [1943] (Vertical file 759.1B, Department of Genealogy and Local History, Fort Worth Public Library). Article extracted from a Fort Worth Chamber of Commerce magazine, month of publication unknown.

[7]Frances Battaile Fisk, *A History of Texas Artists and Sculptors* (Abilene: Frances Battaile Fisk, 1928), 124.

[8]Samuel P. Ziegler, *My Art Background,* written March 1953 at the request of Lorraine Sherley. Collection of the author.

[9]"Art Tours To Be Summer Plan: Many Artists Will Be In Camps, One Will Paint Oil Fields," *Fort Worth Star-Telegram and Sunday Record*, 19 June 1927, 5.

[10]Pauline Naylor, "Wall Visions Great Art Possibility in Oil Field," *Fort Worth Record-Telegram*, 16 April 1927, 10.

[11]Samuel P. Ziegler papers, *Archives of American Art*, Smithsonian Institution, reel 2057, frame 260.

[12]Ibid., frames 262-63.

[13]Ziegler's etchings are often titled in pencil just below the printed image. In addition, images of several Ziegler pencil drawings and etchings, along with typed notes, were microfilmed in 1980 on reel 2058 of the Samuel P. Ziegler papers, *Archives of American Art*, Smithsonian Institution. In contrast, Ziegler's lithographs, which were rarely titled and rarely signed, are not documented in any present-day database.

[14]Samuel P. Ziegler papers, *Archives of American Art*, Smithsonian Institution, reel 2057, frames 392-93, 394-96, 398. Wall wintered in his wife's hometown of La Porte, Texas, for many years. He published two Texas-related books, *Following General Sam Houston, 1793-1863* (Lime Rock, 1935) and *Following Stephen F. Austin: Father of Texas* (Lime Rock, 1936).

[15]Fisk, *A History of Texas Artists and Sculptors*, 125.

[16]Multistory office buildings completed in 1920 through 1930 included the W. T. Waggoner Building (1920), the Neil P. Anderson Building (1921), Farmers and Mechanics National Bank Building (1921), the Hotel Texas (1921), Fort Worth Club Building (1926), Petroleum Building (1927), Medical Arts Building (1927), new Worth Hotel (1927), Blackstone Hotel (1929), Electric Building (1930), Aviation Building (1930), the Fair Building (1930), and the Sinclair Building (1930).

[17]Ziegler, *Archives of American Art*, reel 2057, frame 356. See also, catalogue of the Ninth Annual Exhibition of the Southern States Art League, Witte Memorial Museum, San Antonio, Texas, 1929.

[18]Louise Cox, "Familiar Scenes Give Ziegler Art Strong Appeal to Fort Worthians," *Fort Worth Star-Telegram*, evening edition, 18 January 1933, 7.

[19]*Lecture and Exhibit of His Works by Samuel P. Ziegler, Hotel Wooten, Abilene, Texas, 18 January 1936,* exh. cat. (Abilene: Art Unit of the Abilene Women's Forum, 1936).

[20]Ziegler, *Archives of American Art*, reel 2057, frames 543-48 (checklist of the exhibition).

[21]Ziegler, *Archives of American Art*, reel 2057, frames 521-22 (checklist of the 1942 exhibition). See also, "Paintings by S. P. Ziegler Depict Growth of TCU," *Fort Worth Star-Telegram*, 6 June 1948.

[22]Ziegler, *Archives of American Art*, reel 2057, frames 525-27 (checklist of the exhibition).

[23]*Historical Exhibit: Paintings by Samuel P. Ziegler of Texas Christian University and Fort Worth, 9 October – 31 October, 1949,* exh. cat. (Fort Worth: Texas Christian University, 1949).

Lenders to the Publication

*Sincere thanks to those who generously provided
images to this publication:*

Judy & Stephen Alton

Linda Jo & Scott Barker

The Estate of Beth Lea Clardy

Dow Art Galleries, LLC

Deborah & Gregory Dow

Ann Ekstrom

Jim Finley

The Samye Ziegler Hunt Estate and Suzi Hunt Gamez

Geralyn & Mark Kever

The John L. Nau III Collection of Texas Art

Nancy Ziegler, Frisco, Texas

Acknowledgments

Every book is the product of hard work, cooperation between like-minded people, and serendipity. It was my good fortune that Dr. Ron Tyler took an interest in a booklet on Samuel P. Ziegler's prints and drawings that I assembled in 2004 and pointed out that it could be expanded into a more comprehensive work. Dr. Tyler's encouragement and suggestions on how to do that were the keys to bringing this book to fruition. My deep appreciation also to Dan Williams, Director of TCU Press, for accepting this book for publication and for agreeing to include a selection of color plates. Though this book deals mainly with Mr. Ziegler's graphic work (drawings, lithographs, and etchings), he was one of Texas's earliest impressionist painters, as the color plates will illustrate.

In 1995, Samye Ziegler Hunt, Professor Ziegler's daughter shared with me an extensive collection of her father's prints, drawings, and personal records. It was my first exposure to the depth of Samuel Ziegler's fascination with Fort Worth. Mr. Ziegler's daughter-in-law, Aline Ziegler, likewise preserved and generously shared other important examples of Ziegler's work. Both of these dear ladies are gone now, but their help with the 2004 project underpins almost every phase of this publication.

My sincere thanks also to Samye Ziegler Hunt's husband, Don Hunt, and her children, Suzi Gamez and the late David Hunt. Each of them held the memory of Samuel P. Ziegler particularly close, and that was invigorating for a historian. Aline Ziegler's daughter, Nancy, was likewise extremely helpful and supportive of efforts to assemble and publish a record of her grandfather's accomplishments.

I appreciate Fort Worth businessman Jim Finley, a collector and prescient admirer of Samuel Ziegler's art, who generously shared important works from his collection. My deep gratitude also extends to Fort Worth collectors Judy and Stephen Alton, and to Christopher Beer, curator of the

John L. Nau III Collection of Texas Art, for providing significant artworks to this project. John Roberts, who rigorously maintains the *fortwortharchitecture.com* website as a public service, deserves my thanks and the thanks of everyone who uses this marvelous resource to learn about the architectural history of the city.

None of my projects would go anywhere without the wholehearted support of my dear wife Linda Jo, and I thank her for letting me pursue this one. I also thank Ann Ekstrom, a marvelous artist who has a unique understanding of Samuel Ziegler's art and career. Ann's and Billy Stone's help in recovering examples of Mr. Ziegler's imagery was invaluable. My close friends Ken Jackson and the late Larry Kleinschmidt also assisted me with this project in more ways than I can count. Much appreciated too is the help of senior archivist Mary Saffell and the folks at TCU's Mary Couts Burnett Library, Special Collections. Their assistance with image reproduction came at just the right time.

Finally, I would like to thank my friend and coauthor Gregory H. Dow for bringing his deep knowledge of, and enthusiasm for, the art of Samuel P. Ziegler to this project. Most of what can now be revealed about Ziegler's lithographs is due to Greg Dow's efforts to save them. We have enjoyed many happy hours discussing Mr. Ziegler's notable qualities, particularly his acute sense of place. Greg and I think, and we hope you agree, that Ziegler's sense of place is on full view in the following pages and in these images that have been lost to history for more than half a century, but no longer.

SCOTT GRANT BARKER
March 2022

Photos of the Artist

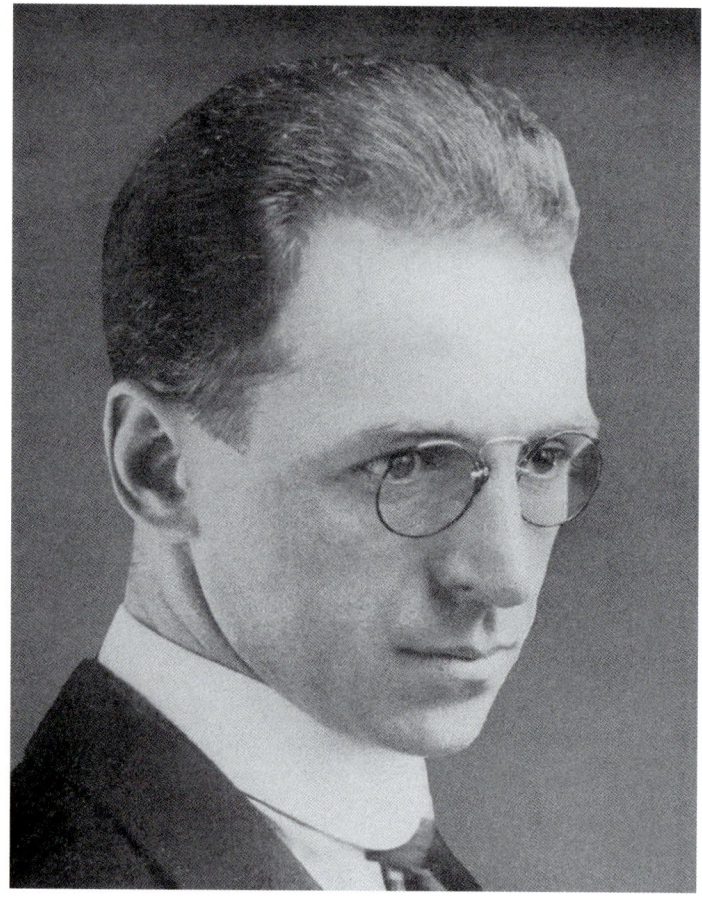

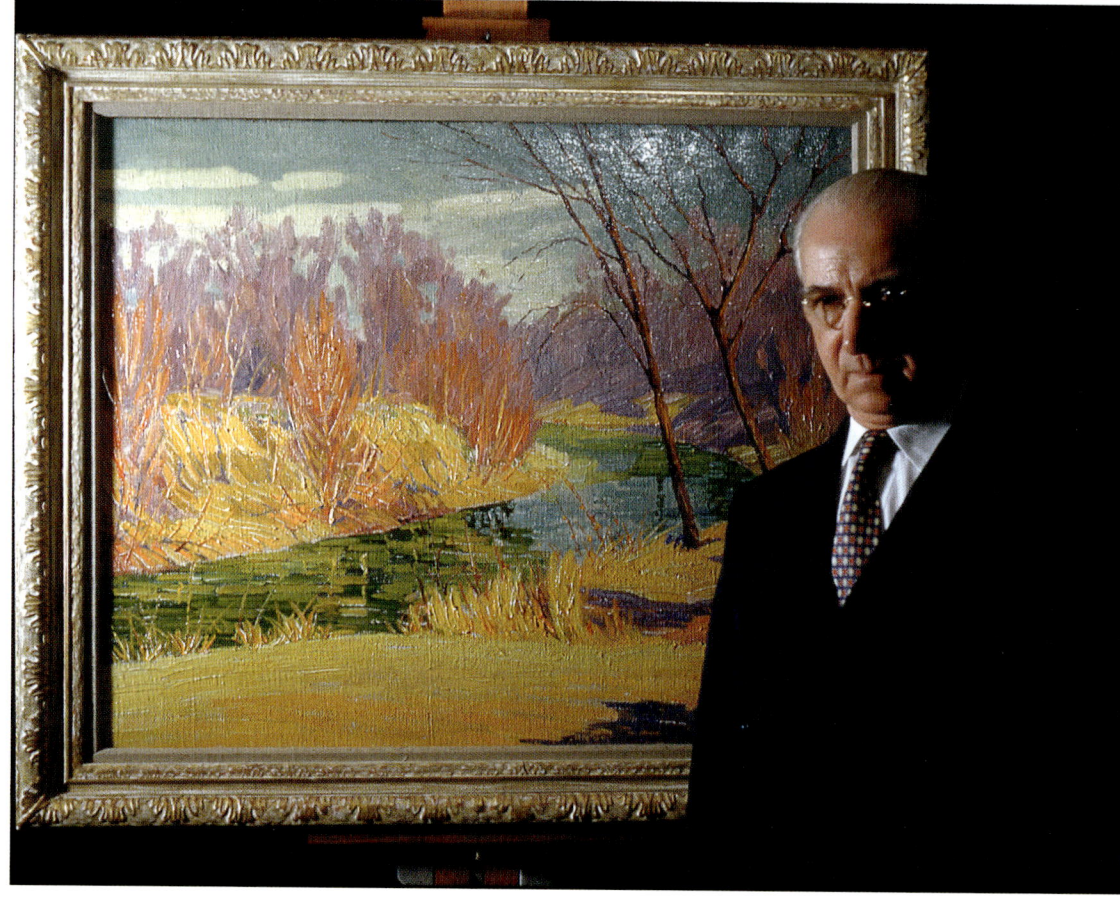

Samuel P. Ziegler, 1921. Faculty photo taken from 1921 yearbook of Texas Woman's College, Fort Worth. Ziegler first arrived in the city in 1917 to work as a music teacher at TCU. Courtesy Linda Jo and Scott Barker Collection.

Samuel P. Ziegler in retirement, ca. 1960. Following Prof. Ziegler's retirement in 1953 as head of the TCU art department, the university provided him with a private studio on campus. There, he posed with *Along the Trinity,* a major early work he had painted in 1930. Courtesy Linda Jo and Scott Barker Collection.

Samuel Ziegler's musical ability was the basis for his initial hiring at Texas Christian University, and he remained musically active throughout his years as a teacher and painter. Mr. Ziegler performed as a cellist with the early-day Fort Worth Symphony Orchestra conducted by Brooks Morris. In 1932, Ziegler and fellow classical string musicians George Orum, Marius Thor, and E. Clyde Whitlock formed the Pro Arte String Quartet. The quartet performed numerous classical chamber music concerts in Fort Worth and elsewhere for seventeen seasons, disbanding in 1949. Courtesy Nancy Ziegler.

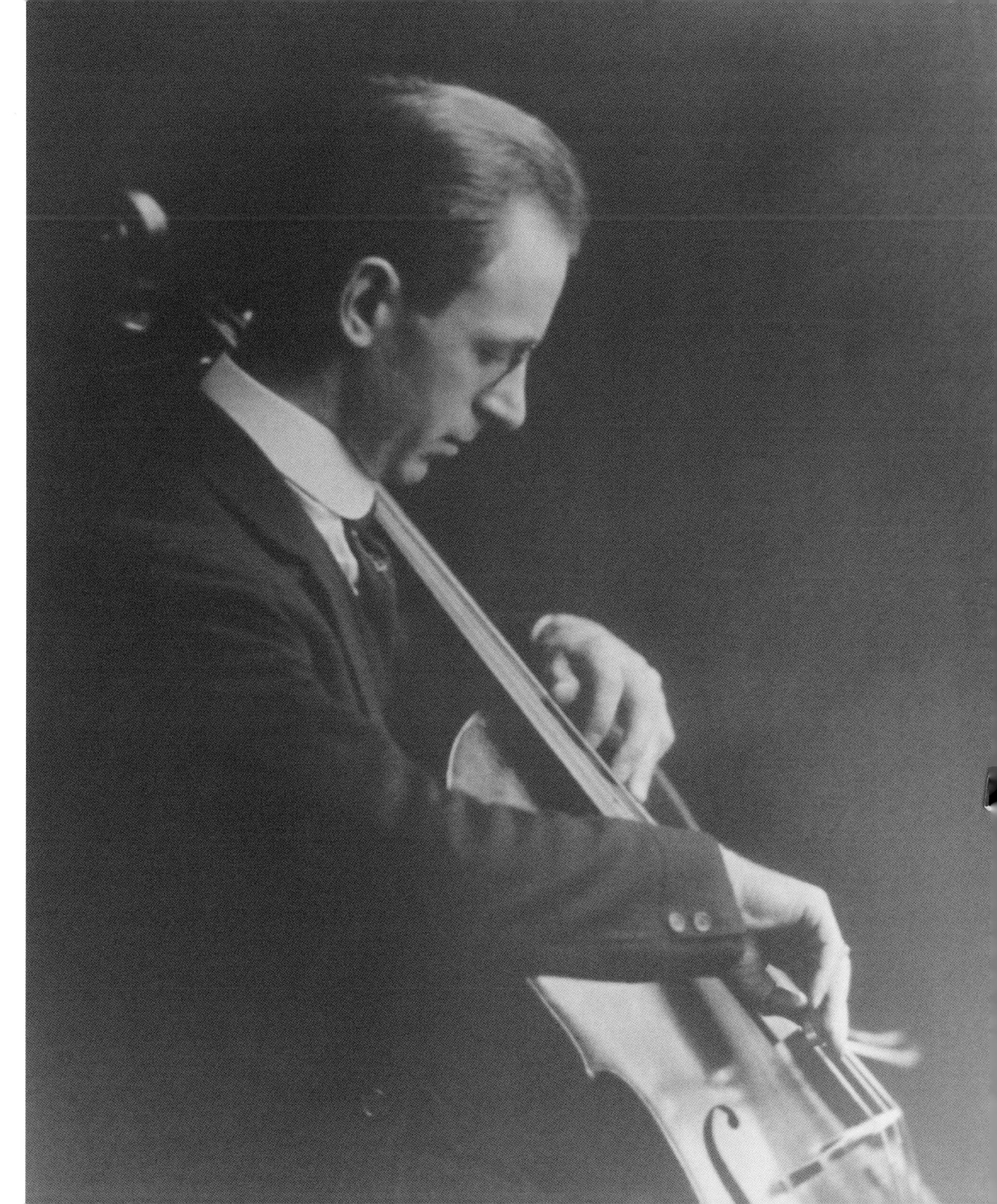

Texas Christian University

T.C.U. Library
(Mary Couts Burnett Library),
1930. Etching.

The Mary Couts Burnett Library opened in 1925. Built adjacent to an early-day Texas Christian University athletic field, it was the first permanent TCU building on the east side of University Drive. The library was designed by Fort Worth architect Wiley G. Clarkson and featured a distinctive neoclassical façade, placing it among the city's most attractive architectural gems. Samuel Ziegler and his family lived at 2908 Cassell Blvd. (later renamed West Lowden Street), directly across the street from the Burnett Library's north side. Professor Ziegler produced a half-dozen prints and paintings of this important campus addition, the earliest image dating to 1924, when the library was under construction.

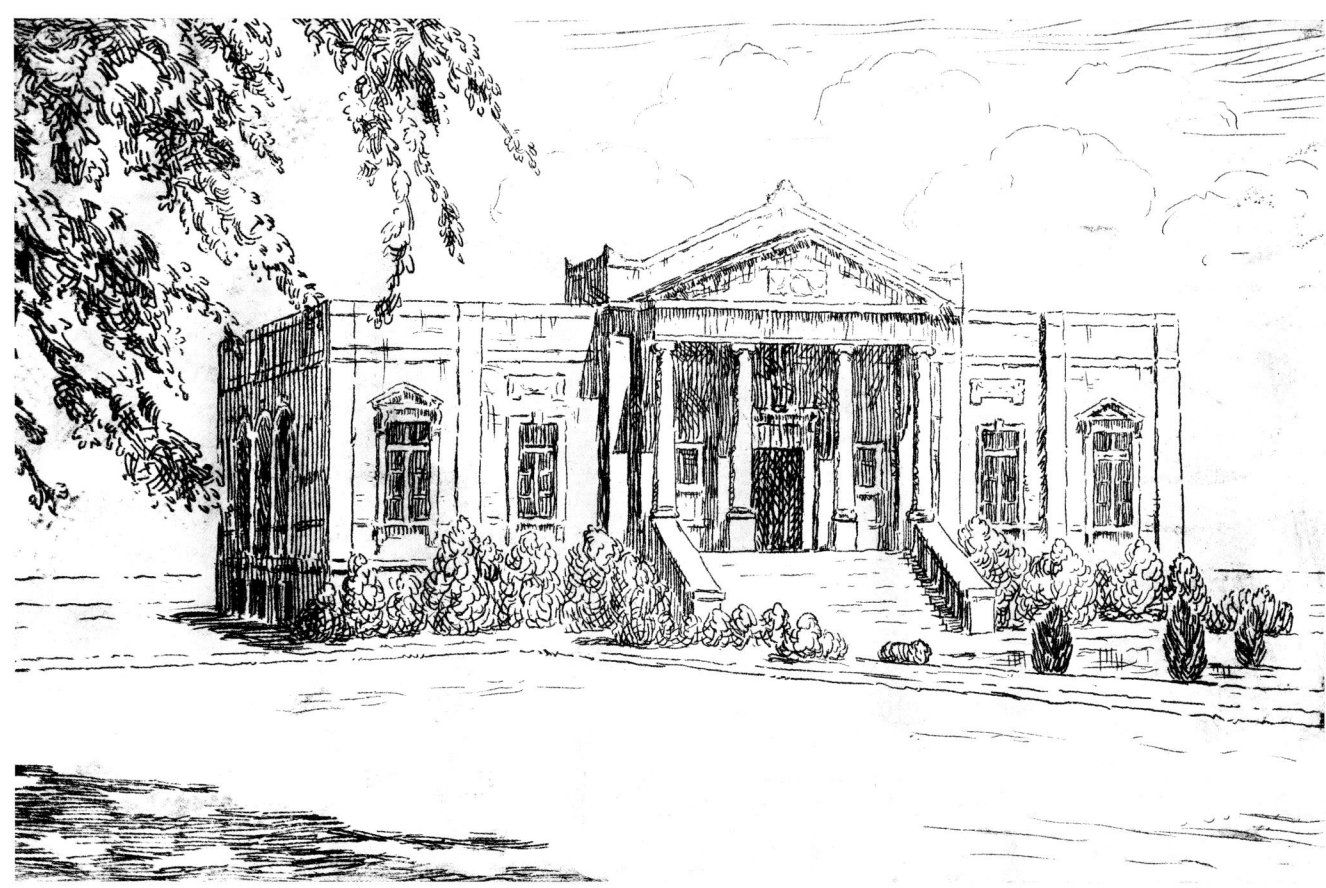

**T.C.U. Library
(Mary Couts Burnett Library),
ca. 1930. Lithograph.**

This Ziegler lithograph depicted a portion
of the Mary Couts Burnett Library façade
from the north, an uncommon view. Minimal
landscaping suggests the newness of
the building.

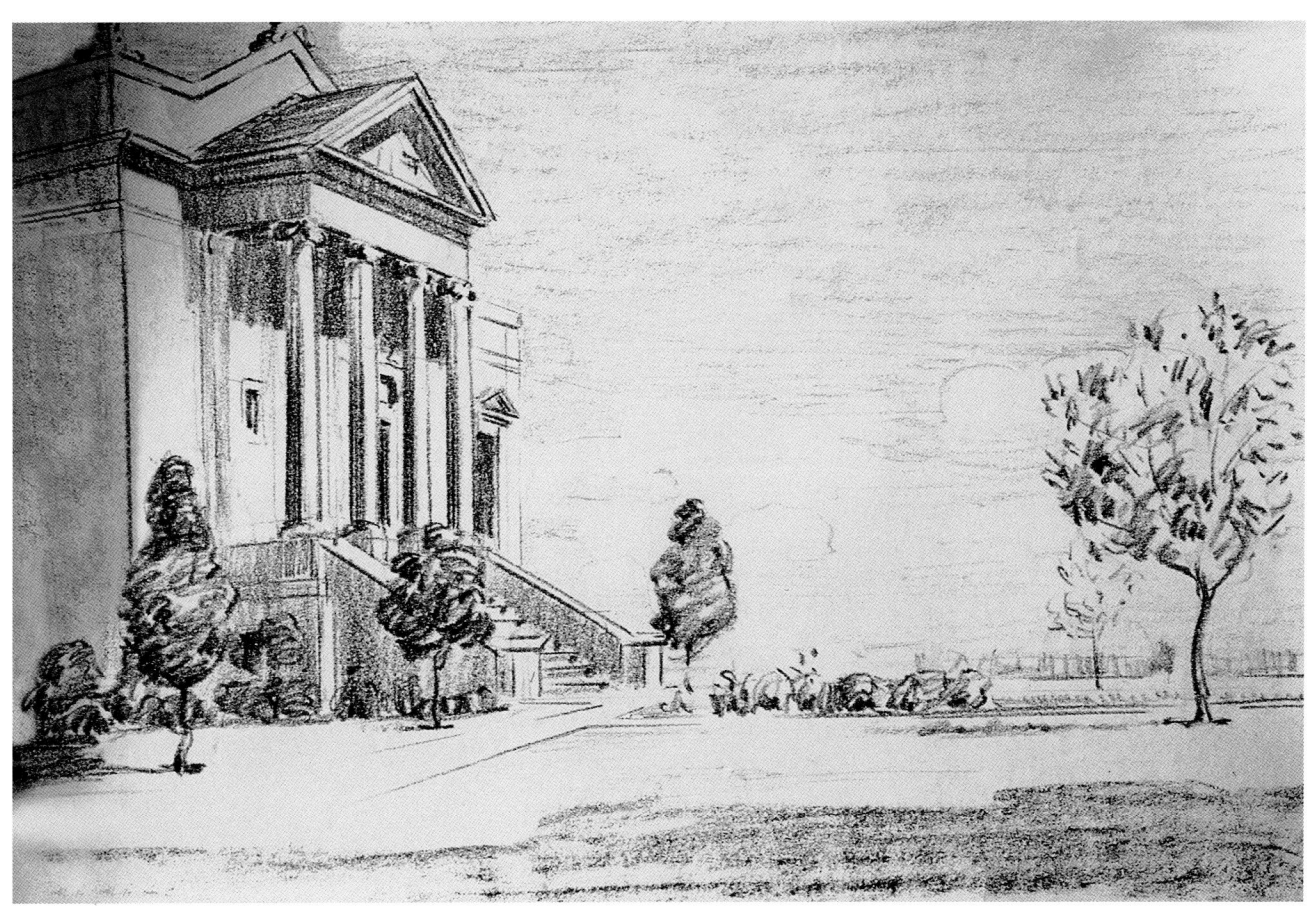

**T.C.U. Library
(Mary Couts Burnett Library),
1931. Etching.**

This small print of the Mary Couts Burnett Library made visual note of the distinctive reflecting pool situated in front of the building. When new, the reflecting pool was equipped with a powerful water fountain illuminated by colored electric lights. At night, Ziegler noted, spectators in slow-moving auto-mobiles crowded onto University Drive to watch the watery fireworks.

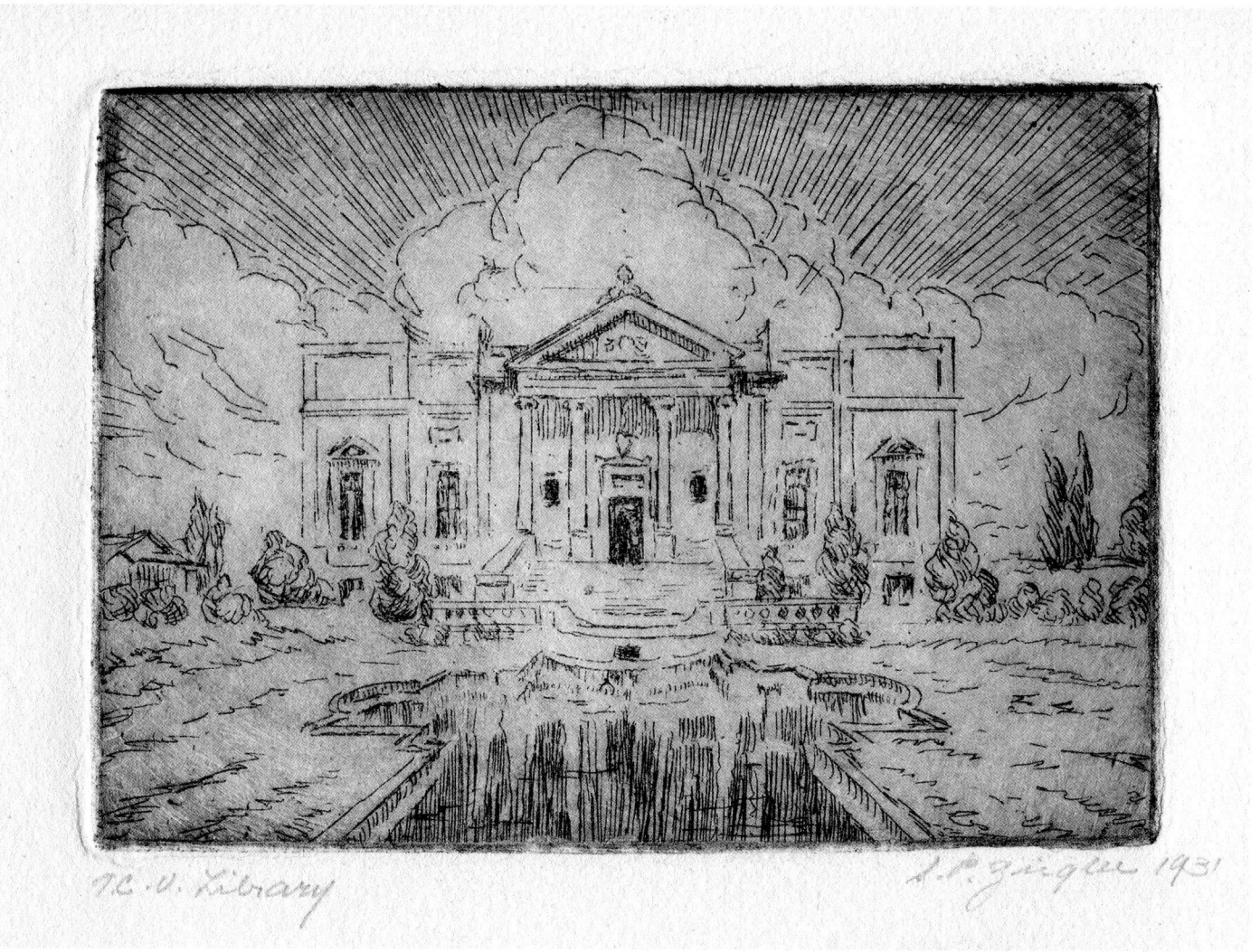

T.C.U. Library   S. P. Ziegler 1931

T.C.U. Library
(Mary Couts Burnett Library),
ca. 1938. Etching.

One of Ziegler's masterpiece prints, this image was etched on a copper plate measuring 6 x 8 inches. This etching was the last in Ziegler's series of Mary Couts Burnett Library images. The print depicted the library's original appearance with mature landscaping and reflecting pool in the foreground. By 1938 the reflecting pool had been modified due to the high cost of maintenance. Its installed fountain was disabled and the reflecting pool stocked with goldfish, leading students to refer to it from that time on as "the fish pond."

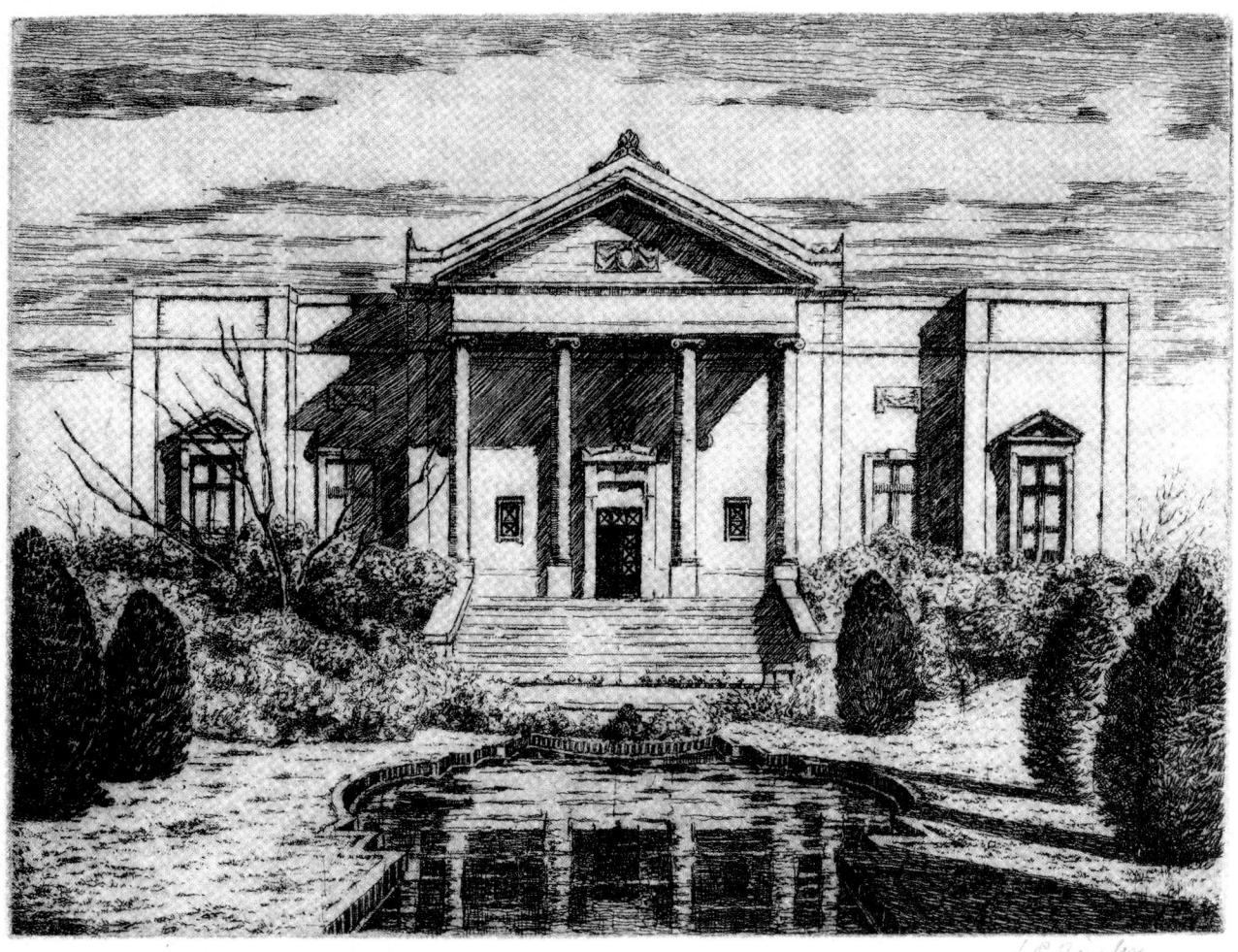

**Brite College of the Bible,
1931. Etching.**

Completed in 1914, Brite College
of the Bible was among the first six
buildings constructed on the Texas
Christian University campus. Brite
College of the Bible housed the
TCU divinity school and provided
the university's first library services.
One of Ziegler's earliest paintings of
TCU campus buildings was based on
the view from the second floor of
the Brite College of the Bible.

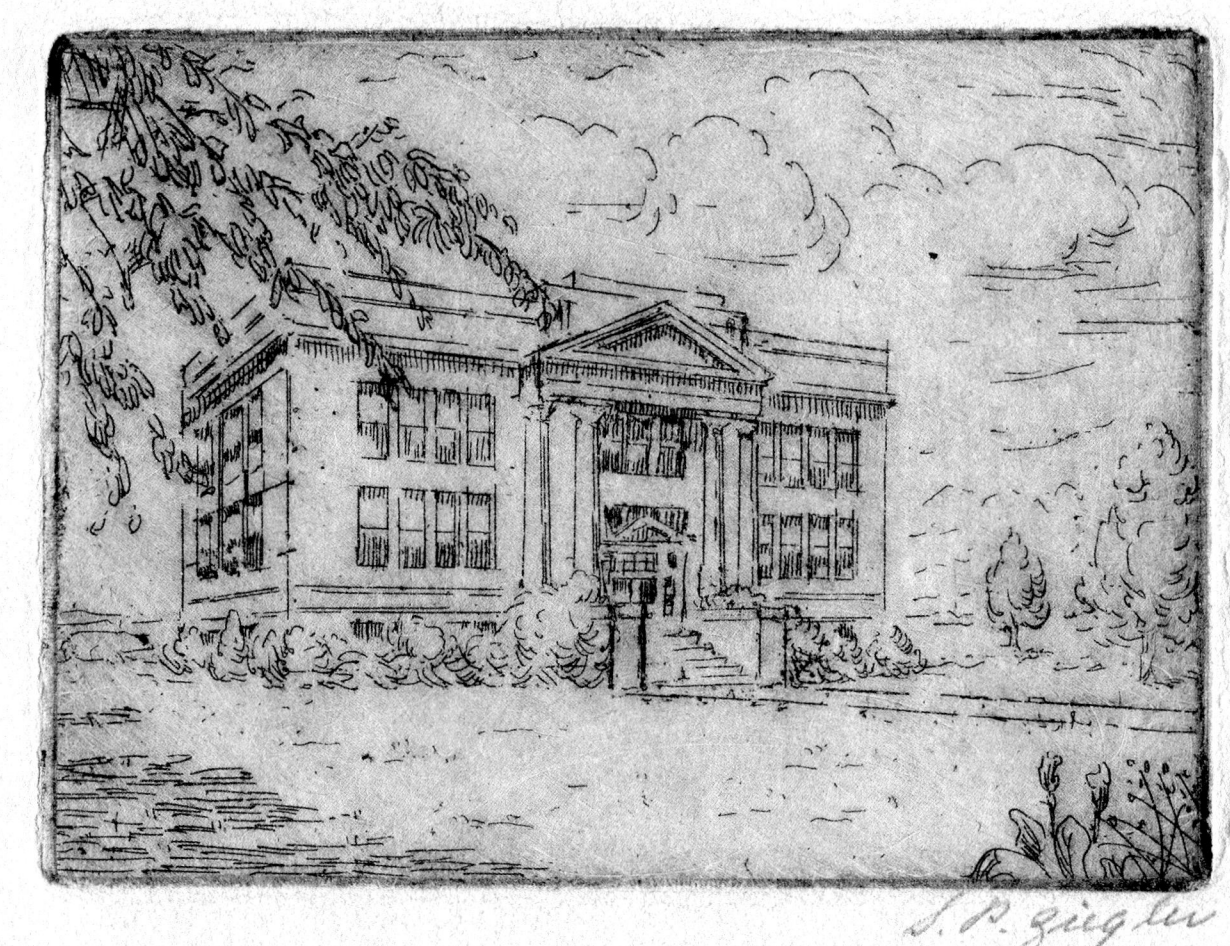

**Brite College of the Bible,
1931. Pen and ink.**

This pen and ink drawing likely served as the preparatory study for Professor Ziegler's 1931 etching of the Brite College building (p. 6).

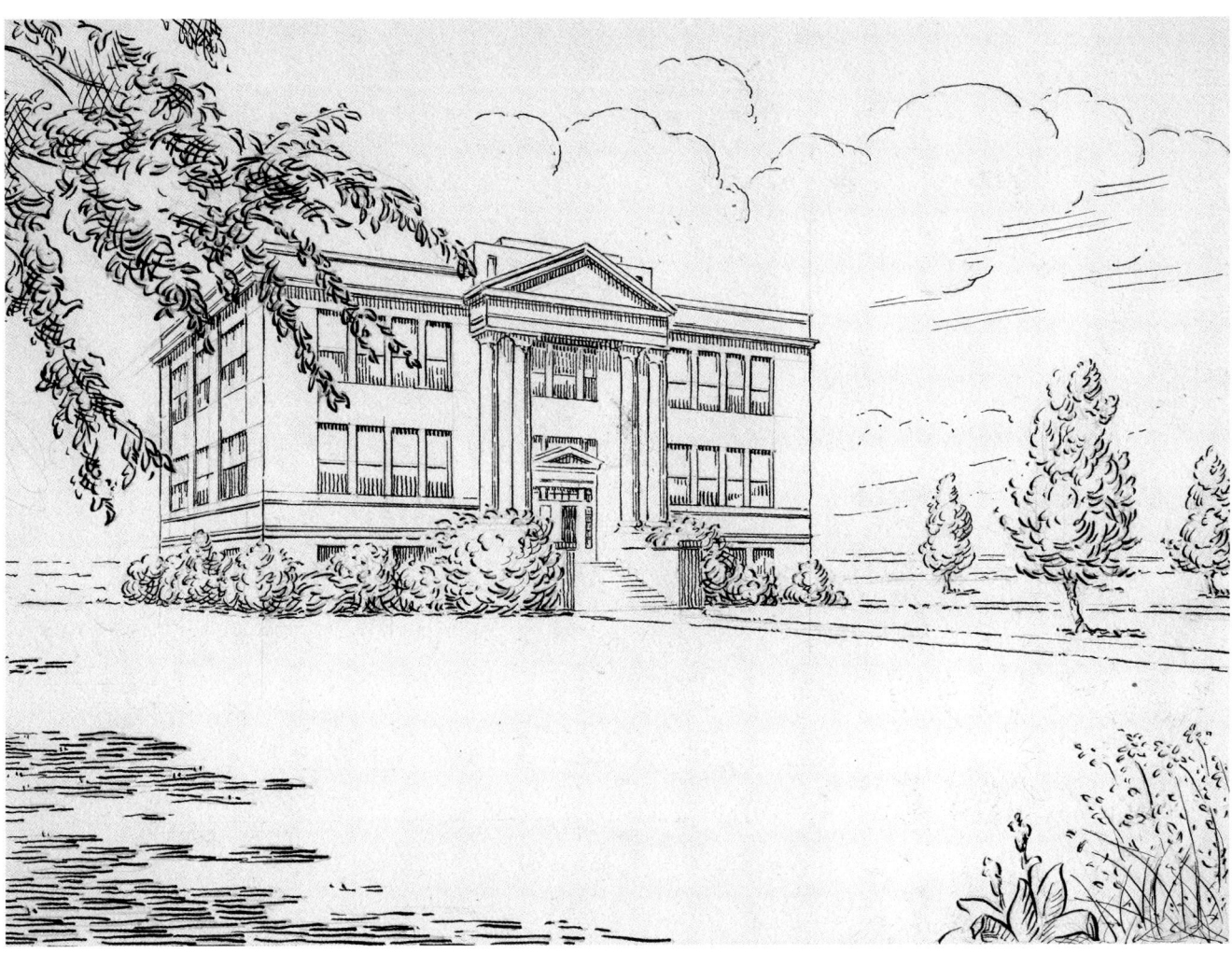

Texas Christian University Gymnasium, **1931. Etching.**

The TCU gymnasium was completed in 1921. It was one of six buildings that comprised the nucleus of the original TCU campus, the campus that Professor Ziegler first saw. All six buildings were arrayed in roughly a straight line along the west side of University Drive.

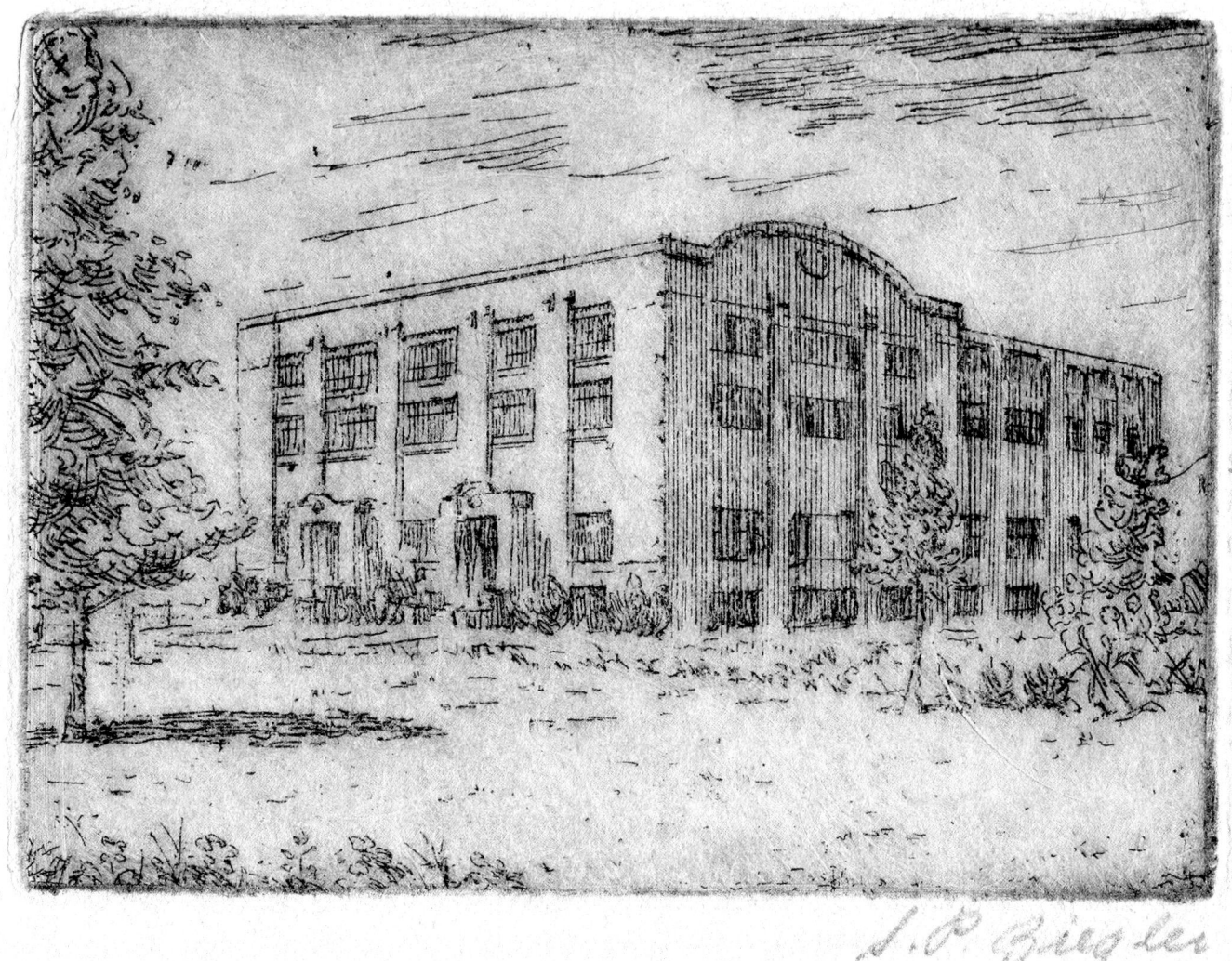

Texas Christian University Gymnasium, ca. 1931. Pen and ink.

This pen and ink drawing likely served as the preparatory study for Professor Ziegler's 1931 etching of the school gymnasium (p. 8).

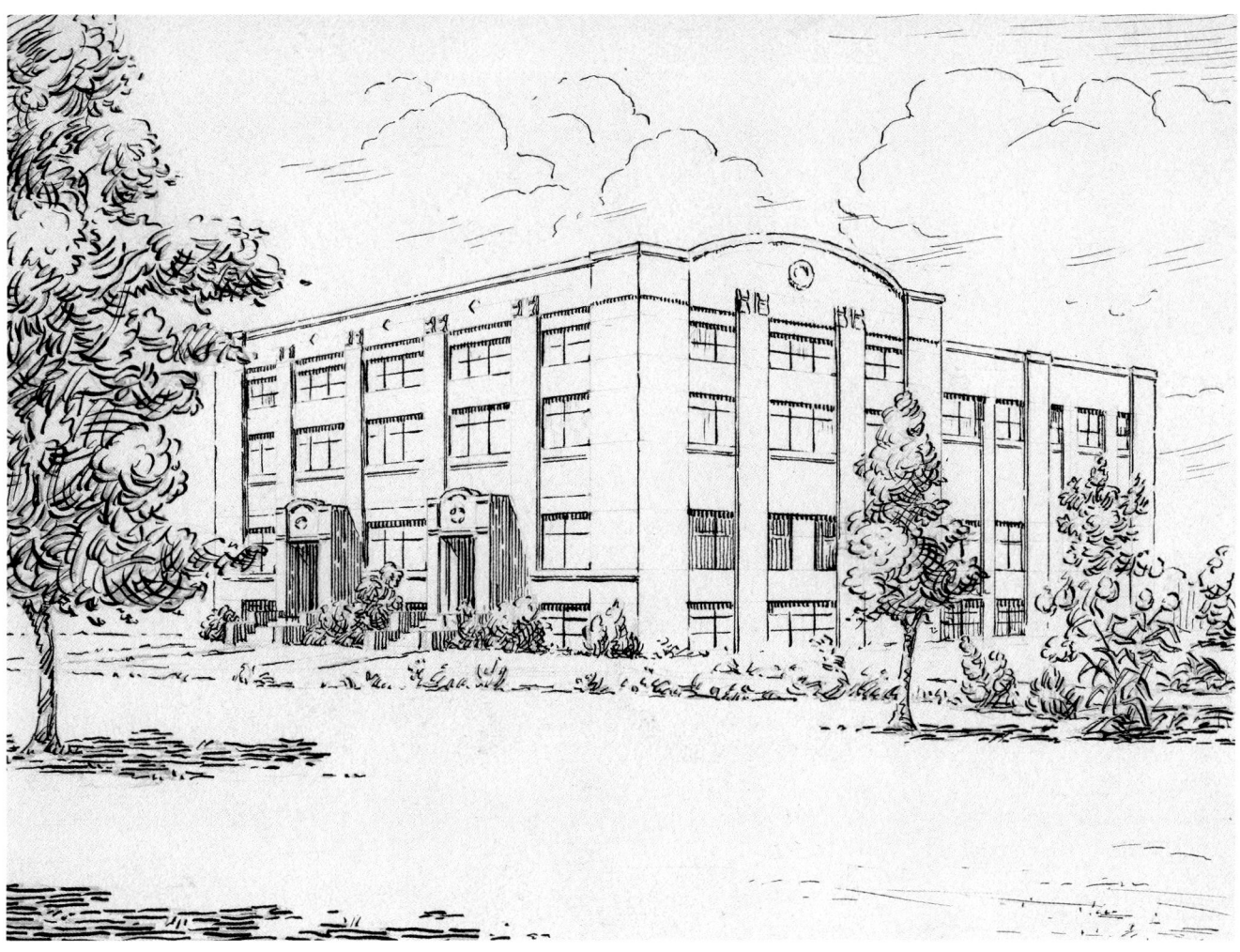

W. T. Hamner Memorial Bandstand, 1931. Etching.

The W. T. Hamner Memorial Bandstand (now demolished) stood on the front lawn of the TCU Main Administration Building. The bandstand was erected shortly after Mr. Hamner's death in 1916 to honor the long-serving professor of English. One evening each fall, freshman men and women attended a traditional mixer at the bandstand. As live music played, couples promenaded or skipped arm-in-arm around the bandstand. It was the closest activity to dancing permitted by university officials at the time.

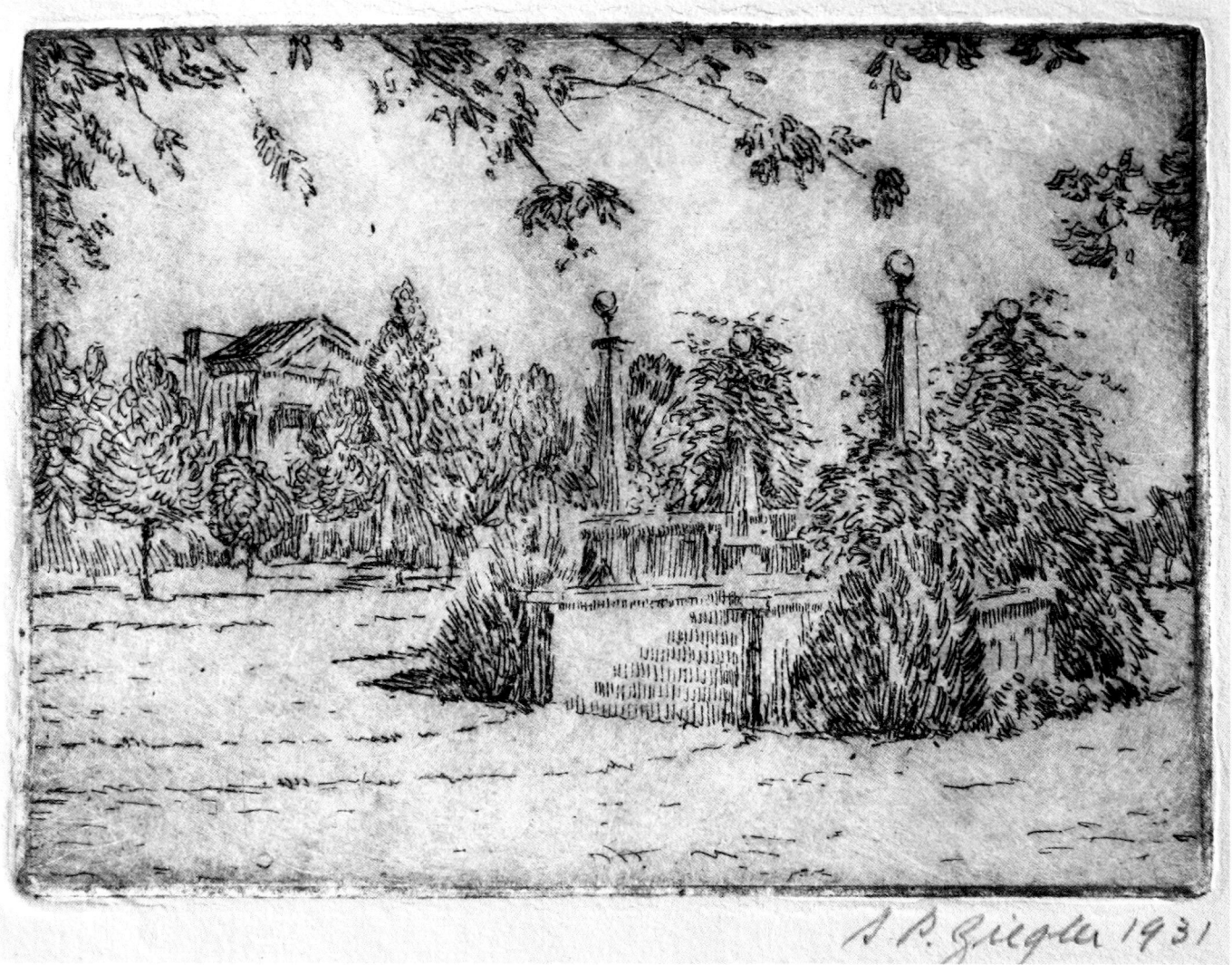

W. T. Hamner Memorial Bandstand, 1931. Pen and ink.

This pen and ink drawing likely served as the preparatory study for Professor Ziegler's 1931 etching of the Hamner Memorial Bandstand (p. 10).

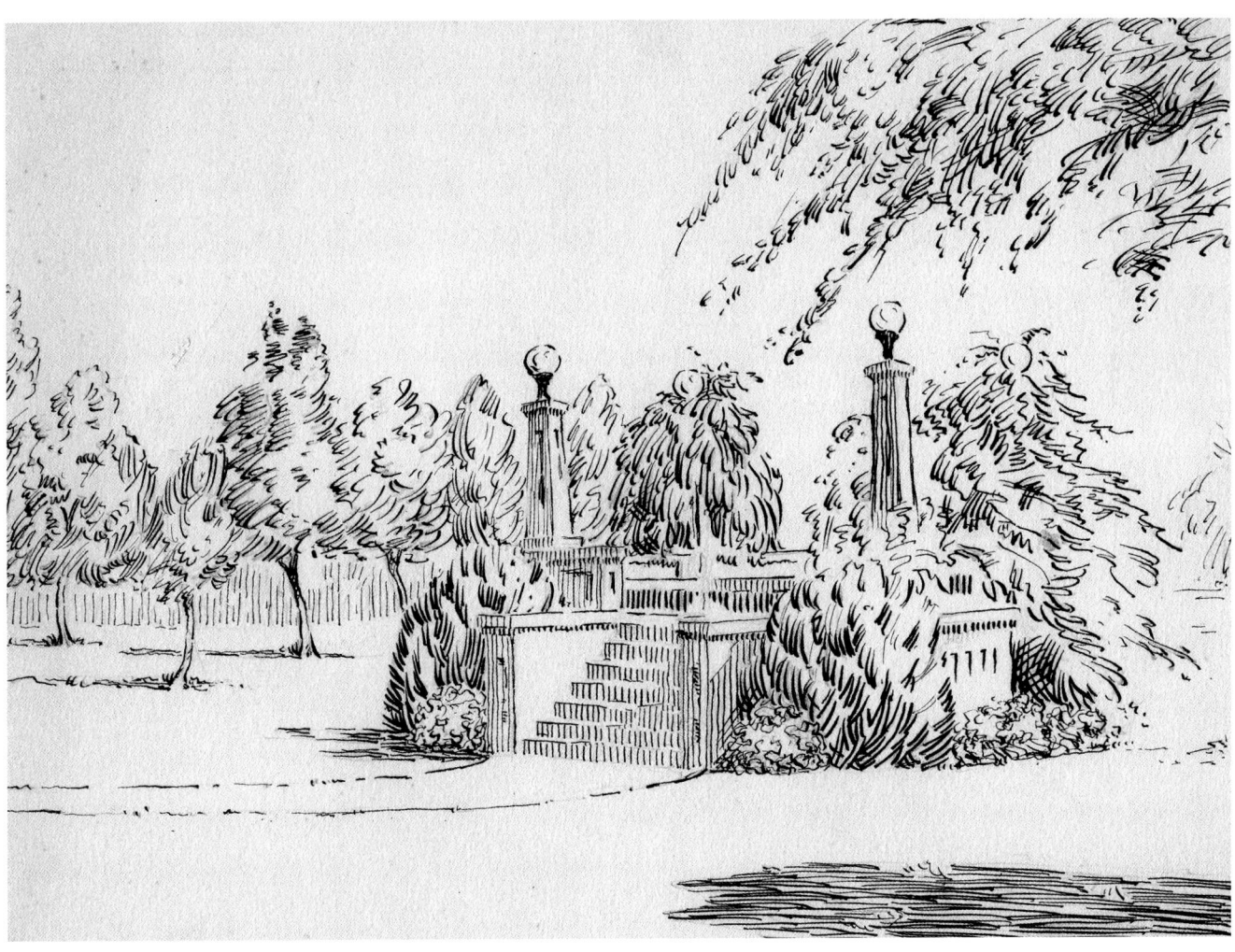

The Memorial Arch,
1931. Etching.

The Memorial Arch was a gift to the university from the graduating class of 1923. The Memorial Arch was erected in recognition of the men and women who served in the US military during World War I and in memory of the three TCU graduates who died in the war. The arch faced University Drive, in front of the Main Administration Building. In this print, the façade of the Mary Couts Burnett Library (across the street) is visible through the archway. The Memorial Arch survived until 1948, when it was demolished as part of the widening of University Drive and replaced by the Memorial Gateway.

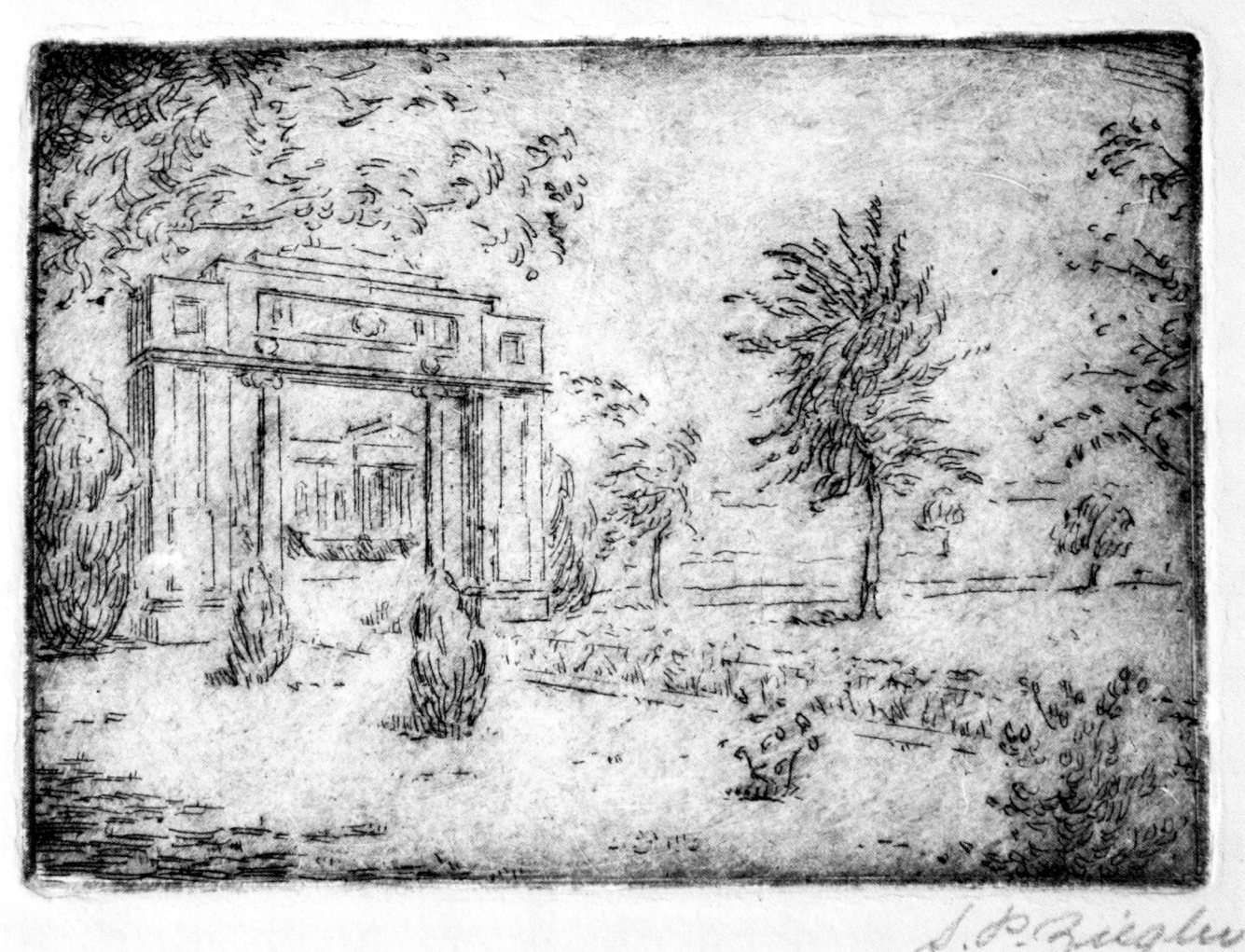

Jarvis Hall, 1931. Etching.

In Professor Ziegler's day, Jarvis Hall served as the women's dormitory. The opening in 1911 of Jarvis Hall, Goode Hall, and the Main Administration Building signaled the creation of Texas Christian University's permanent campus in Fort Worth.

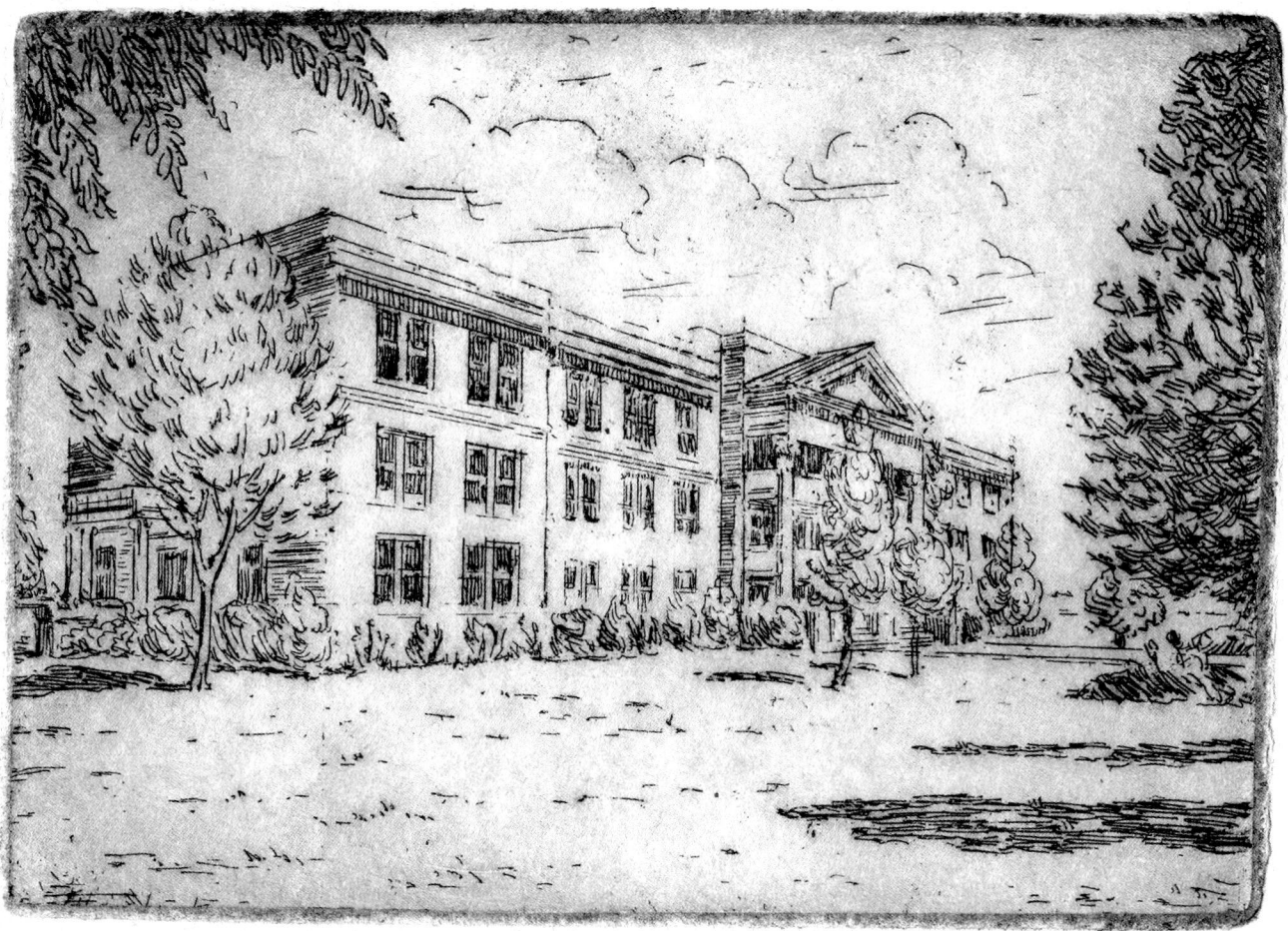

Jarvis Hall, T.C.U., 1931. Etching.

Professor Ziegler's etchings of Jarvis Hall (the TCU women's dormitory) were created in two sizes. This version was the larger of the two and exhibited a higher degree of finish. Image size of the large print was 6 x 8 inches. Both versions were etched on copper plates and printed using a hand-operated press that Ziegler kept in his home.

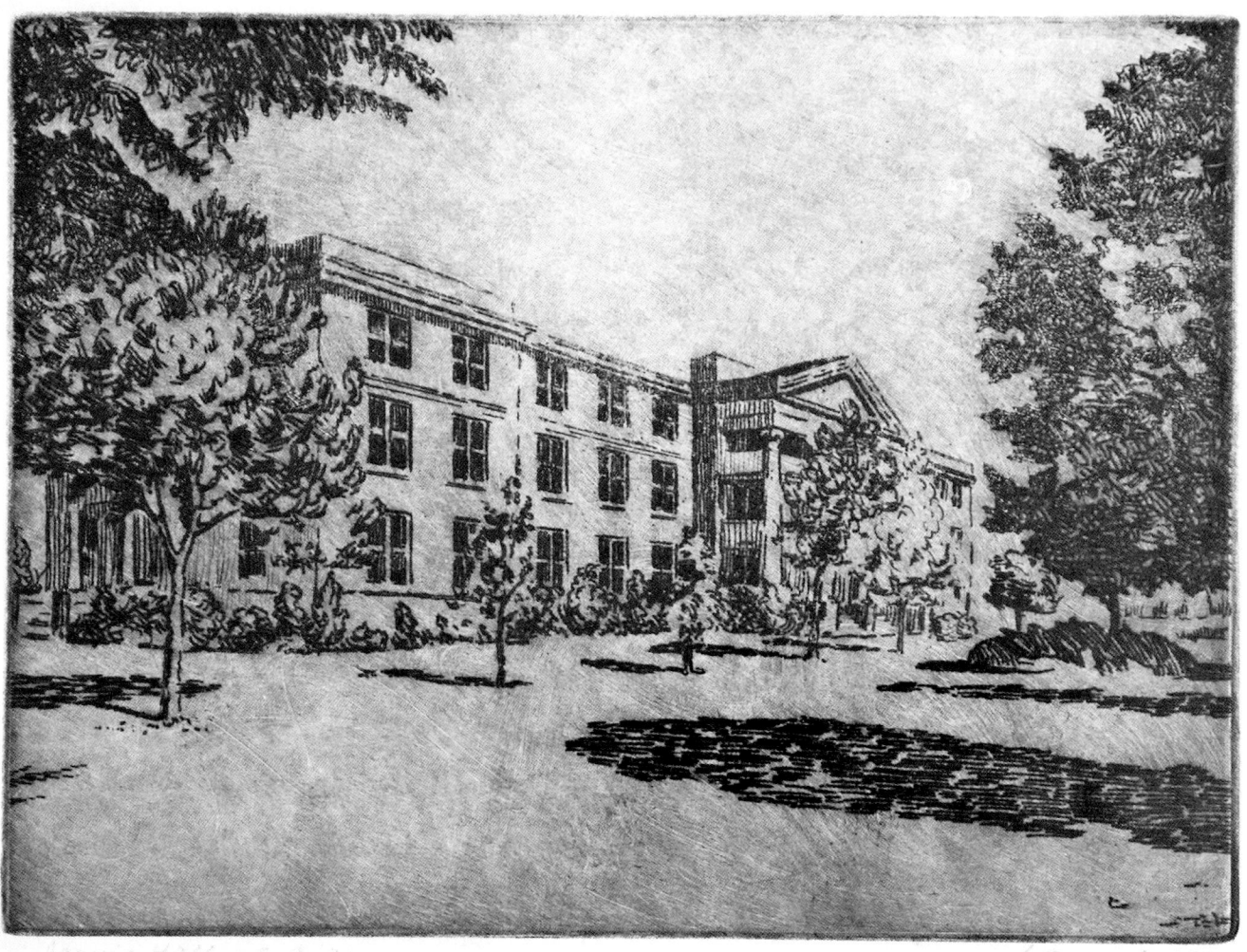

Main Administration Building, 1931. Etching.

The TCU Main Administration Building opened in 1911. In Professor's Ziegler's time, the three-story building housed administrative offices and classrooms and was the hub of Texas Christian University's educational activities. Rooms where Ziegler conducted art classes and student exhibitions were located at the north end of the third floor.

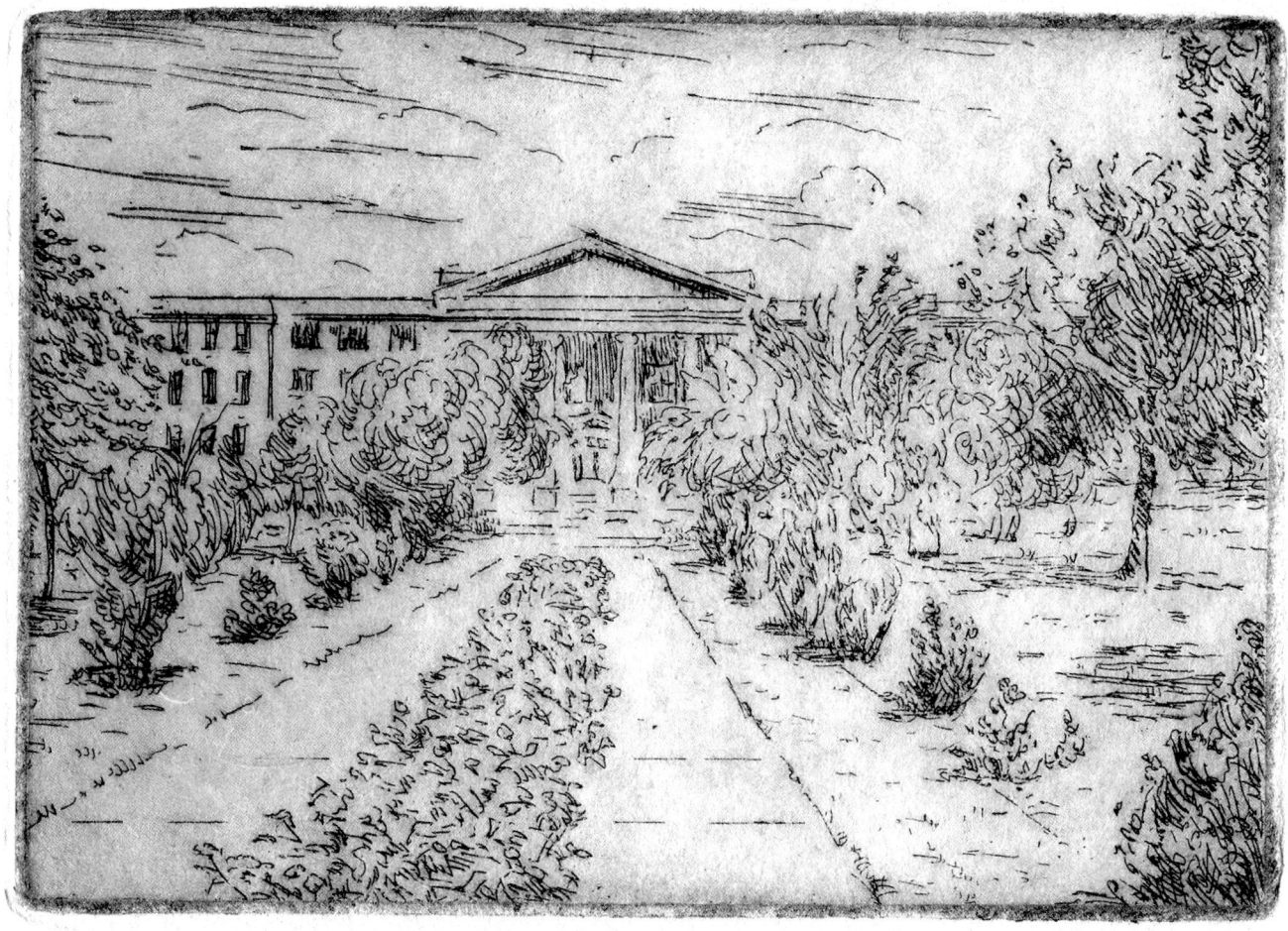

***Main Administration Building, T.C.U., 1931.* Etching.**

Like the prints of Jarvis Hall, Ziegler produced etchings of the Main Administration Building in two sizes. This version was the larger of the two and exhibited a higher degree of finish. Image size of the large print was 6 x 8 inches.

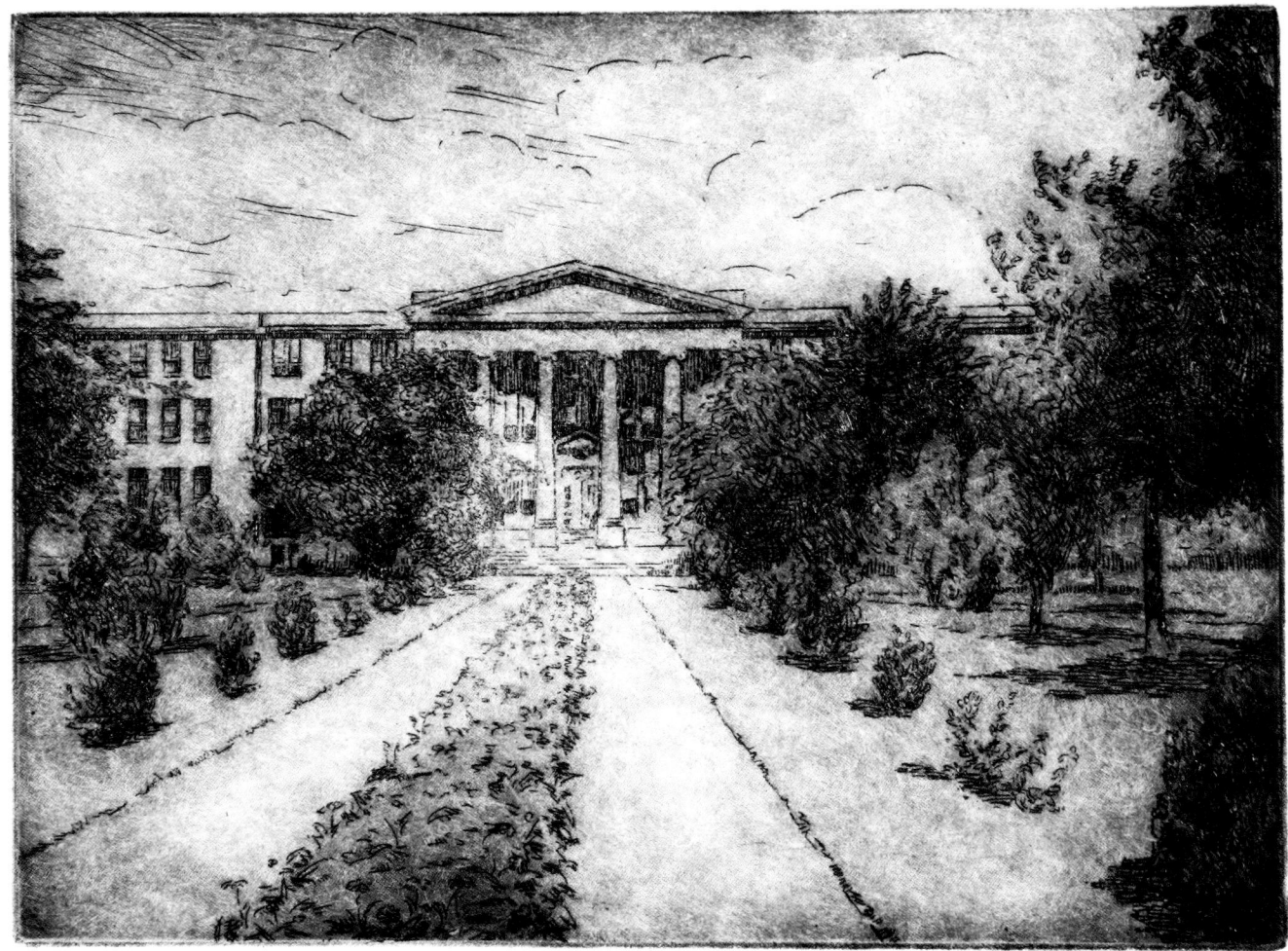

Campus Panorama,
1931. Etching.

Gazing to the west, Professor Ziegler
often stood on the steps of the Mary Couts
Burnett Library and enjoyed the sweeping
view across the street where Texas Christian
University's oldest buildings lined University
Drive. *Campus Panorama* conveys the essence
of what Ziegler saw from that vantage point.
Visible across the street, from left to right,
are Clark Hall, the Main Administration Building
and Jarvis Hall. The scene is bisected by
University Drive, with the manicured lawn
and reflecting pool of the Mary Couts Burnett
Library in the foreground. A few years after
this print was made, Ziegler depicted the
same scene in a formal oil painting.

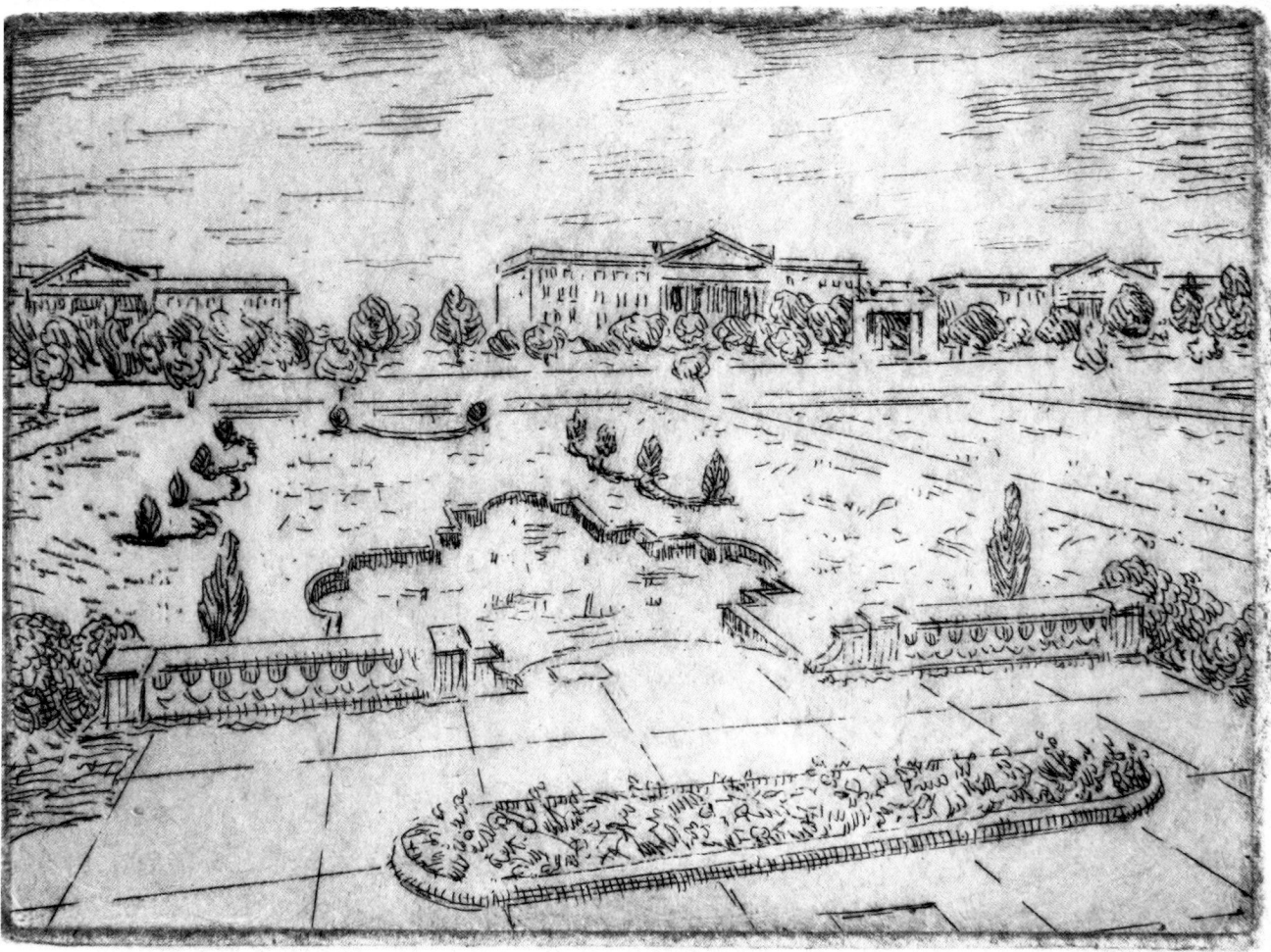

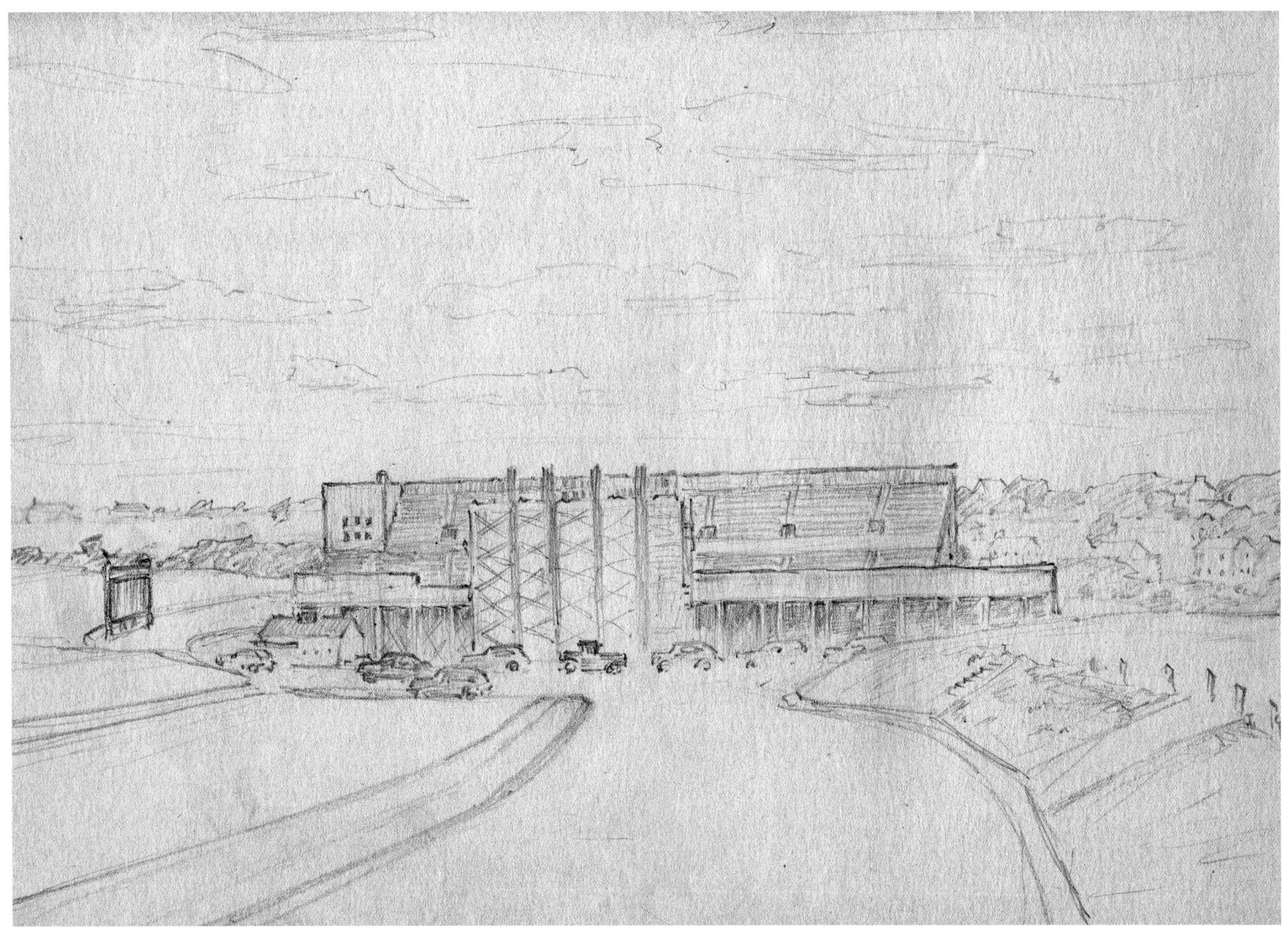

Study for Enlarging Amon Carter Stadium,
1947. Graphite on paper.

Ziegler produced a series of oil paintings of Amon G. Carter Stadium while it was being remodeled and enlarged in 1947. This pencil sketch is one of the preparatory drawings for the series.

Fort Worth Churches

Study of Magnolia Avenue Christian Church, n.d. (early 1930s). **Graphite on paper.**

This drawing served as the preparatory study for Professor Ziegler's etching of the Magnolia Avenue Christian Church (p. 23). A preparatory drawing of his subject allowed Ziegler to solve problems of proportion and perspective before replicating the image on the copper printing plate.

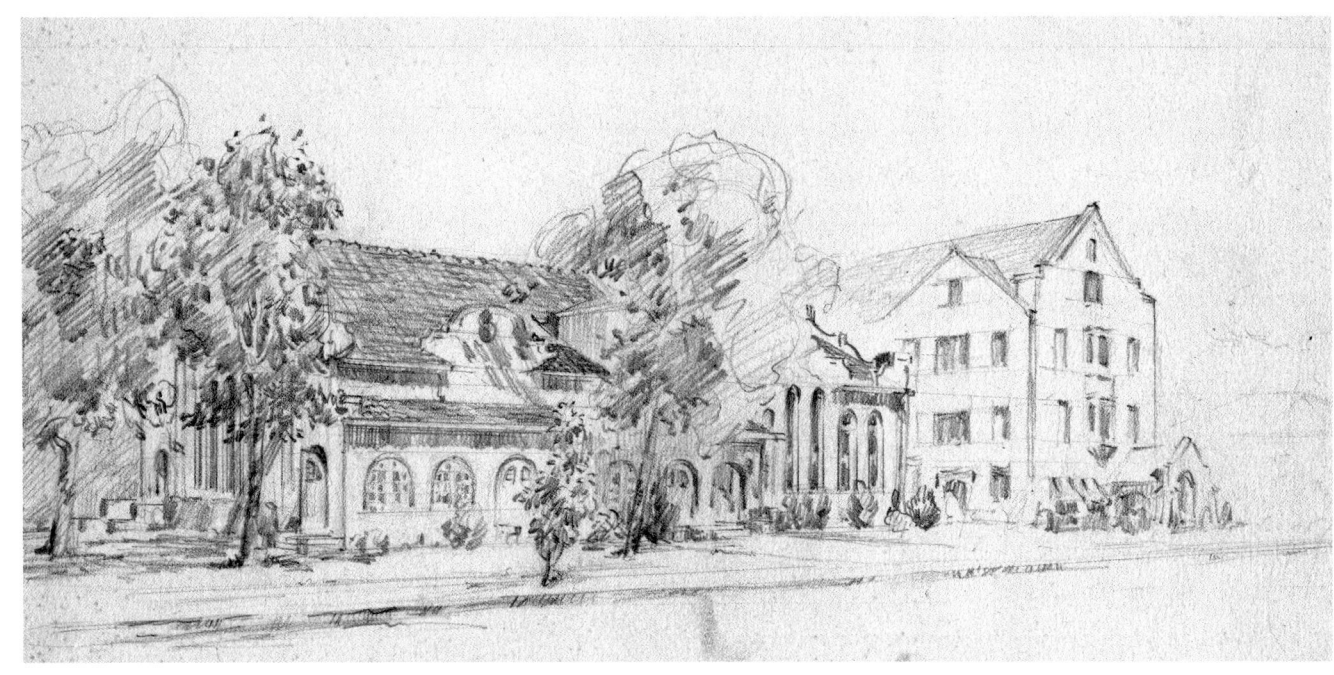

Magnolia Avenue Christian Church, n.d. (early 1930s). Etching.

This 3 x 5 inch print depicted the Magnolia Avenue Christian Church, then located at 950 W. Magnolia Avenue. The church no longer stands.

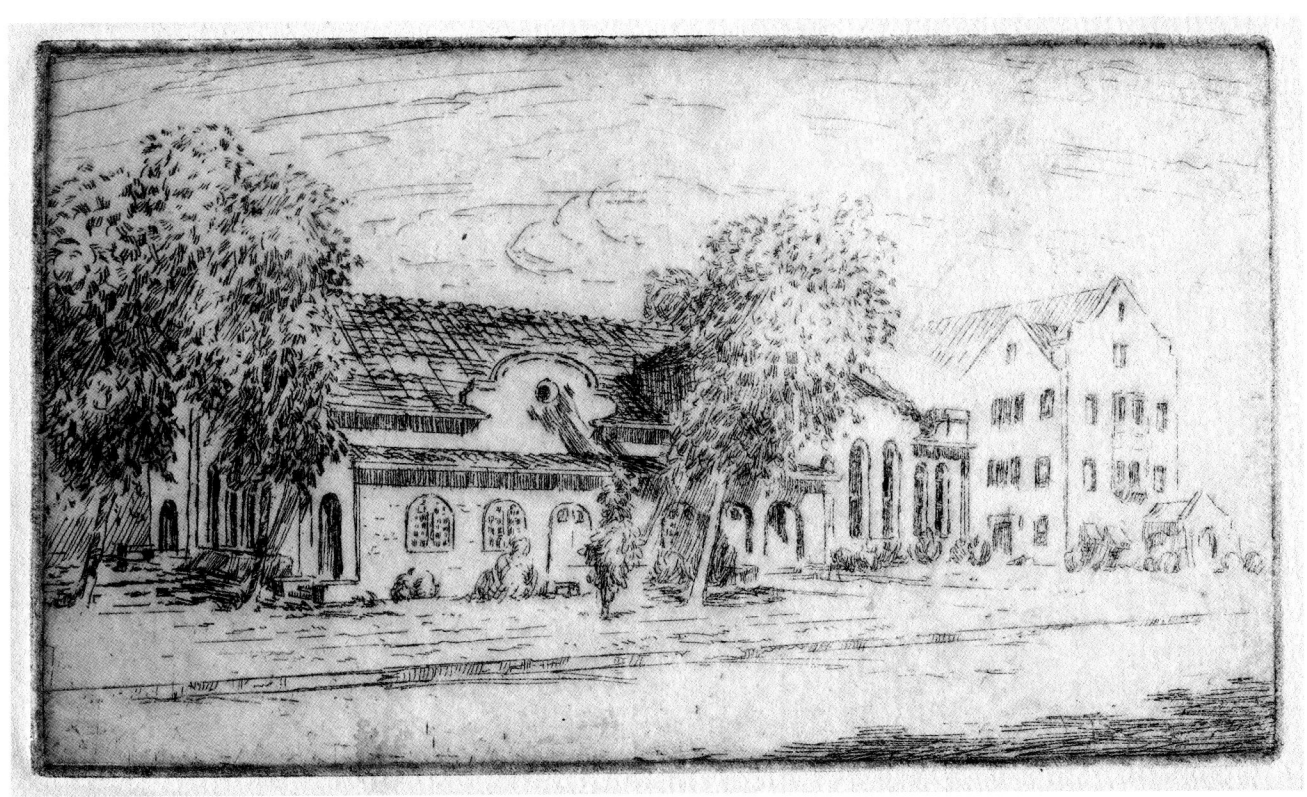

Study of Saint Mary of the Assumption Catholic Church, n.d. (early 1930s). Graphite on paper.

This graphite drawing served as the preparatory study for Professor Ziegler's etching of St. Mary of the Assumption Catholic Church (p. 25). Ziegler's etchings began with a detailed pencil study drawn in correct perspective. The design was then hand-drawn in reverse on a copper plate coated with an acid resistant, tar-like substance called a ground. A hand-held etching needle was used to draw on the surface of the plate.

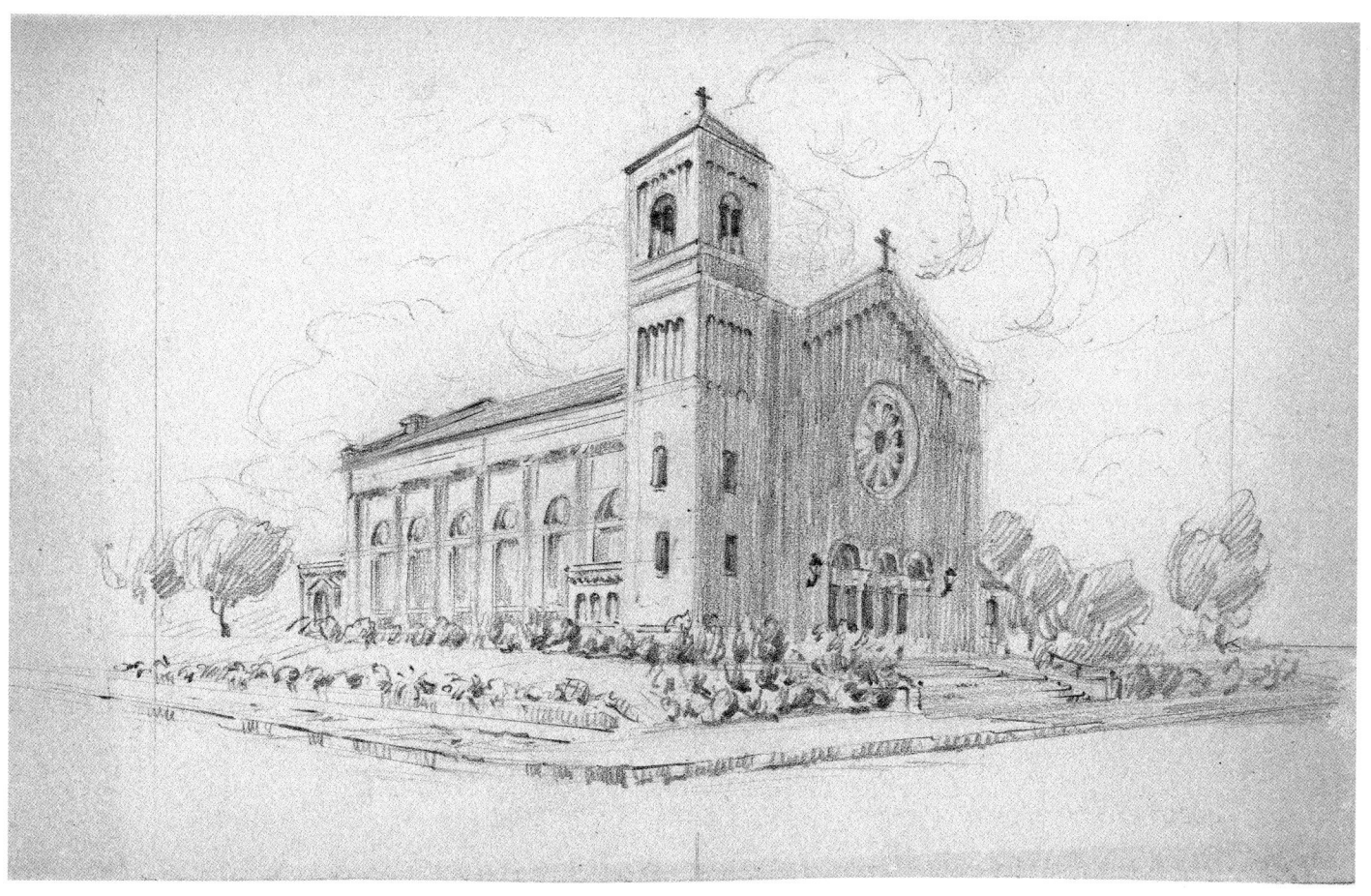

Saint Mary of the Assumption Catholic Church, n.d. (early 1930s). Etching.

After the preparatory drawing was replicated on a coated printing plate, the plate was dipped in acid. Acid ate into the copper surface of the plate wherever ground had been removed by the etching needle, thus transferring the design. The etched plate was cleaned thoroughly and readied for inking. By varying the application of ink to the plate and the amount of pressure applied by the printing press, Ziegler varied the effects of light and dark areas to achieve finished prints. These variations ensured that no two prints were identical. The Romanesque Revival building depicted in this etching is still in use today, located at 509 W. Magnolia Avenue.

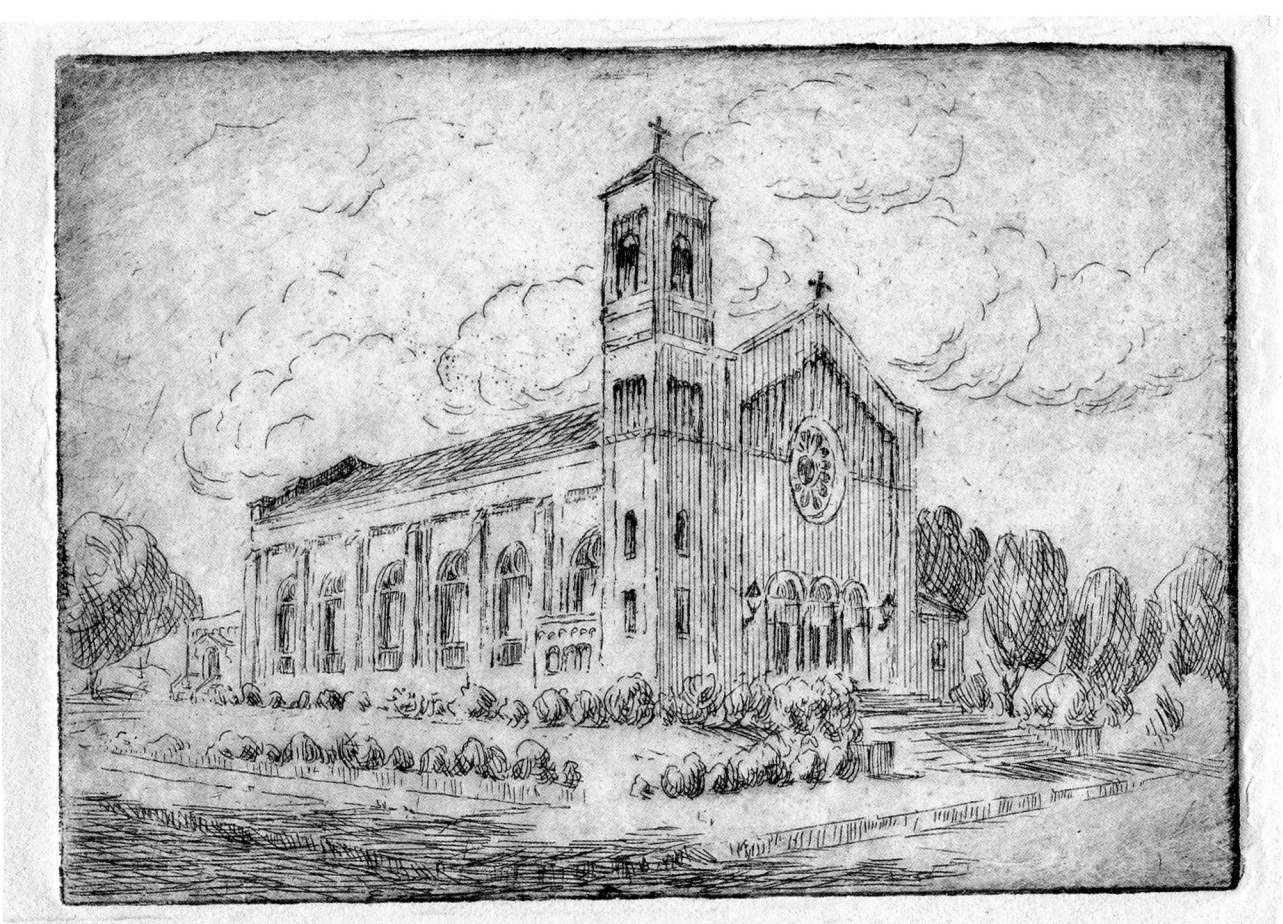

First Christian Church, n.d. (early 1930s). Etching.

This building at 612 Throckmorton Street opened in 1914 and still stands. It houses a congregation that formed in 1865, Fort Worth's oldest congregation. Professor Ziegler's etching of First Christian Church captured a flurry of human activity occurring on the street beneath the copper-clad dome. The lines of the etched plate were bitten with amazing delicacy, given the plate's small size (3 x 4 inches). A year or two before creating this etching, Ziegler produced another view of First Christian Church as part of his series of lithographs of downtown Fort Worth scenes (p. 27).

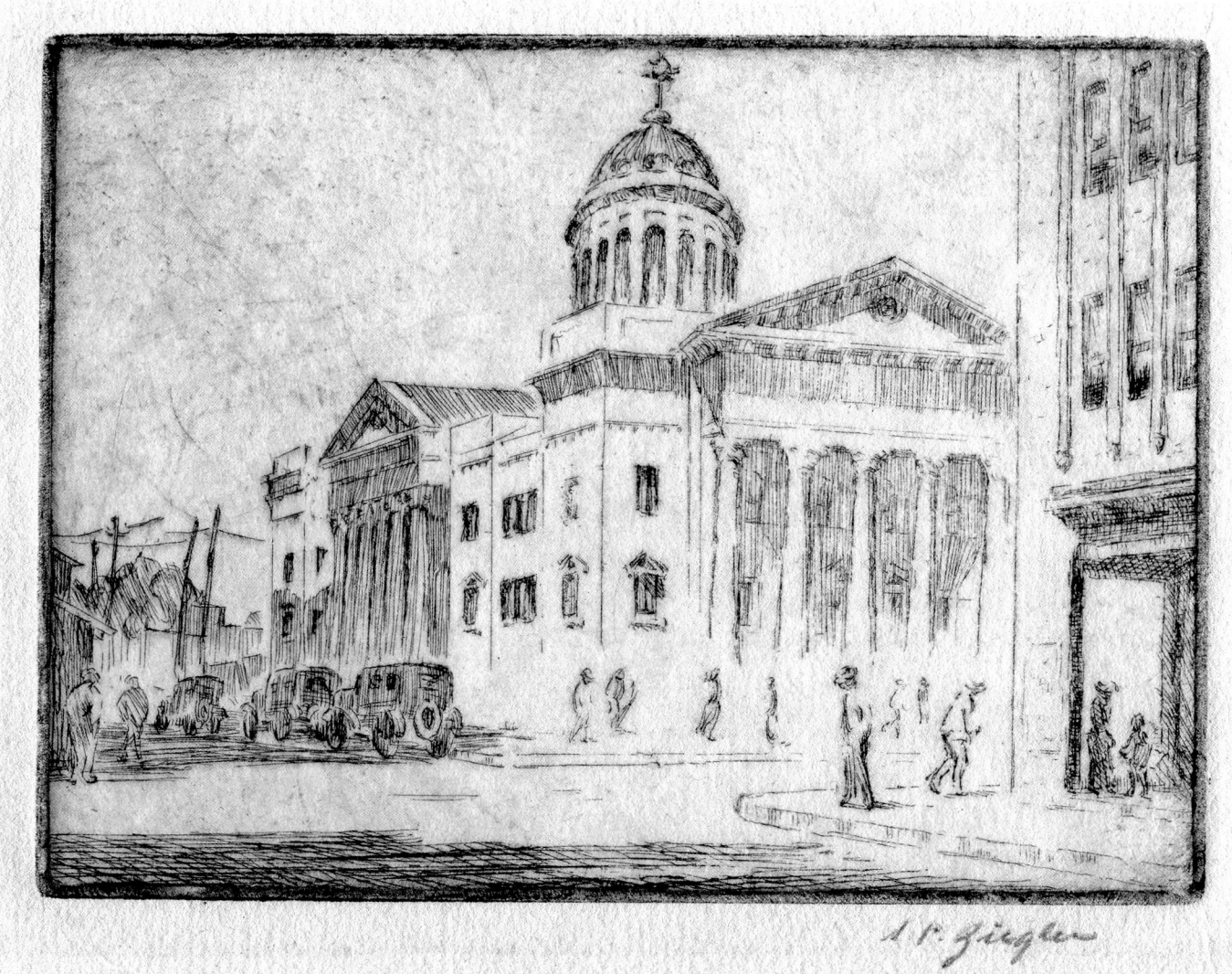

First Christian Church, ca. 1930. Lithograph.

While similar to Ziegler's etching of First Christian Church (p. 26), this lithograph predates the etching by one to two years. The visual perspective of the church is identical in the two prints; however, between them, the scene played out in the street below is quite different. Here, Ziegler records the actions of a masonry crew at work at the northeast corner of Throckmorton and W. Sixth Streets. During the brief period that Ziegler tried his hand at lithography, he produced between 40 and 50 lithographs of Fort Worth churches, office buildings, civic buildings, and West Texas oil scenery.

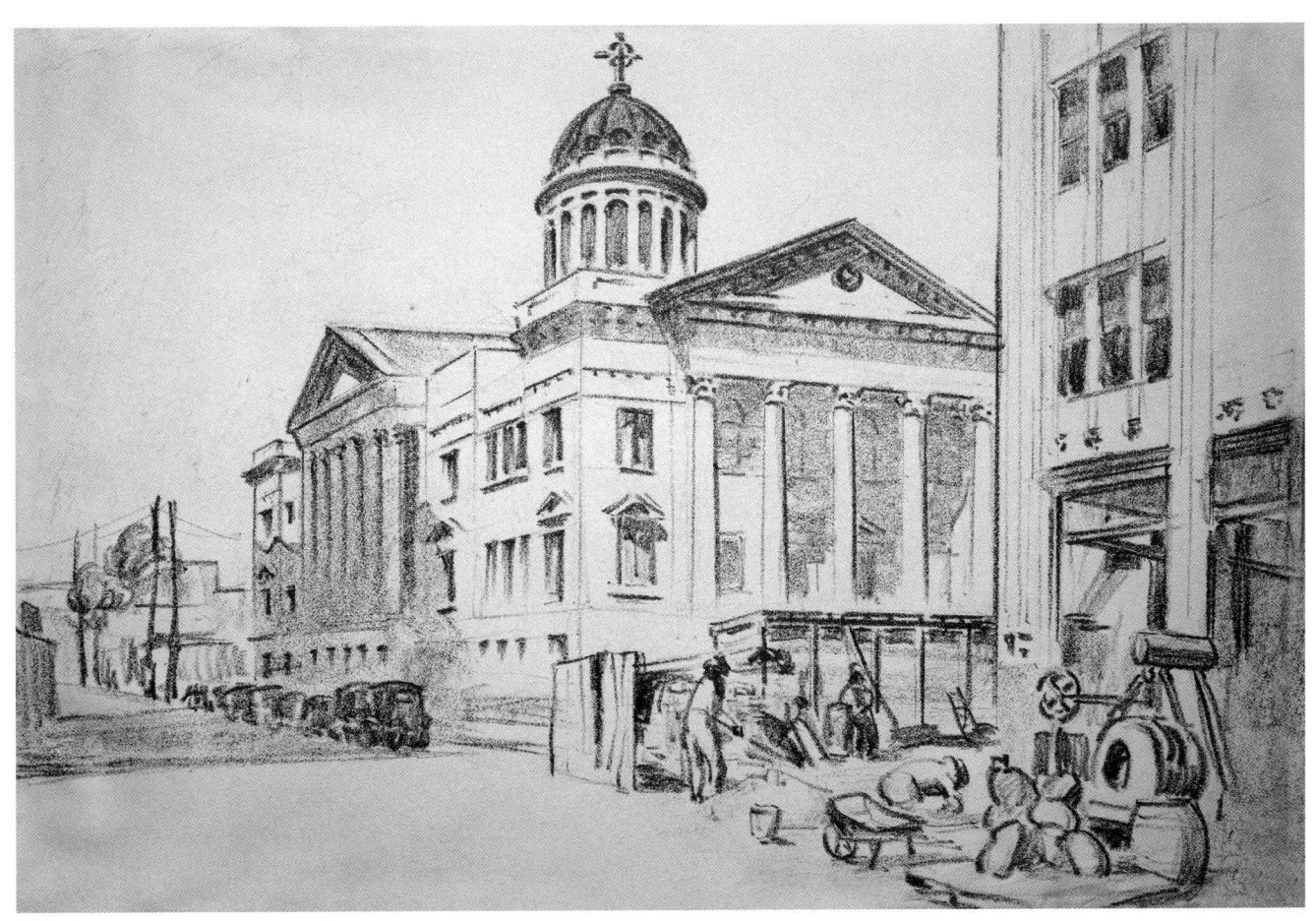

Study of First Methodist Church, n.d. (early 1930s). Graphite on paper.

This pencil study of Fort Worth's First Methodist Church deftly captured the building's Gothic Revival façade; however, for unknown reasons, this preparatory drawing was not utilized as the basis for a fine art print. In the present day, no prints produced by Ziegler of this particular view are known to exist. Instead of utilizing this view of the church's main south entrance, Ziegler made prints of the church as seen from the west (see pp. 29, 30, and 31), perhaps because he felt that the western exposure better conveyed the building's architectural intentions. The First Methodist Church, excluding auxiliary buildings, was modeled after Notre Dame in Paris.

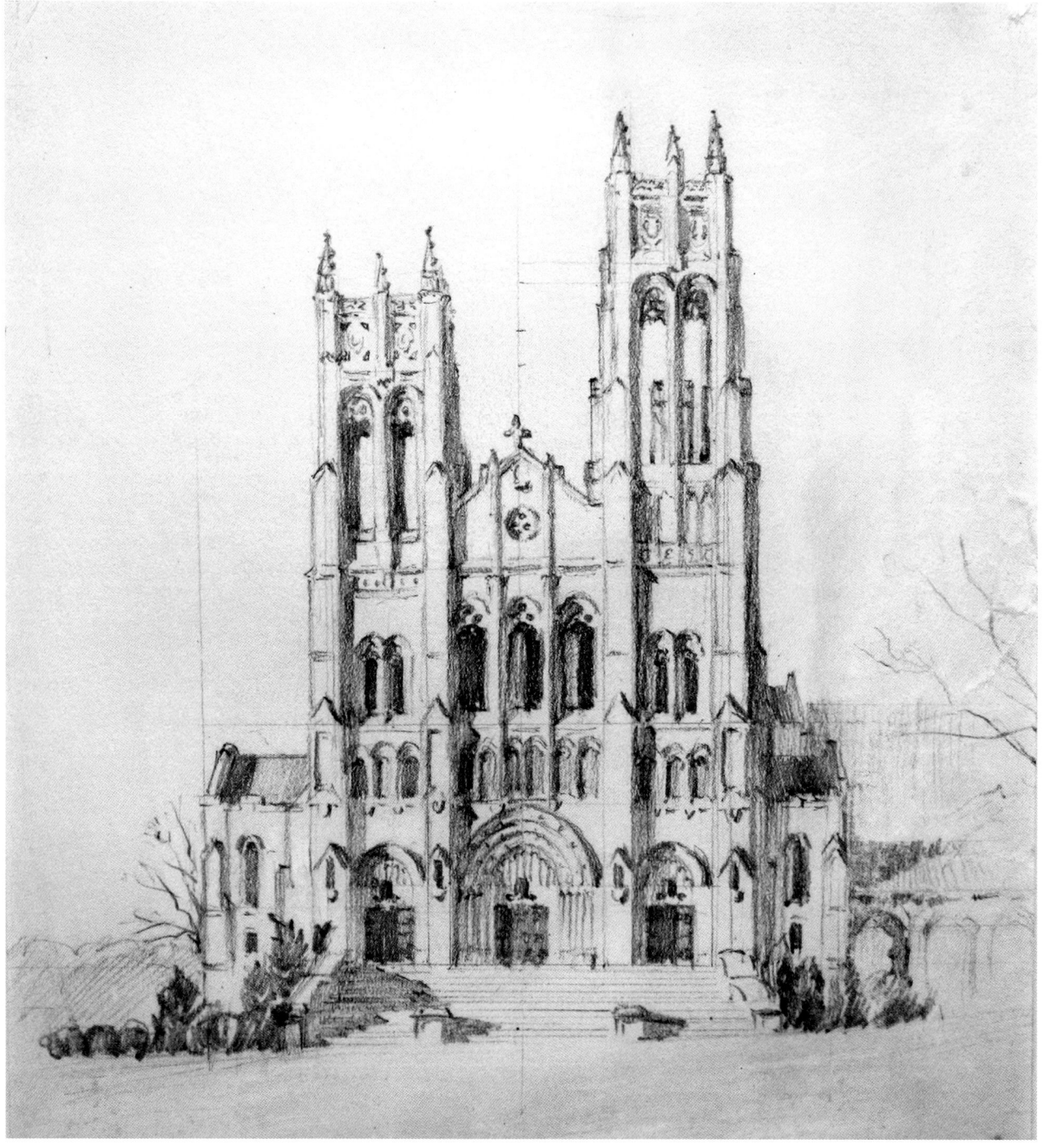

**First Methodist Church,
n.d. (early 1930s). Etching.**

Ziegler produced this view of Fort Worth's
First Methodist Church from the west in both
an etching and a lithograph (see p. 30). In this
view, only the southern half of the sanctuary is
visible. The church's massive rose window is
hidden behind a tree. The Gothic Revival building was designed by Fort Worth architect Wiley
G. Clarkson and opened in 1931 at 800 W. Fifth
Street. The structure still serves in 2023 as the
First United Methodist Church of Fort Worth.

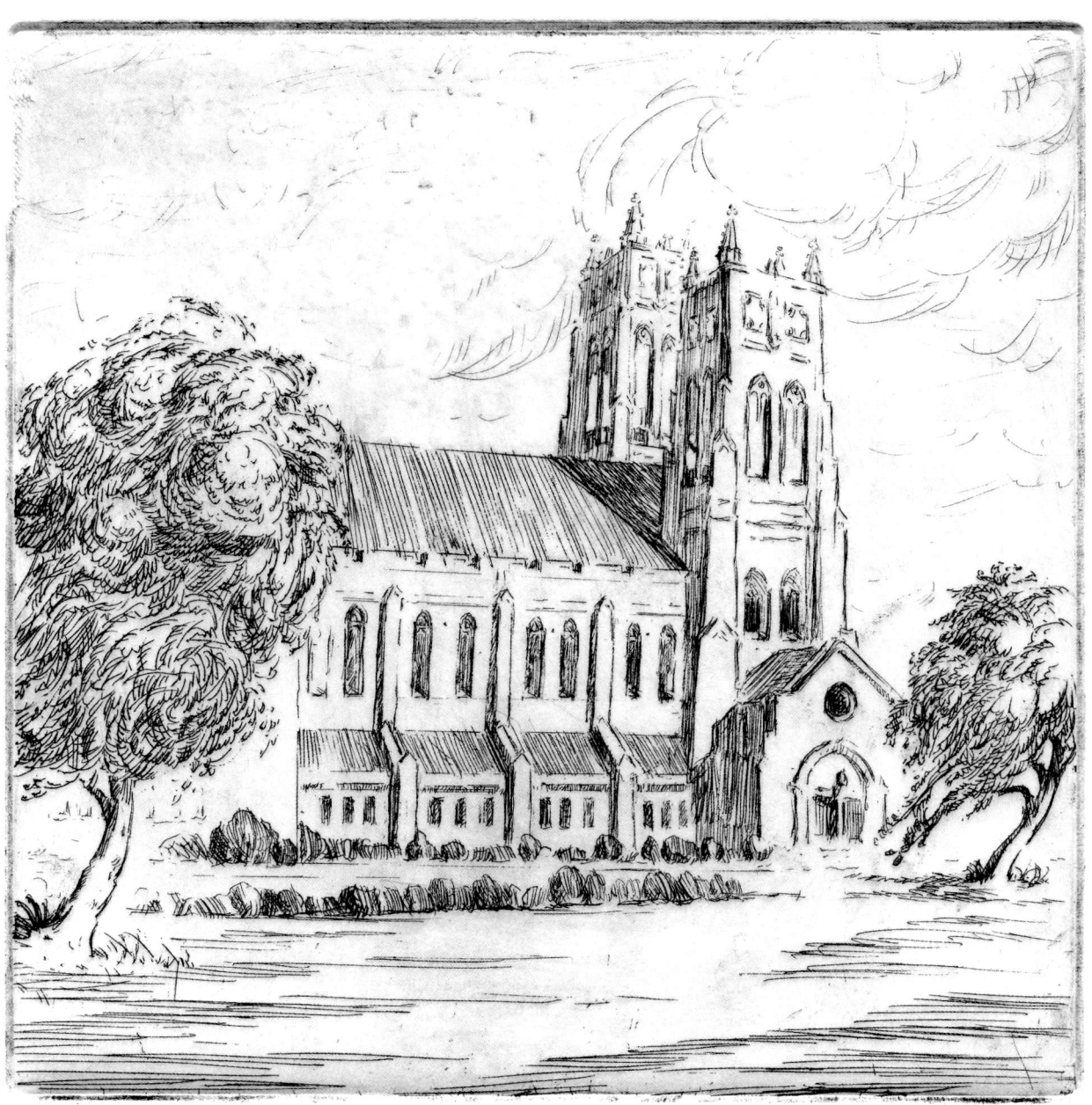

First Methodist Church,
ca. 1930. Lithograph.

The strong similarity between this lithograph of First Methodist Church and Ziegler's etching of the same scene (p. 29) suggests that both prints were based on the same preparatory drawing. Note the spontaneous feel of the lithographic drawing as compared to the carefully designed appearance of the etched image. The lithographic image suggests a building meant to be used, while the etching depicts a building meant to last.

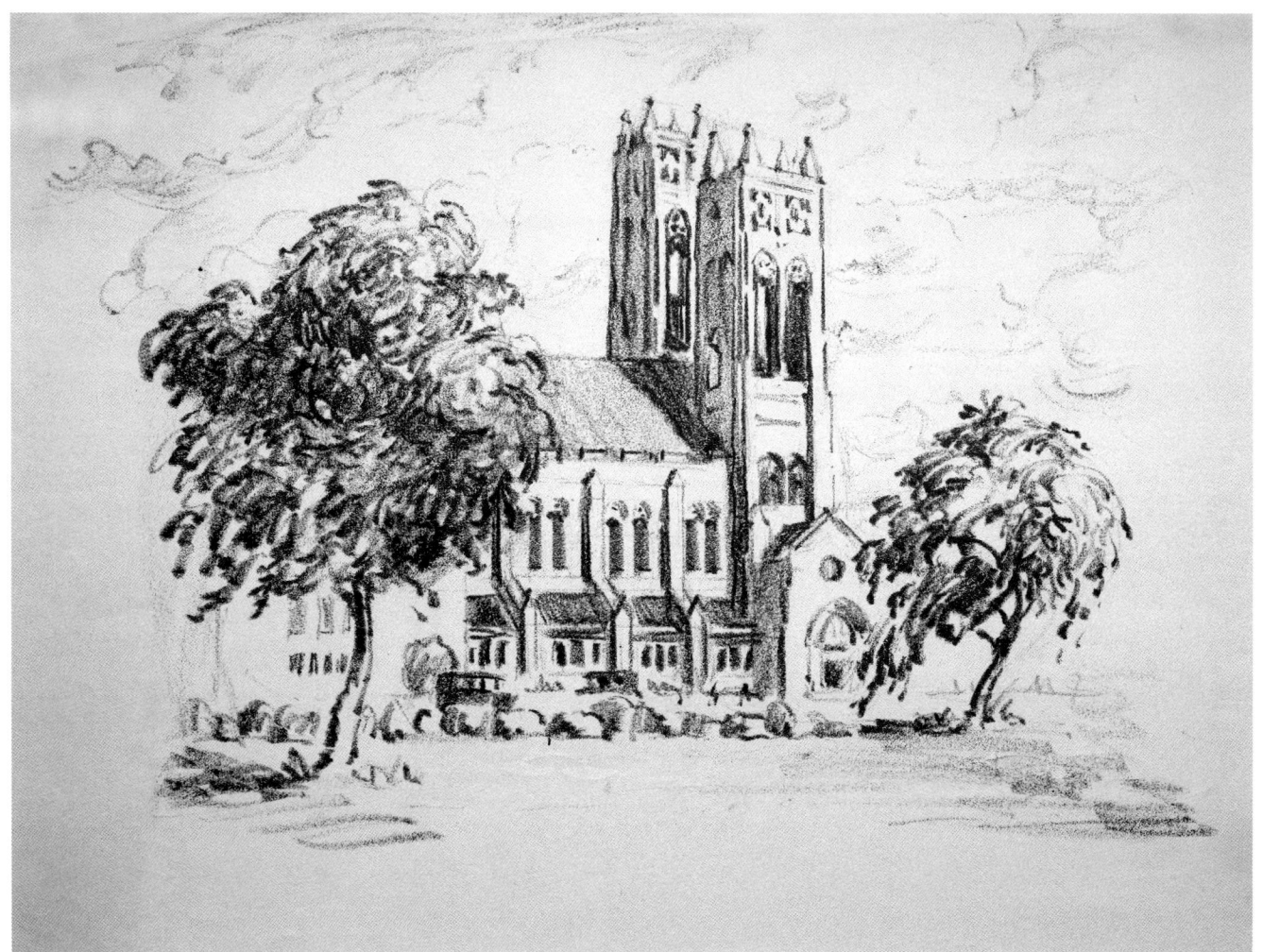

Modern Gothic (First Methodist Church), ca. 1930. Lithograph.

In this second lithographic view of First Methodist Church, Ziegler dispensed with two tree forms in the earlier print, one near the middle of the sanctuary, to reveal the church's arched window and northern apse. He assigned the name *Modern Gothic* to the new image in recognition of the building's medieval ancestry.

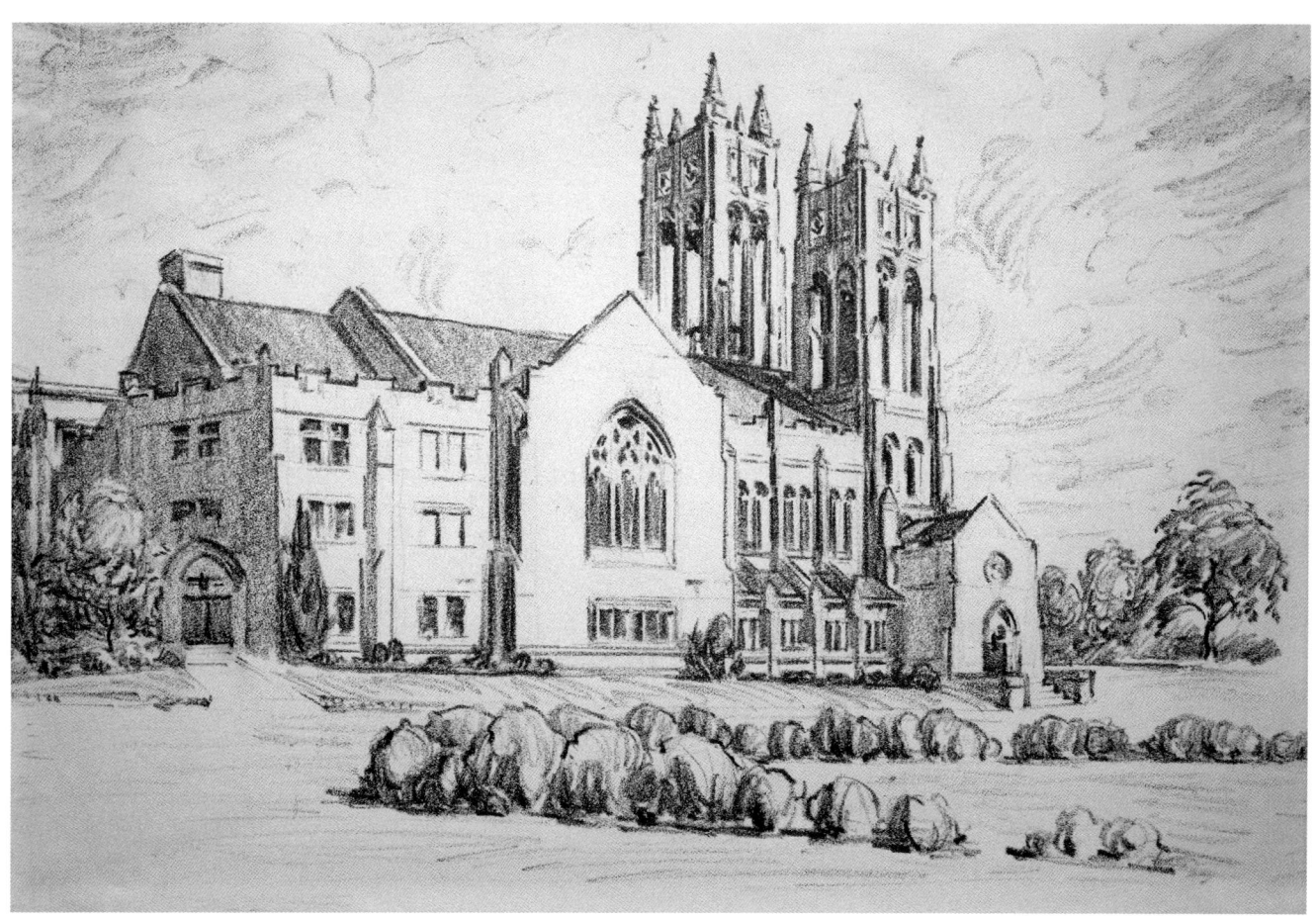

First Baptist Church, n.d. (early 1930s). Etching.

At the time this print was made, First Baptist Church occupied most of the city block from Throckmorton to Taylor Streets, between W. Third and W. Fourth. The church was the exclusive domain of flamboyant pastor J. Frank Norris. One of Norris's enterprises was radio station KFQB, over which his sermons were carried. Here, Ziegler depicted two KFQB broadcast towers on-site, looming over the church. Though the broadcast towers were evidently not in place for long, one of them can be seen in a downtown aerial photo of the period, demonstrating that the towers existed for a time. Today, all traces of the church and towers have vanished from the downtown area.

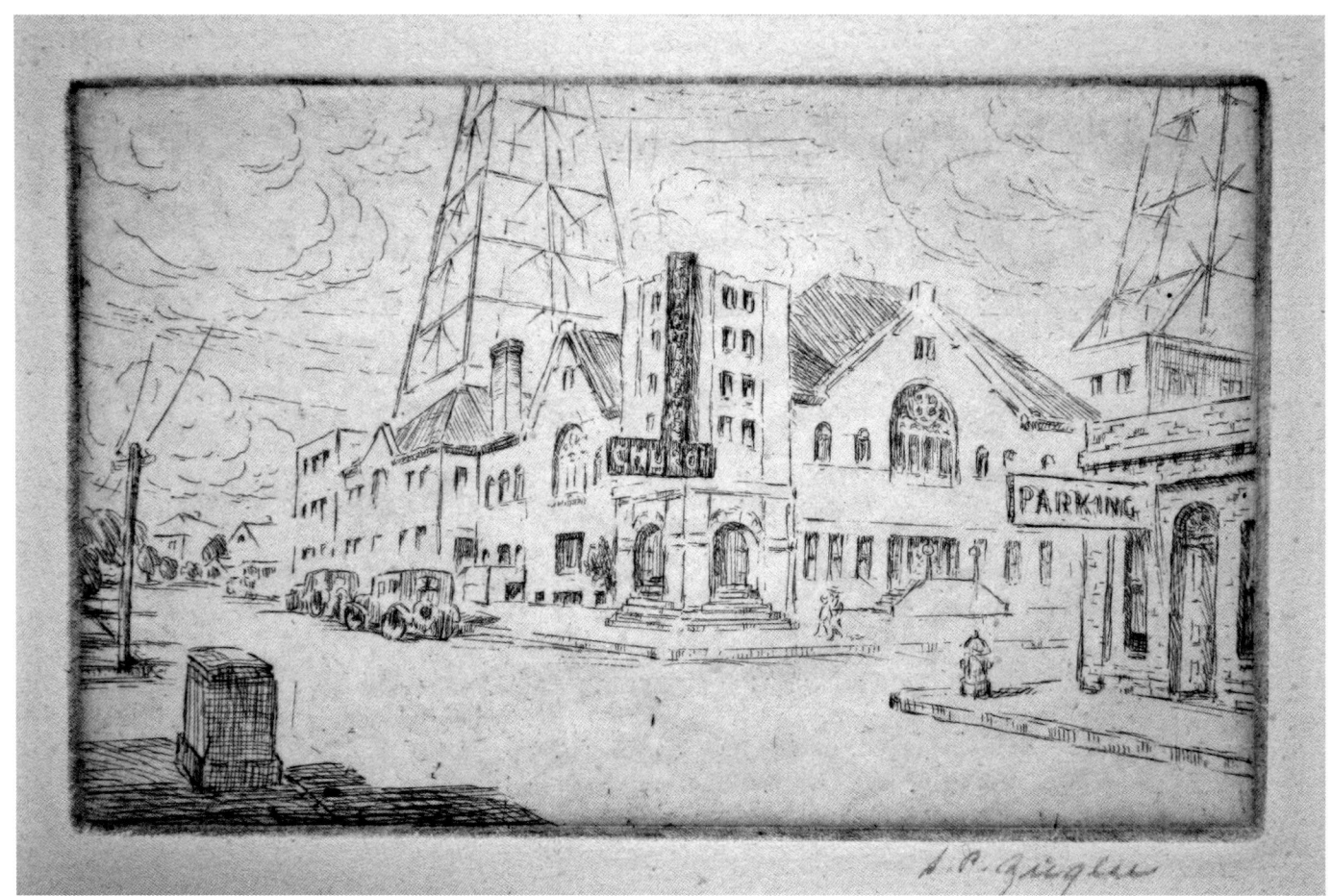

**First Baptist Church,
ca. 1930. Lithograph.**

The content of this circa 1930 lithograph
is substantially identical to Ziegler's etching
of First Baptist Church (opposite). In size,
however, the two prints are vastly different.
The etching measures 3 x 4 ½ inches, while
the lithograph is 12 ½ x 18 inches. The only
known copy of this lithograph resides in the
Dow Art Galleries Collection, Fort Worth, Texas.

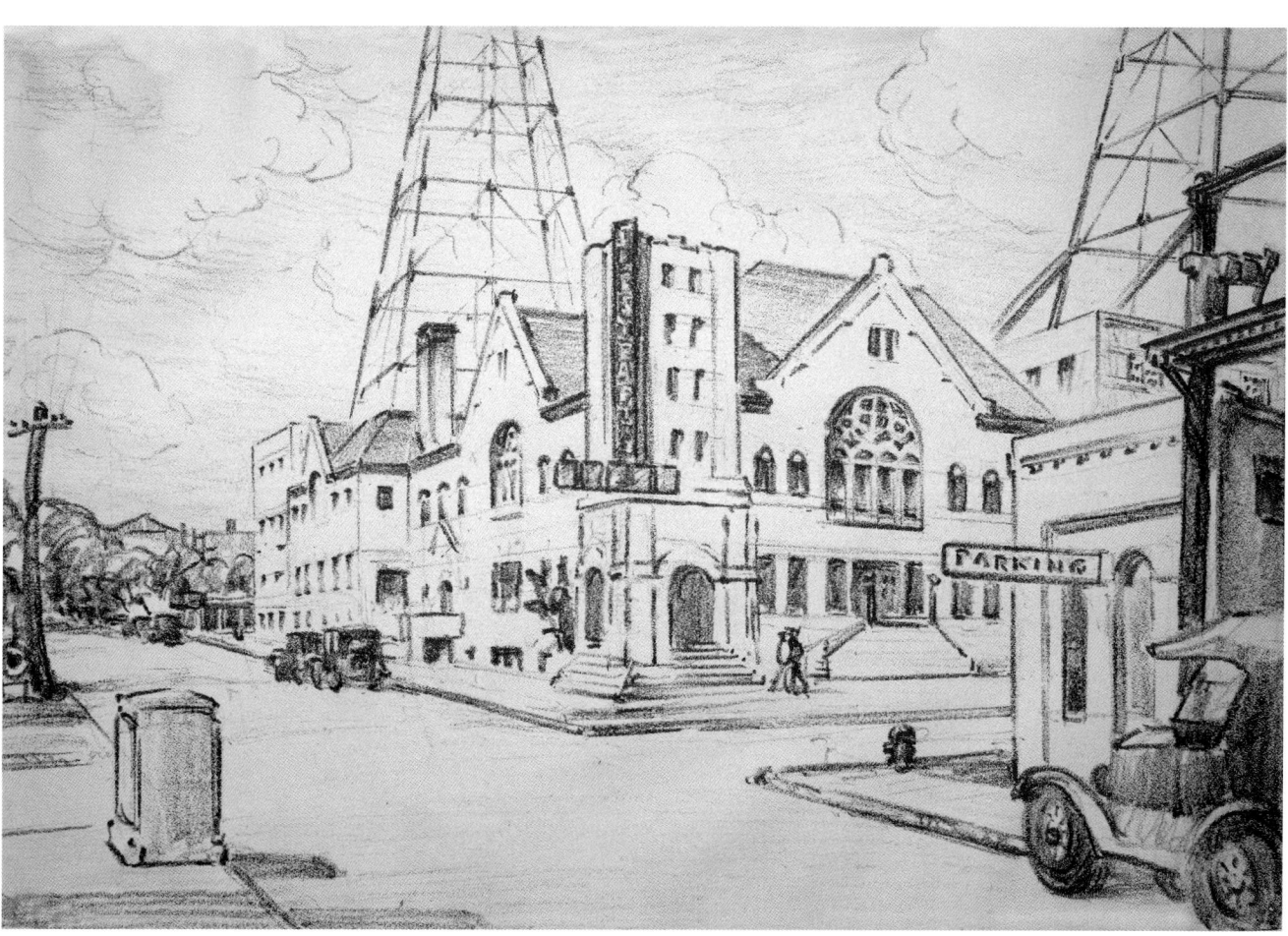

***Study of First Presbyterian
Church,*** n.d. (early 1930s).
Graphite on paper.

First Presbyterian Church (originally
built as Cumberland Presbyterian
Church) was designed about 1890 by
the Fort Worth architectural firm of
Haggart and Sanguinet and located
at the corner of W. Fifth and Taylor
Streets. The church's massive eastern
spire, too tall to fit onto Ziegler's
sketch pad, is depicted in two parts.
For unknown reasons this preparatory
drawing was not utilized as the basis
for a fine art print. In the present day,
no prints produced by Ziegler of First
Presbyterian Church in this location
are known to exist.

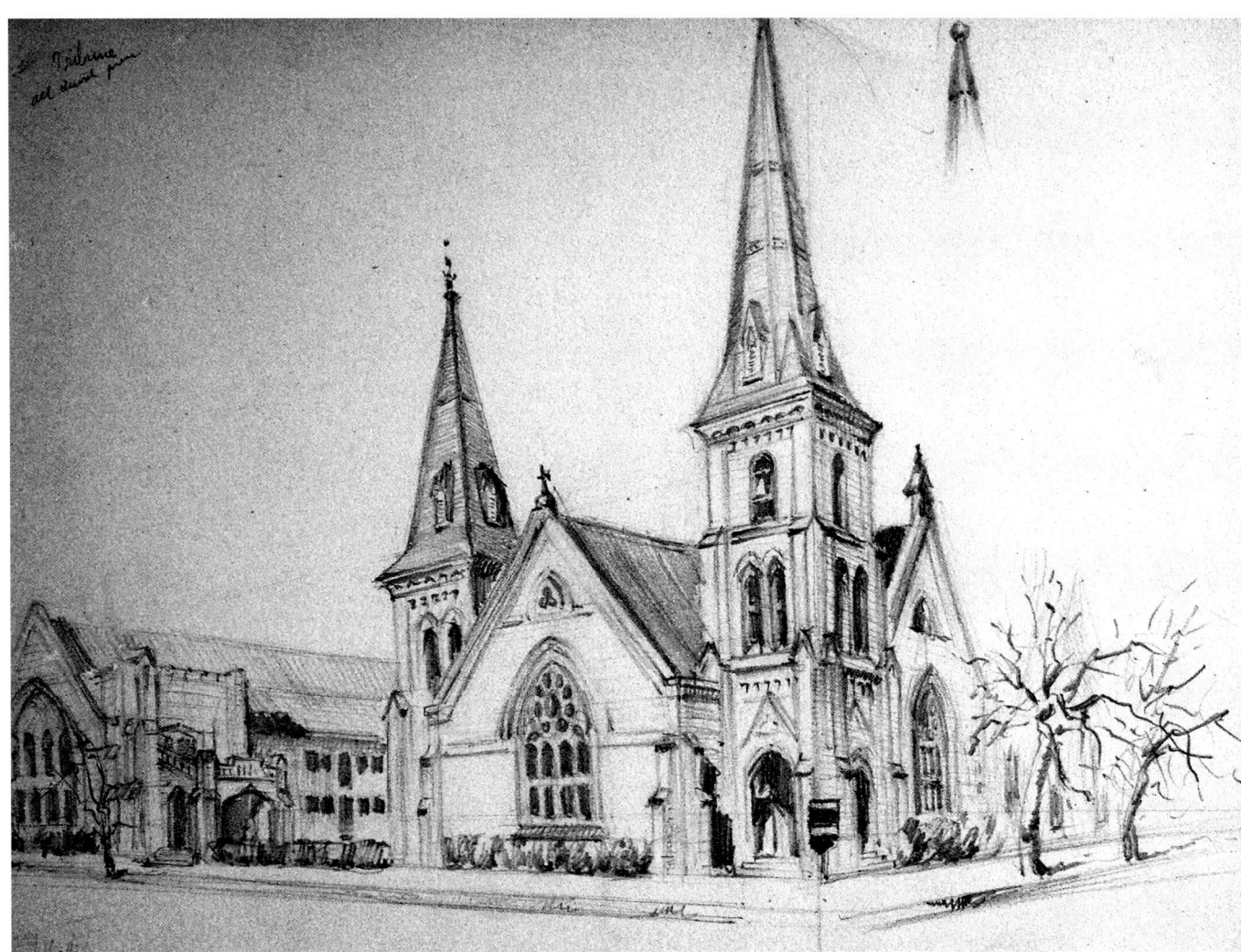

Trinity Episcopal Church,
ca. 1930. Lithograph.

This printed image of Trinity Episcopal Church was part of an extensive series of documentary lithographs of Fort Worth that Ziegler produced around 1930, just prior to his embrace of the etching process. The church still stands at 1501 Lipscomb Street but is no longer used as a place of worship. In Ziegler's day, the building featured a massive arched window pieced together by church parishioners, as the membership could not afford to pay an artisan to do the work.

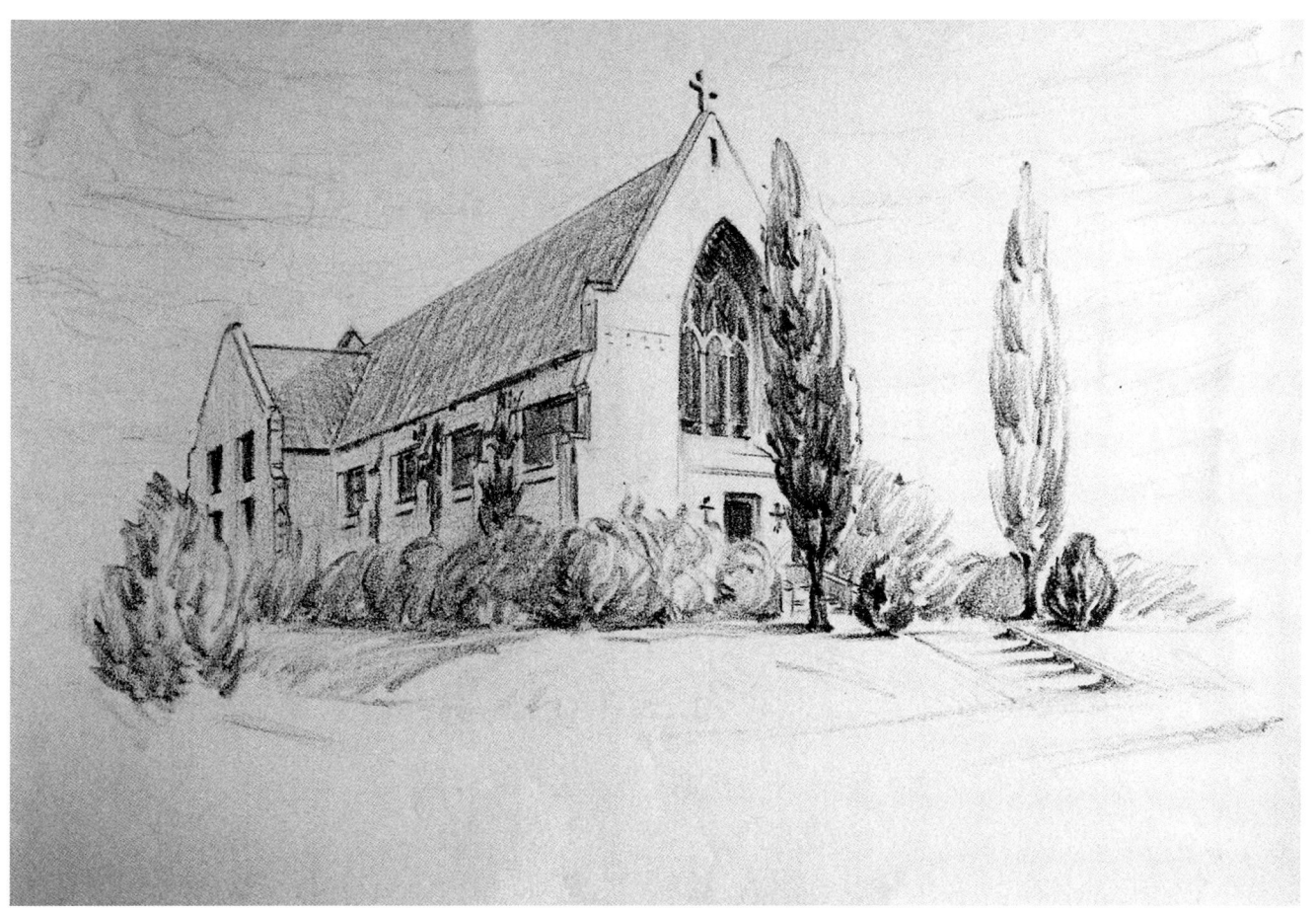

Study of University Christian Church, ca. 1938. Graphite on paper.

This pencil drawing served as the preparatory study for Ziegler's 1938 etching of University Christian Church (opposite). University Christian Church was Ziegler's home church, located two blocks from where he lived. The Spanish-style church was designed by Fort Worth architects A. F. Wickes and Wiley G. Clarkson. Mr. Clarkson had designed the Mary Couts Burnett Library, a short distance south of the church, just a few years earlier.

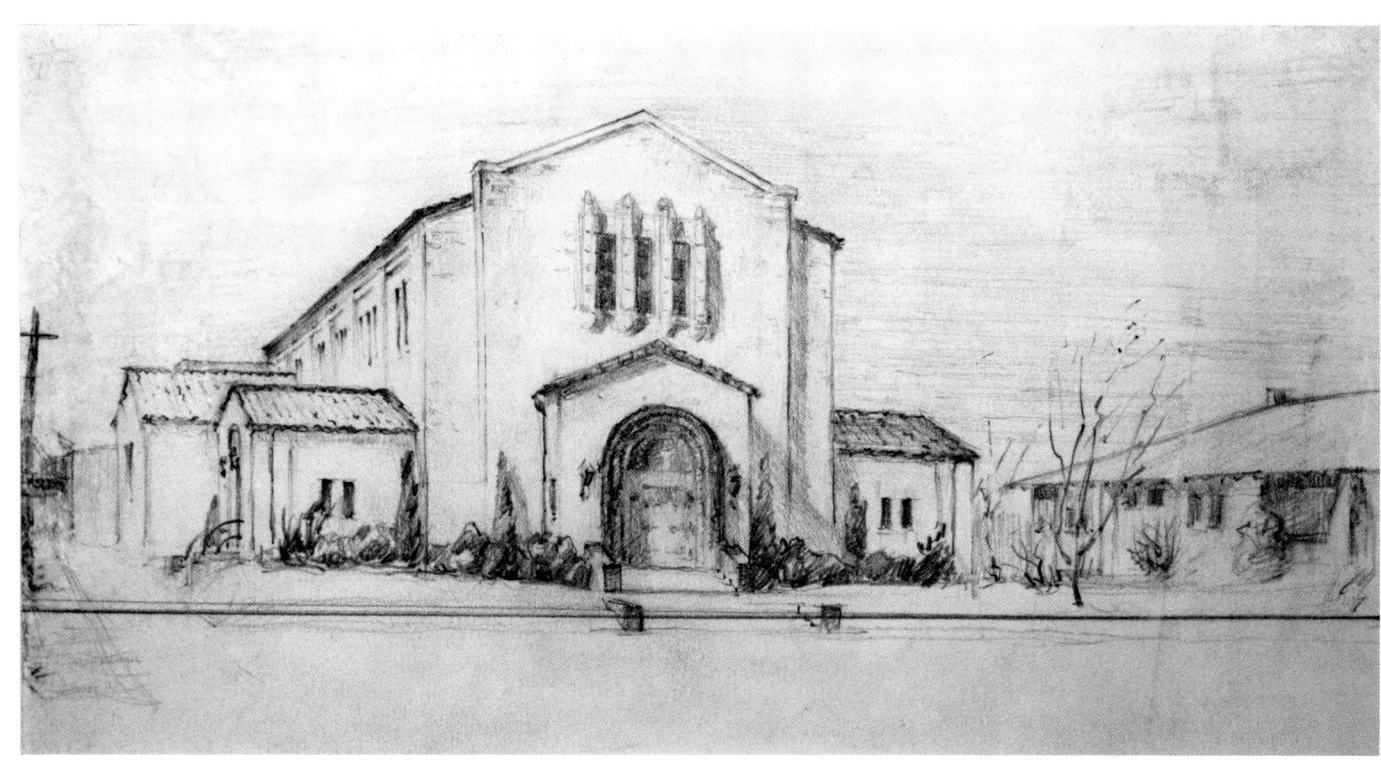

University Christian Church, 1938. Etching.

This beautifully finished print was pulled from a 6 x 8-inch copper plate. The cornerstone for University Christian Church (UCC) was laid in 1933. Prior to that, the congregation had for many years met in various buildings on the Texas Christian University campus. The frame house on the lot next to the church served as the church parsonage. Over a period of time Ziegler created some of the ornamentation that decorated UCC's main sanctuary.

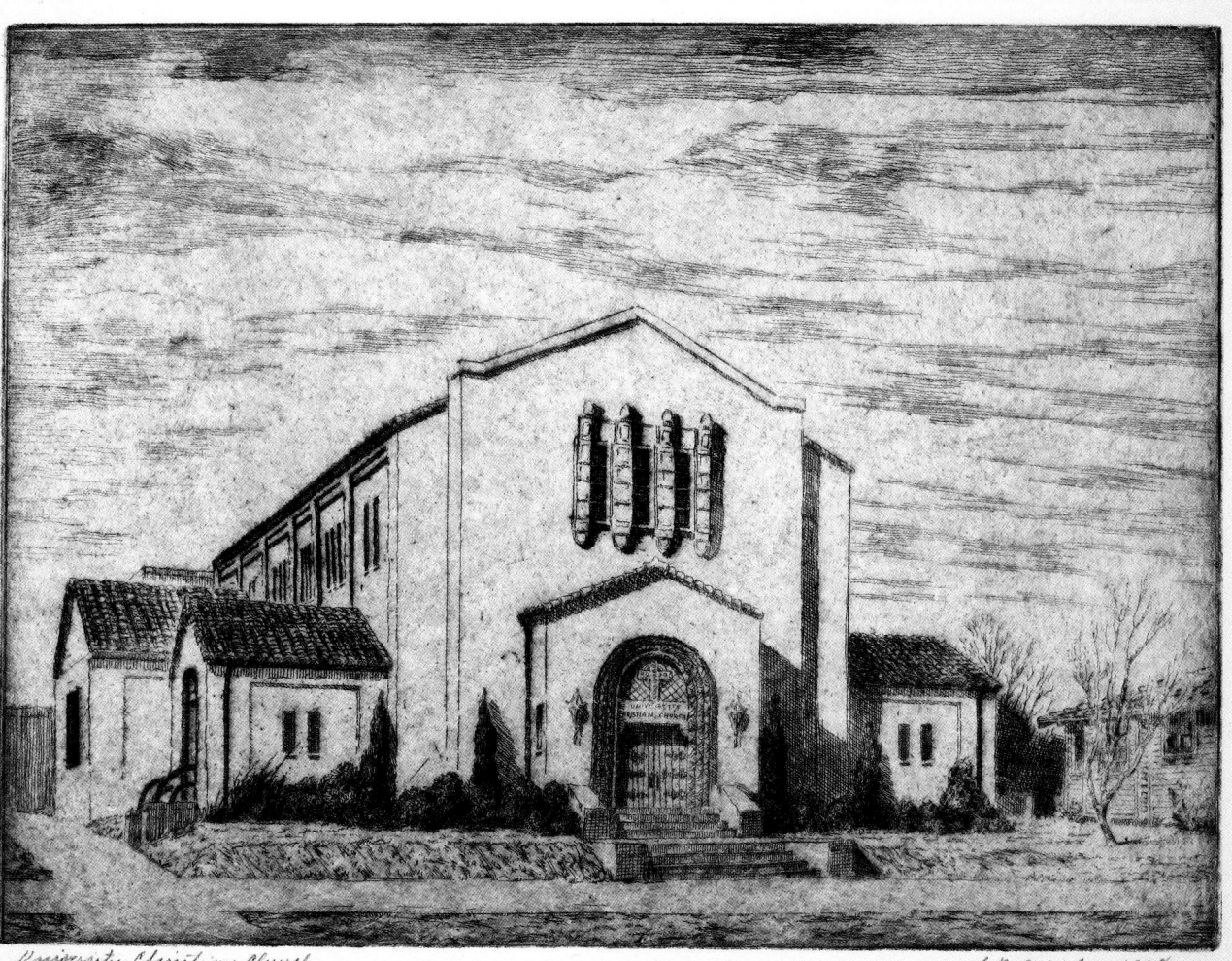

University Christian Church

S.P. Ziegler 1938

**St. Patrick Catholic Church,
n.d. (early 1930s). Etching.**

In this print Ziegler depicted the
Gothic Revival façade of St. Patrick
Catholic Church, as seen from the east.
Housing one of Fort Worth's oldest con-
gregations, the church's cornerstone
was laid in 1888. A photograph taken
in 1890 revealed a cathedral with only
partially completed walls and a construction site with much work left to do.
Prior to producing this etching, Ziegler
created a lithograph of Saint Patrick's
that included glimpses of the Post Office
and Federal Building just to the west
of the church (opposite).

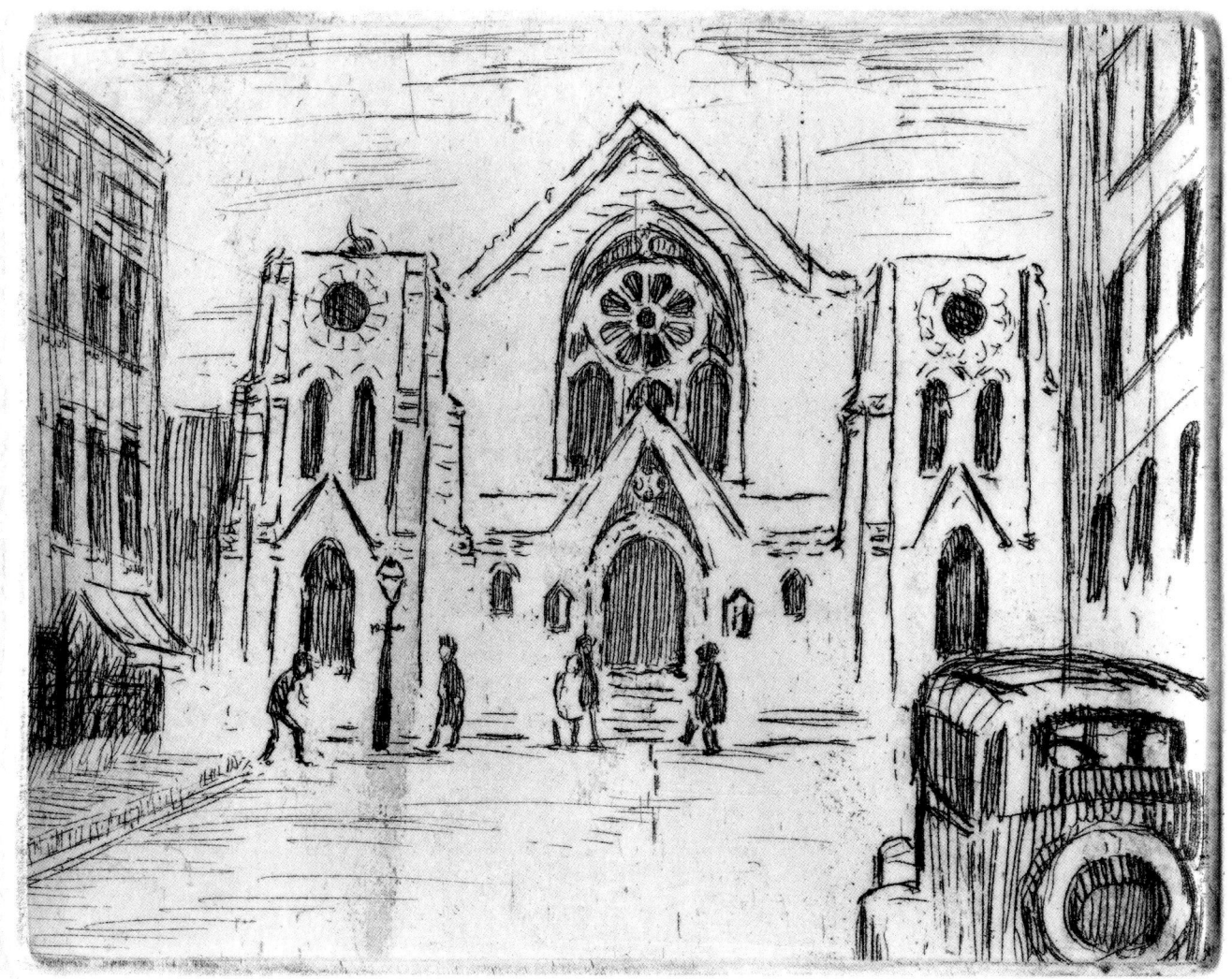

***St. Patrick Catholic Church,*
ca. 1930. Lithograph.**

In this view of the building's façade, Ziegler captured a wide-angle look at St. Patrick Catholic Church. To the west, across Throckmorton Street, the weather station and flag pole atop the nearby Post Office and Federal Building are visible beyond the church's northern tower. Still looking across Throckmorton Street, turrets adorning the post office building are also readily seen beyond the north end of the church building.

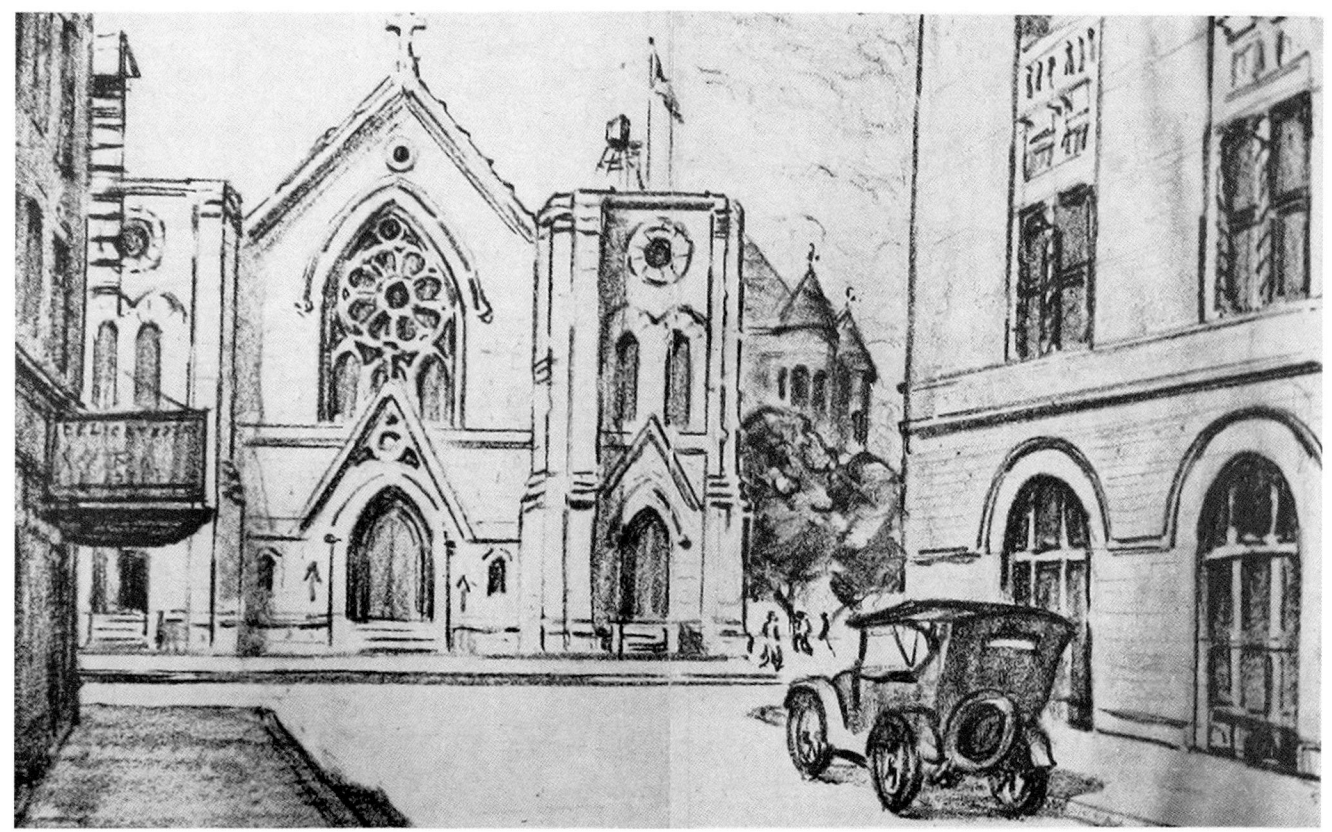

**St. Andrew's Episcopal Church,
n.d. (early 1930s). Etching.**

Services were first held in St. Andrew's
Episcopal Church in 1912, though
the congregation had formed three
decades earlier. The Gothic Revival
church was already a downtown
landmark when Ziegler depicted it
around 1930 in both an etching and a
lithograph (p. 41). In both prints, the
parish hall was hidden by trees
(to the viewer's right), giving the images a rural feel even though the church
occupied a busy downtown location
at 901 Lamar Street.

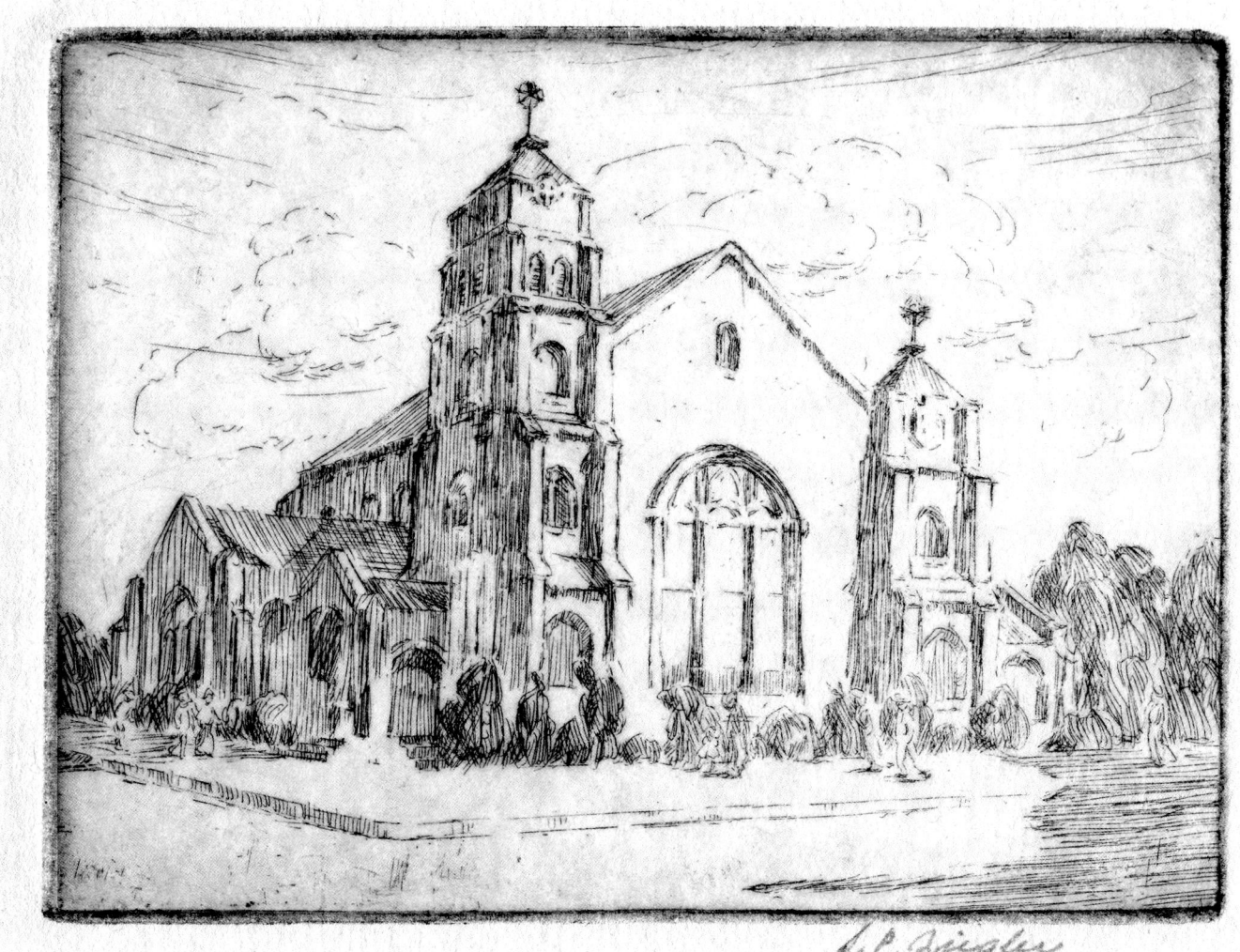

St. Andrew's Episcopal Church, ca. 1930. Lithograph.

The visual content of this lithograph is virtually identical to the etching (opposite), though Ziegler made no effort to depict the sky in the lithographic version. The artist's focus was strictly on the church building.

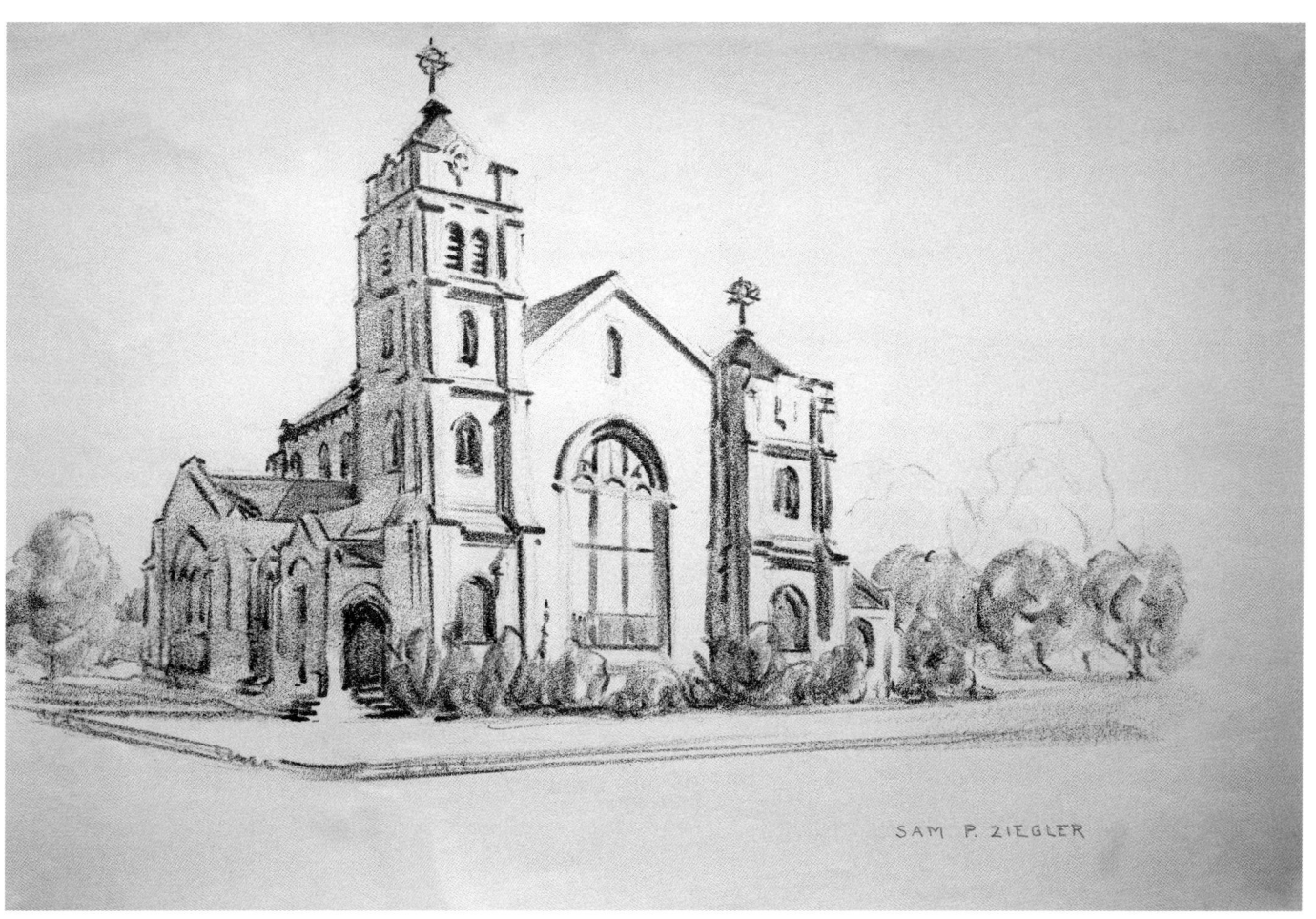

Fort Worth Post Offices
and Railroad Stations

Fort Worth Post Office and Federal Building, ca. 1933. Etching.

The Fort Worth Post Office and Federal Building was completed in 1896 at the corner of Jennings Ave. and W. Eleventh Street. In this fine art print, Ziegler depicted the Pecos red sandstone structure from the south. Along with the post office, the building housed federal courtrooms and offices and served as headquarters for the Eleventh Division of the Railway Mail Service, the coordinating agency for mail delivery in Texas, New Mexico, Louisiana, and Arkansas. Fort Worth's first weather monitoring station was located atop the federal building's gray slate roof.

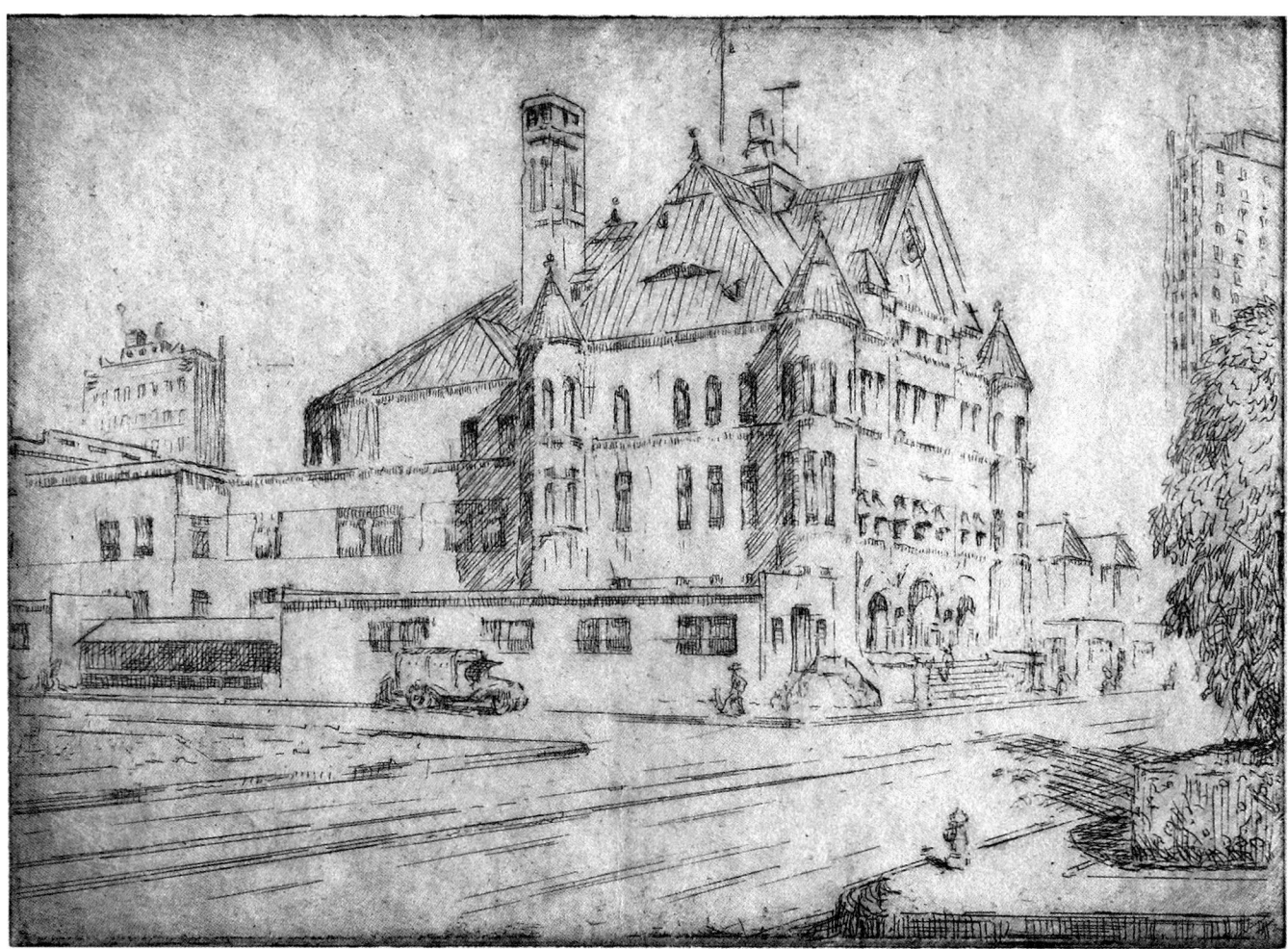

Fort Worth Post Office and Federal Building from the South, ca. 1930. Lithograph.

In this lithograph of the post office and federal building viewed from the south, Ziegler has moved about a block west from the vantage point of his etching of the subject (opposite). In the lithograph, a portion of the twenty-story W. T. Waggoner Building is visible in the upper left. A box-shaped addition to the original post office building is visible to the viewer's left. The rear (west side) of St. Patrick Catholic Church is seen across the street, to the viewer's right.

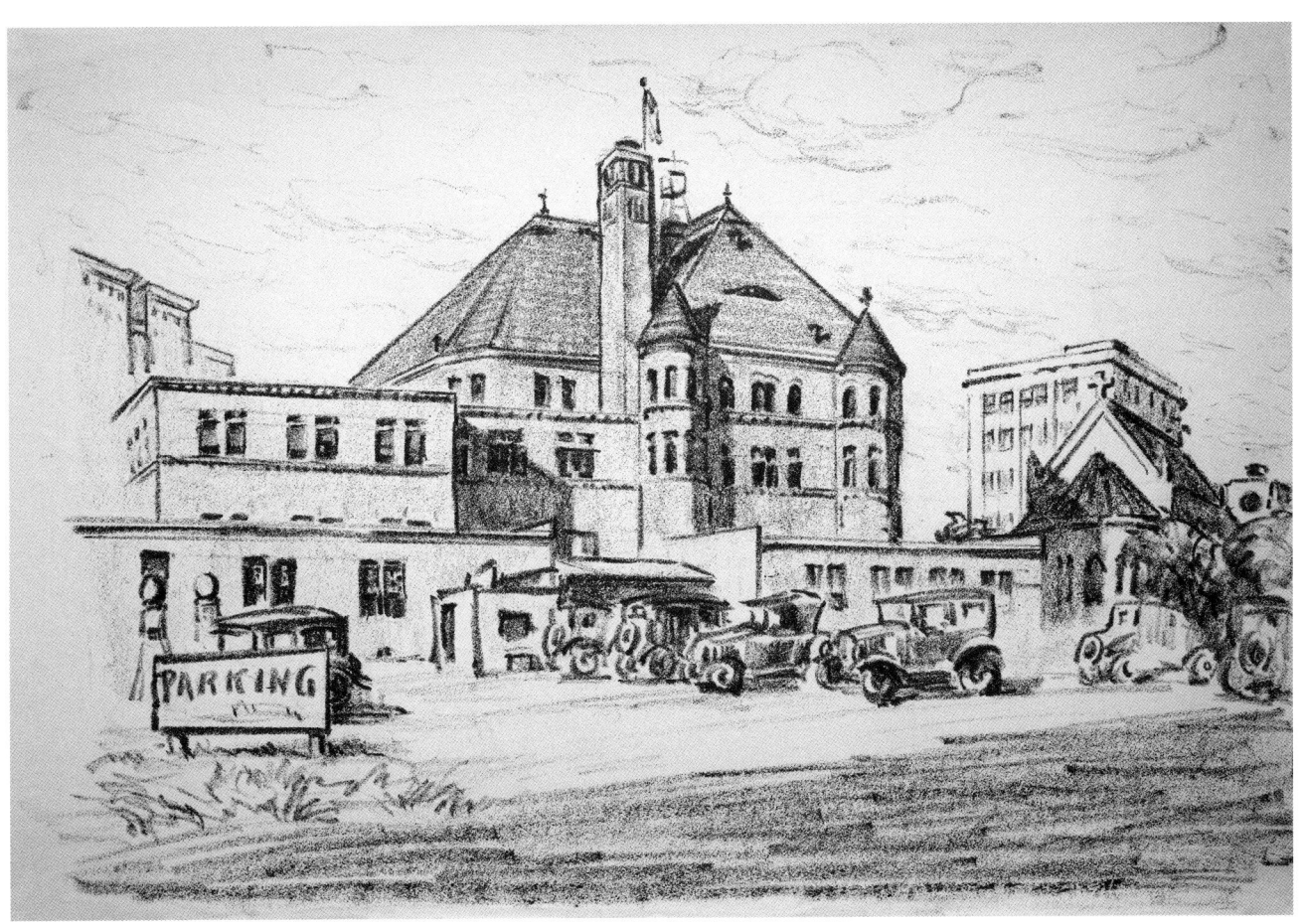

Monroe Street Doorway at Post Office, ca. 1933. Etching.

As the subject of this 3 x 4-inch etching, Ziegler chose the west door of the annex to the post office and federal building, a door that opened onto Monroe Street. He also completed an oil painting of this same scene. As a nod to the building's 19th century inception, Ziegler's oil painting included a woman in Victorian dress standing on the post office steps. The beautiful Romanesque arch over the doorway was a frequently repeated architectural feature of the building's original façade and the later annex.

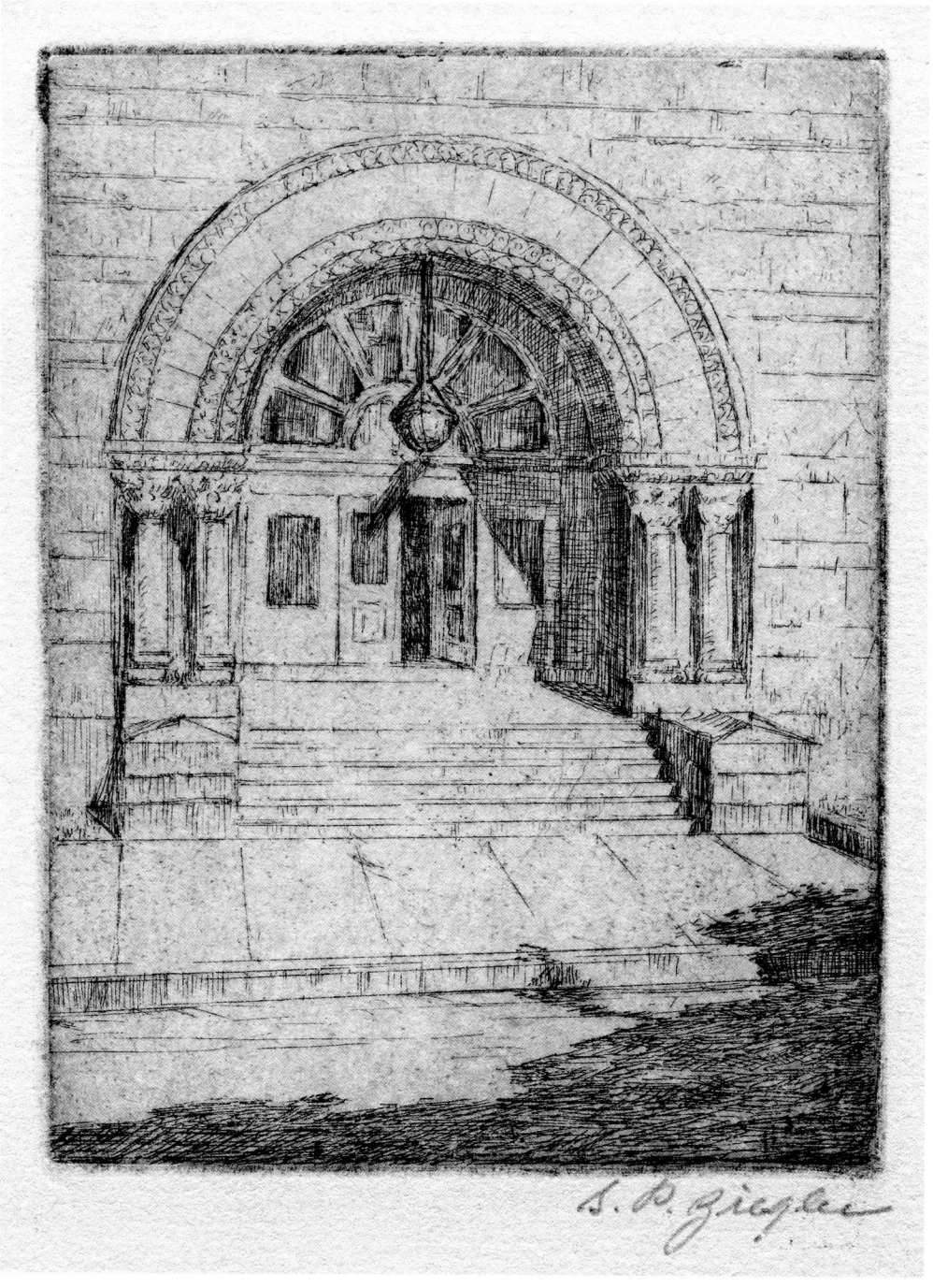

The New Post Office from the East, ca. 1932. Graphite on paper.

In this panoramic pencil sketch, Ziegler recorded construction shacks and workers' automobiles that surrounded the new Fort Worth post office during construction. It opened in 1933, replacing the 19th century post office at Jennings Ave. and W. Eleventh Street. In the Ziegler sketch, what appears to be a flatcar loaded with stone is parked in front of the new post office. The Texas & Pacific (T&P) warehouse is visible just beyond it. Though highly finished, this drawing is unsigned and likely functioned as a preparatory study for a subsequent painting.

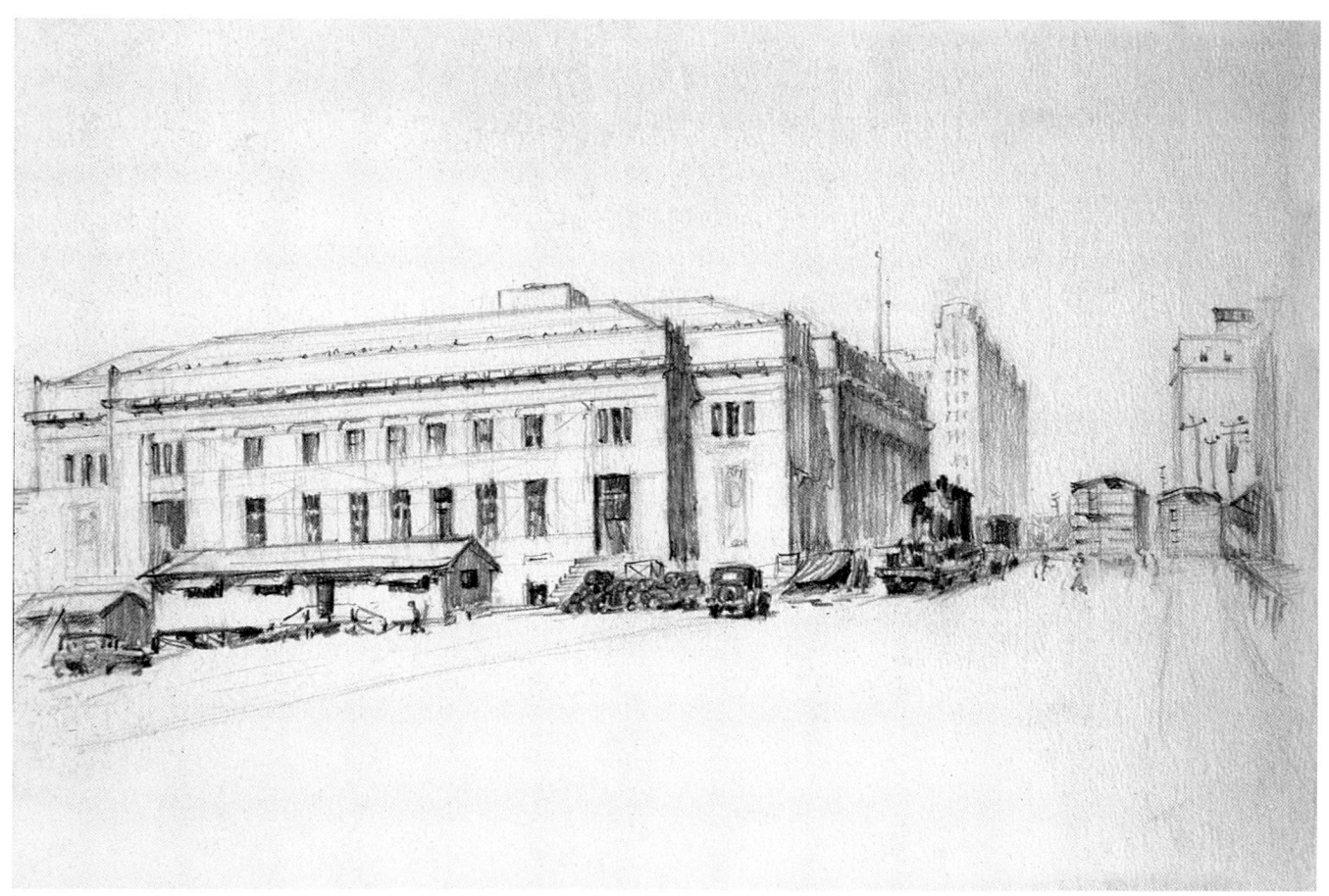

Study of the New Post Office, 1933. Graphite on paper.

This pencil drawing served as the preparatory study for Ziegler's 1933 etching of the new post office (opposite). The building, located at 251 W. Lancaster Ave., was designed by Fort Worth architect Wyatt C. Hedrick in the classical and Beaux Arts styles. Many of the building's architectural ornaments, including the longhorn and shorthorn cattle atop the column capitals, were designed and cast by Fort Worth artist/sculptor Dwight C. Holmes, a friend of Ziegler's.

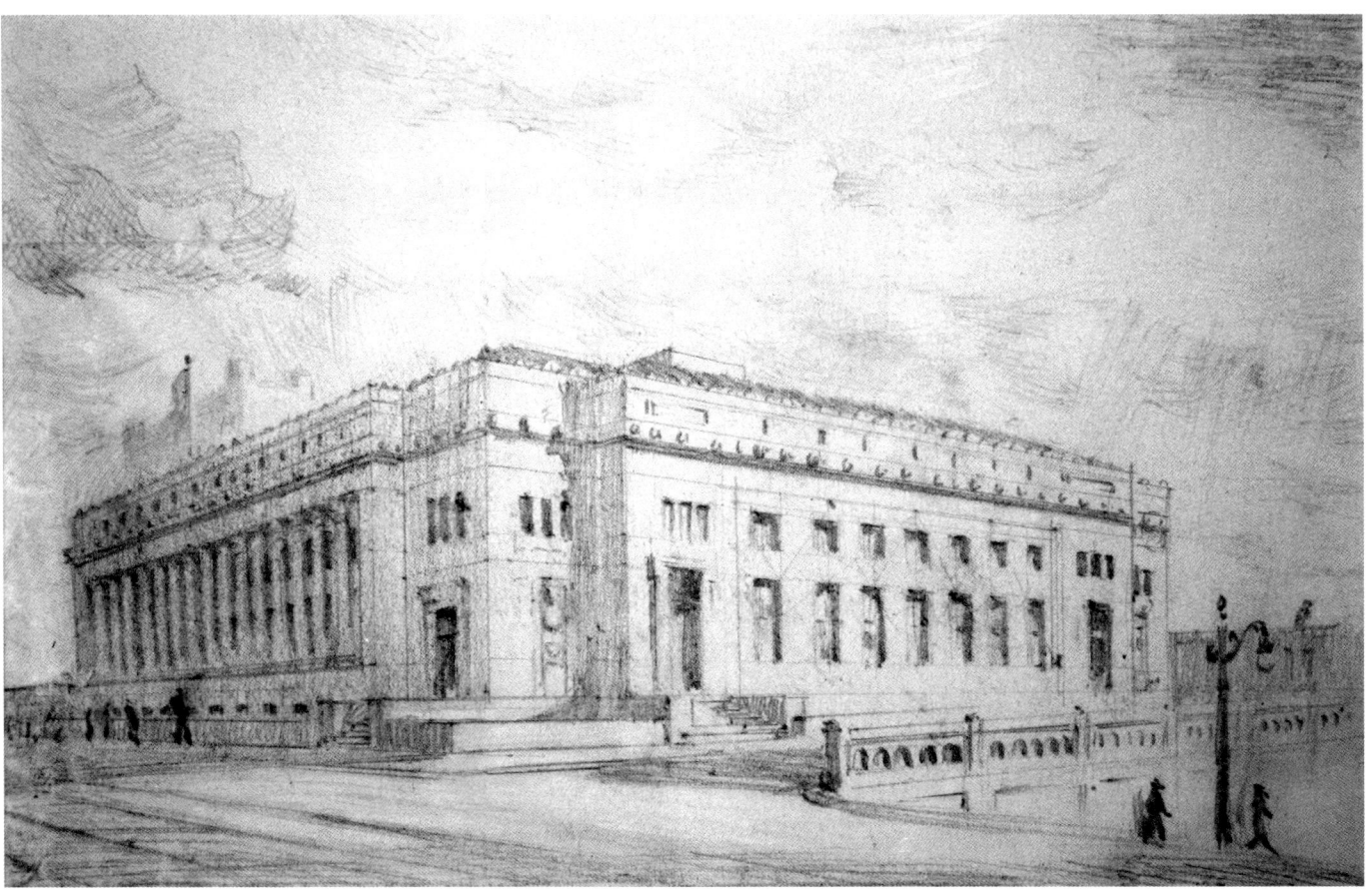

The New Post Office, 1933. Etching.

The temple-like quality of Fort Worth's new main post office was captured with uncanny accuracy in this Ziegler etching from 1933. This etching was printed from a 4 ½ x 6 ½ inch copper plate and demonstrated Ziegler's mastery of architectural perspective. The new post office represented a major addition to Fort Worth's inventory of distinctive public buildings. A mural depicting the evolution of postal delivery in Fort Worth, from ox-drawn wagon to air mail, was installed in the post office in January 1934. The mural was commissioned by the federal Public Works of Art Project and painted by Dwight C. Holmes and William H. Baker, two of Ziegler's fellow Fort Worth artists.

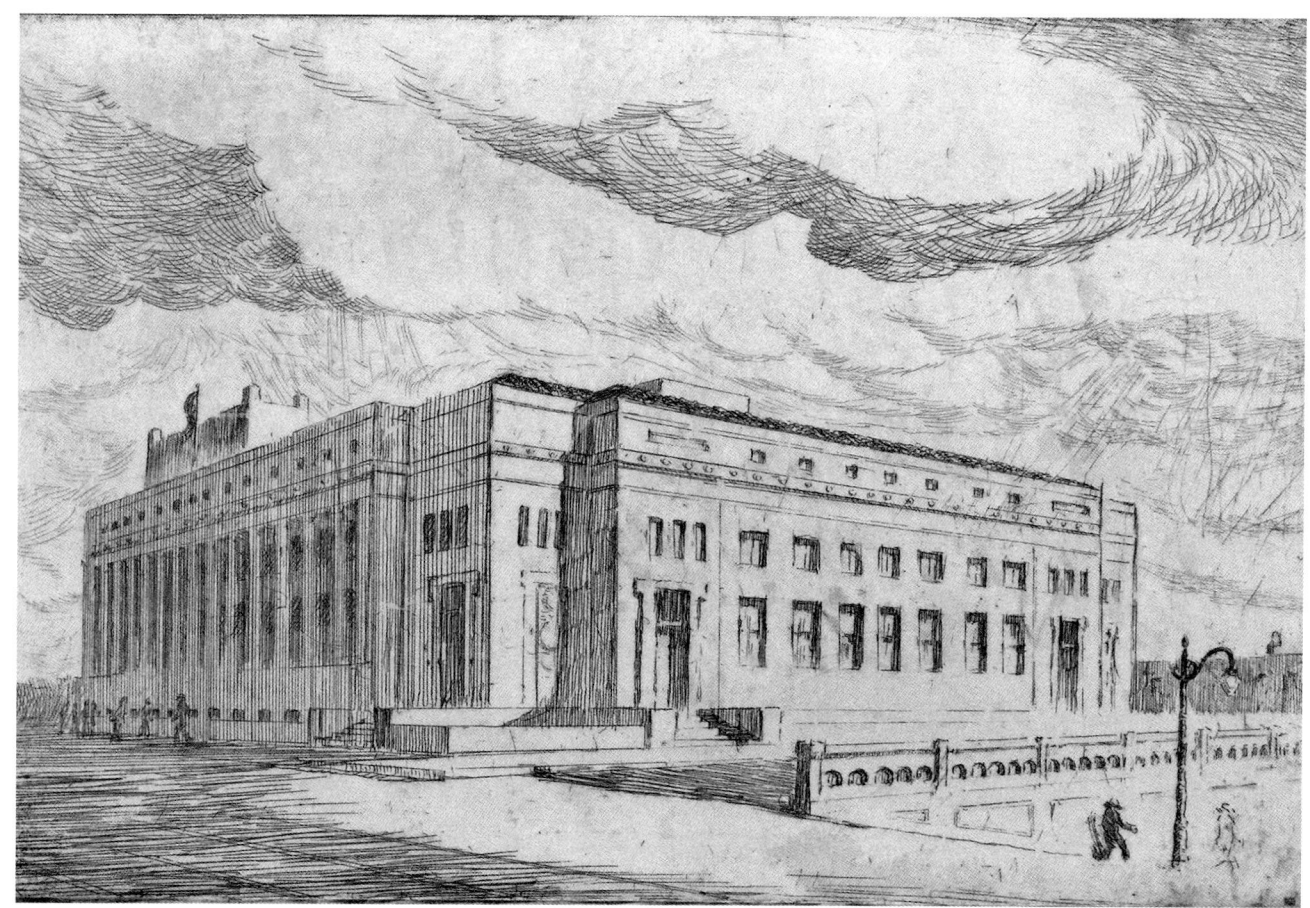

Texas & Pacific Rail Yards from Jennings Ave. Viaduct, n.d. (early 1930s). Etching.

This elevated view of the Texas & Pacific (T&P) rail yards was visible from the Jennings Ave. viaduct looking to the east. The bridge, or viaduct as it was known, spanned the rail yard, connecting Fort Worth's near south side to downtown. The viaduct carried pedestrian and automobile traffic as well as streetcars. Looking east from the viaduct, the T&P freight depot and T&P Passenger Station, with its distinctive dual towers, were on the viewer's left.

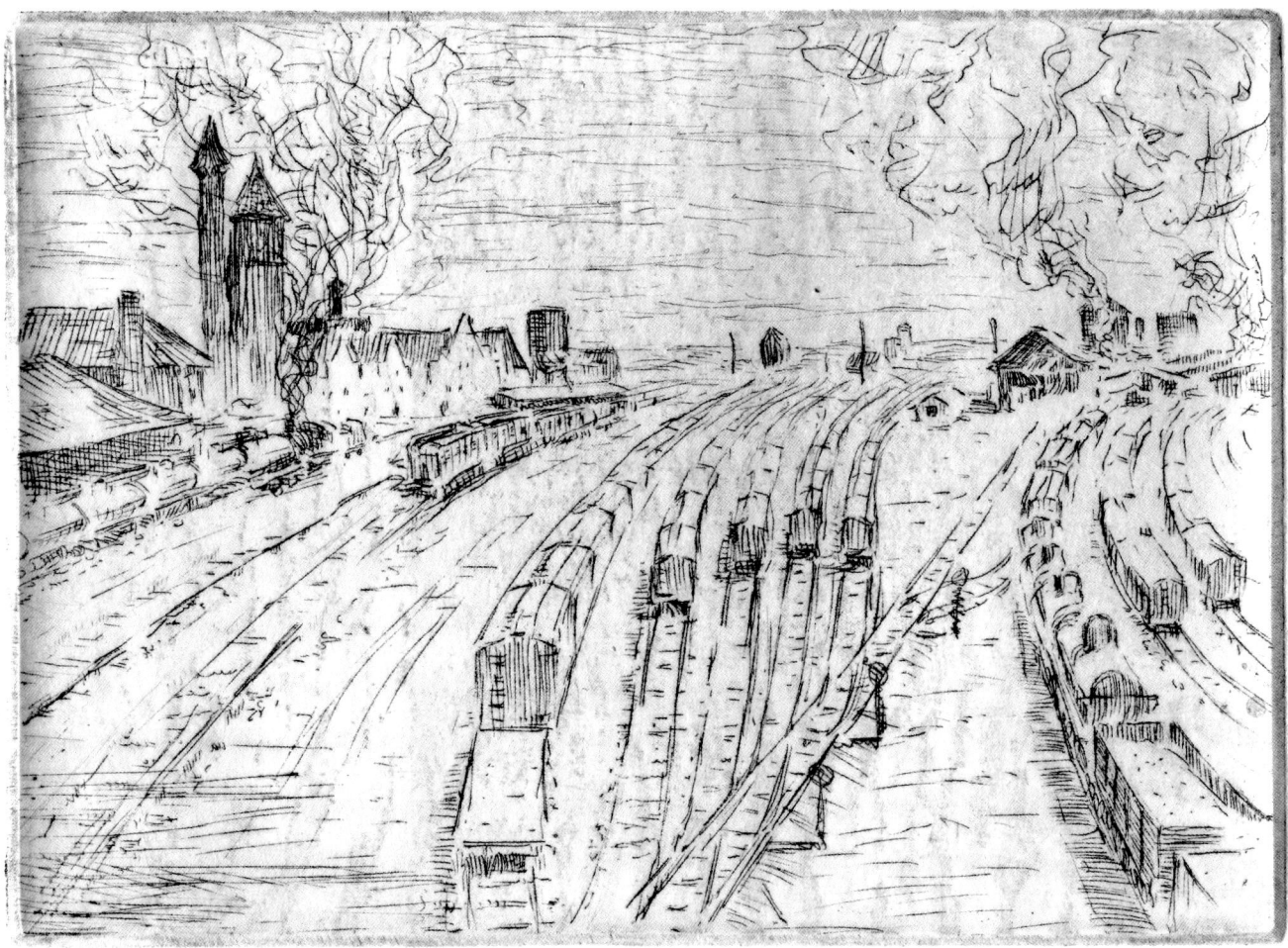

**Texas & Pacific Rail Yards
from Jennings Ave. Viaduct,** ca.
1930. Lithograph.

In this lithograph of the T&P reservation, Ziegler effectively communicated the look and feel of the sooty, hazy atmosphere of the busy rail yard. Coal and coal oil, much of it derived from mining operations in Strawn, Thurber, and other points immediately west of Fort Worth, were the primary fuels for the steam-driven locomotives of the T&P Railway. Despite the obvious pollution, West Texas— mined coal was considered clean burning for its time.

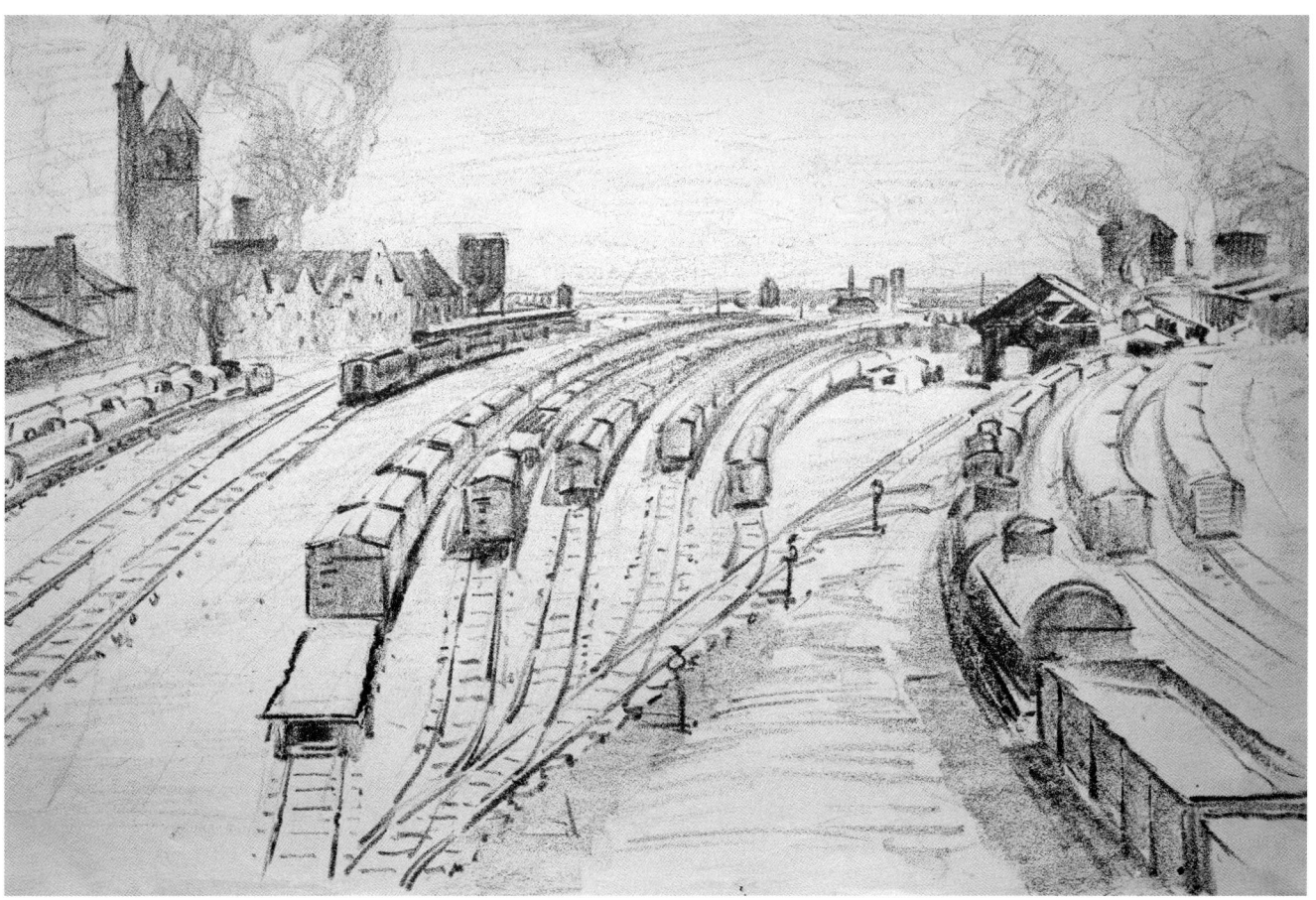

Texas & Pacific Passenger Station Loading Docks, ca. 1930. Lithograph.

The T&P Passenger Station opened in December 1899, burned five years later, and was rebuilt to its original appearance. The restored terminal remained in service until 1931. The terminal was located on present-day Lancaster Avenue at its intersection with Main Street. In this unusual view, Ziegler depicted five loading docks on the terminal's east side, at the rear of the building. The expansive passenger boarding platforms were situated just out of view, to Ziegler's left and also behind him.

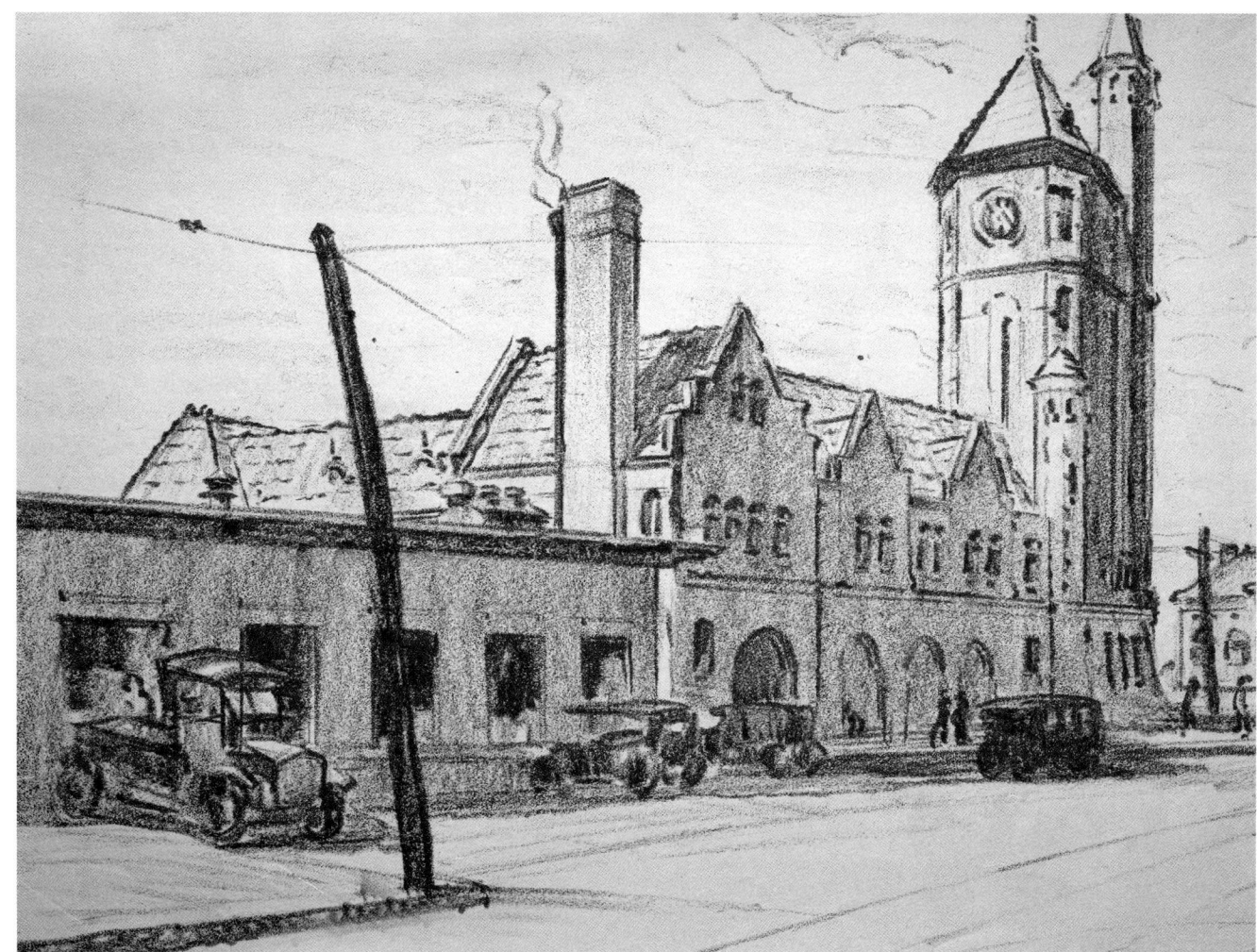

Study of Texas & Pacific Passenger Station from the East, n.d. Graphite on paper.

This drawing was likely an early study for Ziegler's series of documentary lithographs. In this drawing, the 1899 T&P Passenger Station was shown from the east looking west. The terminal's clock tower and companion observation tower were truncated as Ziegler worked to solve problems of perspective.

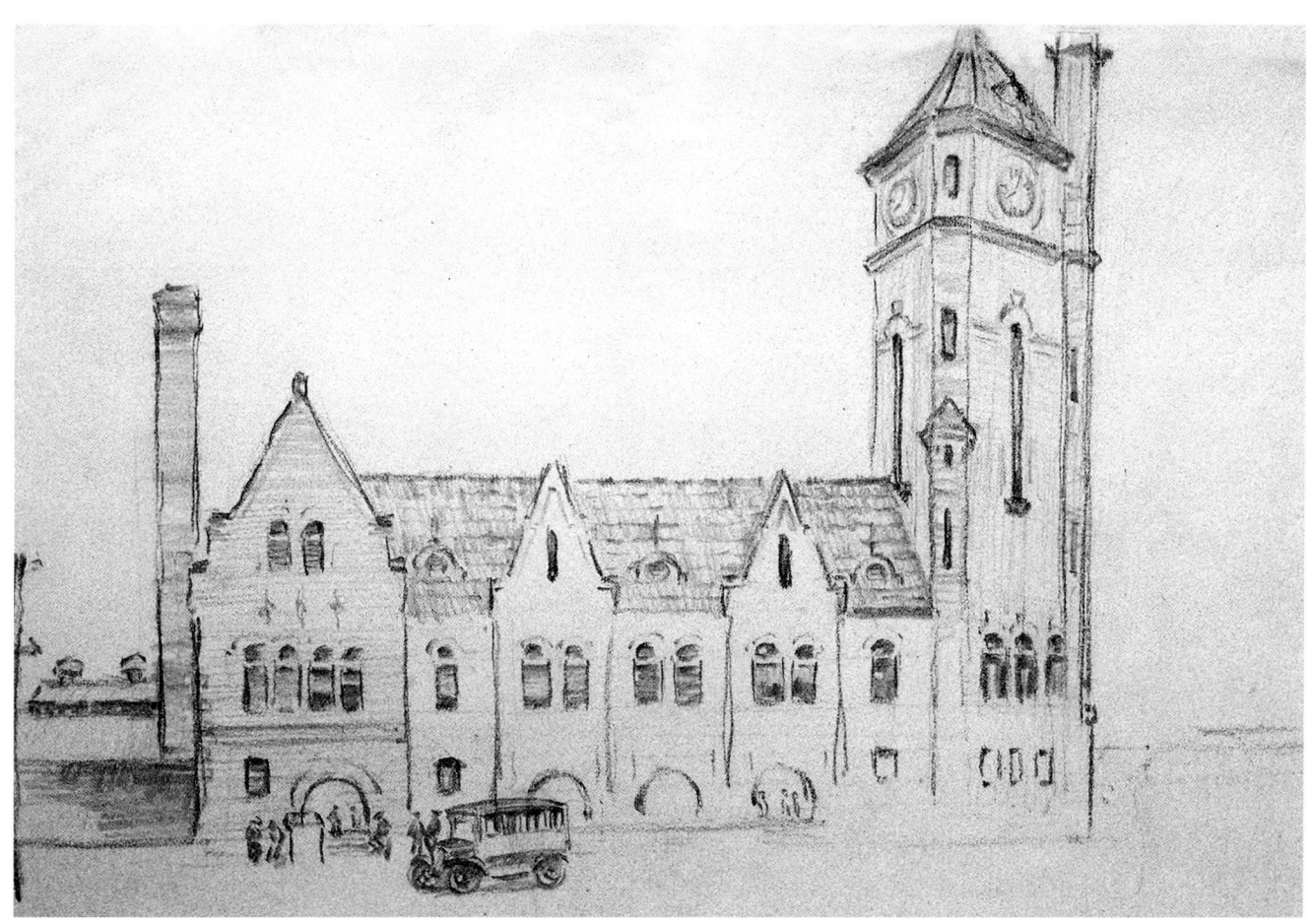

Texas & Pacific Passenger Station from the West, ca. 1930. Lithograph.

Many a traveler's first impression of Fort Worth was the sight of the T&P Passenger Station and its distinctive dual towers. In 1901, local photographer Charles Swartz made his way to the top of the station's narrow observation tower to capture one of the most iconic images of early Fort Worth, a view of the southern end of Main Street looking north to the Tarrant County Courthouse. Rising prominently in the midground of this Ziegler lithograph (on the viewer's left) is the Al Hayne Memorial Fountain. A railway bridge designer, Al Hayne perished in May 1890, just hours after rescuing numerous victims, mostly children, from the Texas Spring Palace inferno. The memorial fountain and bronze bust honoring Hayne were sited only a few hundred feet from where he became a hero.

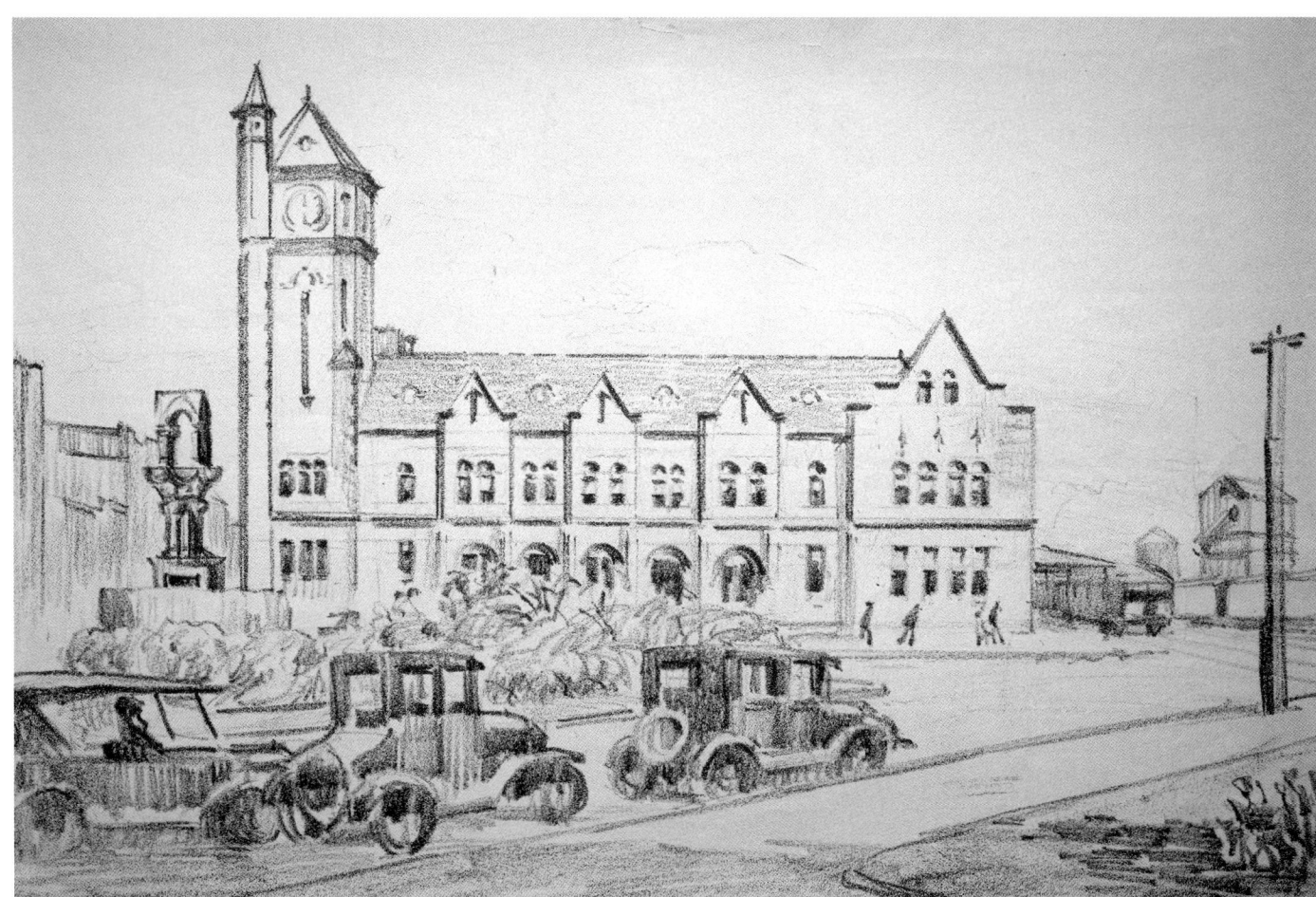

Study for Wrecking the Old T&P Station, 1932. Graphite on paper.

This pencil drawing was the preparatory study for Ziegler's etching of the demolition of the 1899 Texas & Pacific (T&P) Passenger Station (p. 56). A new T&P Passenger Station opened in December 1931, two blocks west of the original terminal, leading to the shuttering and demolition of the 1899 building.

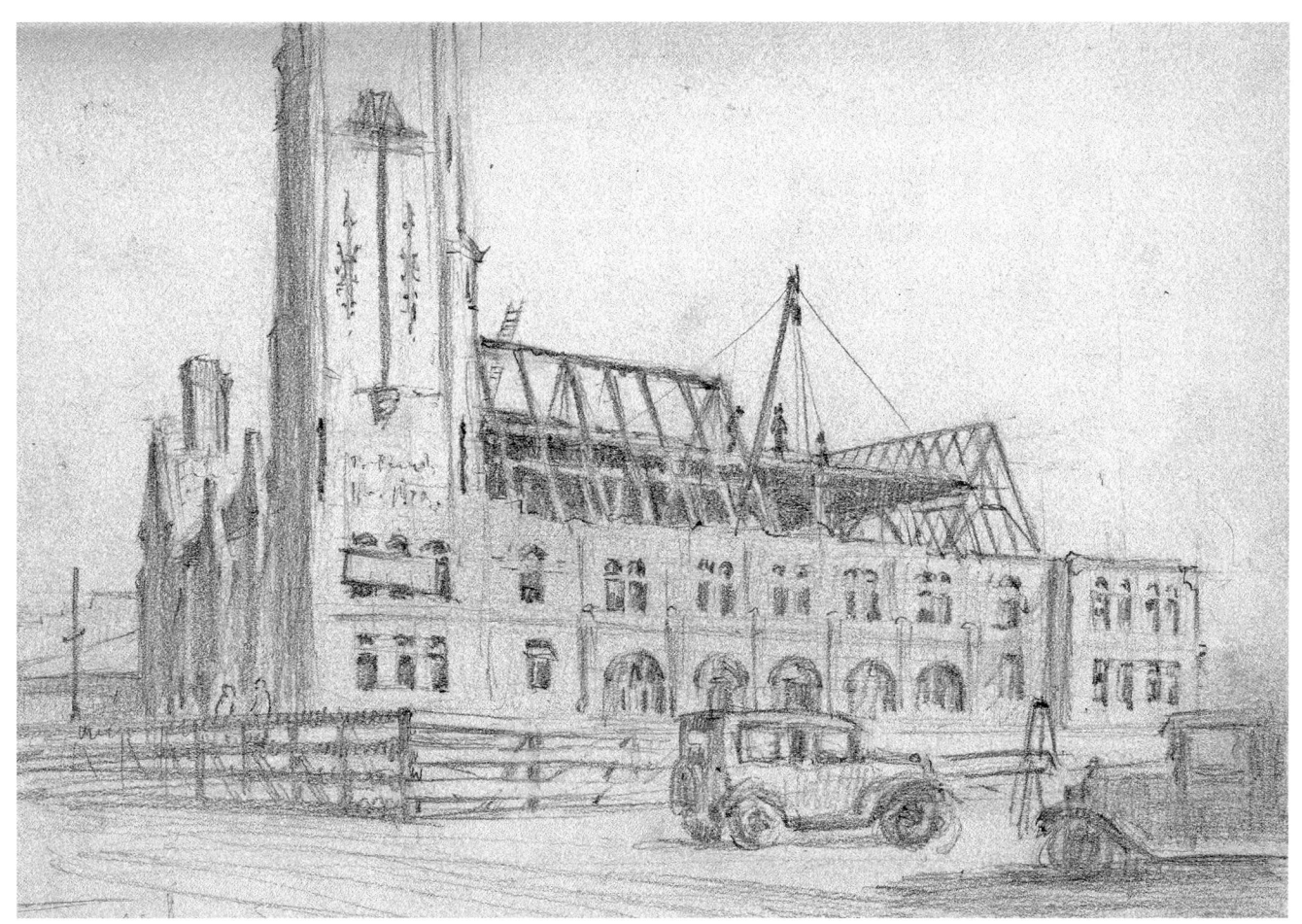

Wrecking the Old T&P Station, 1932. Etching.

With the opening of a new T&P Passenger Station in December 1931, the old terminal at the foot of Main Street became expendable. Ziegler's etching of the demise of the 1899 building revealed that the terminal was disassembled with care from the roof down, and recyclable materials were offered for sale. The sign on the side of the clock tower read "Material for Sale." This interesting image was printed from a 6 x 8–inch copper plate, but the number of copies that Ziegler pulled is unknown.

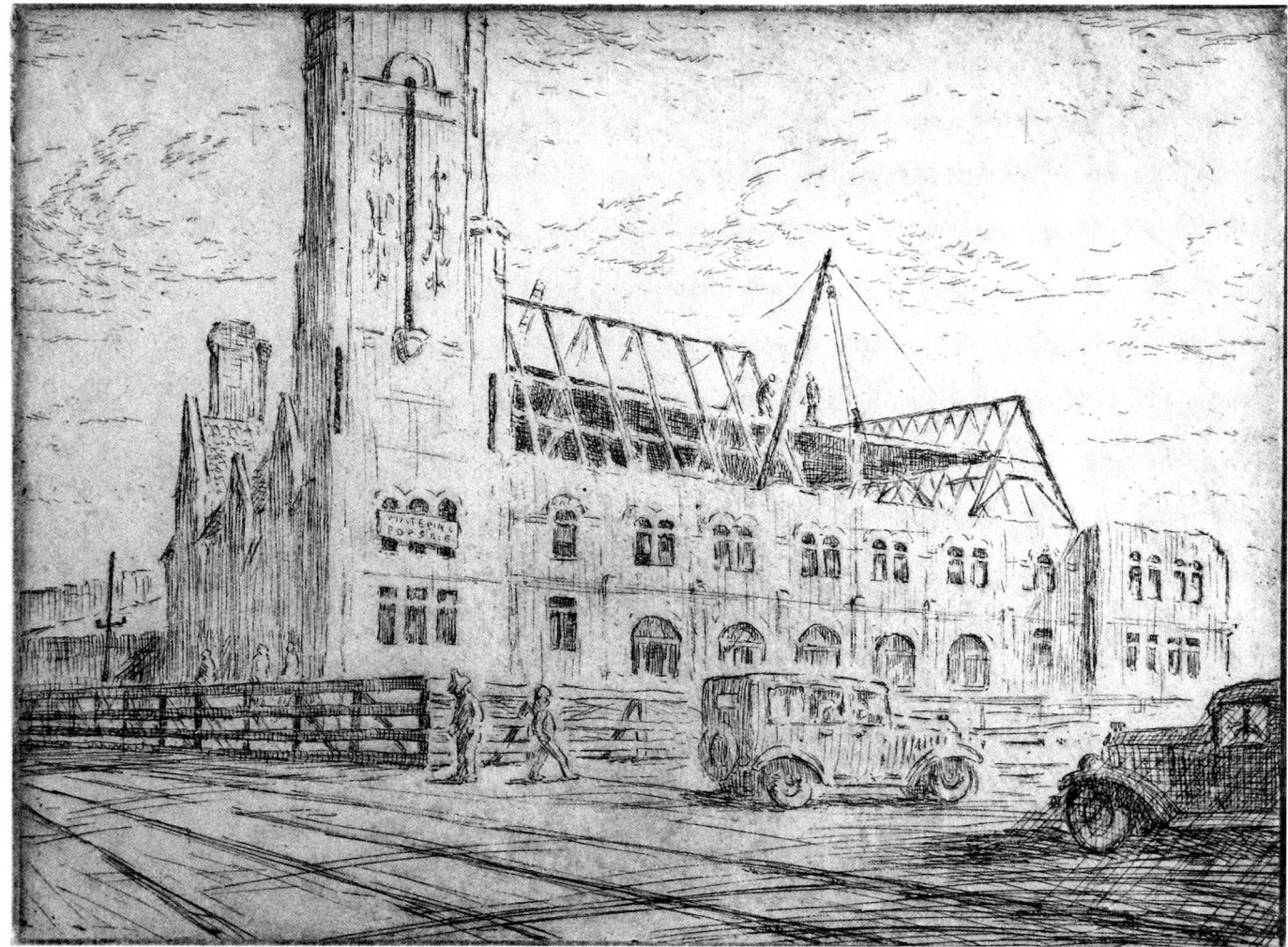

Demolishing the Texas & Pacific Freight Depot, ca. 1930. Lithograph.

From 1900 to 1930, T&P freight trains were loaded and off-loaded at a depot located one block west of the 1899 T&P Passenger Station. In this lithograph Ziegler recorded the depot's demolition during reconstruction of the T&P railway reservation. The freight depot is famously pictured in a photograph from January 1905, when President Theodore Roosevelt used the depot's front steps as a platform from which to deliver a speech to thousands of onlookers. The venue for the president's speech was moved to the freight depot when the original T&P Passenger Station burned in December 1904.

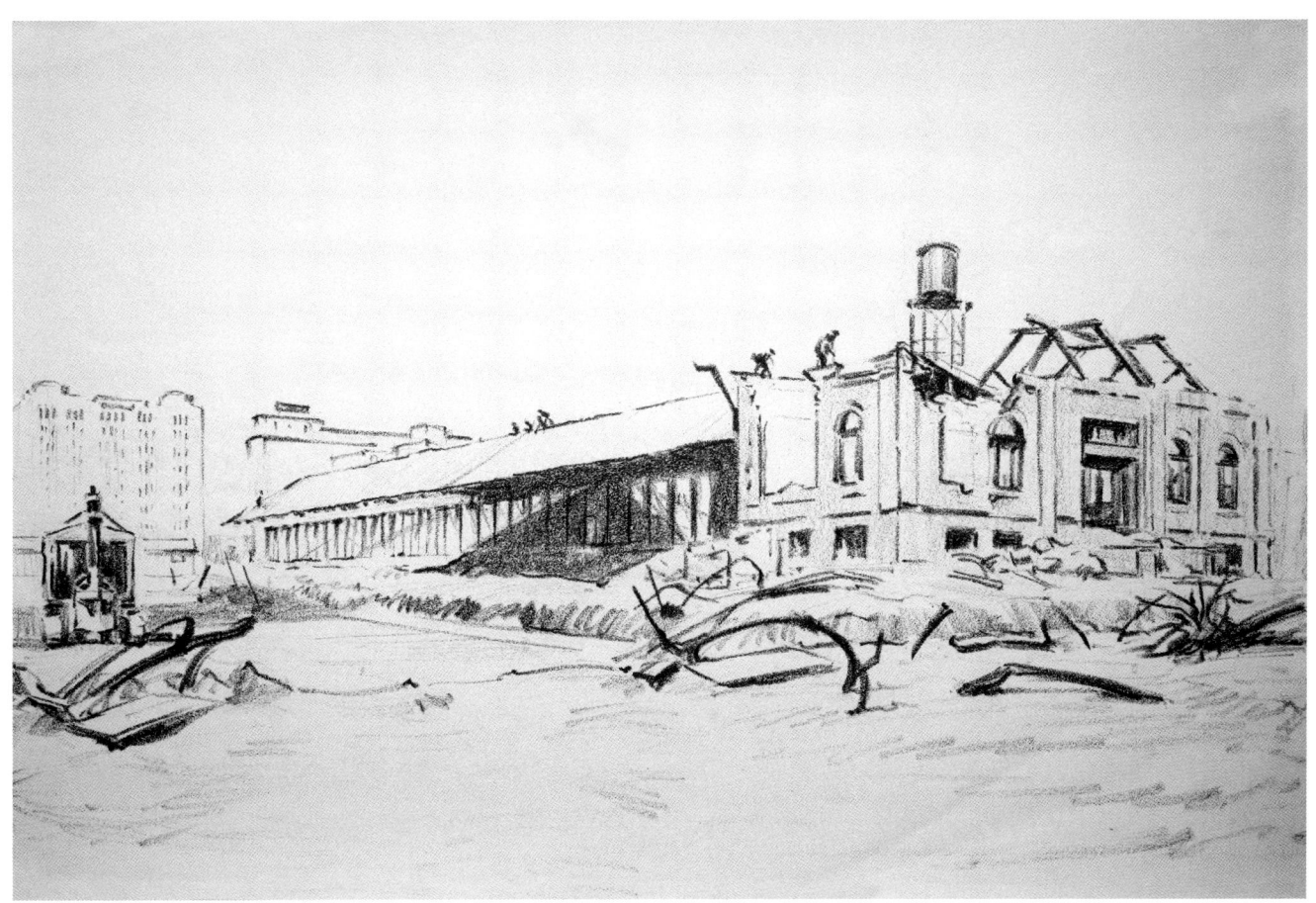

Building the New T&P Station, 1931. Etching.

The new T&P Passenger Station opened in 1931. It was built as part of a massive renovation of the rail and street system on the southern edge of downtown Fort Worth. The renovations were precipitated by ever-increasing automobile traffic through the railroad reservation. Ziegler's etching depicted the new train station under construction and referenced the dual towers of the 1899 passenger station two blocks to the east. The new building was designed in the zigzag Moderne style of art deco by Fort Worth architect Wyatt C. Hedrick. A companion warehouse facility (the T&P Warehouse) was constructed simultaneously, one block west of the new passenger station.

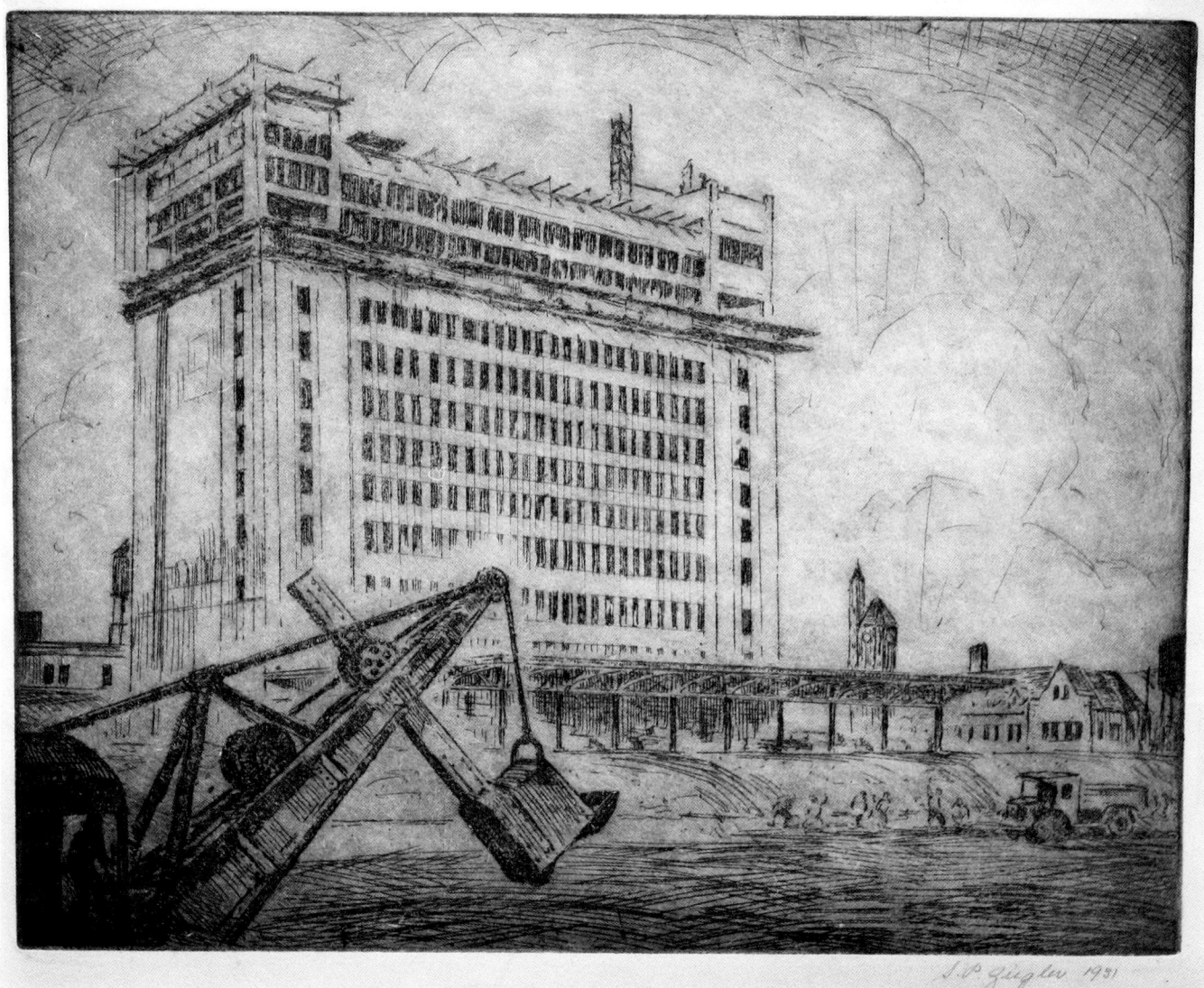

Study for Texas & Pacific Railway / Main Street Underpass, ca. 1932. Graphite on paper.

Reconstruction of the rail and street system around the T&P Railroad reservation in 1930-32 resulted in unimpeded automobile access along the full lengths of south Main Street, Jennings Avenue, and Henderson Street. When completed, automobiles leaving or entering the downtown area from the south were safely routed though underpasses that took them beneath the east-west T&P rail lines. In this pencil sketch, Ziegler depicted the juxtaposition of train and automobile in the new alignment along South Main Street. A neon sign advertising rail service to St. Louis commanded the attention of motorists leaving downtown. Ziegler also completed an oil painting of this scene and exhibited it under the title *T&P Overpass at Main Street*.

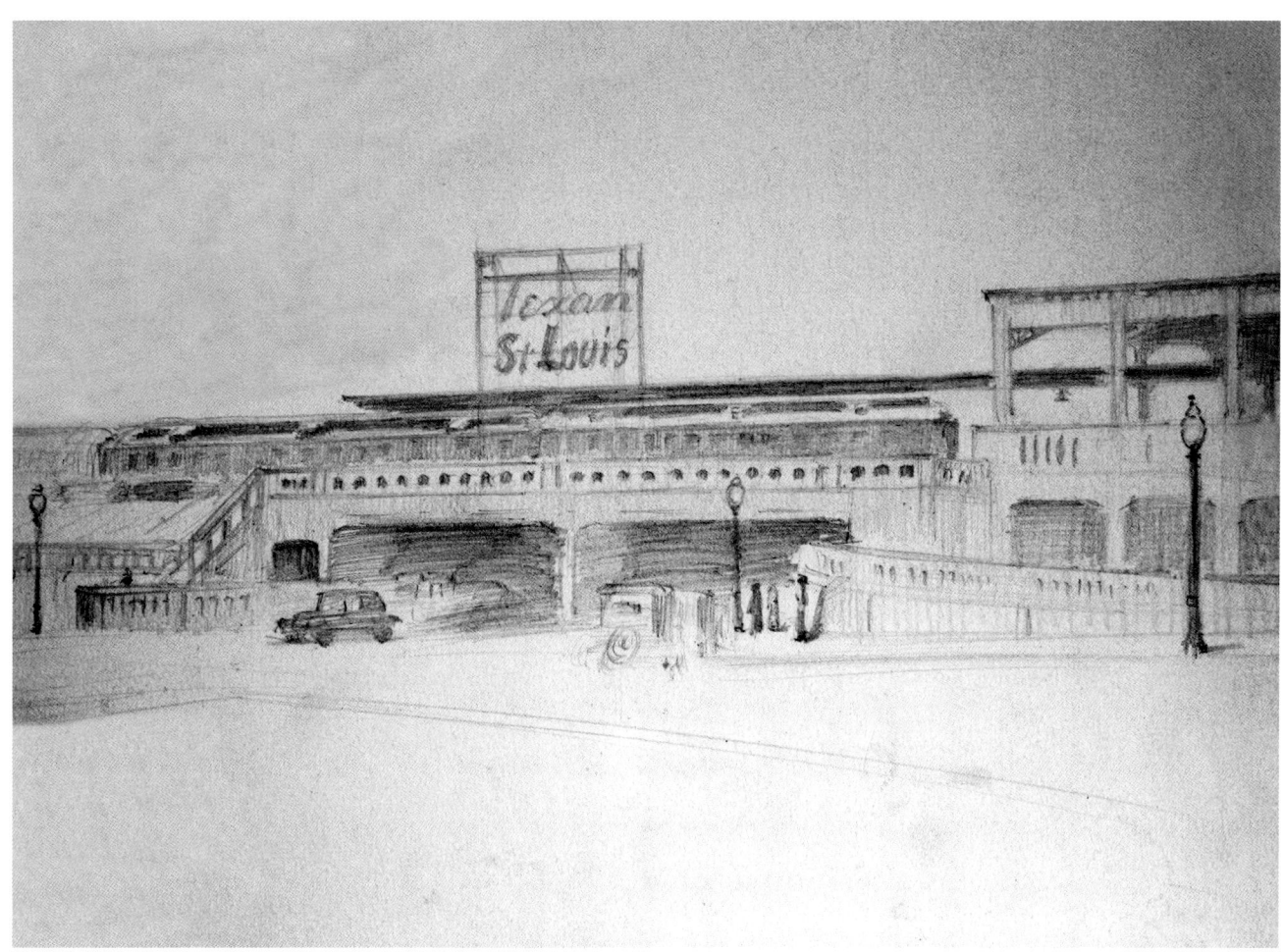

Views of Downtown Fort Worth

Carnegie Public Library, 1919.
Graphite on paper.

A rapid pencil drawing from Ziegler's
pocket sketchbook captured the allure
of the Carnegie Public Library's neoclassical façade. The building stood as a cultural
counterweight to Fort Worth's infamous
red light district a few blocks away. The
library opened in 1901 on West Ninth Street
between Houston and Throckmorton Streets.
It housed a public art gallery on the second
floor, the first such art exhibit venue in the
city. The observation towers of the Central
Fire Hall were a block north, visible through
the branches of a tree. Ziegler signed the
drawing with his initials and dated the
work April 6, 1919.

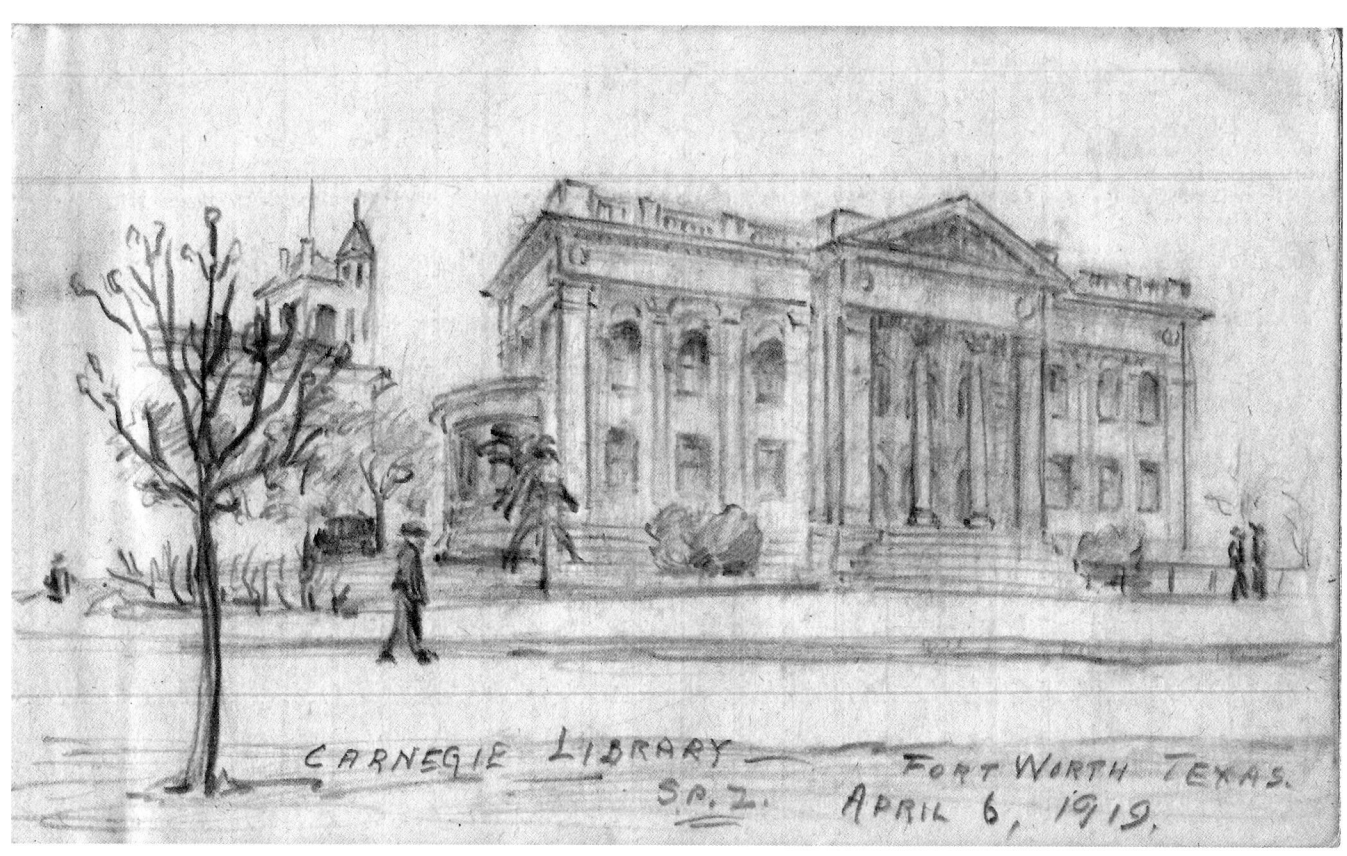

Carnegie Public Library, n.d.
(early 1930s). Etching.

In this print Ziegler depicted the Carnegie
Public Library as seen from Houston Street.
The clock tower of Fort Worth City Hall is
visible just beyond the library. The Carnegie
Library survived until 1938, when it was
torn down and replaced by a larger library
building on the same site. The Carnegie was
demolished in spite of efforts by patrons to
save it. The rationale for demolishing the
Carnegie Library involved the city's inability
to obtain an alternate site for the new
library building.

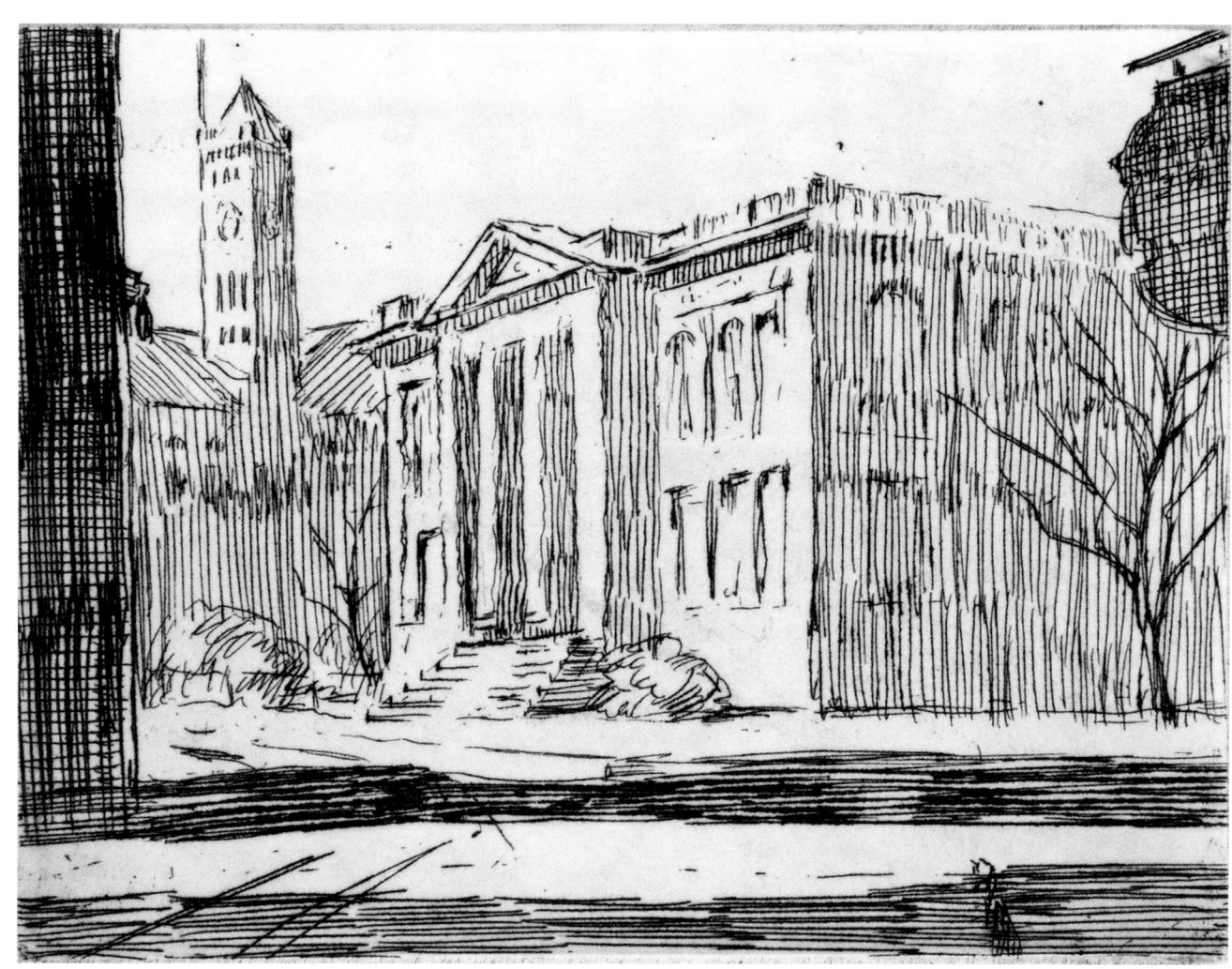

Looking North from Ninth Street and Throckmorton, **1919–1920. Graphite on paper.**

The John Peter Smith Triangle provided the vantage point for Ziegler's pencil study of the intersection of Throckmorton and West Ninth streets. Looking to the north on Throckmorton, Ziegler captured several prominent buildings including (L-R) the Fort Worth City Hall (far left), the Central Fire Hall, Ellison's Furniture (at Throckmorton and West Seventh Street), and the Carnegie Public Library. The drawing's most striking image is of the unfinished W. T. Waggoner Building. Soaring twenty stories, for a brief time the W. T. Waggoner Building was the tallest structure in Fort Worth.

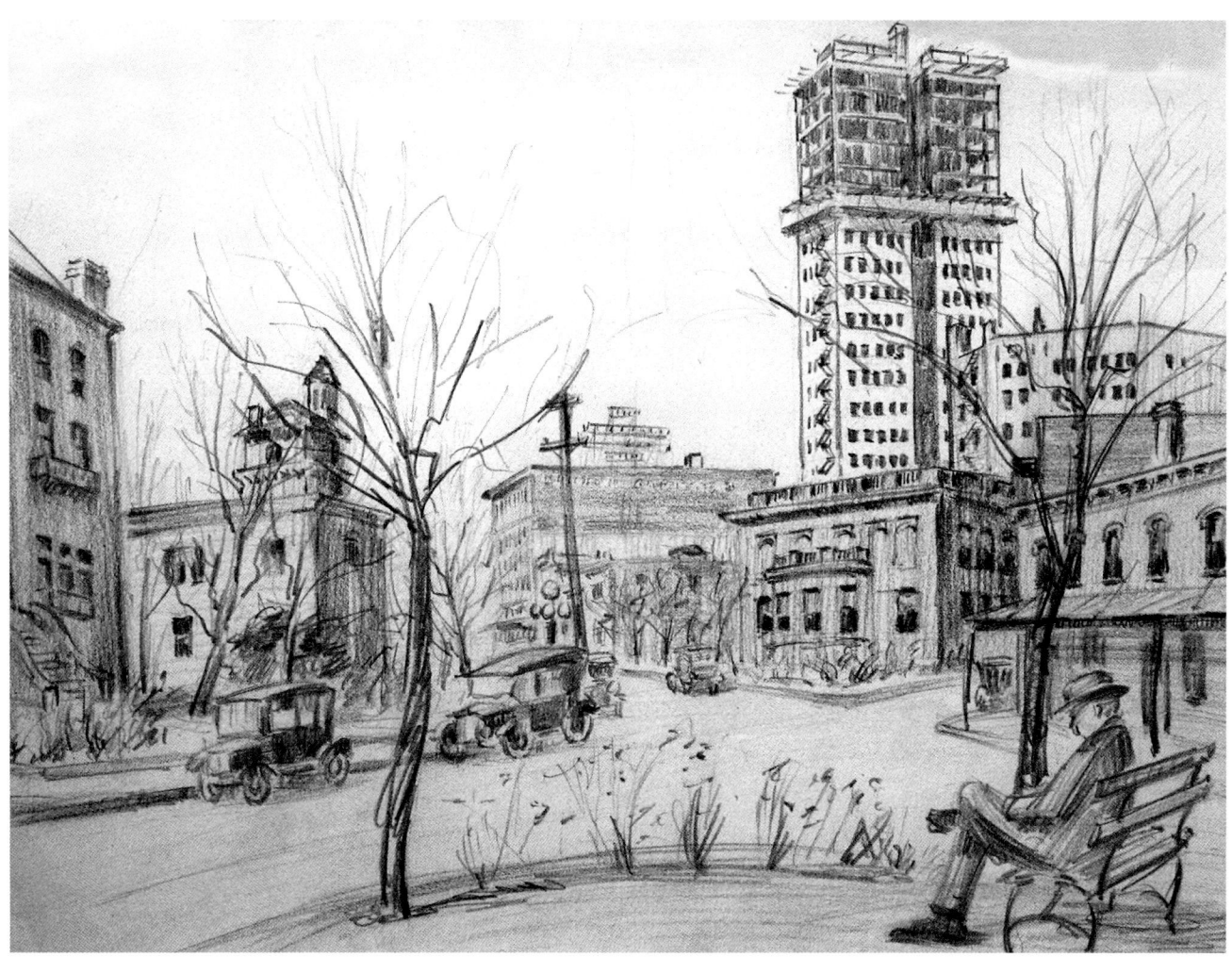

W. T. Waggoner Building under Construction, 1919–1920. Graphite on paper.

Ziegler chose the 900 block of Main Street as his vantage point to depict the W. T. Waggoner Building under construction. A corner of the Metropolitan Hotel is visible on the far-right side of the pencil drawing. Directly in front of the artist was the National Business College, located at 912 ½ Main Street. Construction of the W. T. Waggoner Building began in 1919. The building topped out in March 1920 when its namesake, rancher and oil man W. T. Waggoner, unfurled an American flag from the roof. For a few months the twenty-story skyscraper at Main and Eighth Streets was the tallest building in the Fort Worth skyline, but was soon eclipsed by the twenty-four-story Farmers and Mechanics Federal Bank building at West Seventh Street and Main.

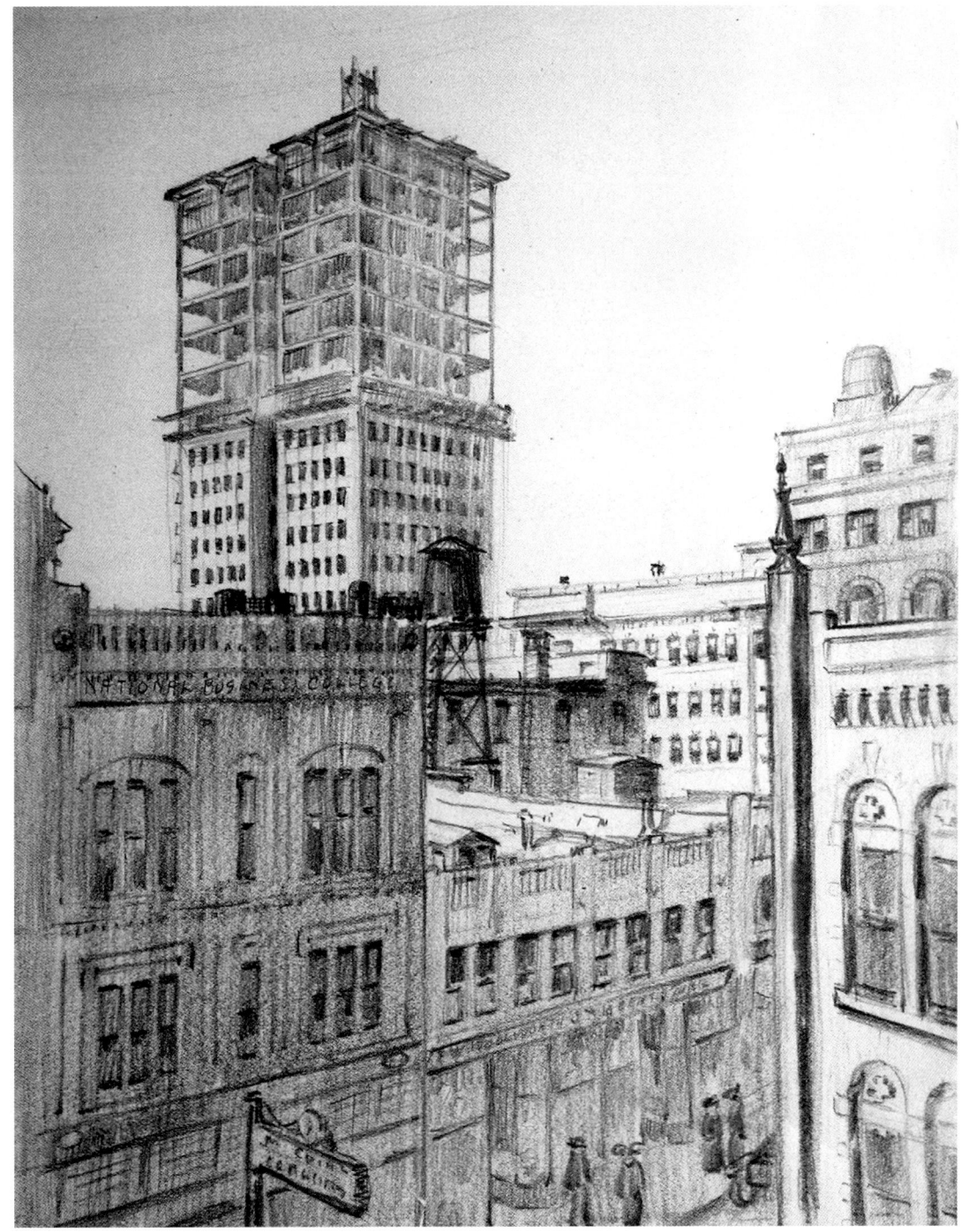

Sinclair Building at Night, 1931.
Drypoint etching.

Sinclair Building at Night was one of Ziegler's most successful etchings, recalling the renowned New York night scenes of printmaker Martin Lewis. The crown of the zigzag Moderne building was accentuated after dark by installed floodlighting, creating an irresistible motif for the artist. The building, standing sixteen stories, opened in 1930 at the corner of West Fifth and Main Streets. The Sinclair Building was wholly owned and developed by Fort Worth investors. The sixth through eleventh floors were occupied by the southwestern offices of the building's namesake tenant, the Sinclair Oil and Refining Company. Ground floor tenants in 1930 included a Renfro Drug Store and a Western Union telegraph office.

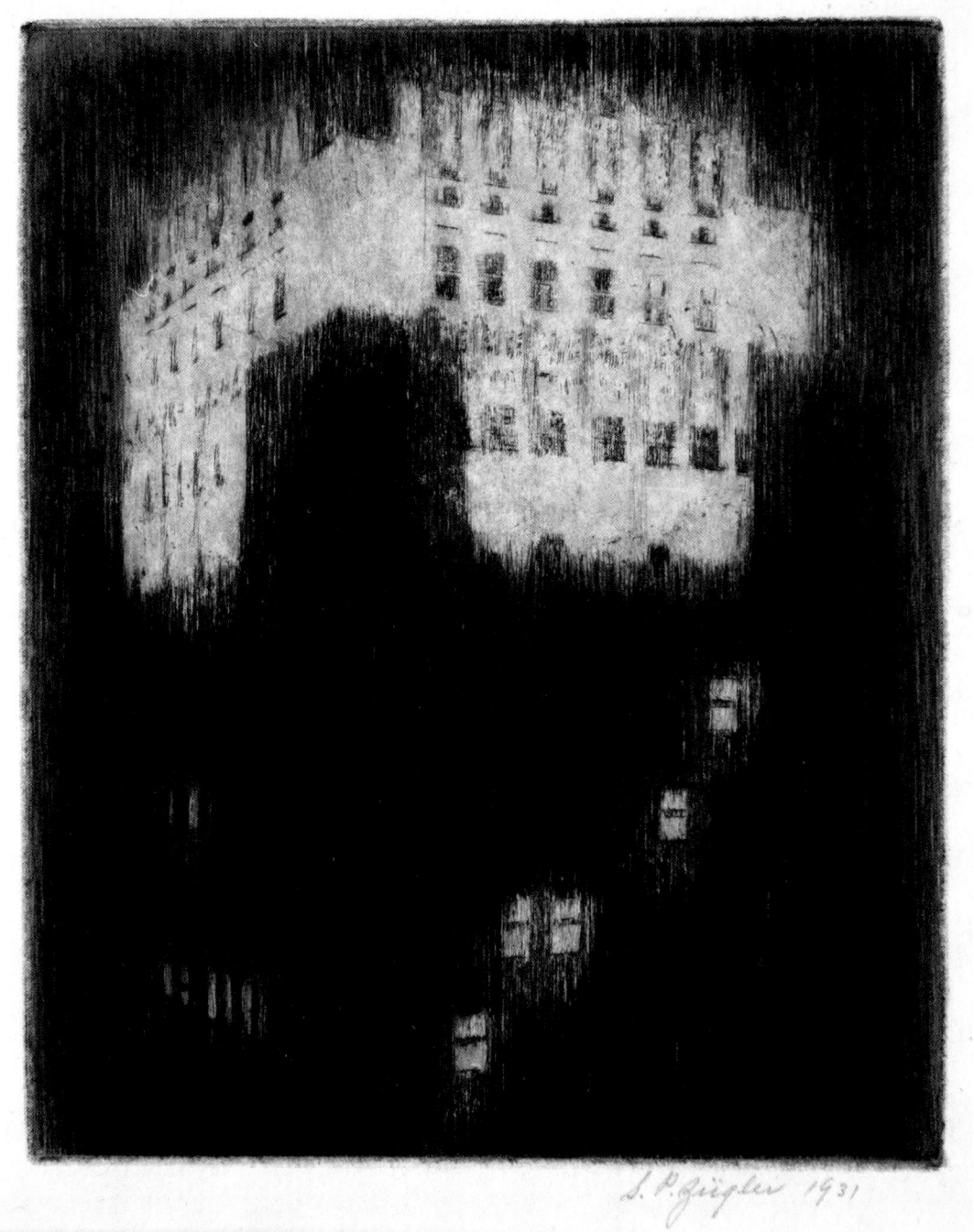

Study of Box Seating, Majestic Theatre, 1919.
Graphite on paper.

Samuel Ziegler was both an artist and professional musician. He supplemented his teacher's salary by playing cello in the Majestic Theatre's orchestra. This pencil study of the theater's box seating was probably based on the view from the orchestra pit where Ziegler sat during performances. Ornate box seating flanked both sides of the proscenium stage. The sketch was dated March 31, 1919.

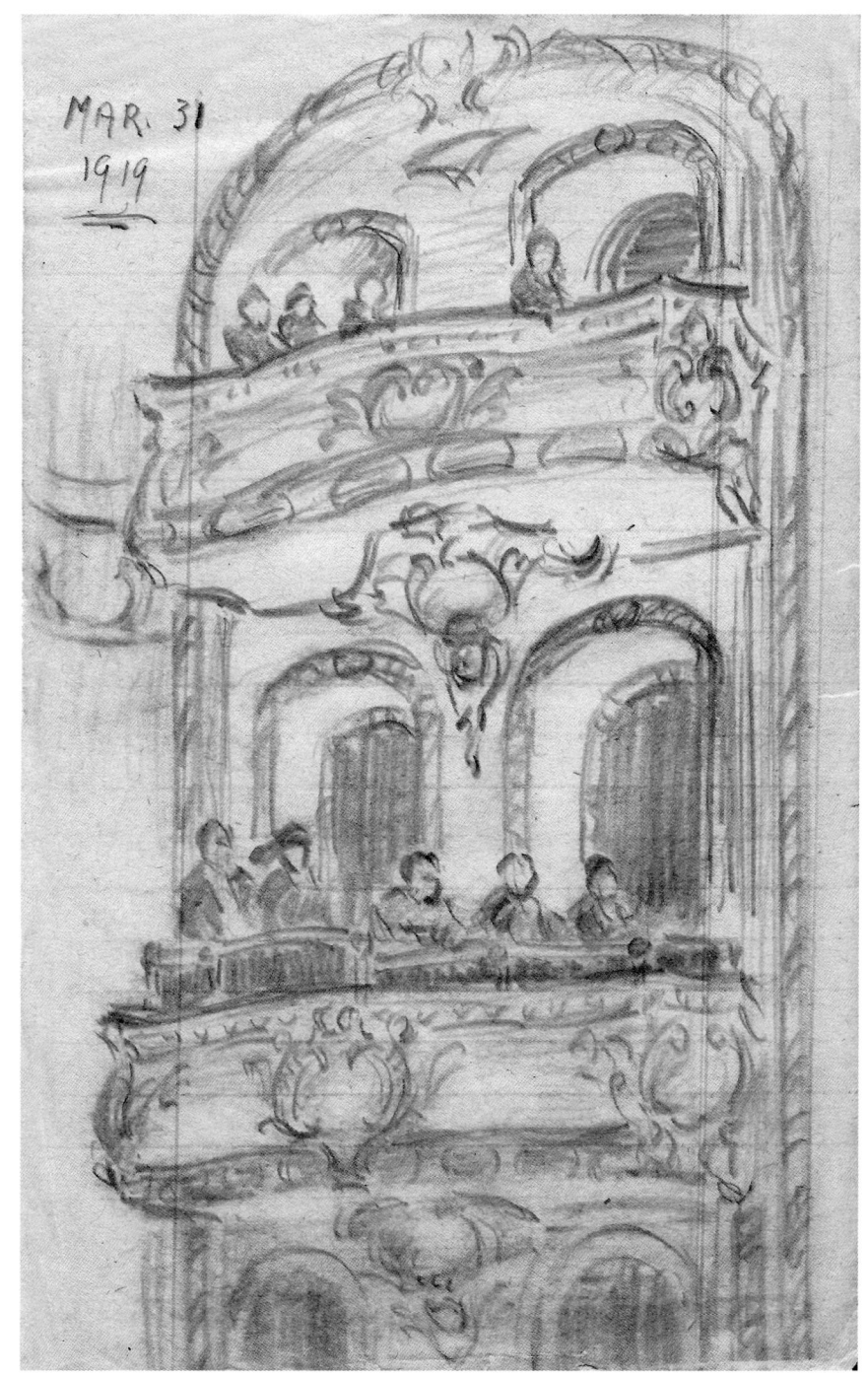

**Proscenium Boxes,
Majestic Theatre, ca. 1920.
Graphite on paper.**

The Fort Worth Majestic Theatre,
1101 Commerce Street, was a Vaudeville
theater renowned for its live entertainment
and ornate interior. It was owned and
operated by the Interstate Amusement
Company as part of a chain of Vaudeville
theaters designed and controlled by
company president Karl Hoblitzelle.
The building was constructed in 1911 on
Commerce Street (originally Rusk Street)
and was sometimes referred to as the
New Majestic Theatre, as it replaced the
theater's original location on Jennings
Avenue. The Commerce Street structure
stood until 1966. Ziegler's highly finished
pencil drawing (shown here) gives a sense
of the baroque architectural theme used
inside the performance hall. Box seats
depicted in this drawing overlooked both
sides of the main stage and were officially
known as Proscenium Boxes.

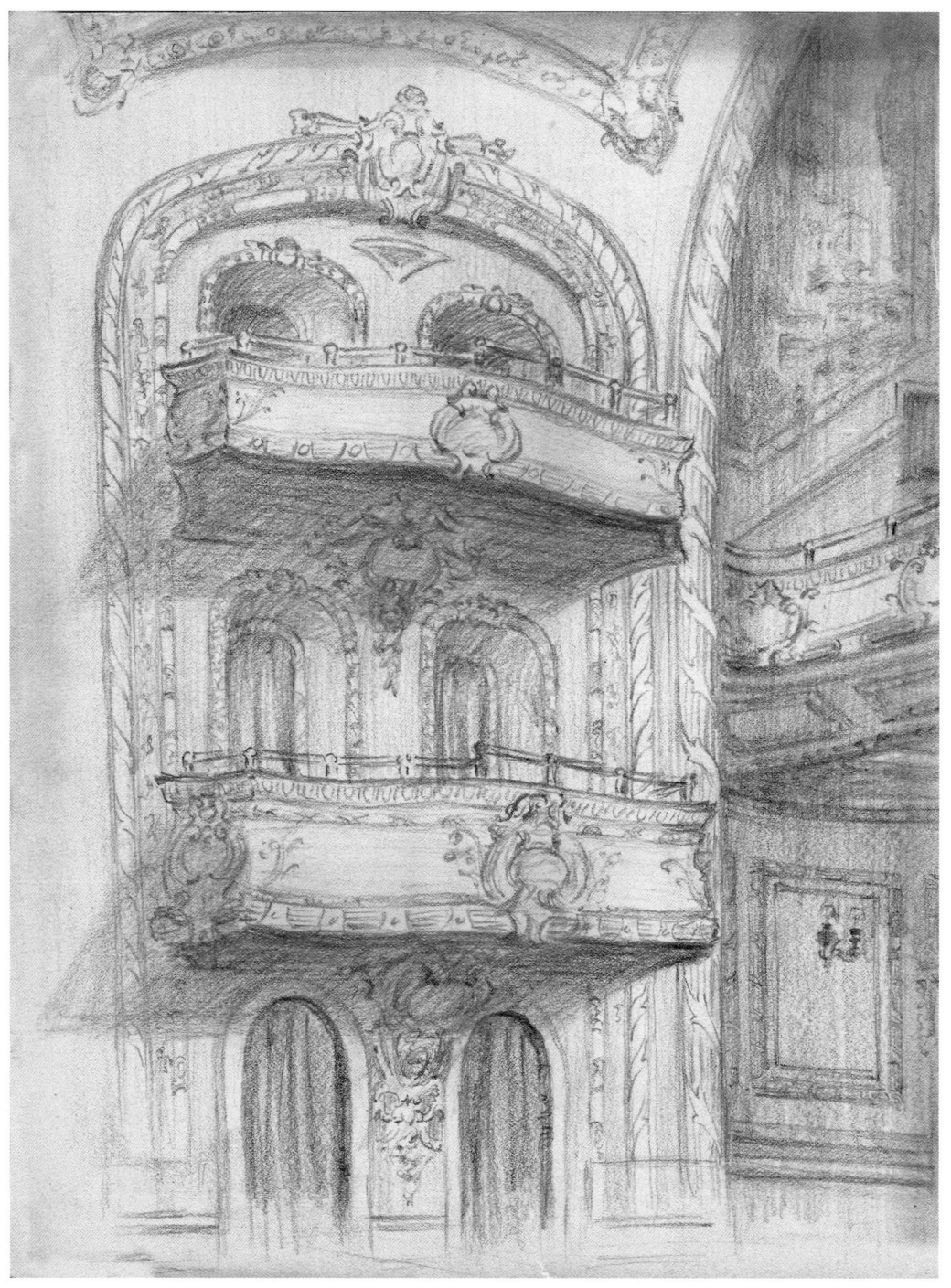

Backstage at the Majestic Theatre,
ca. 1920. Graphite on paper.

The backstage area of the Majestic Theatre
was the vantage point for this Ziegler pencil
drawing. Some of the theater's box seats
were visible beyond the proscenium stage.
The rectangle in the center of the stage
floor suggested an elevator mechanism for
raising and lowering props and set pieces.

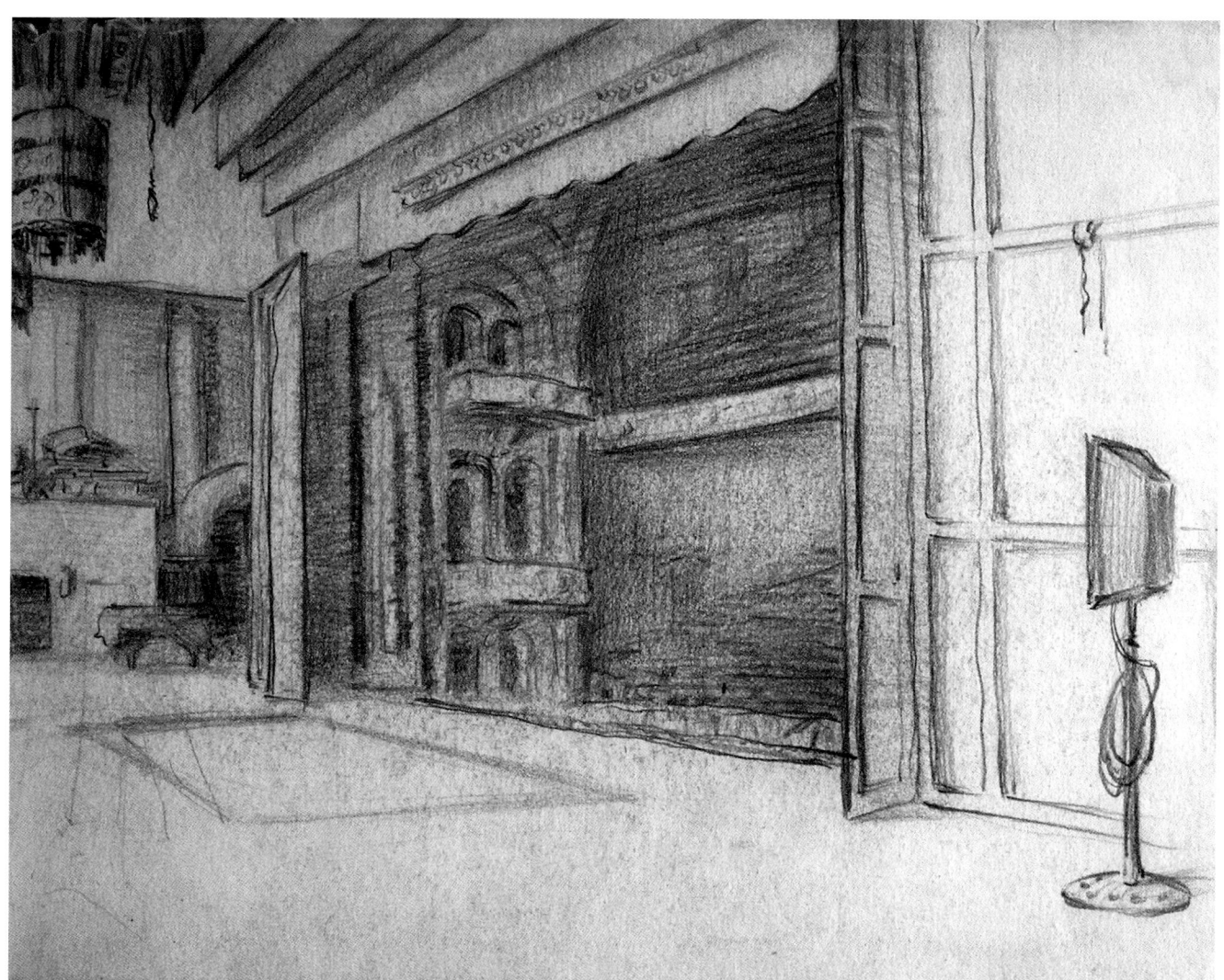

Fort Worth City Hall, ca. 1930. Lithograph.

Fort Worth's nineteenth-century City Hall building was still in use but nearing the end of its useful life when Ziegler made this lithographic drawing of it around 1930. City Hall was located at Throckmorton and West Tenth Street, across the street from the post office and federal building. This seat of city government was constructed in the 1890s at a cost of $72,500. Its distinctive clock tower was captured in many period photographs of the downtown area. Fort Worth City Hall, badly outdated, was demolished in November 1937. It was replaced the following year by a new building constructed with federal funds. Fort Worth Wrecking & Lumber Company, the city hall demolition contractor, salvaged a lengthy list of building materials from the demolition site and offered them for sale. Included were circular steel fire escapes, 150,000 board feet of long-leaf lumber, and a complete steam heating system, including the boiler.

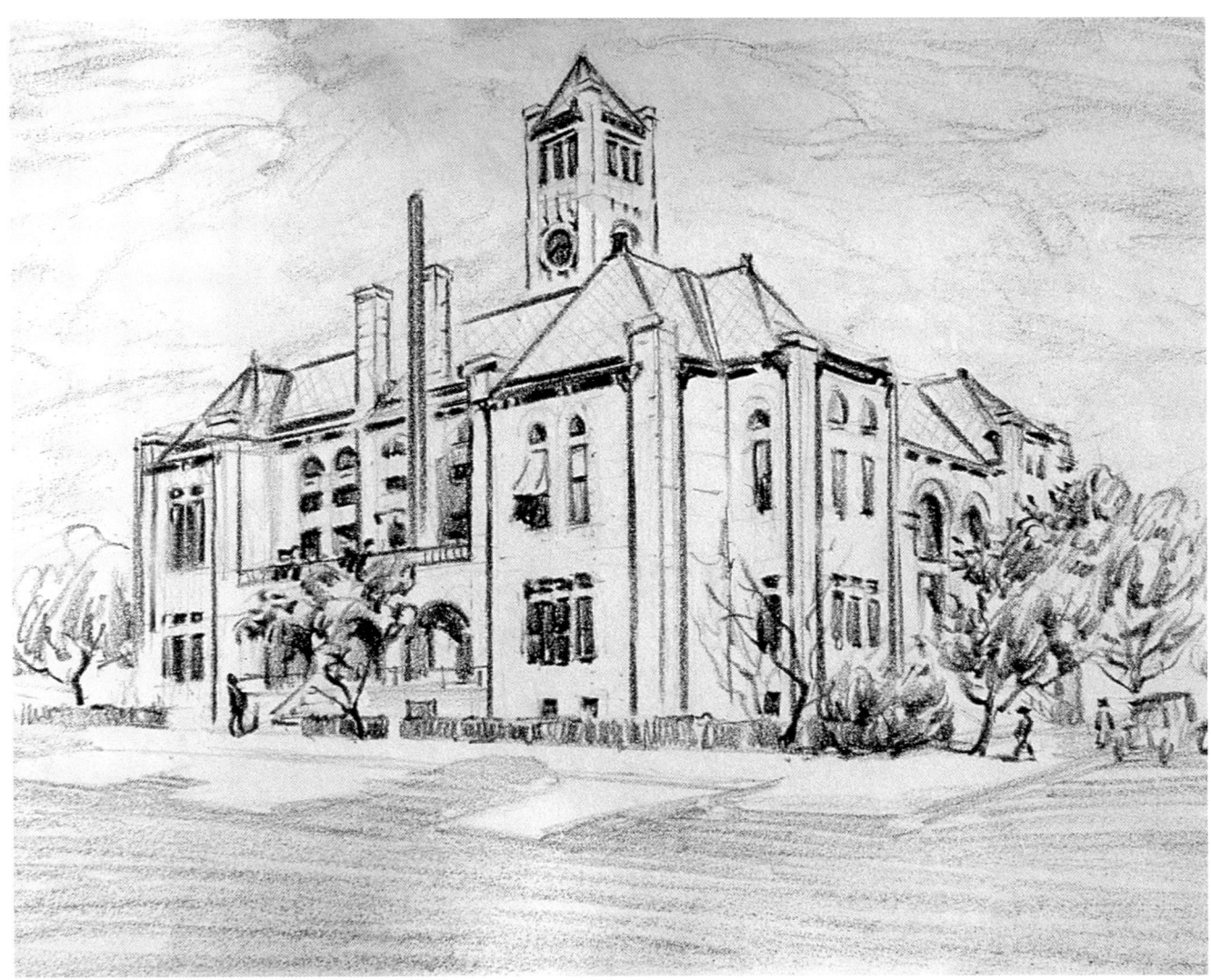

Skyline Fort Worth, ca. 1930. Etching.

This detailed etching captured an impressive panoramic sweep of the Fort Worth skyline about 1930. Each major building between the Paddock Viaduct to the north (far left) and the Medical Arts Building to the west (far right) was carefully observed and recorded. The original copper printing plate for this image was permanently kept in Professor Ziegler's studio; however, there is some evidence that the plate was etched by Lottie Martin, a noted Ziegler student. The only known signed copy of this print carries Martin's signature. It is entirely possible that Martin created the image and Ziegler supervised its printing or printed it for her. Other Ziegler printmaking protégés at Texas Christian University included Lucille Richhart and Sarah Smith.

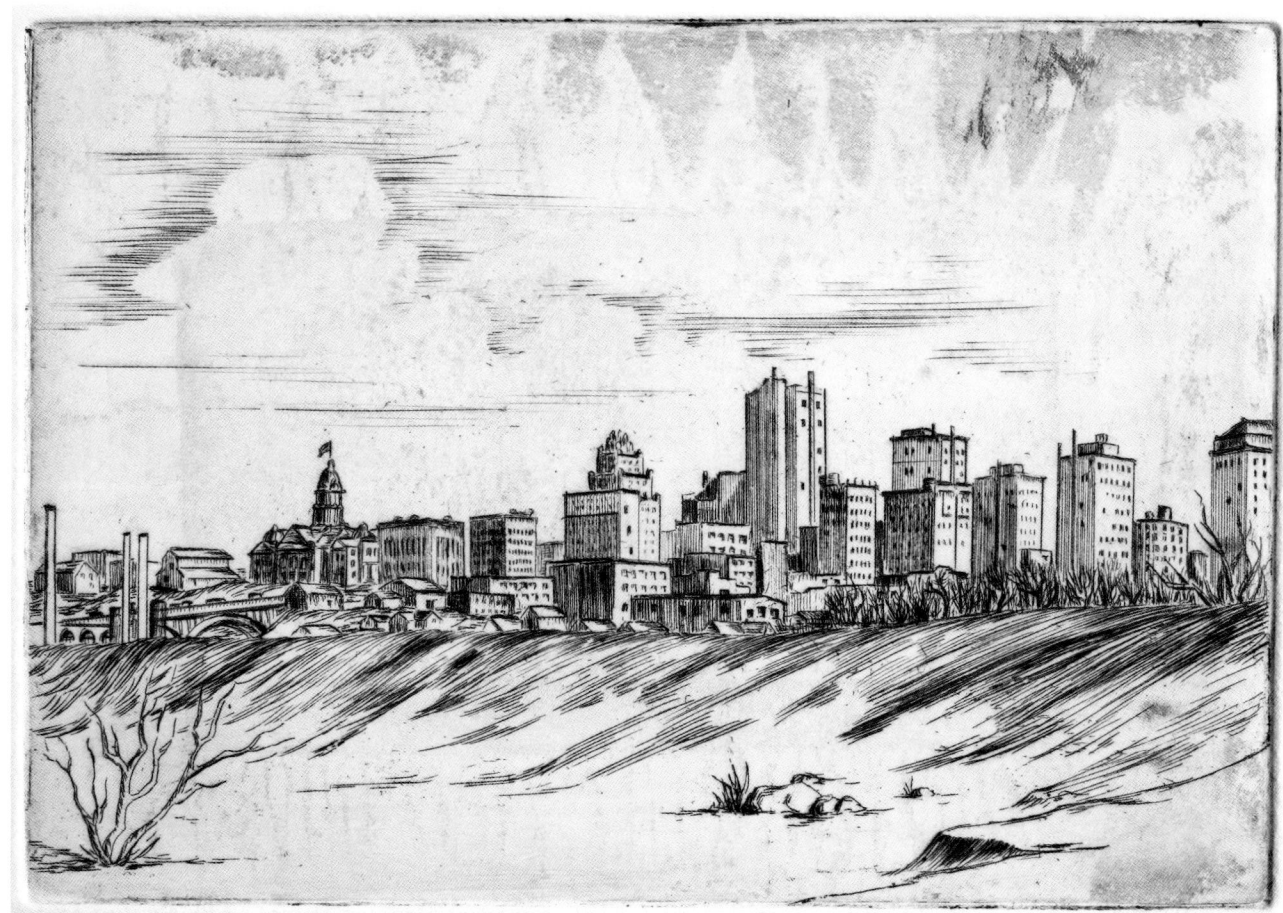

Fort Worth Skyline from the West, ca. 1930. Pen and ink.

The vantage point for this pen and ink study of the downtown skyline was near present-day University Drive and West Seventh Street. In the left foreground was the new Montgomery Ward store (opened 1928) which, from this vantage point, partially obscured the view of the Tarrant County Courthouse and the North Main Power Plant. Only the power plant smoke stacks were visible. In the center and right foreground were the former Chevrolet assembly plant and the Bain Peanut Company elevator complex. It is unknown whether Ziegler used this study to produce other versions of the image via a lithograph, etching, or oil painting. Stylistically, this drawing strongly echoes the draftsmanship seen in the etching on p. 71, and is therefore possibly the work of Lottie Martin.

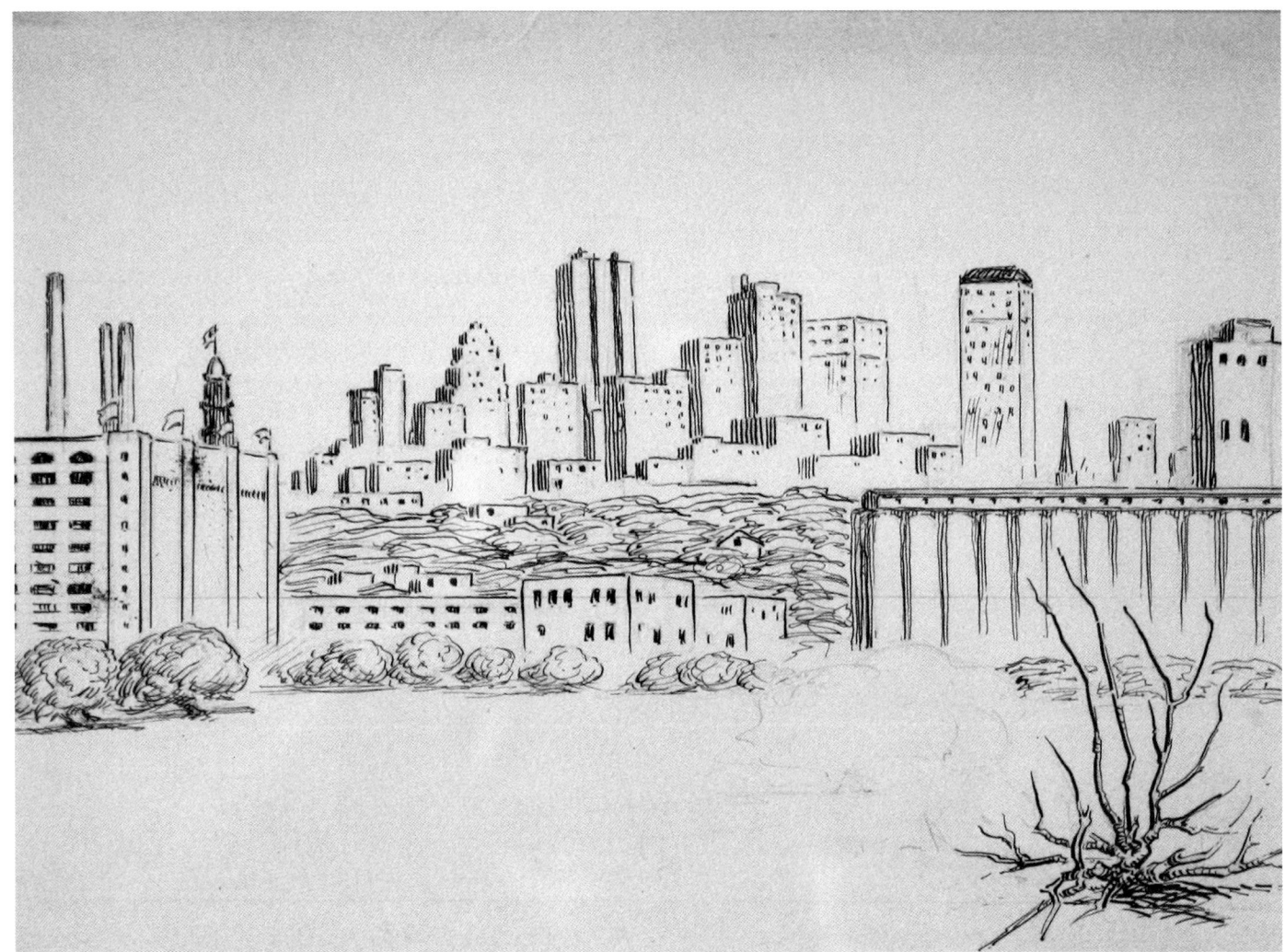

Fort Worth Skyline Over Campus Tree Tops, **ca. 1930. Lithograph.**

The Fort Worth skyline as seen from the Texas Christian University campus was one of Ziegler's earliest painting motifs. His first depiction of the skyline from this vantage point was executed in 1925. In this lithograph, the positioning of the Medical Arts Building (at left-center) and the 1899 T&P Passenger Station (at far right) is consistent with the panoramic view of downtown as seen from Ziegler's art classroom, located on the third floor (north end) of the TCU Main Administration Building. The city street in the foreground is University Drive. By 1930 (the approximate date of this lithograph), neighborhood development northeast of the school campus was well underway, as demonstrated by the dense cluster of rooftops in the mid-ground.

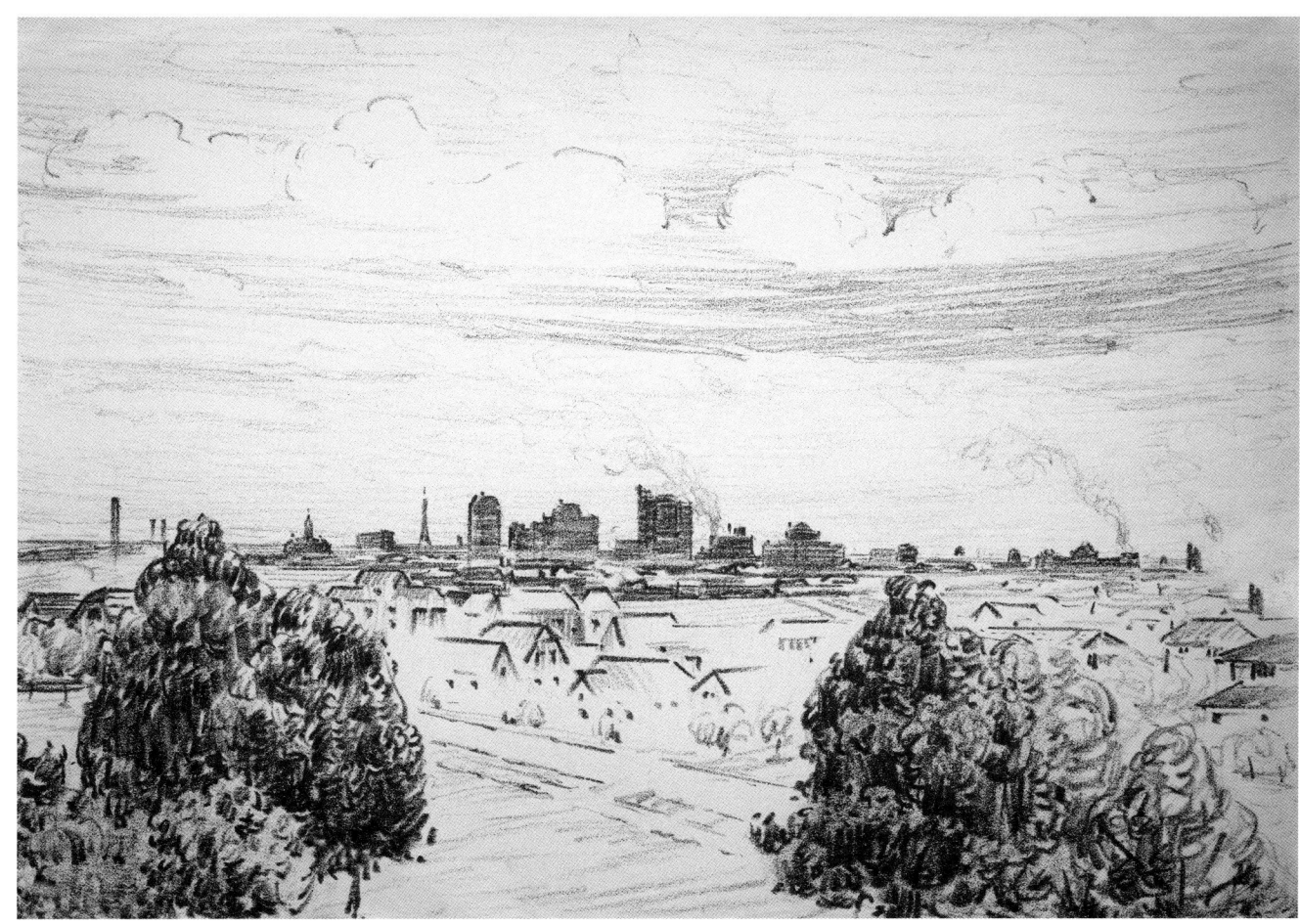

**Tarrant County Courthouse,
ca. 1930. Lithograph.**

Since its completion in 1895,
Fort Worth's signature architectural
landmark is the Tarrant County
Courthouse. In this lithograph Ziegler
captured the dome and west façade
of the courthouse as seen from Weath-
erford Street looking eastward. With
the demolition of the Tarrant County
Civil Courts Building in 2013, this view
of the courthouse from the west is
again available to observers. Reconstruction of the courthouse's west
entrance has restored the scene
to almost exactly what it was in
Ziegler's time.

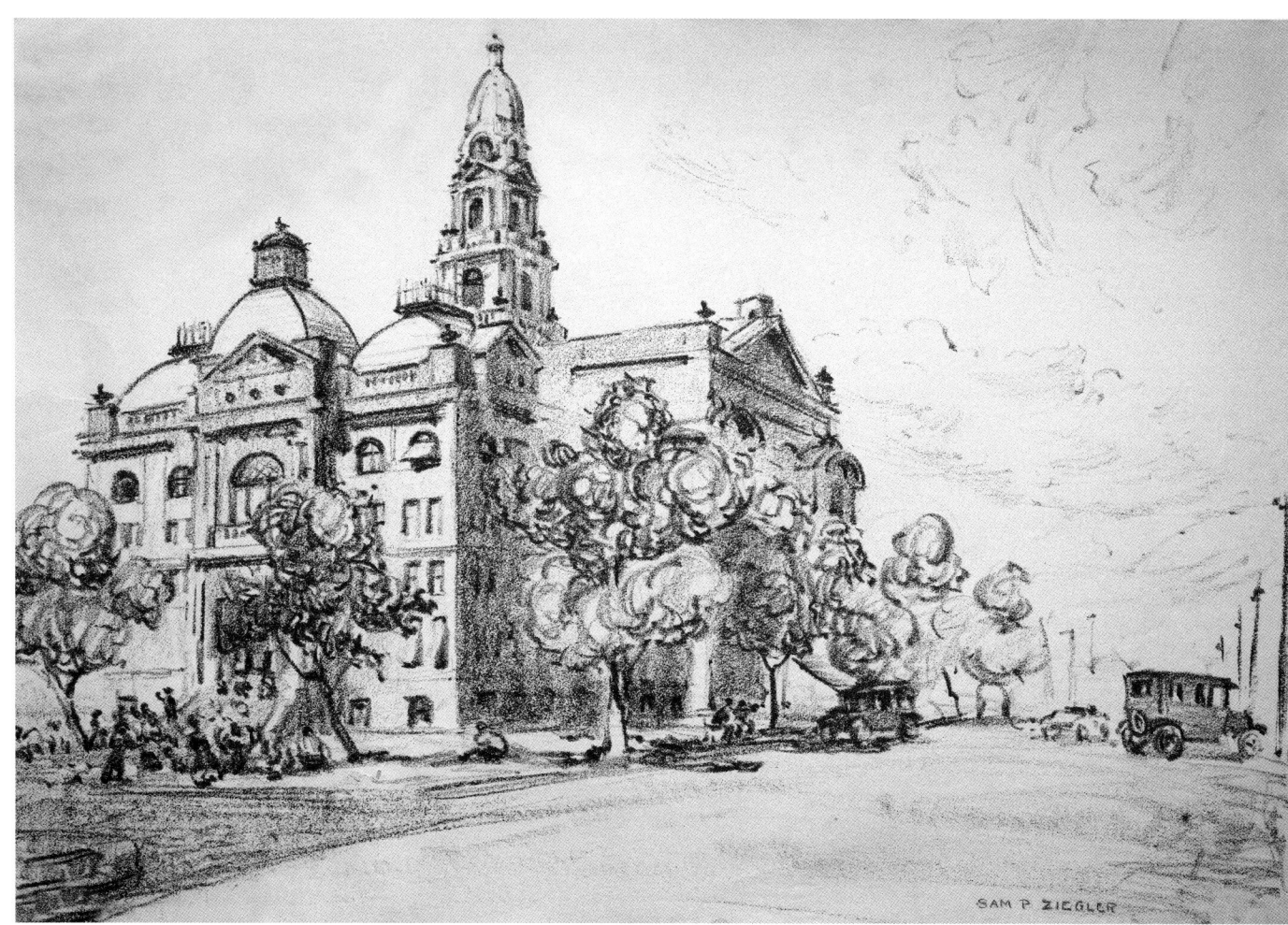

Court Buildings from Trinity River Flats, n.d. (early 1930s). Graphite on paper.

Ziegler's pencil drawing captured this most interesting view of the Tarrant County Courthouse. His vantage point was near the corner of N. Houston Street and Fourth Street SW, north of the Trinity River. Dual exhaust stacks of the North Main Power Plant occupied the center of the scene. The Tarrant County Criminal Courts Building sat in the distance to the right of the stacks.

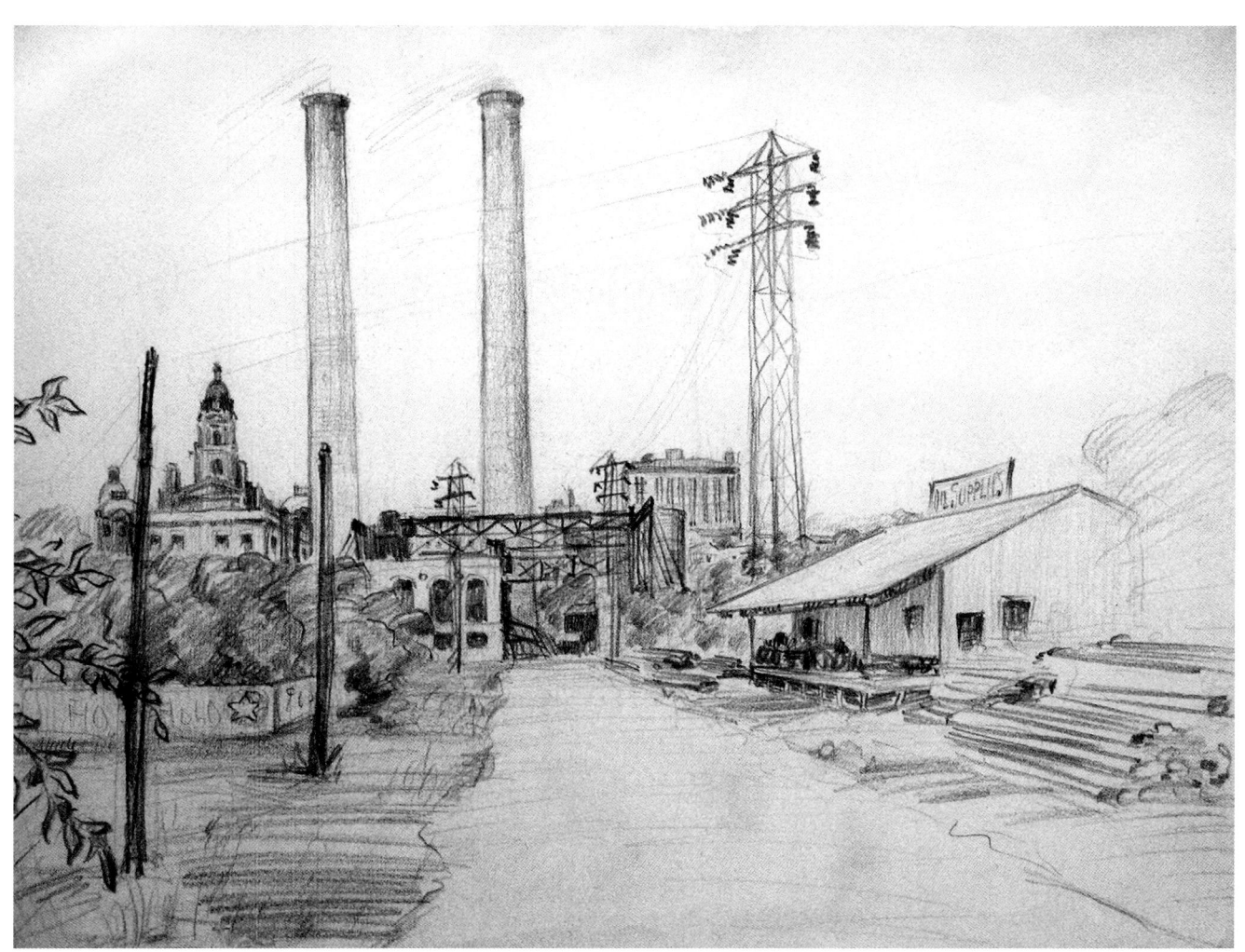

Looking North on Main Street,
n.d. (early 1930s). Etching.

This iconic view of the Tarrant County Courthouse from the south was often captured by photographers but rarely depicted by local artists. Ziegler returned to this scene in 1936 when he produced an oil painting entitled *Looking North on Main Street*. The etching reproduced here was pulled from a small copper plate measuring 3 ½ x 2 inches.

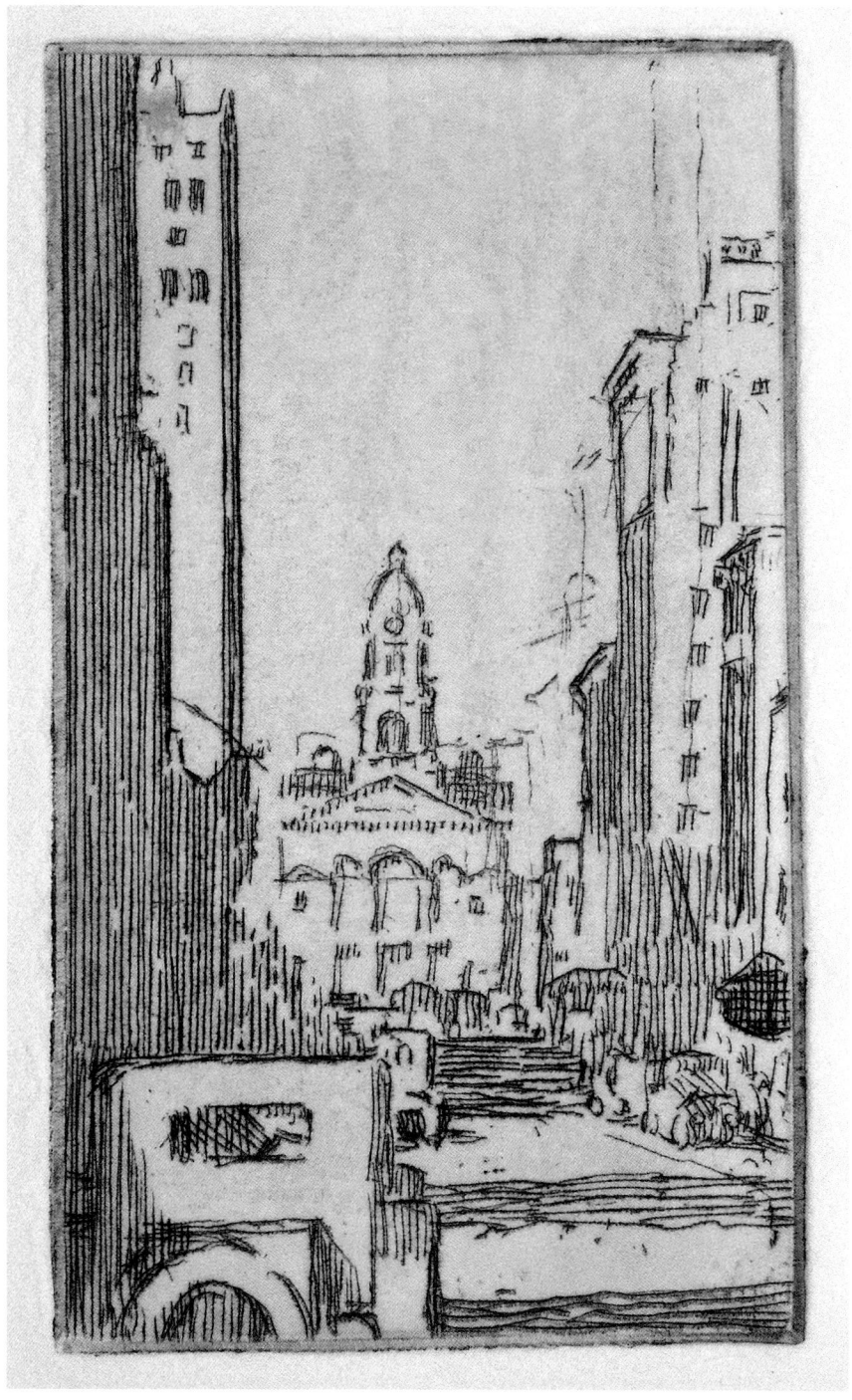

Fort Worth Star-Telegram Building, ca. 1929. Lithograph.

The *Fort Worth Star-Telegram* Building was built in 1921 at 400 West Seventh Street, the northwest corner of West Seventh and Taylor Streets. The new four-story building, complete with printing presses in the basement, housed the powerhouse newspaper led by Amon G. Carter Sr. This Ziegler lithograph depicted the *Star-Telegram* offices as seen from the next block east on West Seventh Street. In addition to newspaper publishing, the *Star-Telegram* Building housed the first broadcast studio of WBAP, Amon Carter's AM radio broadcasting venture. WBAP went on the air in 1922 and quickly attracted listeners who, in search of WBAP's daily programming schedule, purchased copies of the *Star-Telegram*. The radio station's first transmission tower was on top of the *Star-Telegram* Building. In later years, broadcasts originated from a series of other locations, including the Montgomery Ward building on West Seventh Street. Permanent broadcast facilities for WBAP were eventually built on high ground in east Fort Worth.

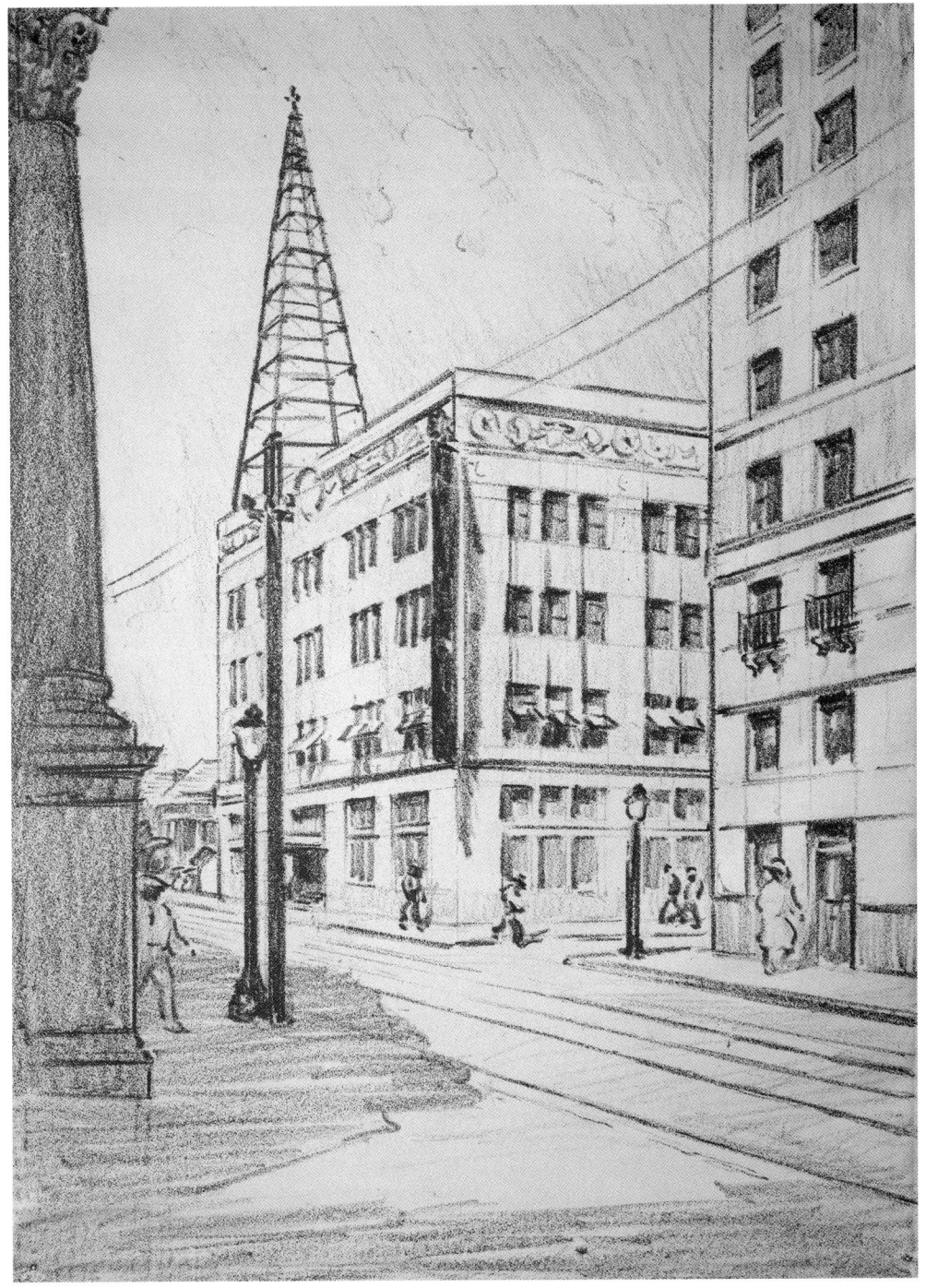

View from Burnett Park, ca. 1929. Lithograph.

From Burnett Park looking eastward Ziegler captured a wealth of visual information about downtown Fort Worth. On his left was the stately Elks Club, located at the northwest corner of West Seventh and Lamar Streets. The four-story *Star-Telegram* Building, with WBAP broadcast tower atop its roof, was in the center of Ziegler's field of view. Immediately beyond the *Star-Telegram* Building was the new multistory Worth Hotel. The distinctive curvature of the Neil P. Anderson Building can be seen to the right of the *Star-Telegram* Building. At the time this lithograph was made, the *Star-Telegram* Building and Worth Hotel were clearly visible from the park because ground for the new Electric Building (constructed 1929-30 at 410 West Seventh Street) had not yet been broken.

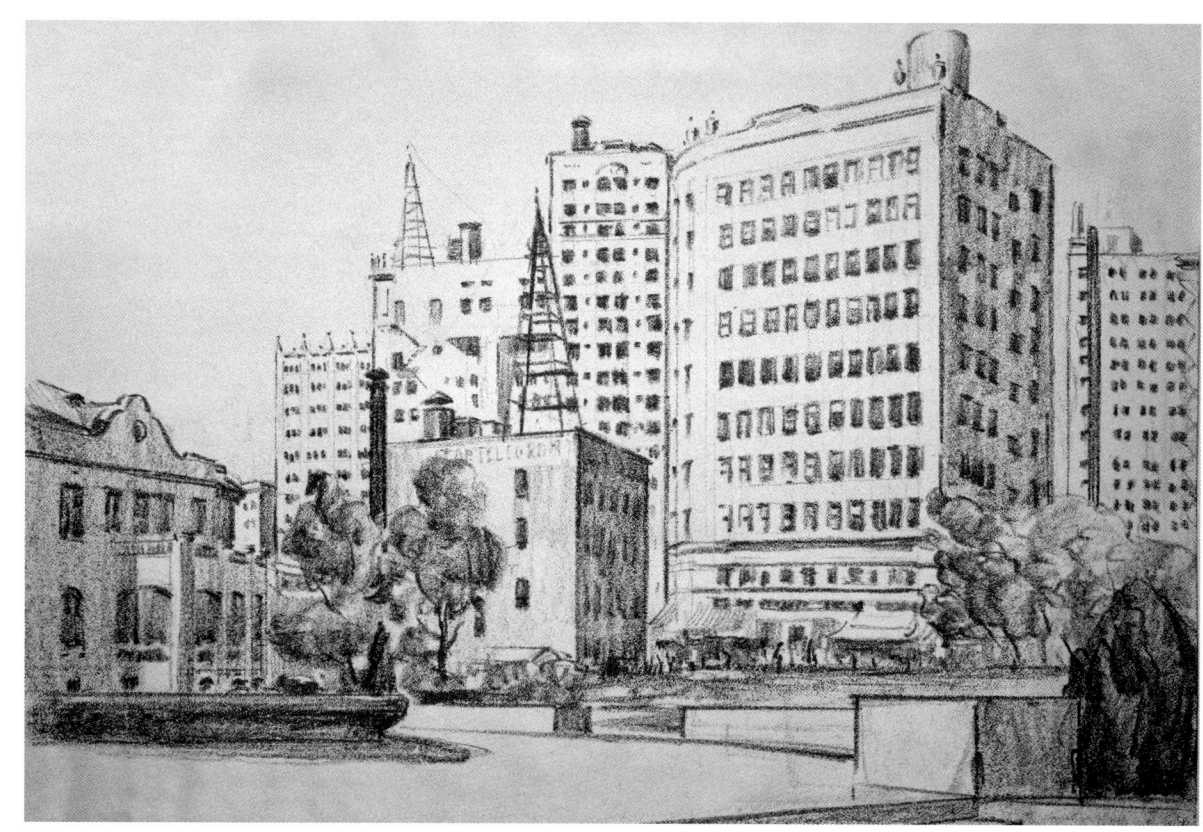

Skyline from Post Office Roof,
ca. 1929. Lithograph.

The roof of the post office and federal building
provided Ziegler with a classic birds-eye view of the
Fort Worth skyline from the southwest. Directly across
the street was Fort Worth City Hall with its distinctive
clock tower. The mid-ground to the right of City Hall
was occupied by the Carnegie Public Library. Major
office buildings in the background were (left to right)
the Worth Hotel, the Fort Worth Club Building, the
Petroleum Building, W. T. Waggoner Building,
Fort Worth National Bank Building, and the Texas
National Bank (just beyond the Carnegie Library).

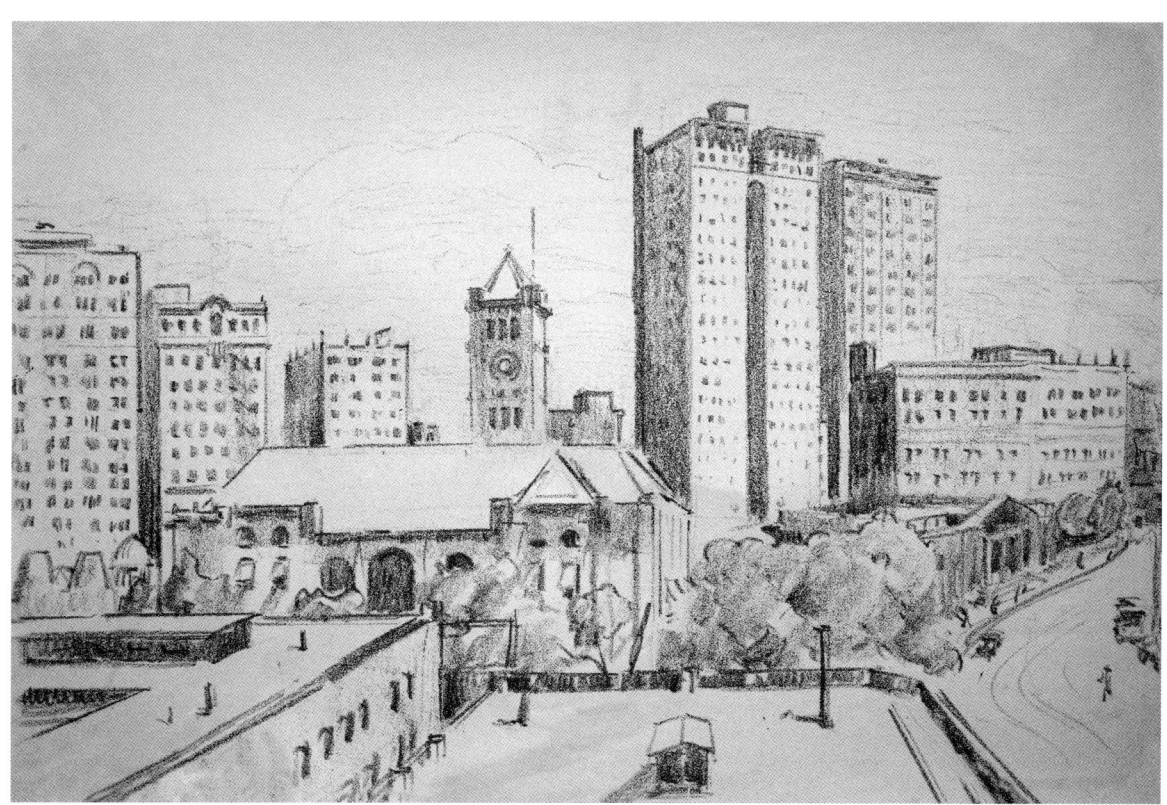

In and Around Fort Worth I

Study for Fort Worth Conservatory of Music, n.d. (early 1930s). Graphite on paper.

This pencil sketch served as the preparatory drawing for the related etching (opposite). In his travels around Fort Worth, Ziegler was attracted to buildings of cultural significance as well as buildings of civic importance. Ultimately, all were historically worthwhile in his estimation. The Fort Worth Conservatory of Music (later the Fort Worth Conservatory of Music and Fine Arts) represented a note-worthy effort by local musicians to deliver youth-oriented music education outside of the public school system.

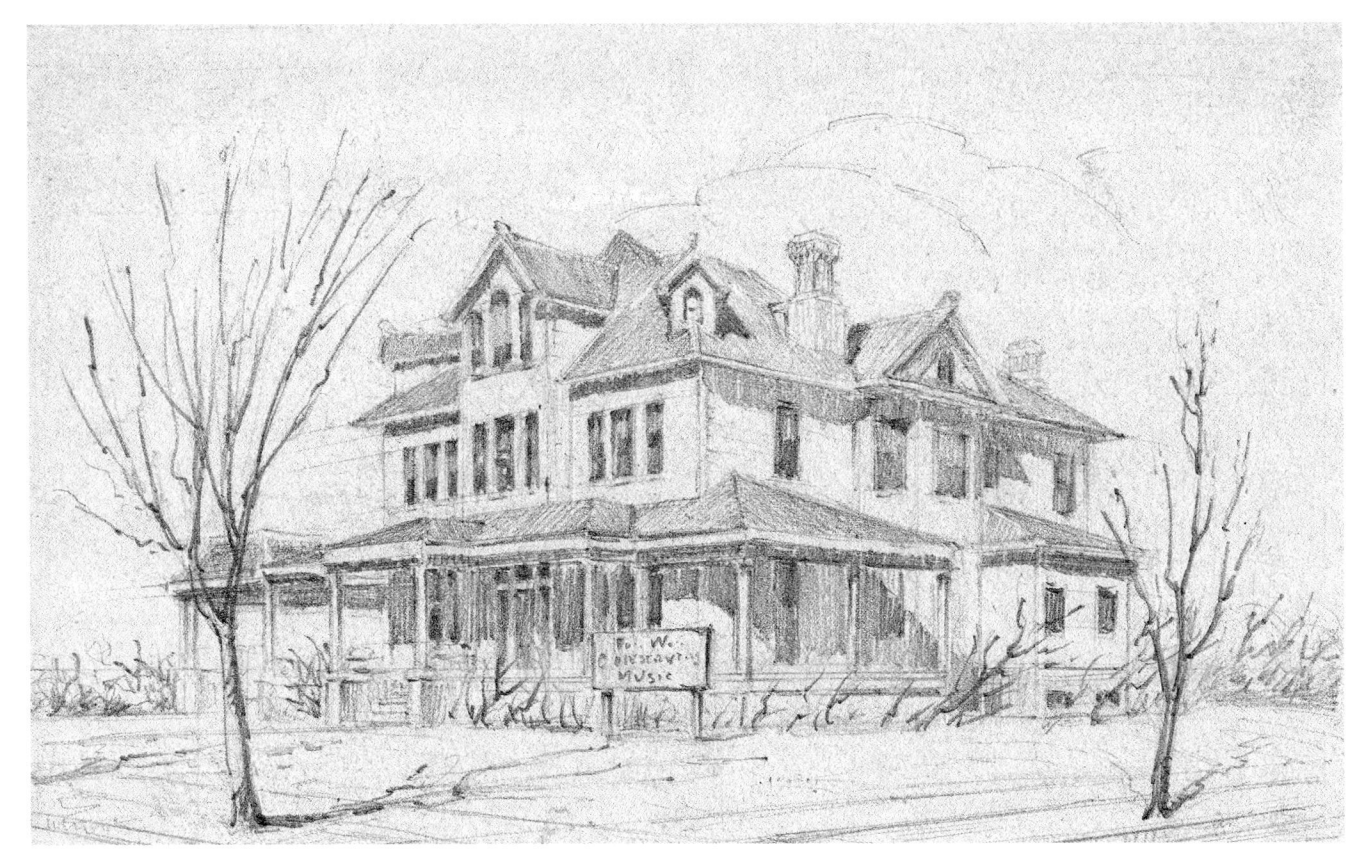

Fort Worth Conservatory of Music, n.d. (early 1930s). Etching.

The Fort Worth Conservatory of Music was founded in 1924. It was located in a converted house at 1100 W. Cannon Avenue, across the street from Fort Worth Central High School (which later became R. L. Paschal High School and then Green B. Trimble Technical High School). The conservatory catered to young musicians and offered after-school instruction by local luminaries such as pianist Jeanette Tillett and violinist E. Clyde Whitlock. Samuel P. Ziegler, who was a trained cellist as well as a painter, and E. Clyde Whitlock had a long association as principals in the popular Pro Arte String Quartet. The conservatory at 1100 W. Cannon Avenue is no longer standing.

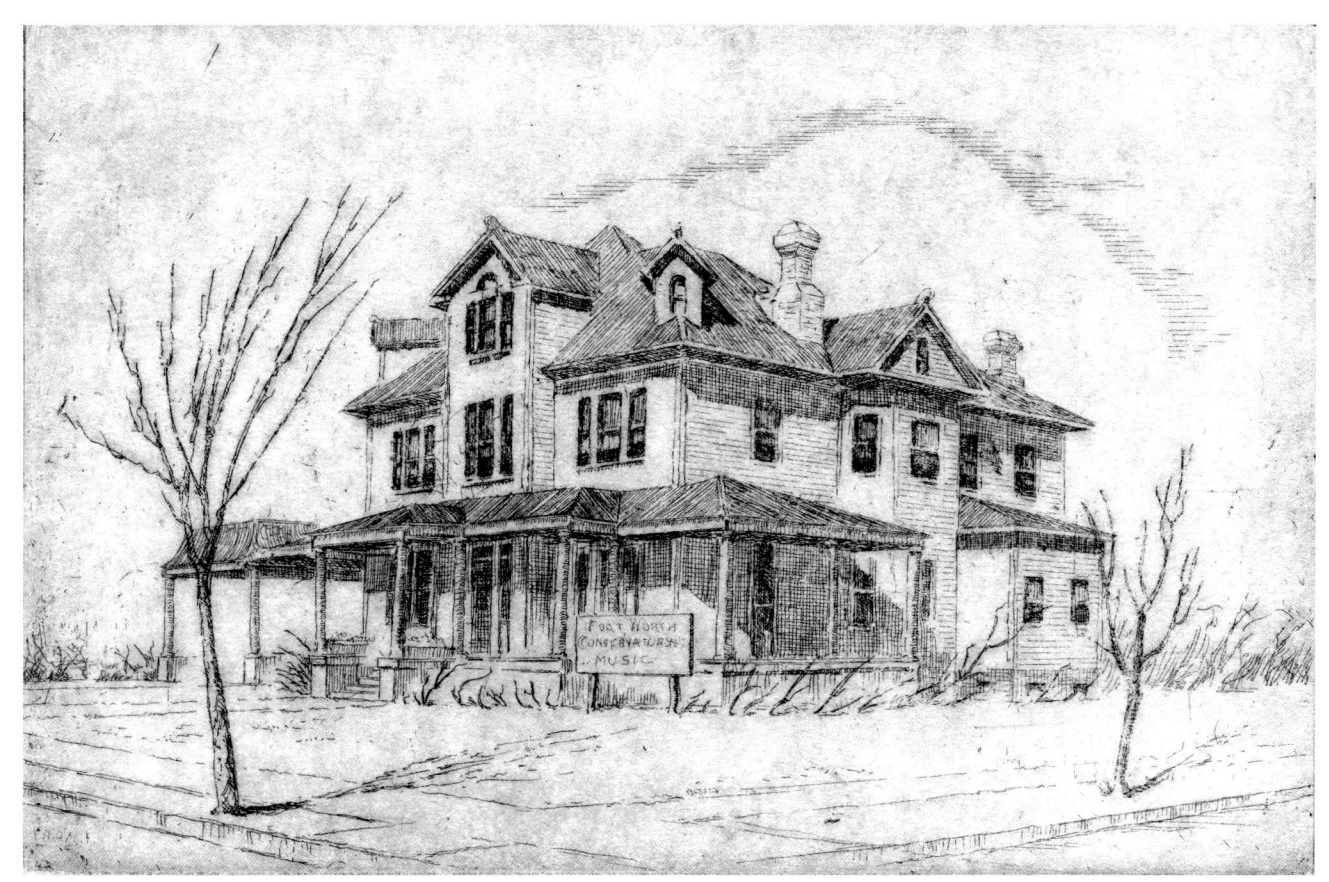

The Music Box, ca. 1930.
Lithograph.

The Music Box was built by the Woman's
Club of Fort Worth in 1925. It was located at
1312 W. Tucker Street, behind the Woman's
Club compound on Pennsylvania Avenue. The
building was designed pro bono by architect
Wiley G. Clarkson to serve as the clubhouse and
performance venue for the Euterpean Club and
the Harmony Club. Among the several clubs
that operated under the Woman's Club umbrella,
the Euterpean and Harmony clubs were uniquely
devoted to the study of music. From 1925 to
1933 the Music Box also hosted live theater
productions put on by the Fort Worth Little
Theater, the city's first true community theater
company. The building was put to a new use in
1933 when the back half of the structure was
converted into the Fort Worth School of Fine
Arts and used full time as a school for visual art
instruction. As the Fort Worth School of Fine Arts,
the Music Box facility provided a vital educational option for working-age Fort Worth artists
looking to expand their skills during the Great
Depression.

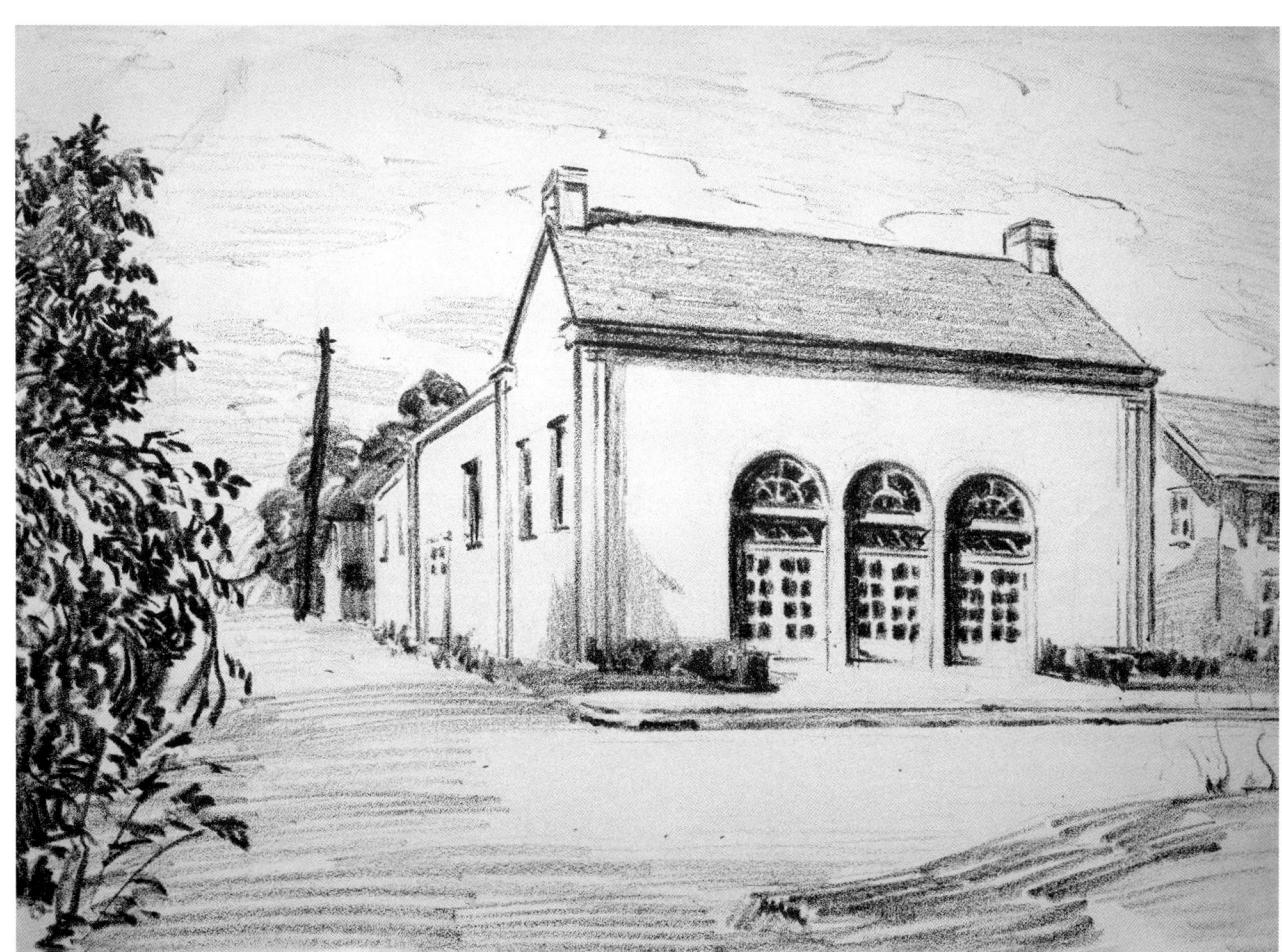

Athens Pottery Company – Kiln, ca. 1930. Lithograph.

The Fort Worth branch of Athens Pottery Company was located at 701 North Hampton Street. The pottery made flower pots, stoneware crocks, butter churns, water jars, kitchen utensils, and bowls and vases suitable for hand painting. Advertising stated that the company's vases and clay products were used in schools, colleges, and art classes all over the country. Athens Pottery Company began in Athens, Texas, and operated potteries in seven Texas cities at its peak. The Fort Worth plant opened in 1914 and was the largest of the seven by virtue of a one-hundred-foot-long, continuously operated tunnel kiln. In the Ziegler lithograph, a beehive kiln next to the main building is pictured. The beehive kiln supplemented the plant's capacity and was used when needed. A railroad semaphore (upper left) marked the pottery's proximity to nearby rail lines. Clay used in production was mined in Henderson County, near Athens, and shipped to Fort Worth by boxcar. In the late 1920s the Fort Worth plant tried unsuccessfully to make building tile from clay mined near Arlington. The Fort Worth plant failed in the early years of the Great Depression, but the company retrenched and continued operations in Athens.

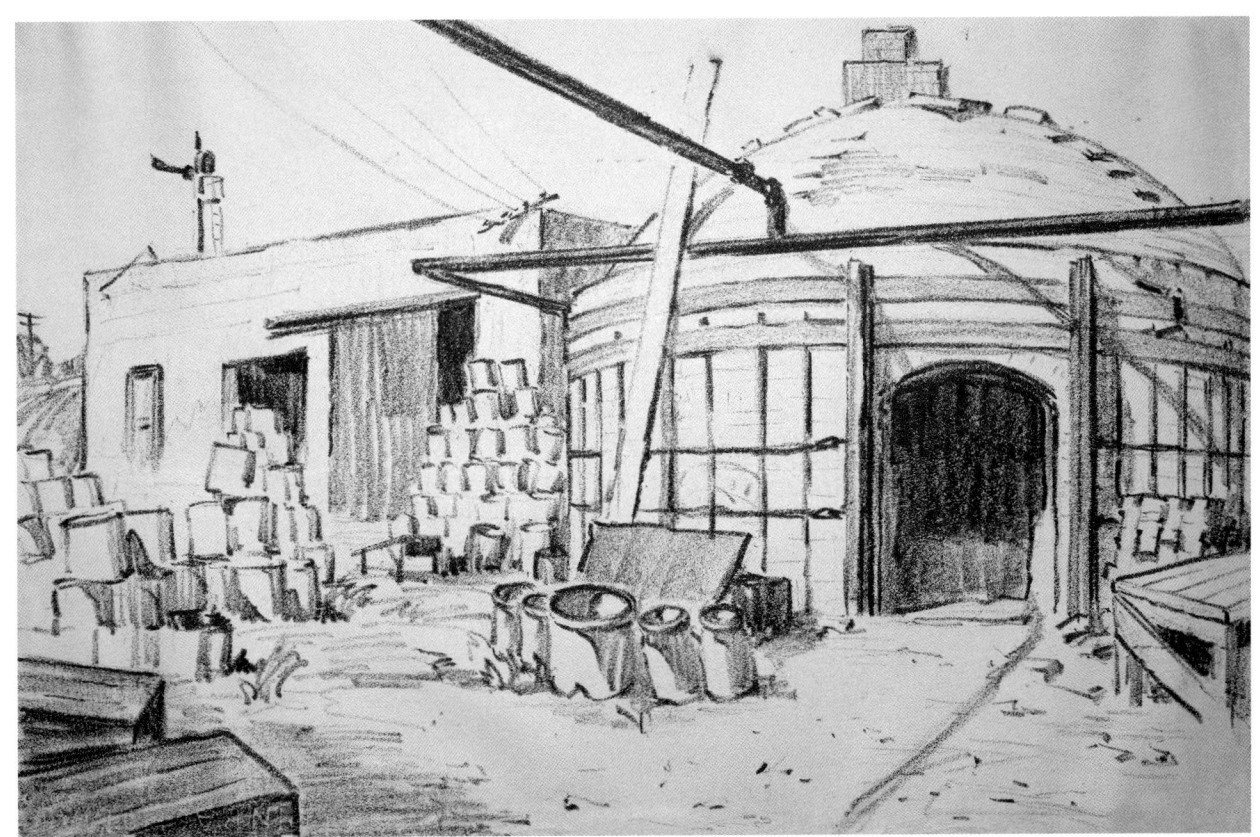

Athens Pottery Company – Clay Mixing Machine, ca. 1930. Lithograph.

Operations of the Athens Pottery Company at 701 North Hampton Street were labor intensive. One mechanized aspect of the pottery-making process was clay grinding and mixing. In this lithograph, Ziegler depicted the machine used to transform raw clay into usable pottery clay. The mixer, powered by a kerosene-fueled industrial engine, featured a large-diameter rotating steel pan into which several wheelbarrow loads of raw clay were poured. The gearing and shaft needed to drive the rotating pan were housed in an A-frame structure that straddled the spinning pan. As the pan spun, clay was pulverized by the motion and weight of two upright steel wheels which contacted the bottom of the pan. Added water brought the pulverized clay to consistency. Individual clay items were then formed either by machine or by hand turning.

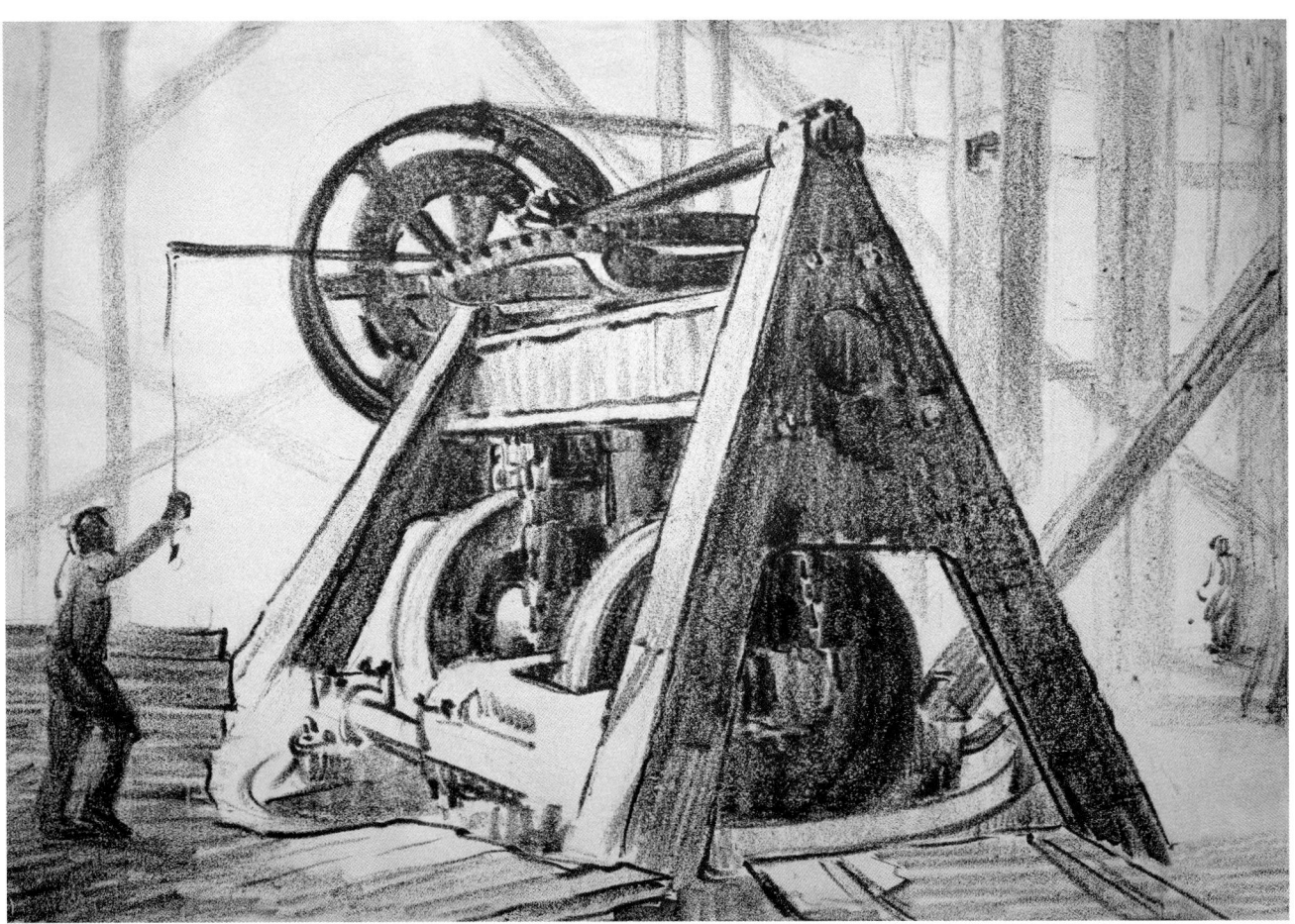

**Study for Building the
Masonic Temple – Ionic Peristyle,
ca. 1931. Graphite on paper.**

All of the hustle, bustle, and human effort
expended in the construction of the new
Masonic Temple was skillfully captured by
Ziegler in this pencil study. Work on the Ionic
peristyle (the upper section of the building)
was in full swing when Ziegler recorded
the scene.

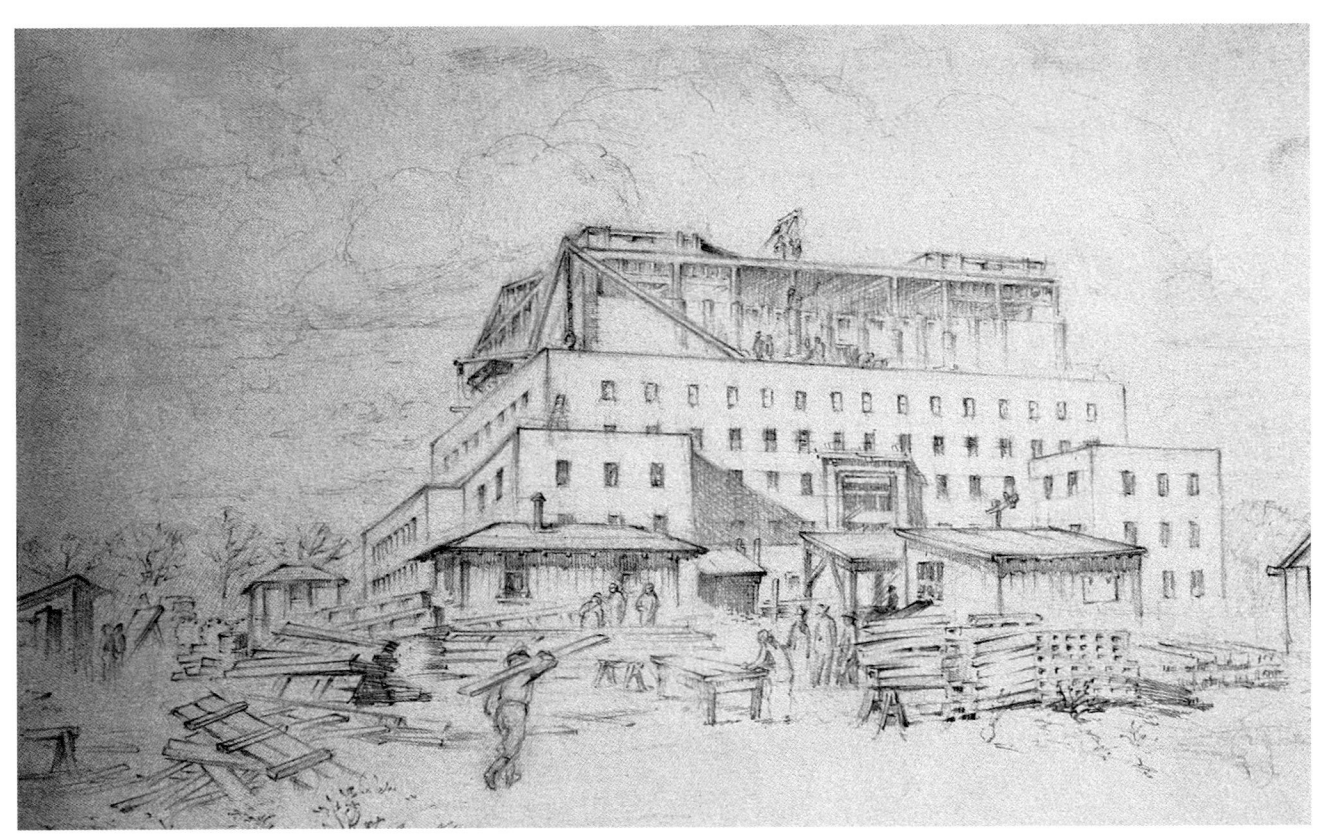

Study of Masonic Temple Under Construction – South End, ca. 1931. Graphite on paper.

This interesting pencil study by Ziegler recorded the maze of contractors' shacks and building materials that occupied a staging area on the south end of the Masonic Temple construction site at 1100 Henderson Street. Ground for the new temple was broken in November 1930, and construction was completed in 1931.

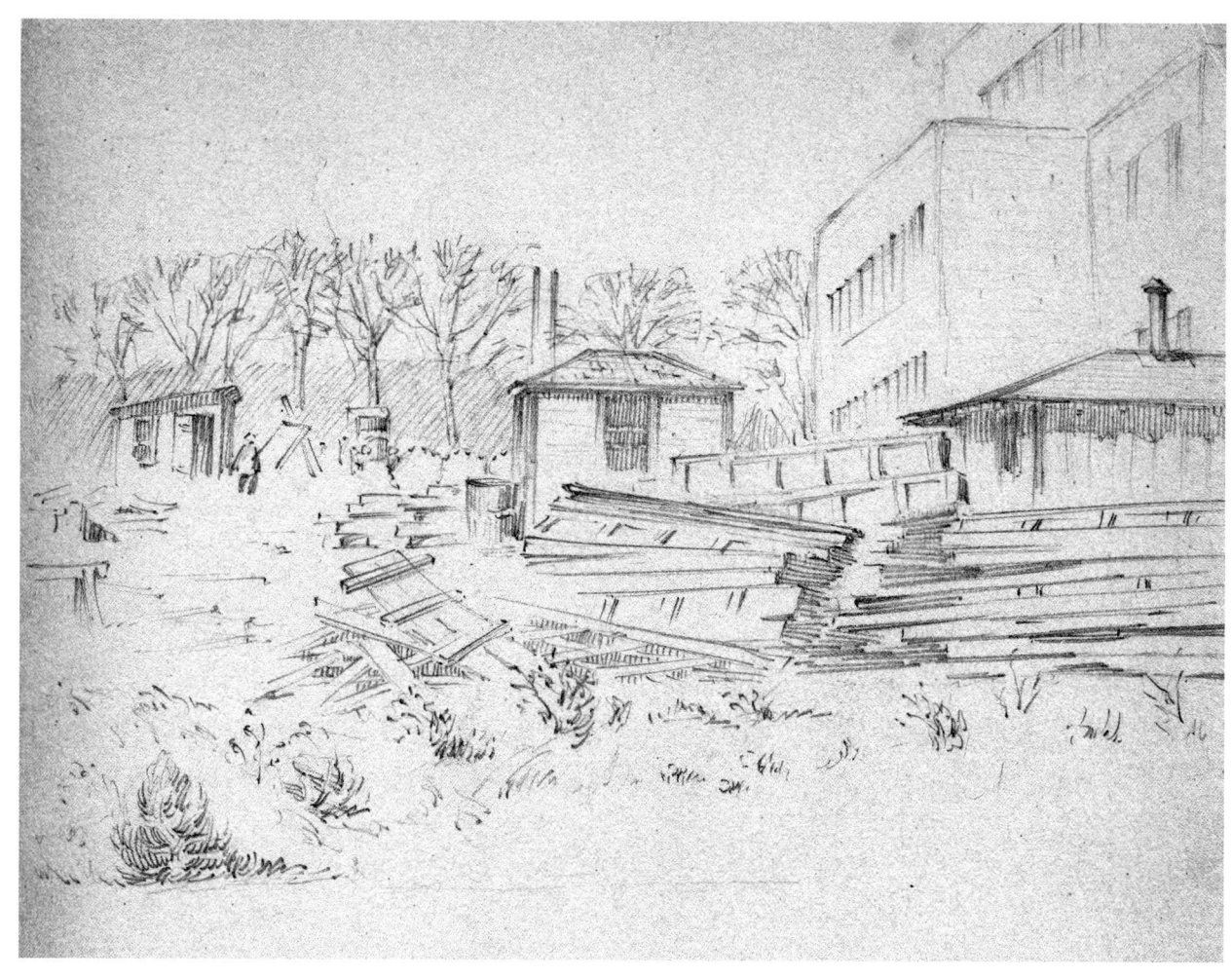

**Building the Masonic Temple,
ca. 1931. Lithograph.**

The steel skeleton of the Masonic Temple
was substantially complete when Ziegler produced this lithograph of the busy construction
site. The building's hillside location at 1100
Henderson Street elevated the temple well
above street level and offered temple visitors
an impressive view of downtown Fort Worth
from the west looking east.

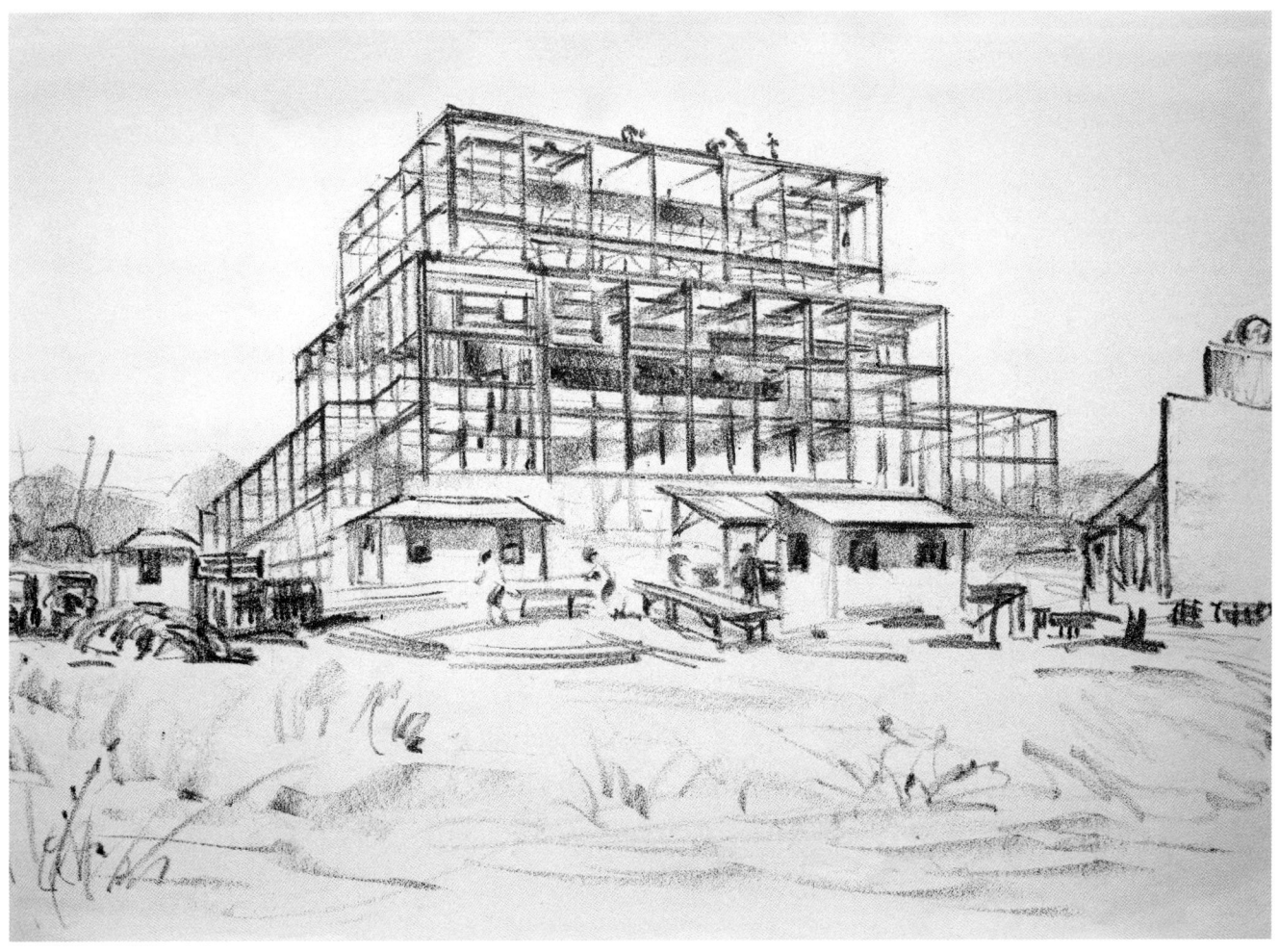

Building the Masonic Temple – Ionic Peristyle, ca. 1931. Lithograph.

Like most forms of printmaking, lithography allows for many copies of an original drawing to be made. For that reason, Ziegler probably intended this lithograph to become the permanent record of the Masonic Temple's appearance as it neared completion. One copy of this print is known to survive and is reproduced here, thus fulfilling the artist's intentions. Period photographs of the Masonic Temple under construction are preserved in the *Fort Worth Star-Telegram* Photograph Collection housed at the University of Texas at Arlington library, Special Collections division.

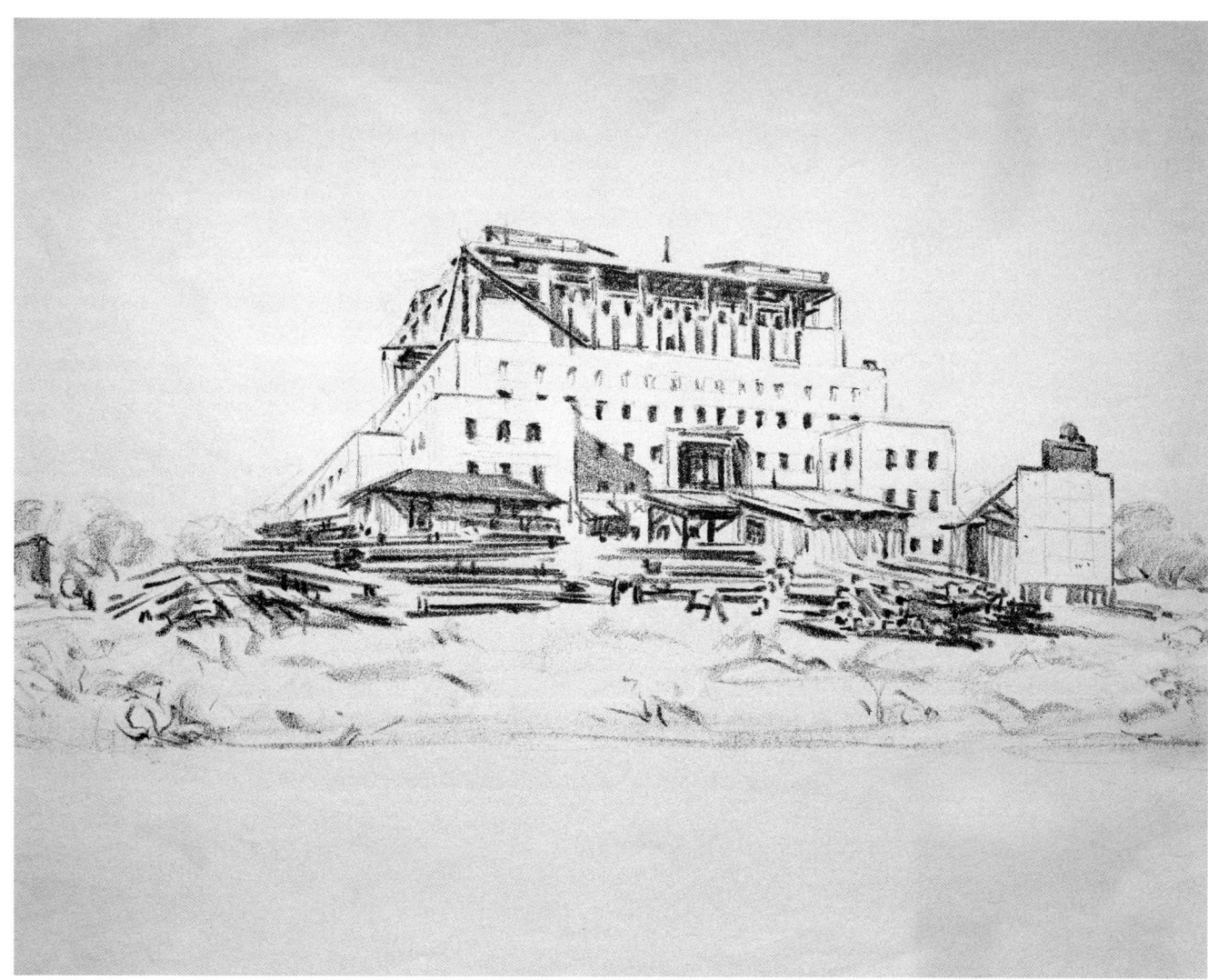

W. I. Cook Memorial Hospital, 1930. Lithograph.

The architectural splendor of the W. I. Cook Memorial Hospital presented a fitting subject for this rare Ziegler print. Construction costs for the new Fort Worth hospital, said to be the highest per square foot of any American hospital of that era, were borne by Missouri Matilda Nail Cook of Shackelford County. Mrs. Cook conceived of the hospital as a memorial to her late husband and daughter Jessie, who died bearing Mrs. Cook's only grandchild. The hospital was paid for by royalties from oil production on Mrs. Cook's Shackelford County ranch. Doctor Heb Beall, a Fort Worth physician for whom Mrs. Cook had a special admiration, was handpicked by Mrs. Cook to run the new hospital and carry out its mission of caring for women regardless of their ability to pay. A progenitor of the Cook Children's Medical Center, the W. I. Cook Memorial Hospital building opened in 1929 at 1212 W. Lancaster Avenue.

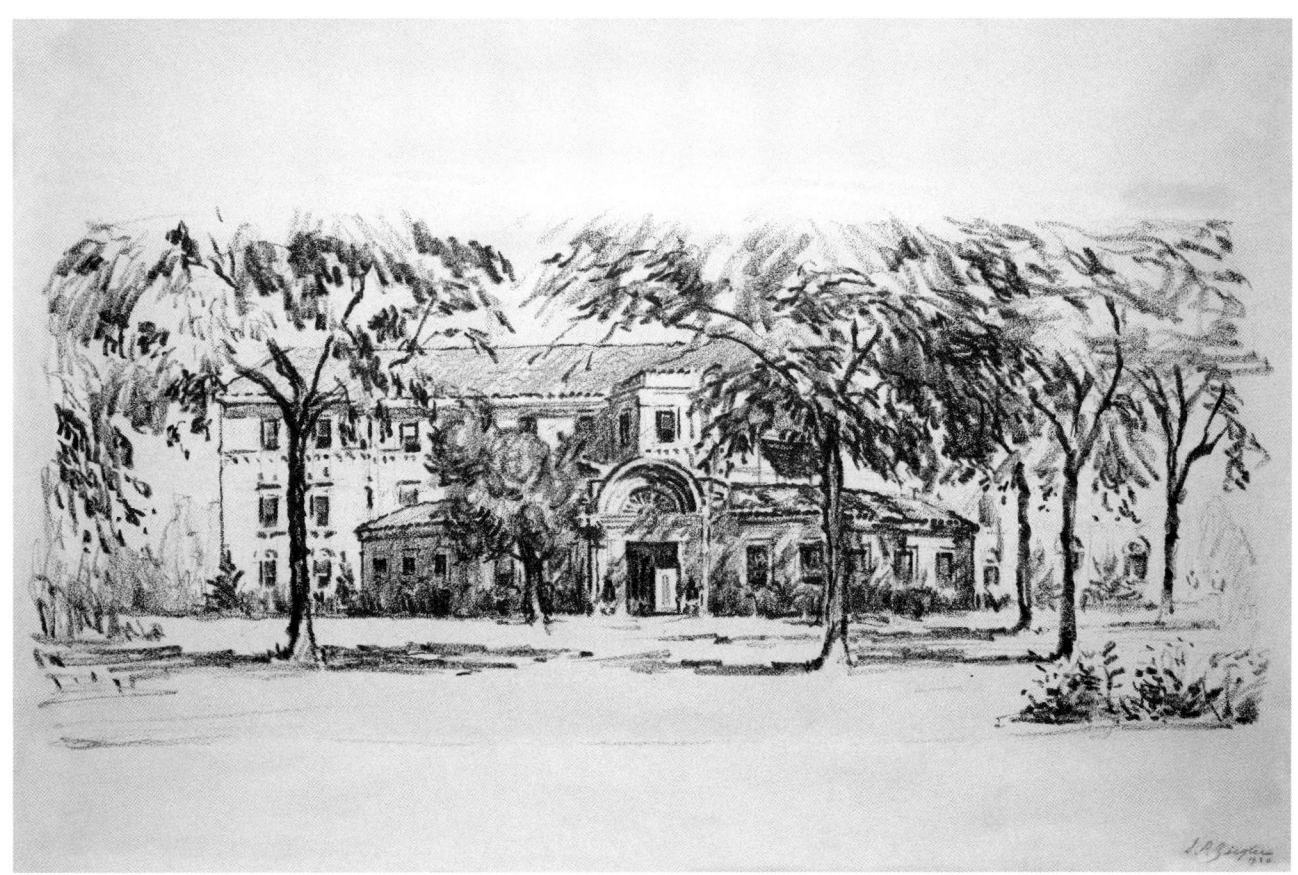

Paddock Viaduct from Below, ca. 1930. Lithograph.

The Paddock Viaduct (commonly called the North Main Bridge) was less than twenty years old when Ziegler produced this lithographic drawing of it. It was named for Col. Buckley B. Paddock, a former mayor, who was one of Fort Worth's most ardent civic boosters in the late nineteenth and early twentieth centuries. The bridge was built in 1913–14 to replace an earlier iron bridge that spanned the Trinity River in the same location. The Paddock Viaduct provided, and still provides, a primary transportation link between Fort Worth's north side and the downtown area. By depicting the bridge from the riverbank looking upward, Ziegler focused on the bridge's grand scale and hinted at the cutting-edge engineering feats contained in the span's design.

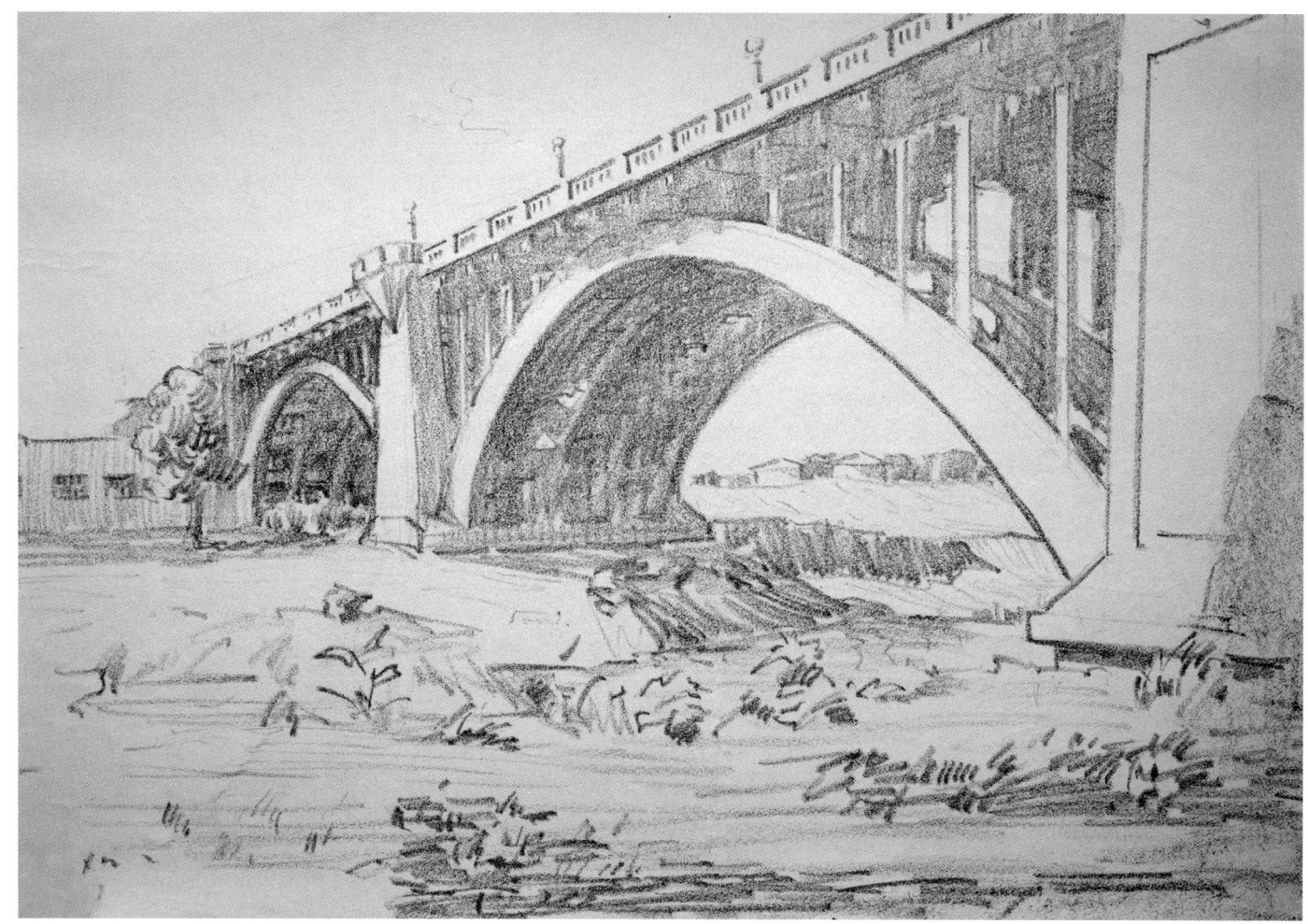

Northside Coliseum,
ca. 1930. Lithograph.

The Northside Coliseum on East Exchange Avenue in the Fort Worth Stockyards opened in 1908. For almost thirty years, the coliseum served as home to the annual feeders' and breeders' livestock show for which Fort Worth became famous. When Ziegler produced this lithograph, the coliseum was also noted for hosting the annual Queen of the Horse Show Pageant, one of Fort Worth's most opulent social events. The yearly pageant provided a high-profile "coming out" opportunity for the daughters and sons of Fort Worth's socially prominent families, particularly those families involved in ranching and cattle raising.

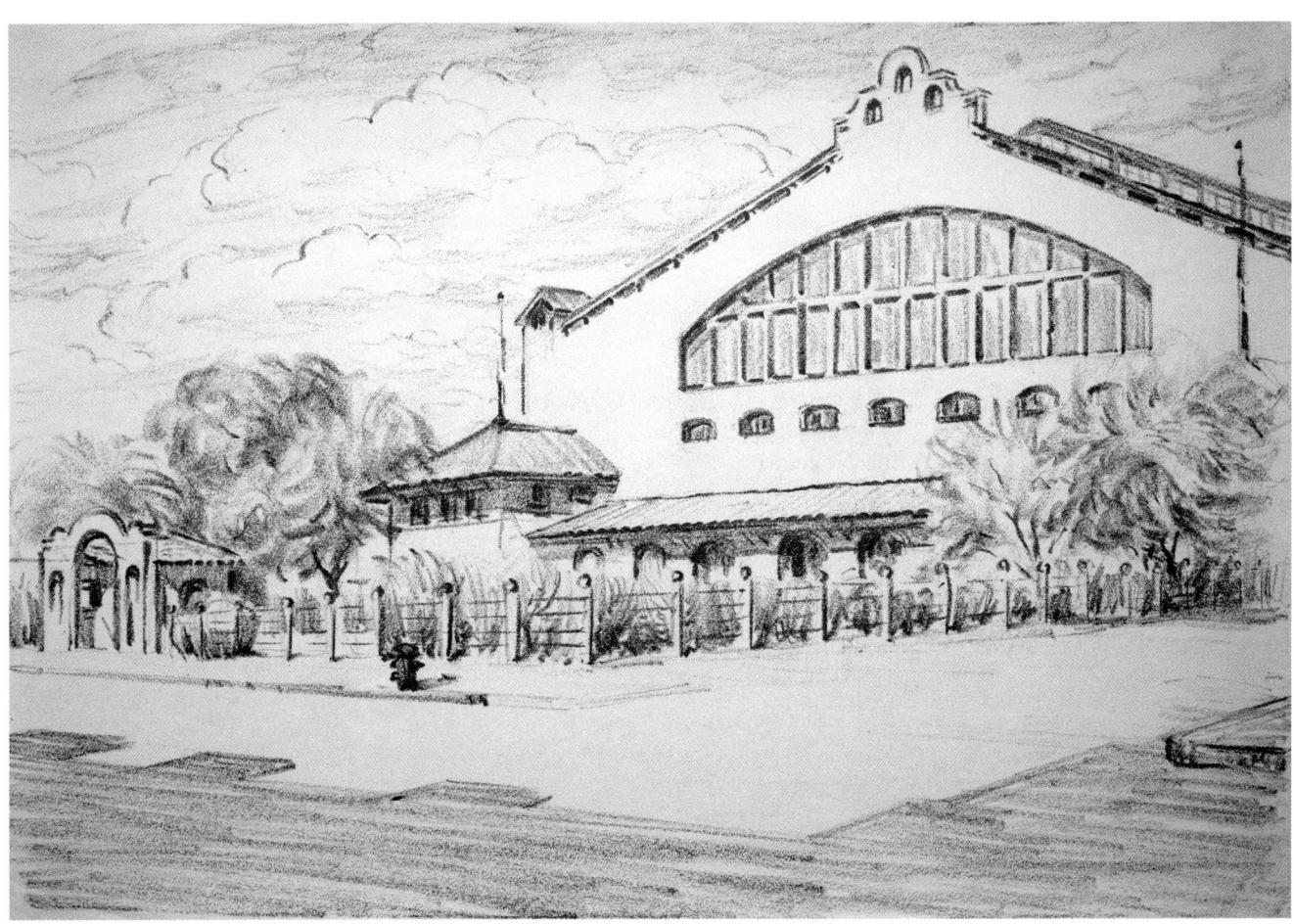

Southern Cabin,
ca. 1930. Lithograph.

The location of this rural homestead
is unknown. The lithograph's title and
inclusion in Ziegler's series of Fort
Worth images suggests that the
farmhouse was located near or
just outside the city limits.

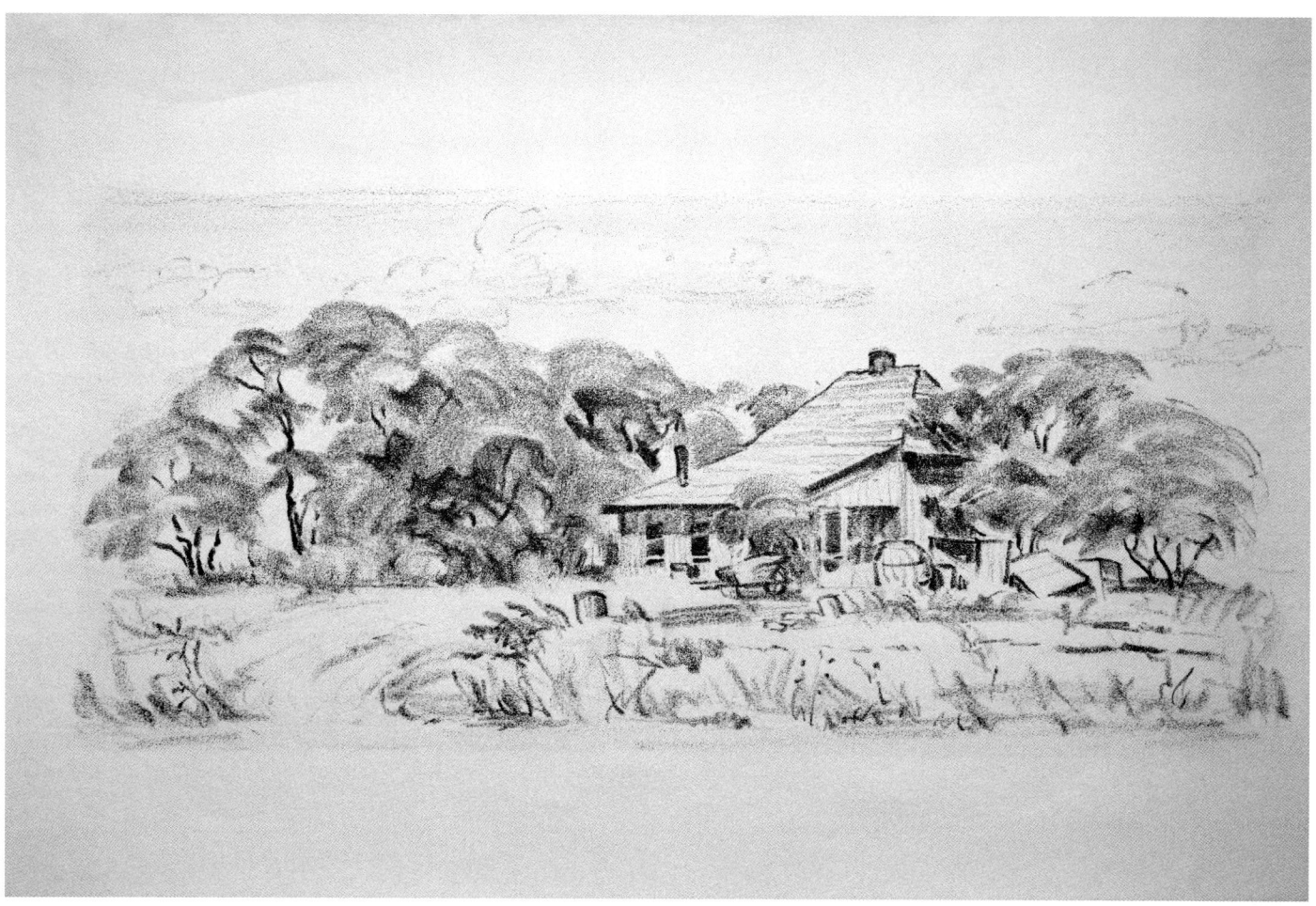

Constructing the West Berry Street Underpass, 1927. Lithograph.

In 1927 the City of Fort Worth moved forward with plans to transform West Berry Street into a major crosstown thoroughfare. The plan included construction of a new railway underpass just west of the intersection of West Berry and Henderson Streets in order to create grade separation between West Berry and the tracks of the Gulf, Colorado and Santa Fe Railway. The project unfolded not far from Ziegler's TCU-area home, which gave him the opportunity to observe and document road construction practices of the time. The underpass, now expanded, is still in use.

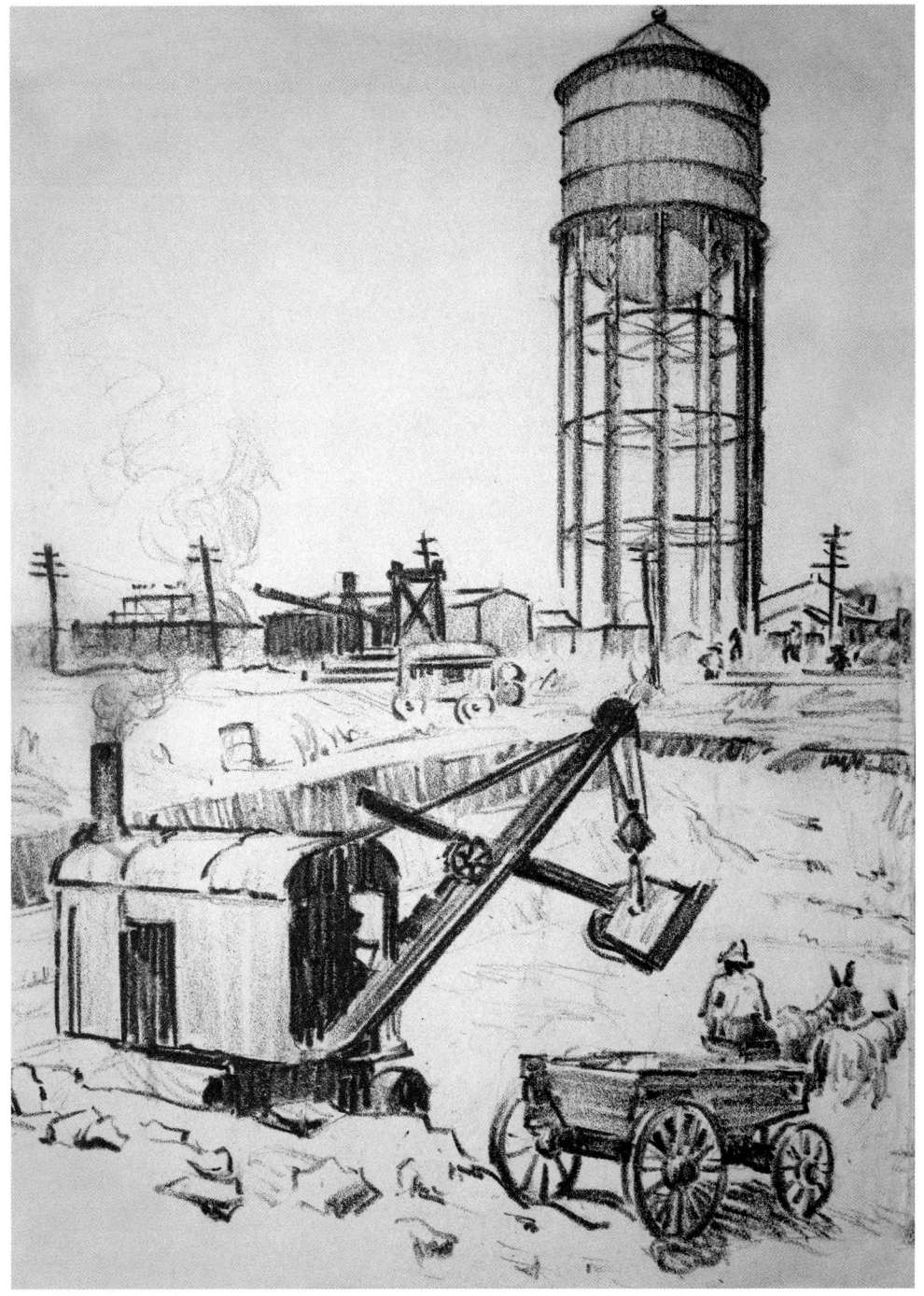

Color Plates

Untitled (open country south of TCU campus), 1918.

Oil on canvas, 36 x 38 in.

Collection of Dow Art Galleries, LLC

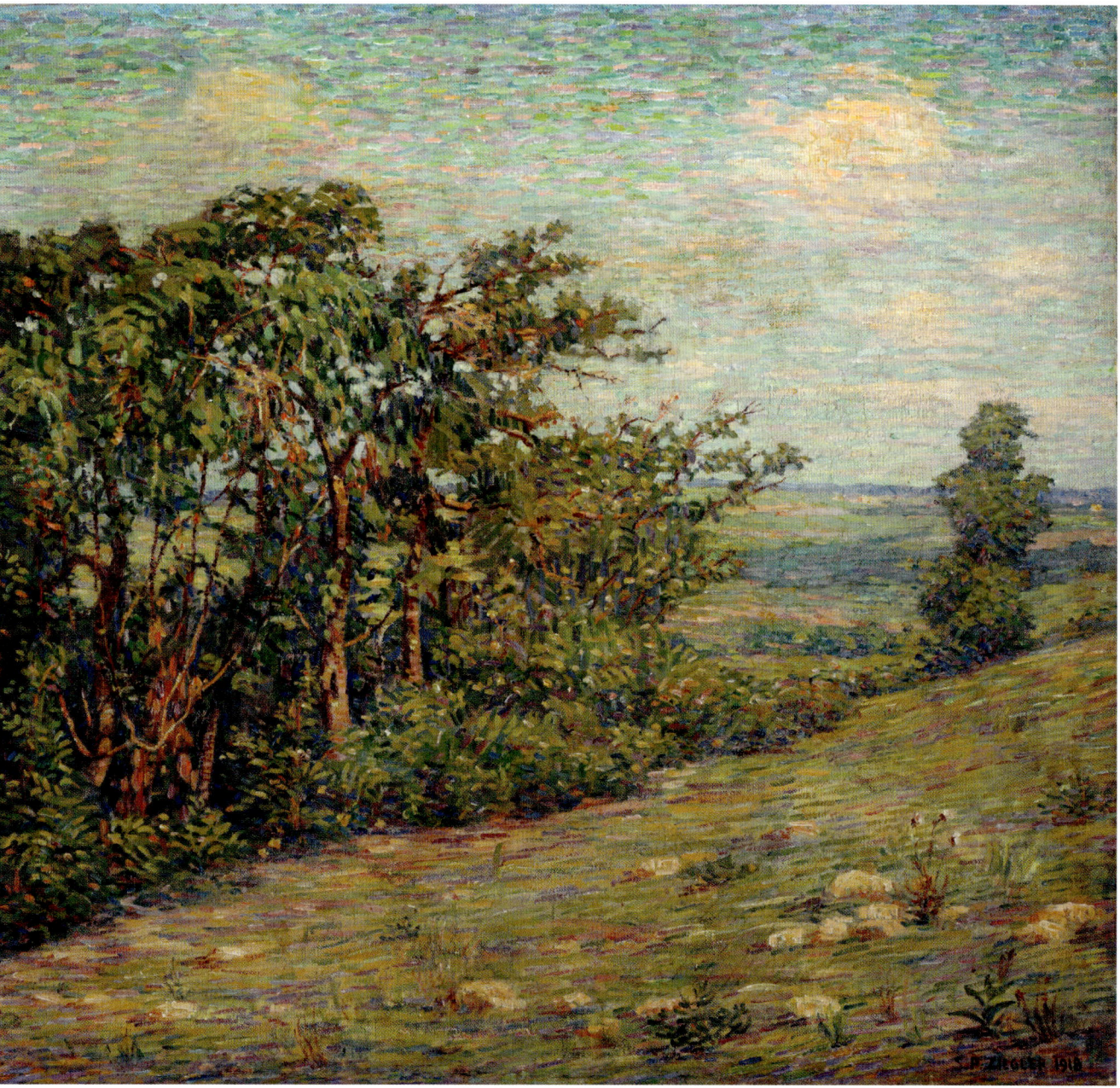

Texas, 1922.

Oil on canvas, 18 x 20 in.

Collection of Dow Art Galleries, LLC

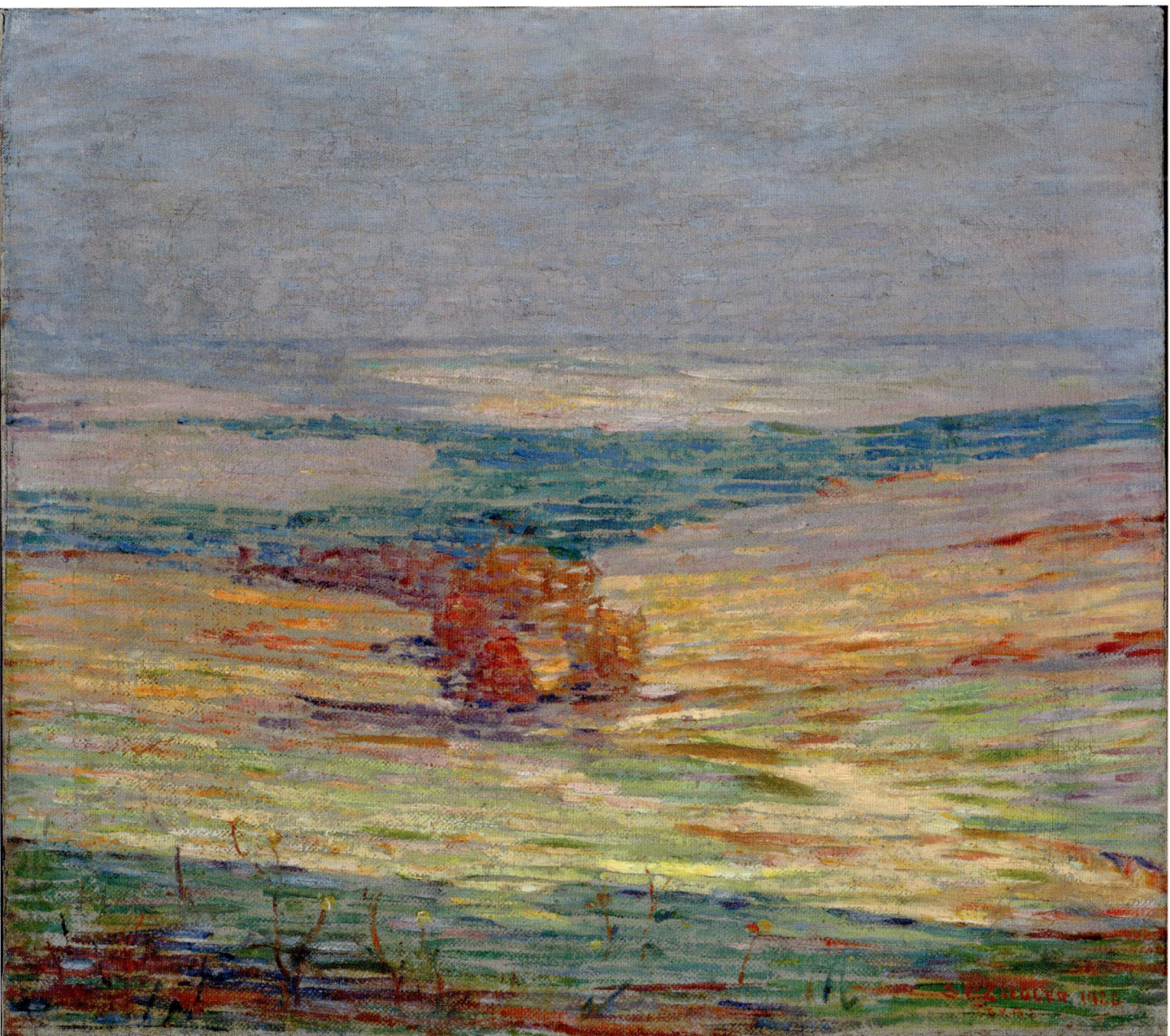

Untitled (field of Texas wildflowers), 1925.

Oil on canvas, 16 x 20 in.

Collection of Dow Art Galleries, LLC

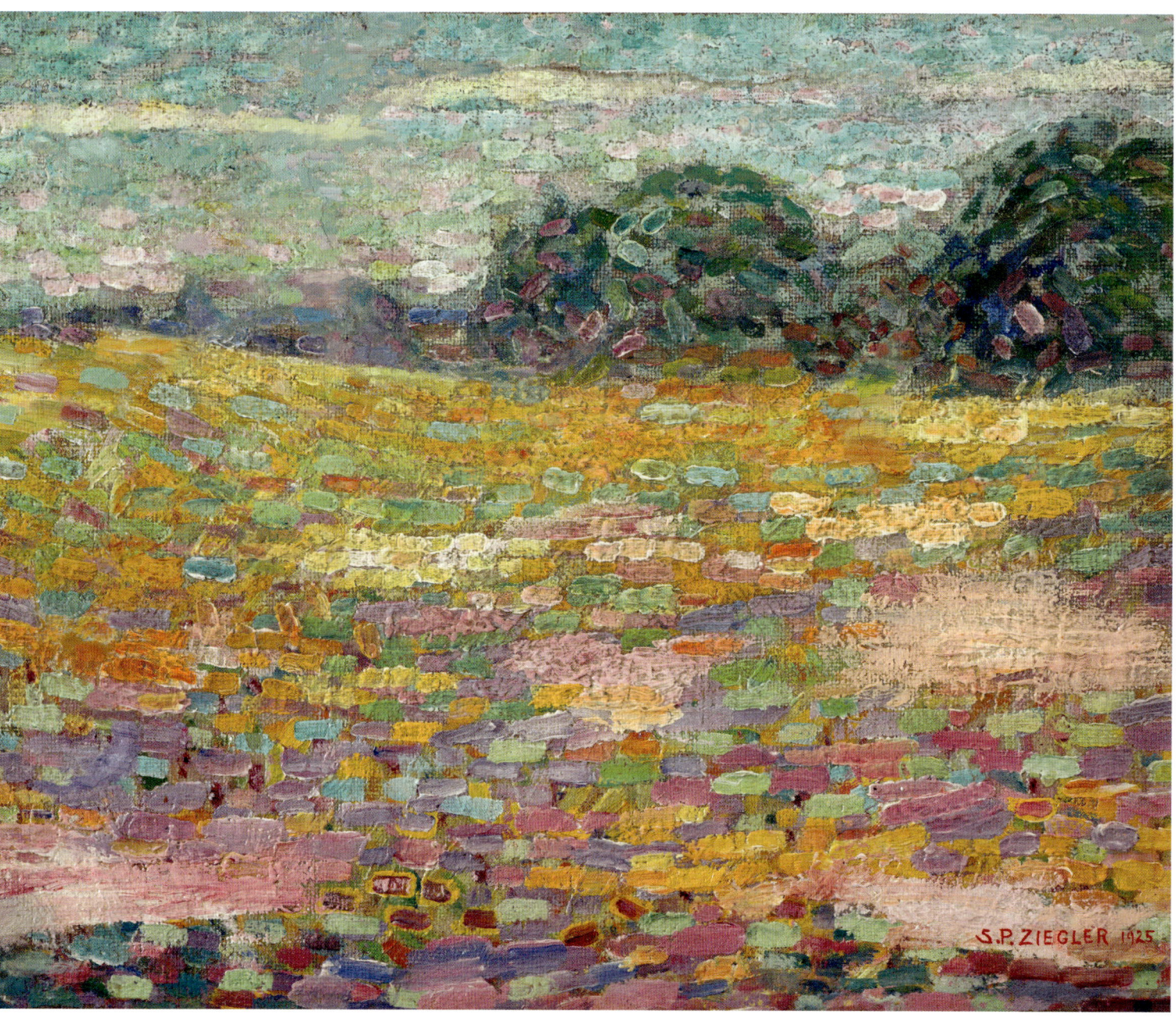

Untitled (scene near Santa Fe, New Mexico), 1925.
Oil on canvas, 20 x 24 in.

Ziegler made his first visit to Santa Fe and Taos, New Mexico, in 1925. This experience inspired a series of prints and paintings of the New Mexico landscape.

Collection of Dow Art Galleries, LLC

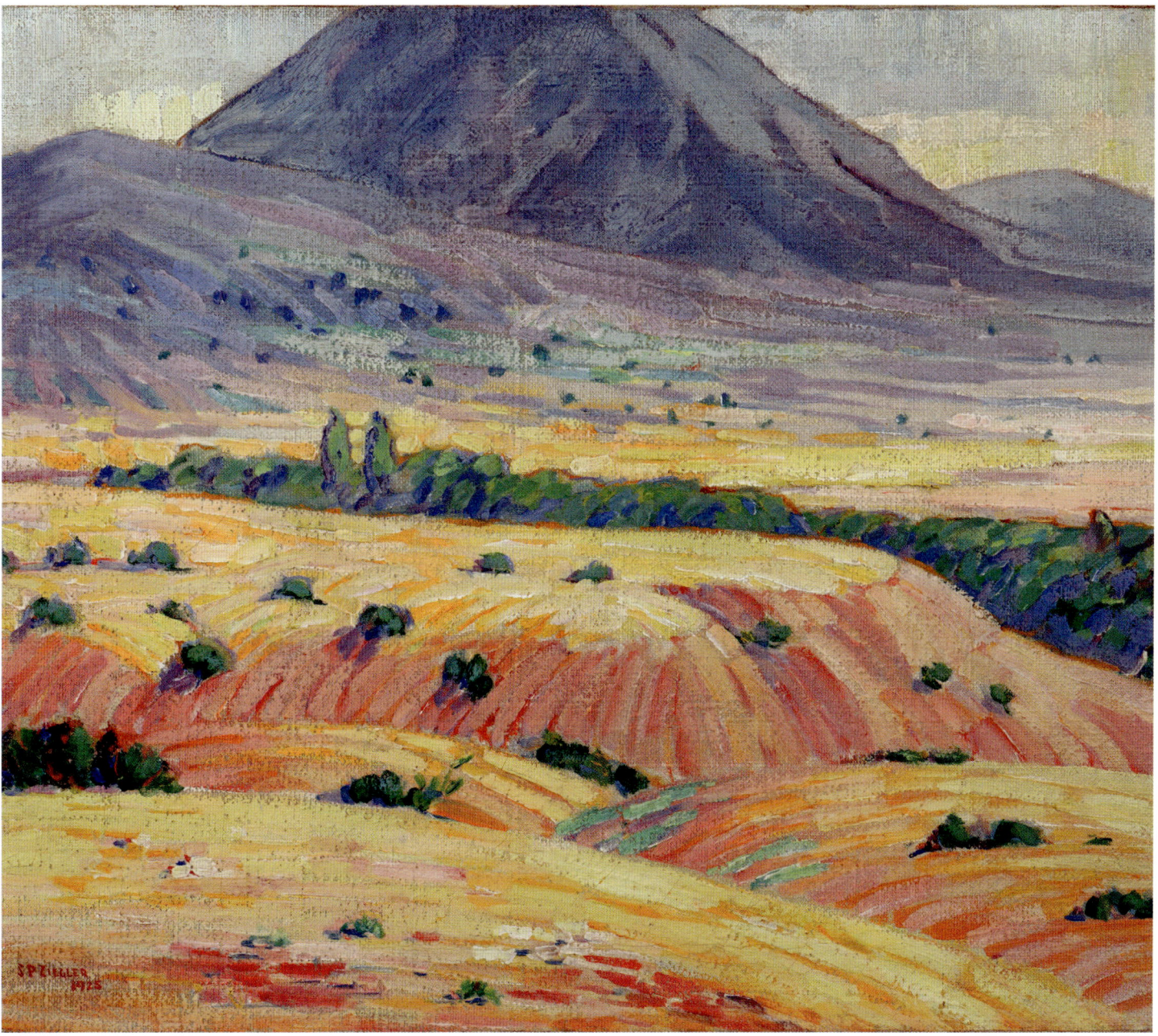

Trinity River Flats, ca. 1935.

Oil on canvas, 14 x 18 in.

Collection of Nancy Ziegler, Frisco, Texas

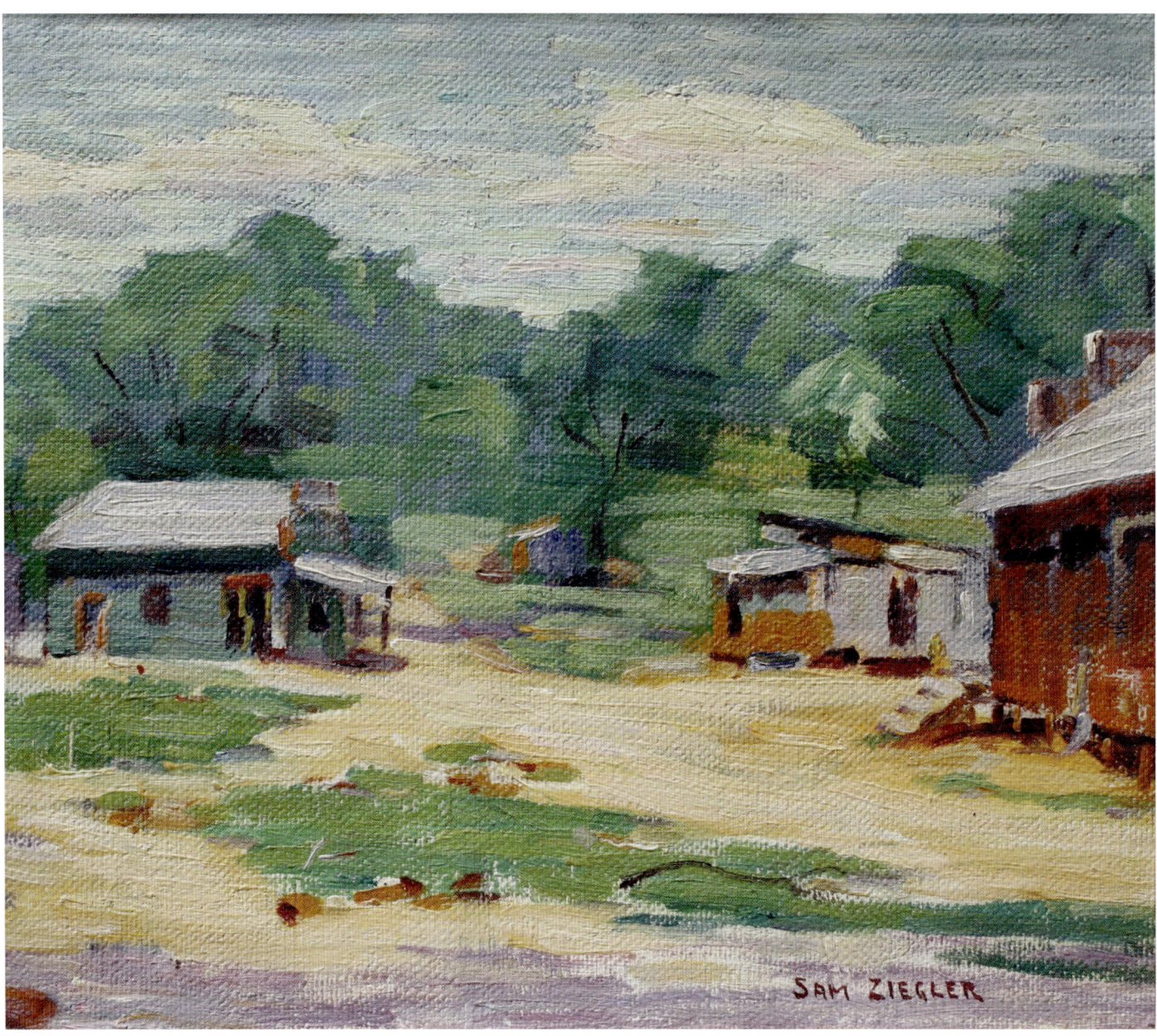

Untitled (creek near Forest Park Zoo), 1929.

Oil on canvas, 18 x 20 in.

Collection of Dow Art Galleries, LLC

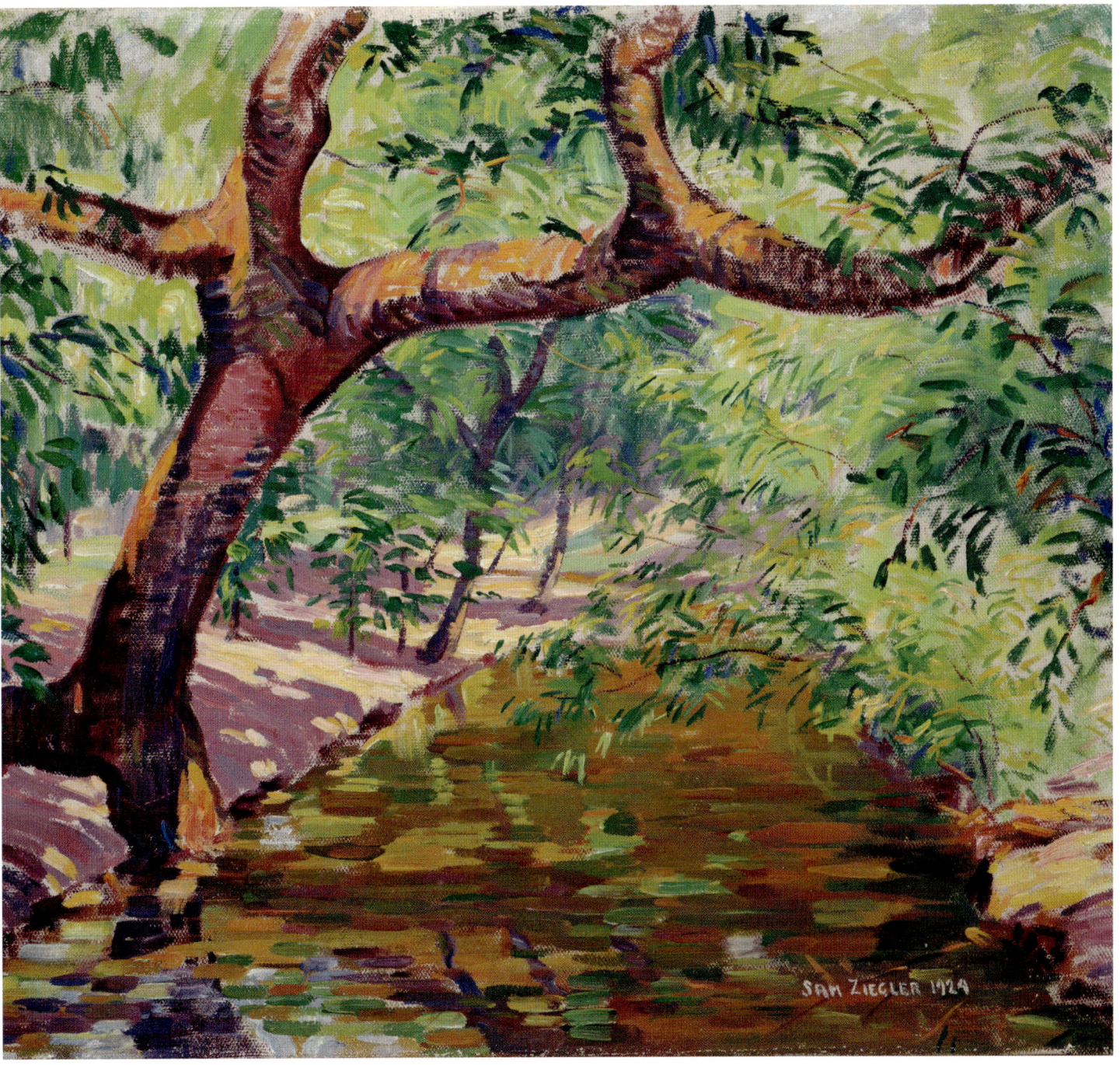

Along the Trinity, 1930.

Oil on canvas, 36 x 38 in.

Collection of Nancy Ziegler,
Frisco, Texas

Bend in the Trinity River, 1934.

Oil on canvas, 18 x 20 in.

Collection of Dow Art Galleries, LLC

Burning the Slush Pit, 1934.

Oil on canvas, 14 x 16 in.

Courtesy of the Samye Ziegler
Hunt Estate and Suzi Hunt Gamez

**W. T. Waggoner Building
Under Construction, 1919.**
Oil on board, 12 x 10 in.

Geralyn and Mark Kever Collection

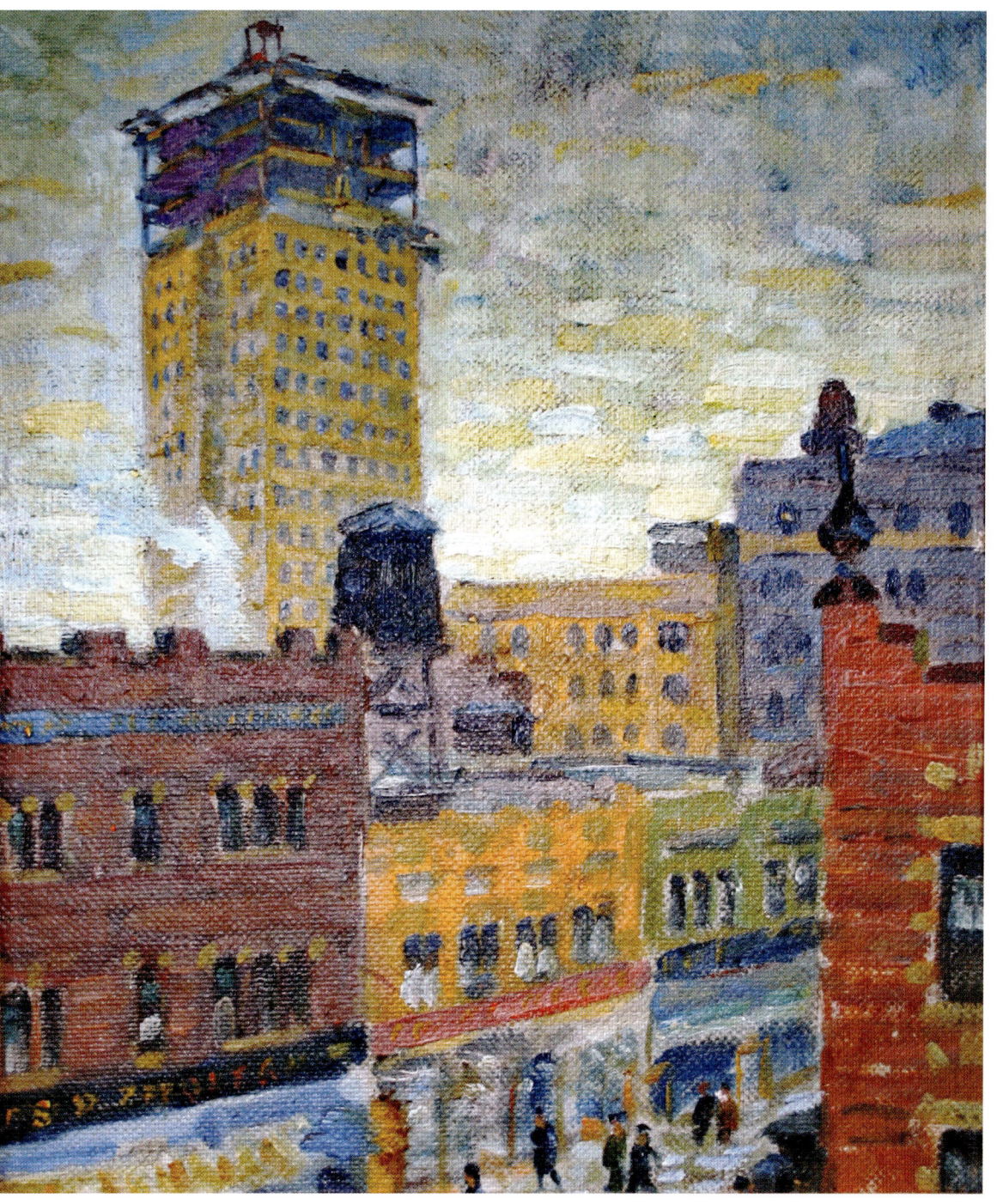

Carnegie Public Library
at Night, 1922.

Oil on canvas, 36 x 38 in.

For over fifty years, the Carnegie Public Library (1901-1938) and the new library building that replaced it served as the city's main art exhibition space. Dozens of major art shows were hosted at the library prior to the opening of Fort Worth's first public art museum in 1954. Professor Ziegler often lectured at the Carnegie Public Library about the current art exhibit.

Collection of Dow Art Galleries, LLC

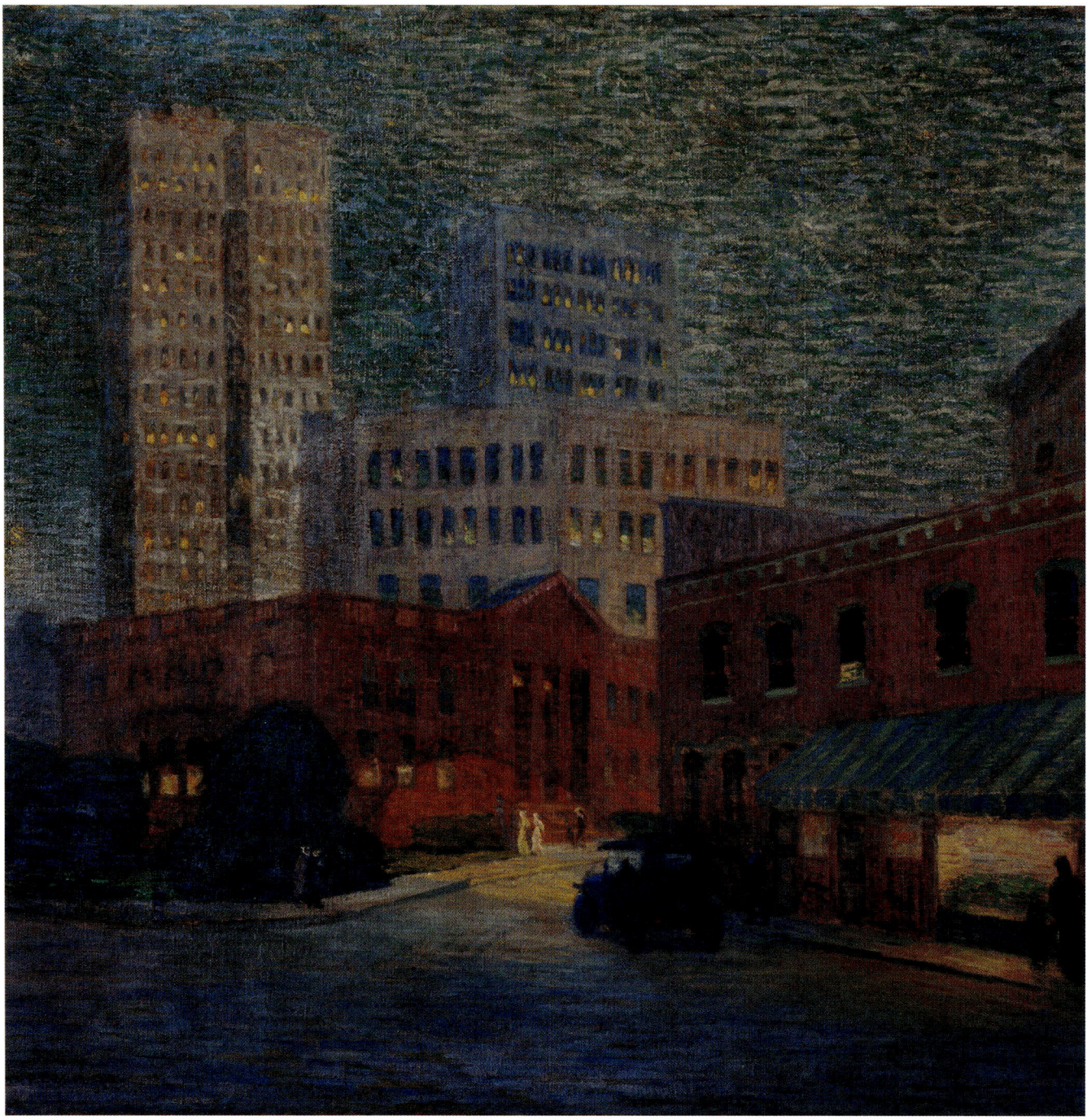

Looking North on Main Street, 1936.
Oil on canvas, 16 x 12 in.

This iconic view of Main Street and the Tarrant County Courthouse was painted by Ziegler during Texas's centennial year, 1936.

The John L. Nau III Collection of Texas Art

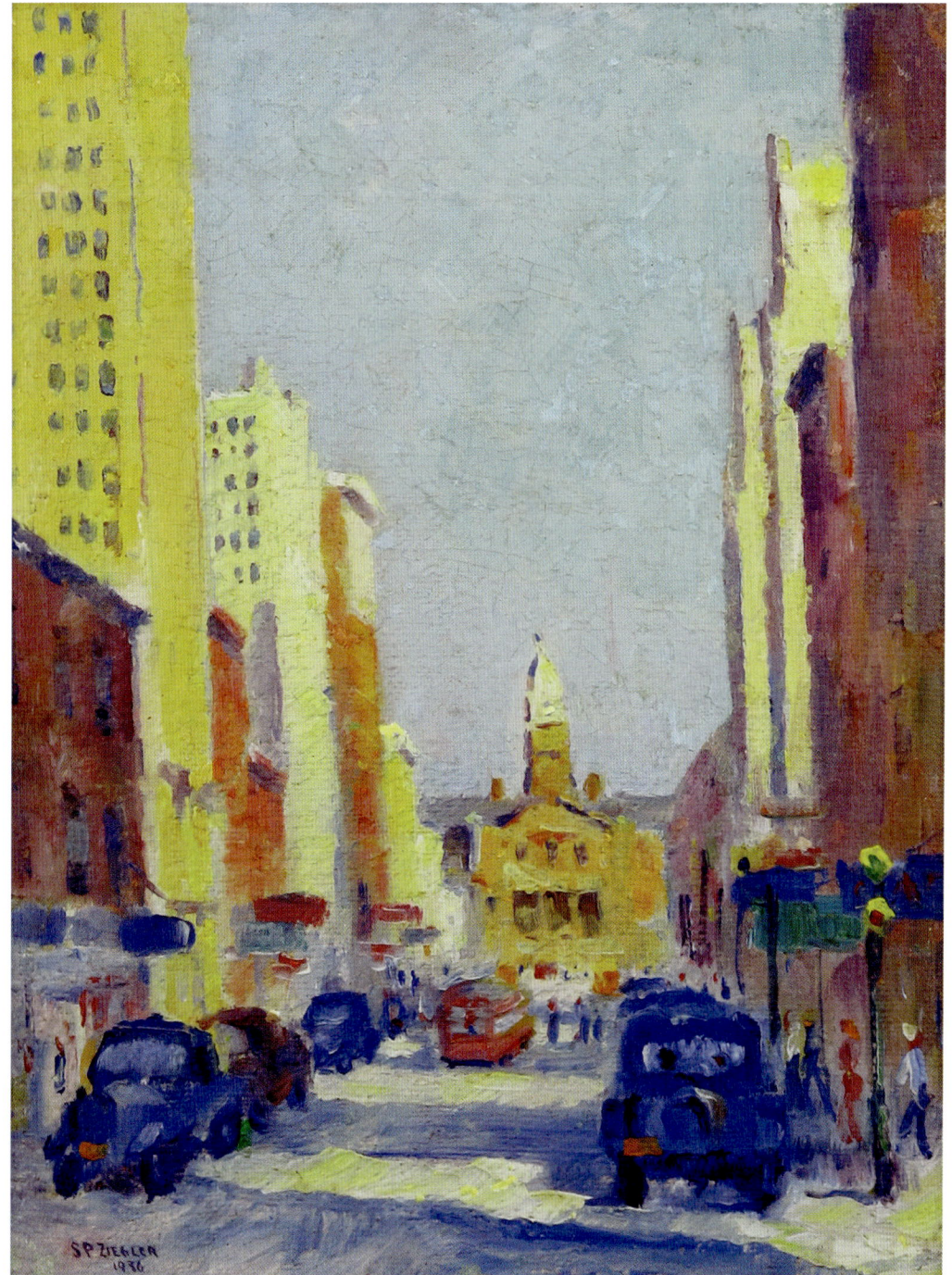

Looking North on Throckmorton Street, ca. 1935.

Oil on canvas, 14 X 16 in.

Fort Worth's nineteenth-century fire hall at 908 Throckmorton is seen on the left, distinguished by its red-turreted towers. The red sandstone wall of the Carnegie Public Library, located at the corner of W. Ninth Street and Throckmorton, is visible in the right foreground.

Collection of Nancy Ziegler, Frisco, Texas

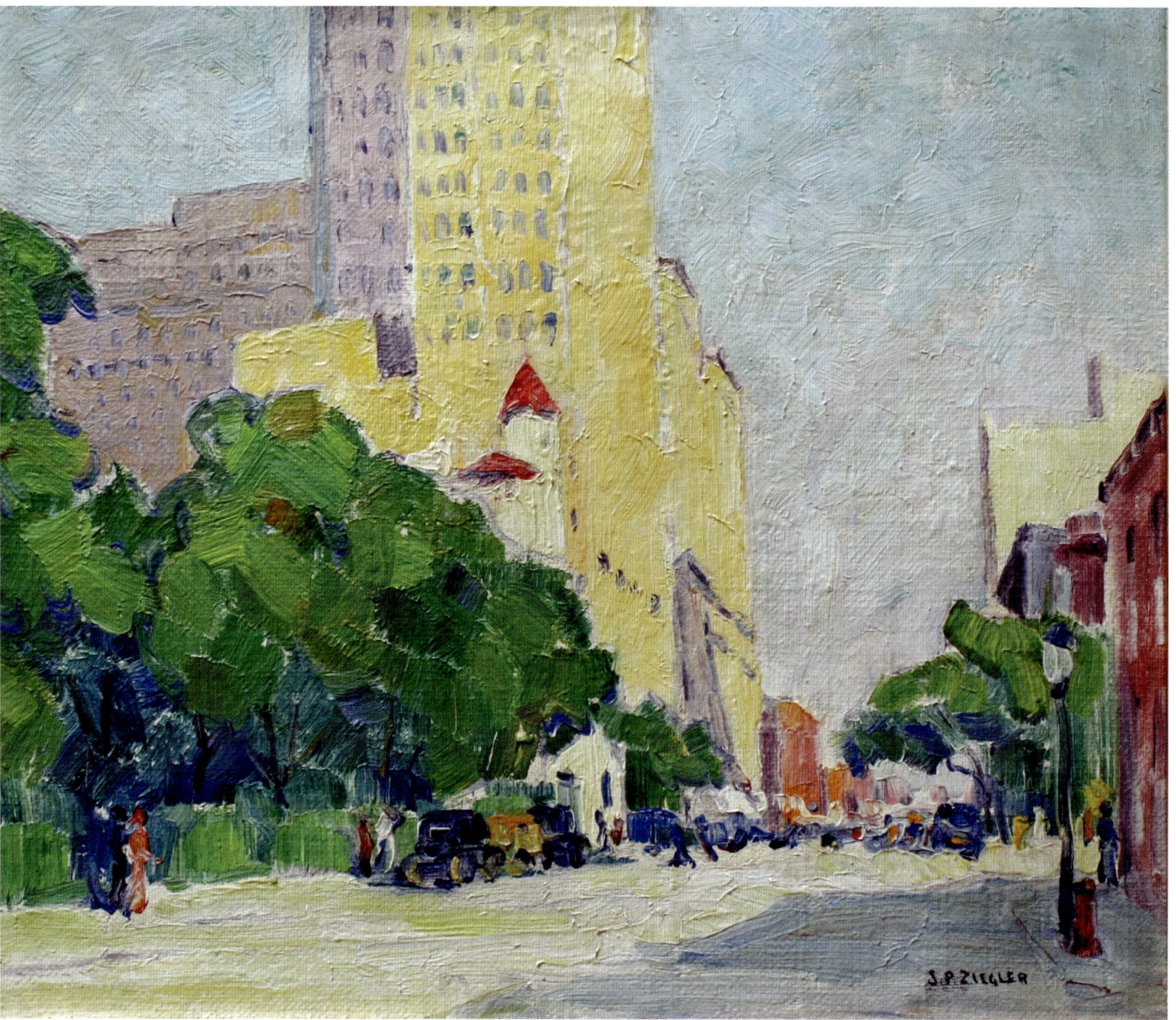

Towers of the Old Fire Hall and City Hall, ca. 1935.
Oil on canvas, 14 x 16 in.

In the nineteenth and early twentieth centuries, the central fire hall's observation towers were used by dispatchers to pinpoint the location of fires within the city. Fort Worth City Hall, with its four-sided clock tower, sat at the corner of Throckmorton and W. Tenth Street, a block south of the fire station.

Linda Jo and Scott Barker Collection

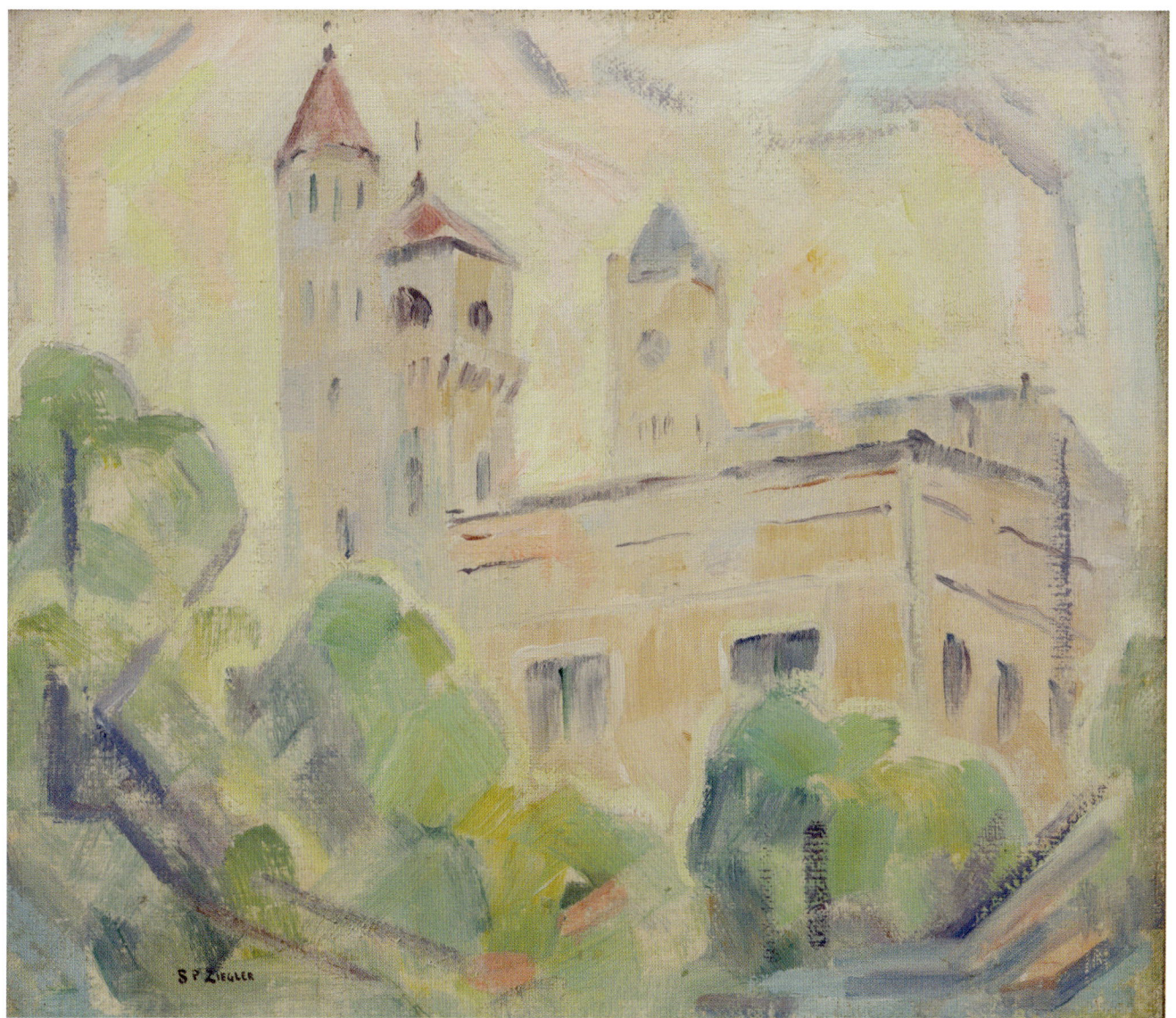

New Amon G. Carter Stadium at TCU, 1930.

Oil on board, 12 x 16 in.

Collection of Dow Art Galleries, LLC

Campus Panorama, ca. 1930.
Oil on canvas, 24 x 36 in.

Ziegler's unorthodox palette was applied throughout this painting in contrasting, broken strokes that moved in concert like flowing water. See caption for *Campus Panorama* (p. 17) for a description of this view from the steps of the Mary Couts Burnett Library.

Collection of Ann Ekstrom

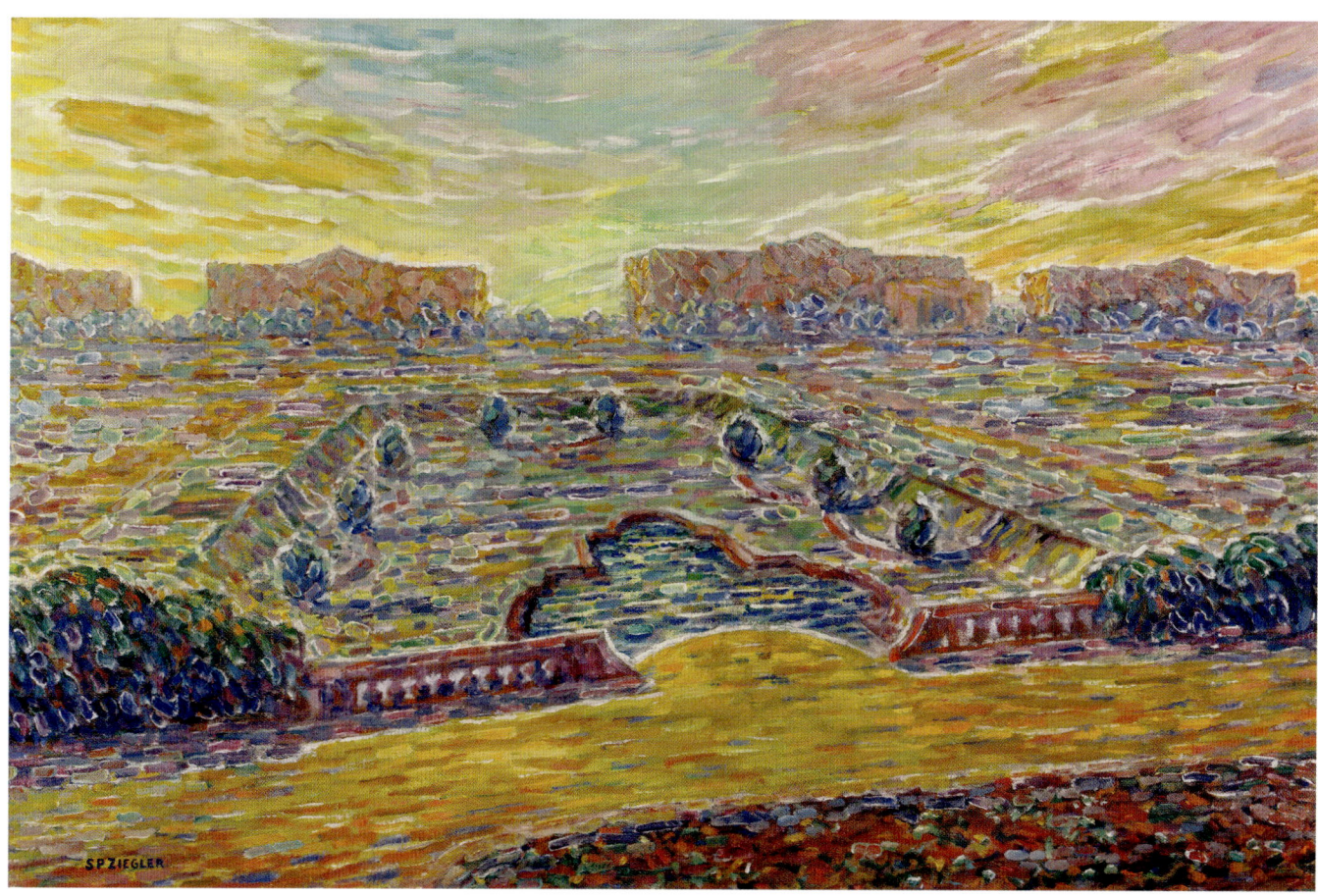

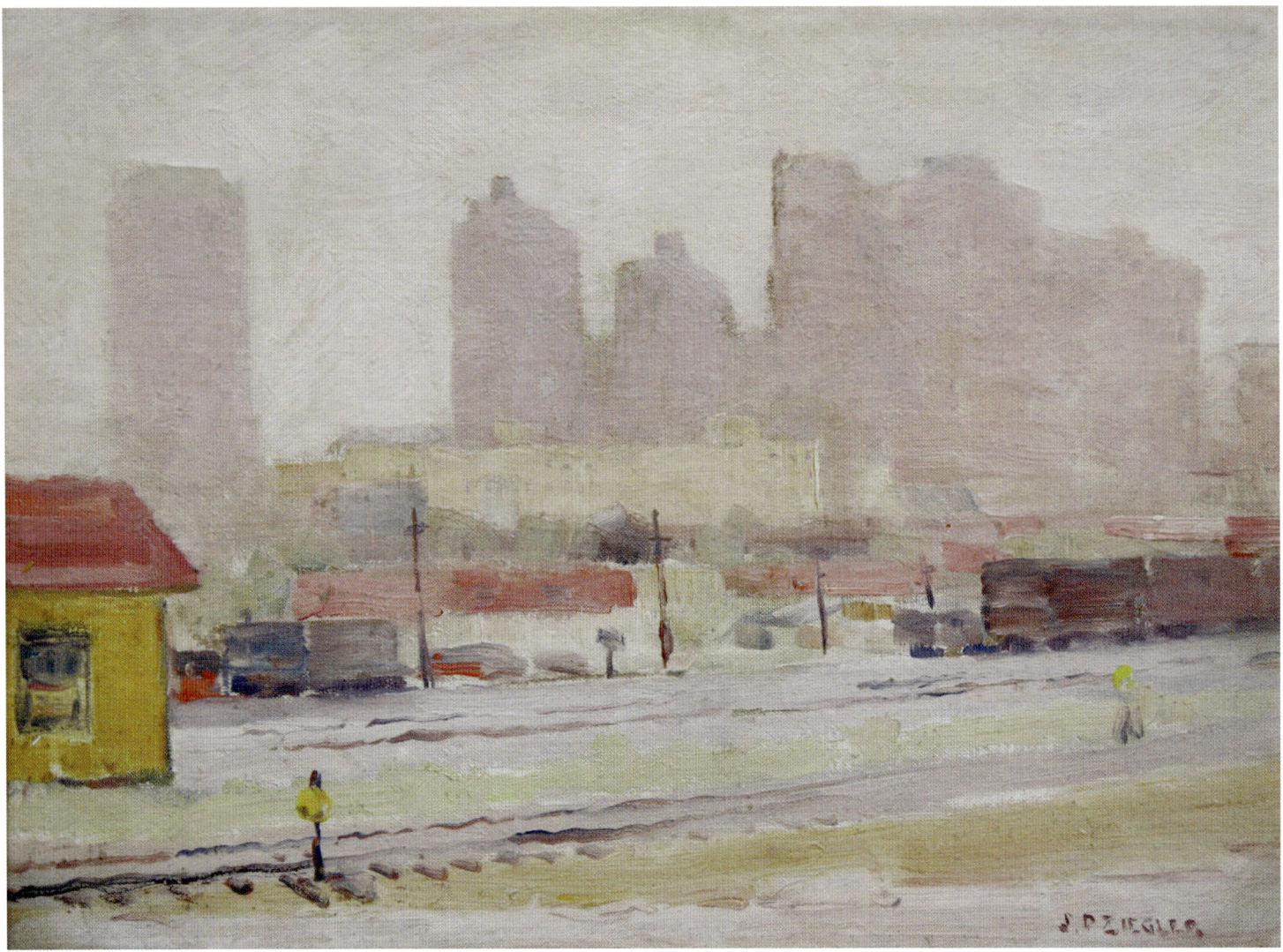

Study for Downtown on a Gray Day, ca. 1935
Oil on canvas, 12 x 16 in.

The Medical Arts Building—
first high-rise on the left—anchors
this view of downtown Fort Worth
from the T&P railroad reservation.

Judy and Stephen Alton Collection

**Discovery Field –
Lake Eastland, 1927.**

Oil on canvas, 30 x 40 in.

Discovery Field – Lake Eastland was completed soon after Samuel Ziegler returned to Fort Worth from his first summer sketching tour through the oil fields of Eastland County. He undertook the trip at the invitation of George W. Briggs, secretary of the Eastland Chamber of Commerce. This initial foray into West Texas was the genesis of several other expeditions by Ziegler into Texas oil country in the coming years. Lake Eastland, the site of this painting, was a small lake located northwest of the City of Eastland. In one of his letters to Ziegler, George Briggs wrote, "Lake Eastland is partly surrounded by wooded hills, with oil derricks scattered here and there. One derrick is on a little island near the shore. I have often thought it would be a fine setting for a picture." Mr. Ziegler obviously agreed.

*Collection of Nancy Ziegler,
Frisco, Texas*

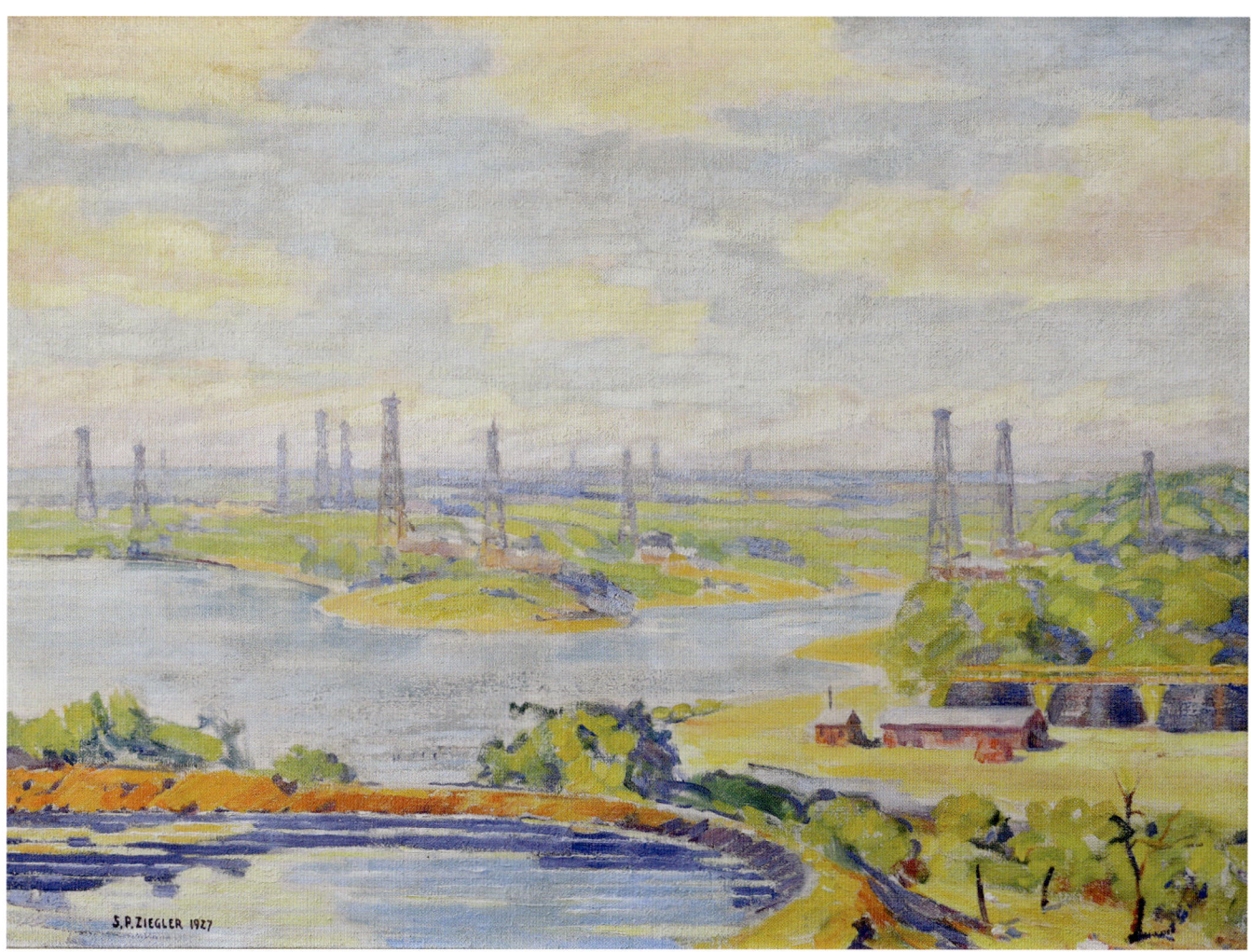

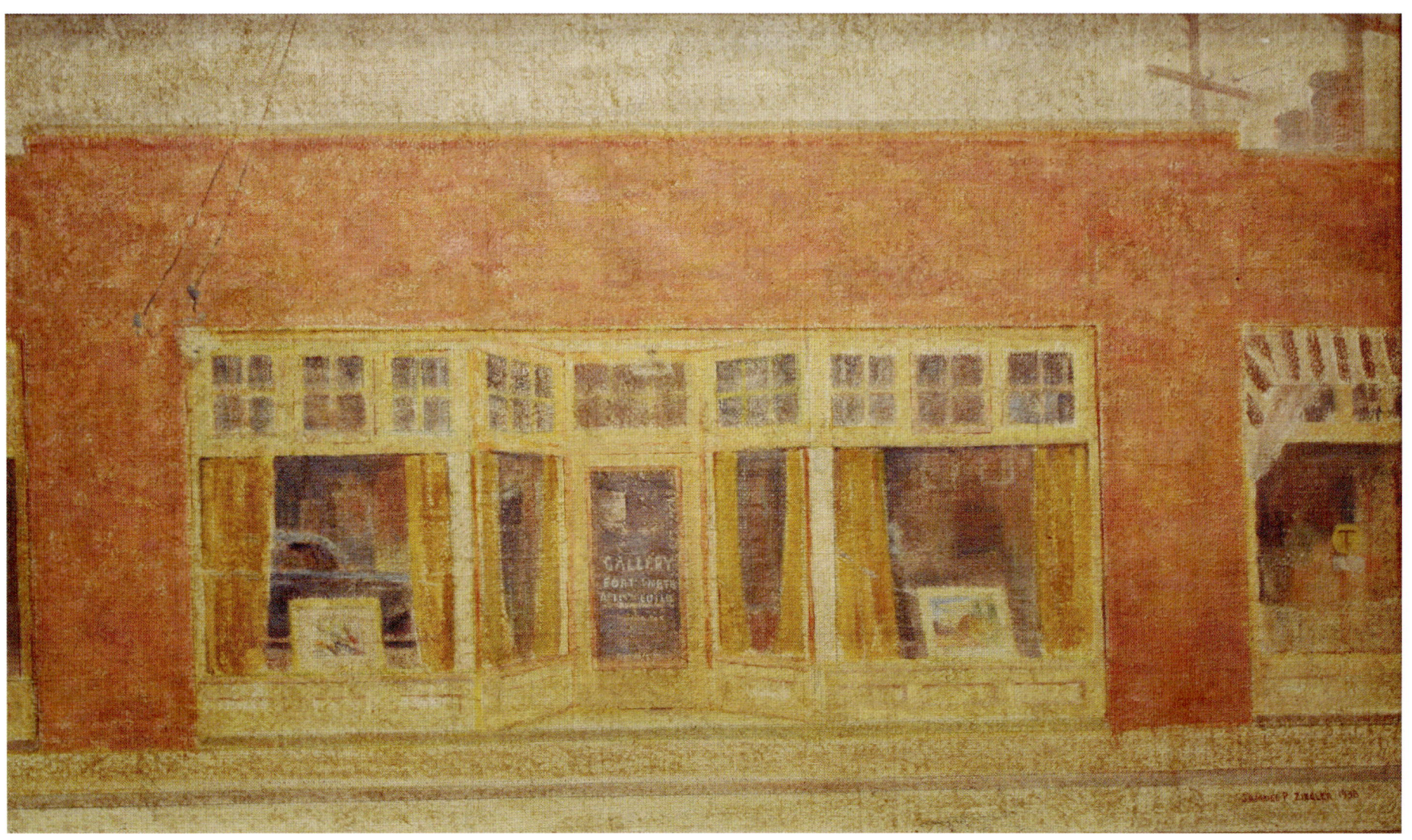

Art Gallery of the Fort Worth Artists Guild, 1938
Oil in canvas, 18 x 32 in.

Networking opportunities among local artists, amplified by the opening of the Fort Worth School of Fine Arts (see p. 84, *The Music Box*), led to formation of the Artists Guild of Texas – a.k.a. Fort Worth Artists Guild – in 1935. Eighteen months later, guild members opened a small art gallery in a vacant storefront at 1414 W. Tucker St., a space that formerly housed a neighborhood grocery store. Samuel Ziegler, a guild member, made this unassuming storefront the subject of a painting. The art gallery operated for fewer than three years, but during that time Fort Worth collectors could view and purchase paintings and prints by the city's top local artists in one convenient place. The Artists Guild of Texas disbanded during World War II.

Collection of Dow Art Galleries, LLC

In and Around Fort Worth II

Aeroplane – Reg Robbins Tri-Motor Ford, 1930. Etching.

Fort Worth aviator Reg Robbins ran one of the city's first air transport services. Based at Meacham Airport, the service was known as the Reg Robbins Flying Service. Robbins flew the Ford Tri-Motor, an aircraft made by the Ford Motor Company. On weekends Robbins offered rides in the aircraft for five dollars per person, making his flying machine a popular attraction for Fort Worthians looking for adventure. An empty field in Bluebonnet Hills, just south of TCU, was one of Robbins's departure points, and that may be where Ziegler documented this scene. During the short flights, the uncomfortably high decibel level inside the aircraft made as much of an impression on Robbins's passengers as the view.

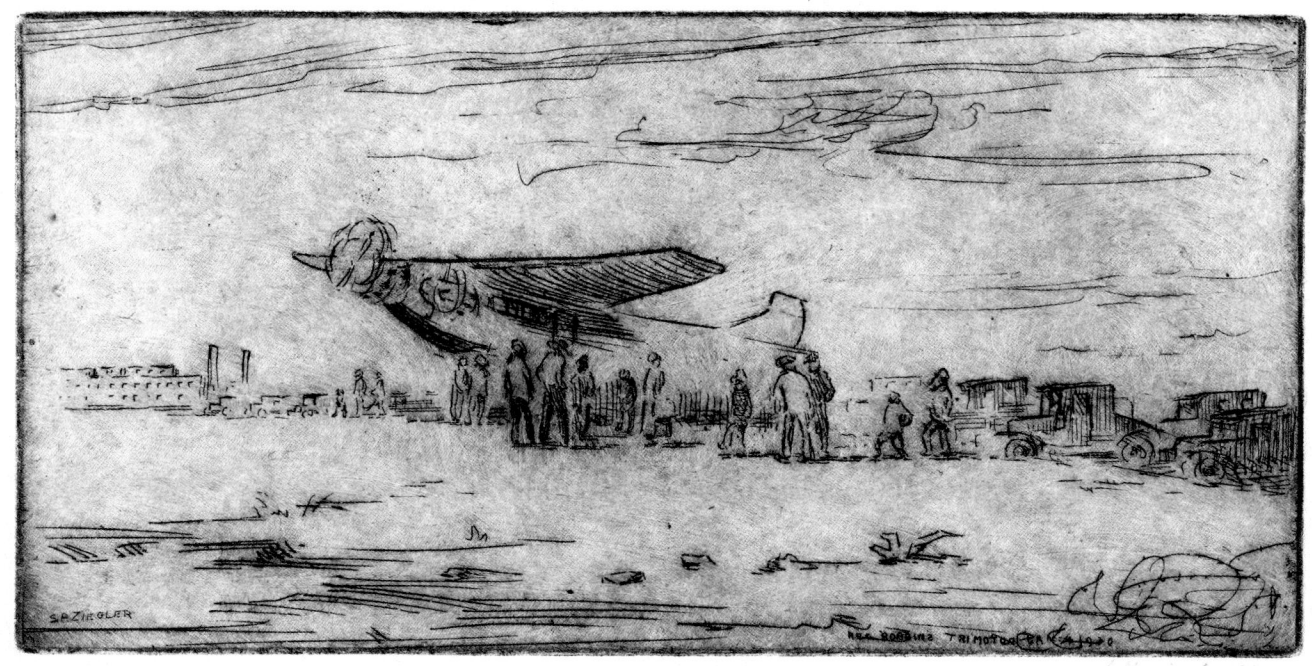

On the Grease Rack, n.d.
(early 1930s). Etching.

Professor Ziegler's Nash automobile was
an object of artistic attention in this unusual
depiction of periodic automobile maintenance. The scene was probably recorded at
a service station near Ziegler's home. Note
that the auto mechanic wore shiny, high-top
boots for protection. This print received
mention in the *Fort Worth Star-Telegram*
in 1933 when it was first exhibited.

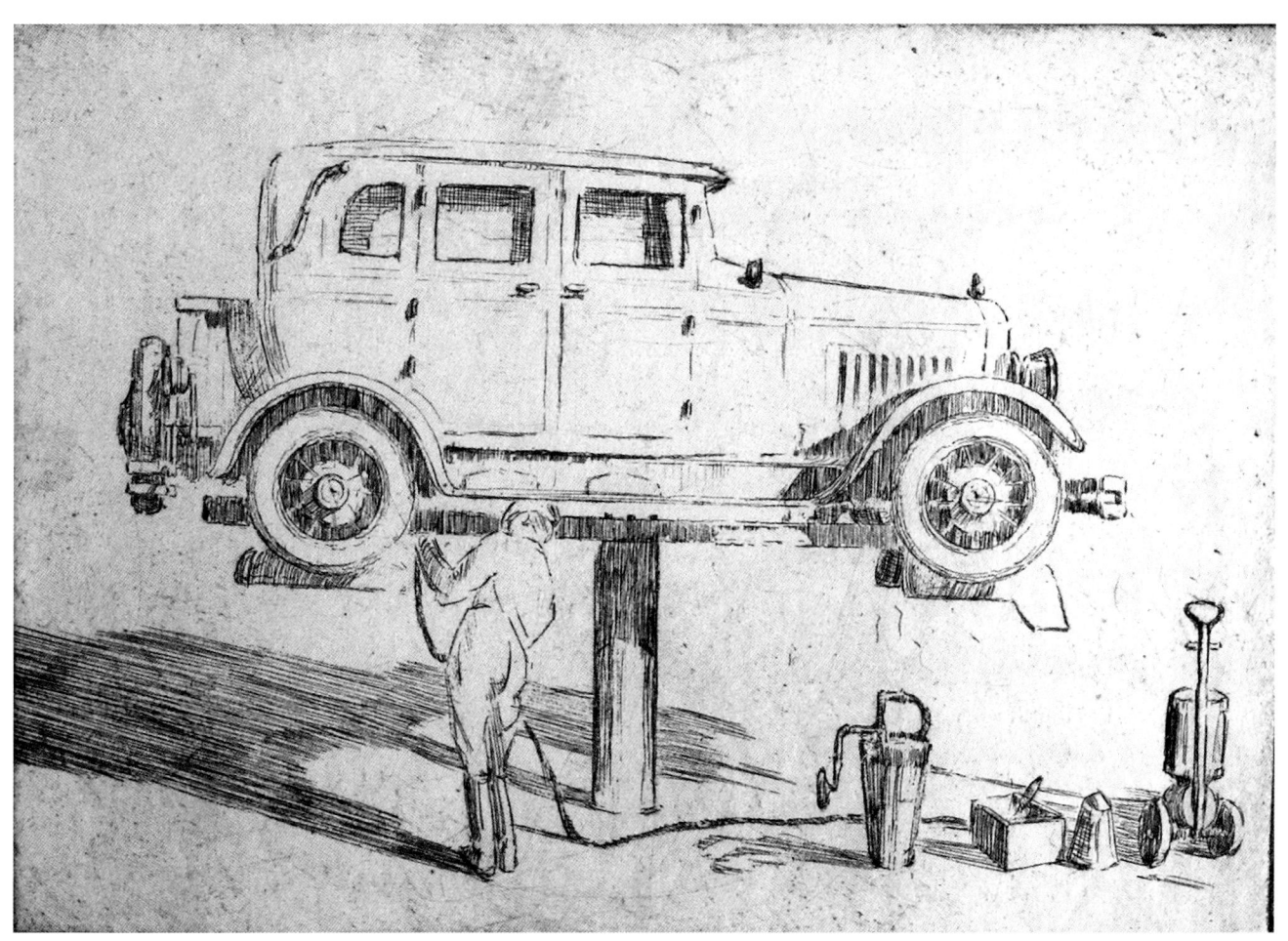

**Study for Gulf Refinery, n.d.
(early 1930s). Graphite on paper.**

Crude oil refining was big business in Fort Worth when Professor Ziegler focused on the Gulf Oil refinery on Brennan Avenue (see commentary on p. 123).

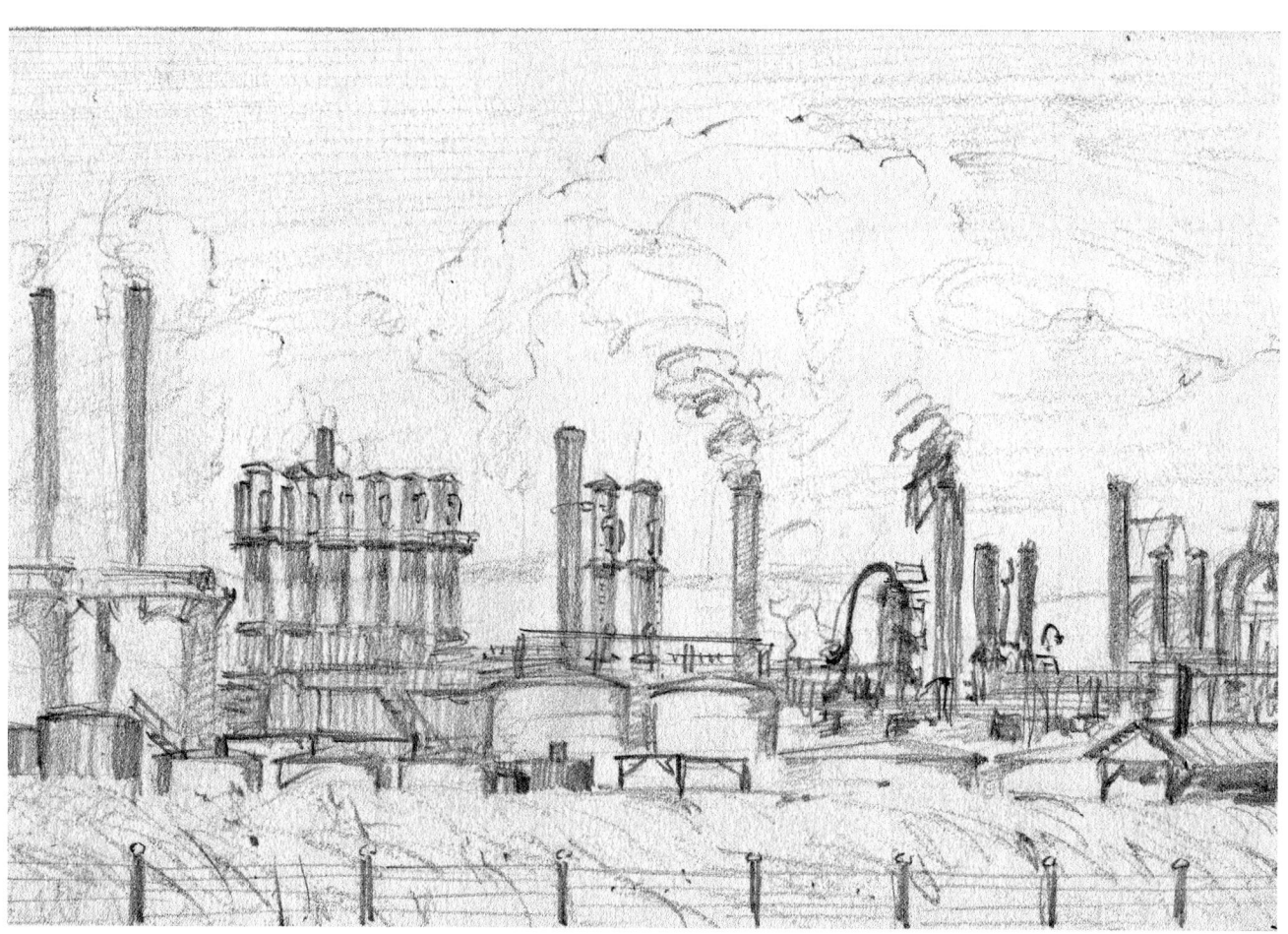

**_The Gulf Refinery,_ n.d.
(early 1930s). Etching.**

In 1911, Gulf Refining Company chose Fort Worth
as the location for its second oil refinery in Texas,
the first being located in Port Arthur. One hundred
acres of land along Brennan Avenue, east of the Fort
Worth stockyards, was acquired for the refinery site.
The facility opened in 1912 and produced all of the
Gulf Oil Company's brands of kerosene, gasoline,
and lubricating oils. Crude oil from Oklahoma,
brought in through a newly laid pipeline, provided
the raw material for the new Fort Worth operation.
By the time Ziegler produced this print, discoveries
in Texas had placed Fort Worth at the geographical
center of the world's richest oil-producing region,
and the city was home to seven petroleum refineries
of varying capacity. Much of the gasoline produced
by these refineries was sold through chains of com-
pany-owned filling stations located across the area.
In 1930, Gulf Refining Company operated twenty-four filling stations in Fort Worth proper.

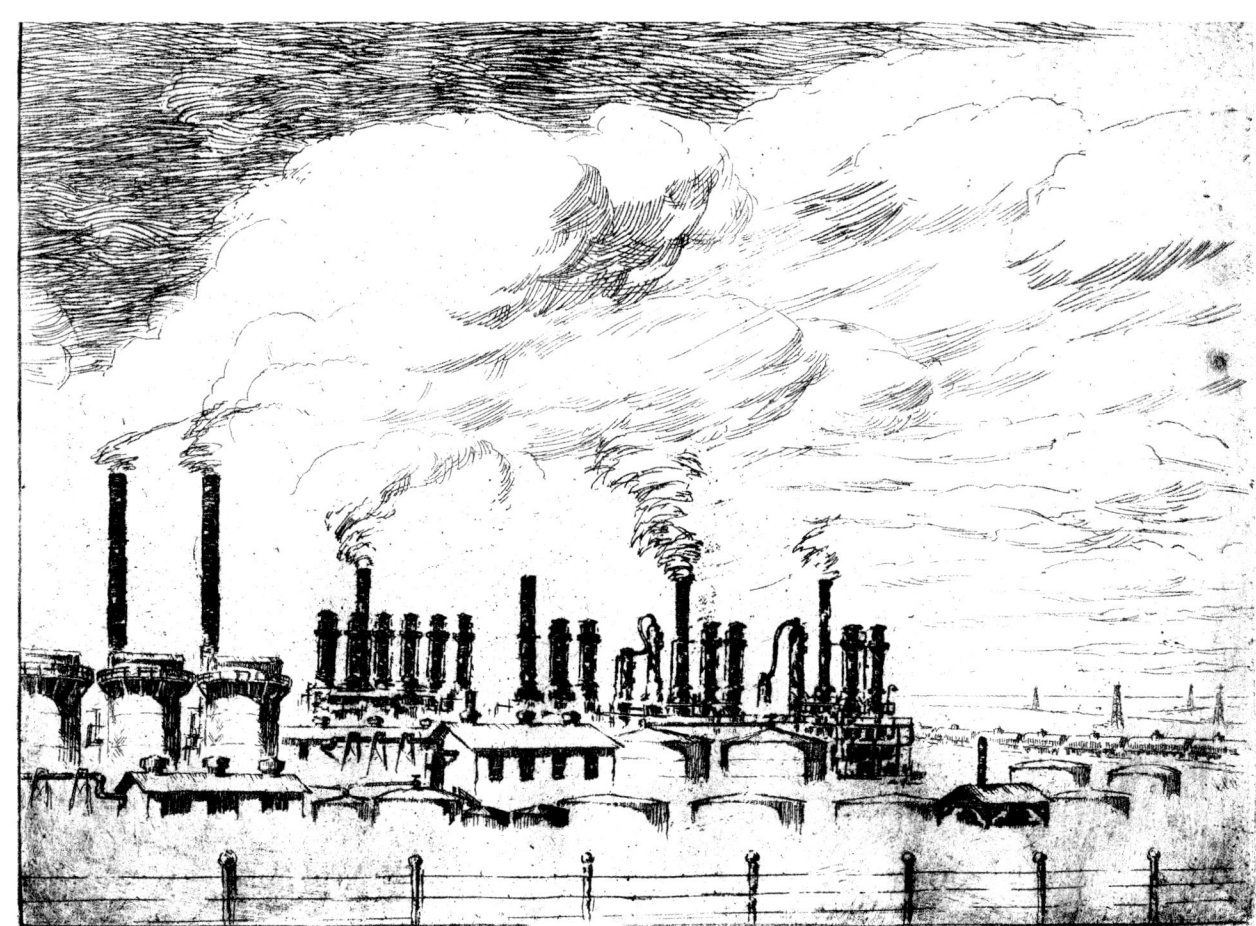

The Forest Park Gates, n.d.
(late 1930s). Graphite on paper.

The twin stone towers of the Forest Park Gates
were handsomely depicted in this 1930s masterpiece drawing by Ziegler. The twelve-story Forest
Park Apartments (constructed 1927-28) stood
just beyond the gates. The gates were built by the
City of Fort Worth to flank the entrance to Forest
Park, home of the city's public zoo. Restoration of
the gates in the 1980s has allowed this scene to
remain little changed up to the present day.

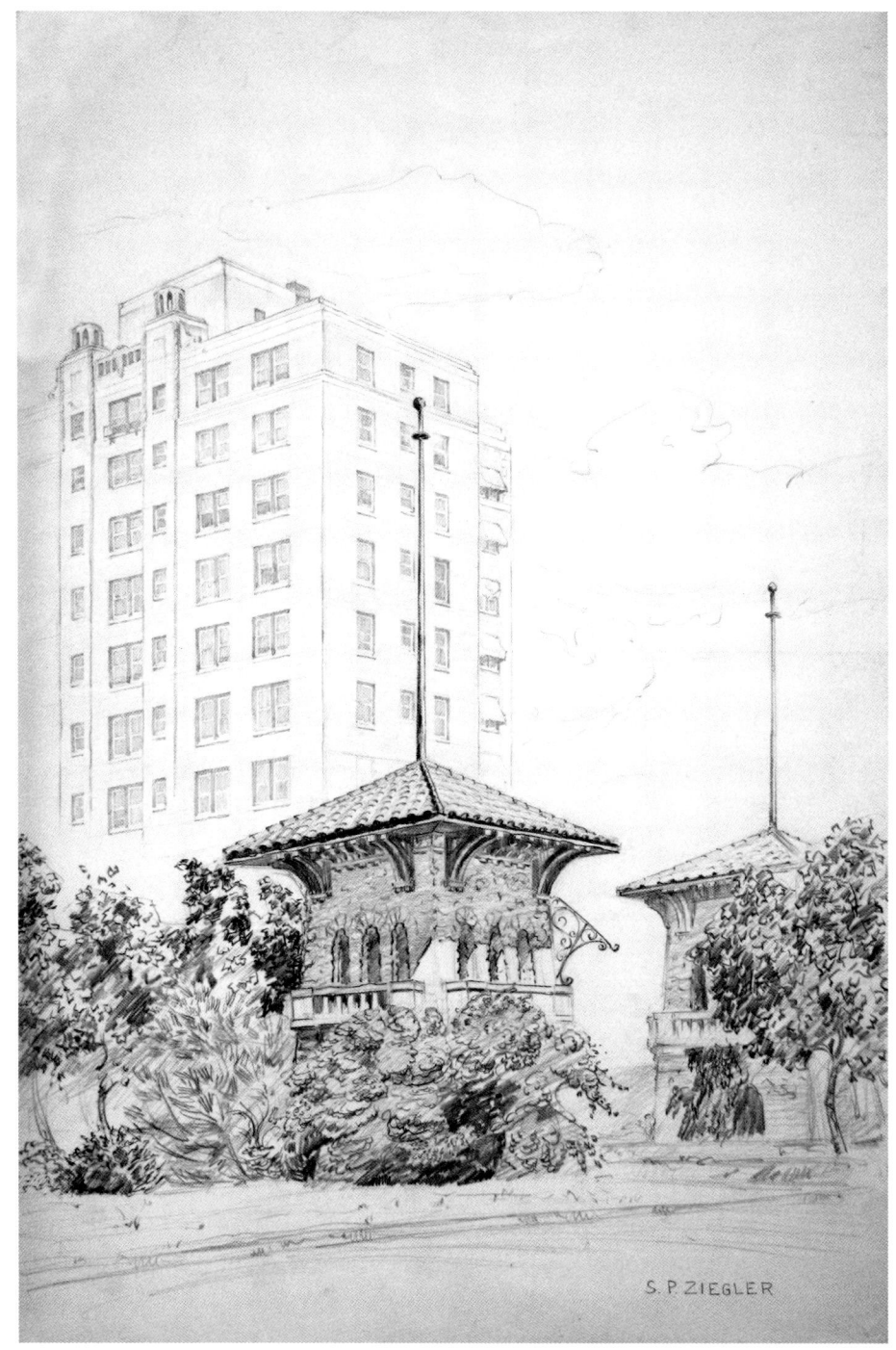

S.P. ZIEGLER

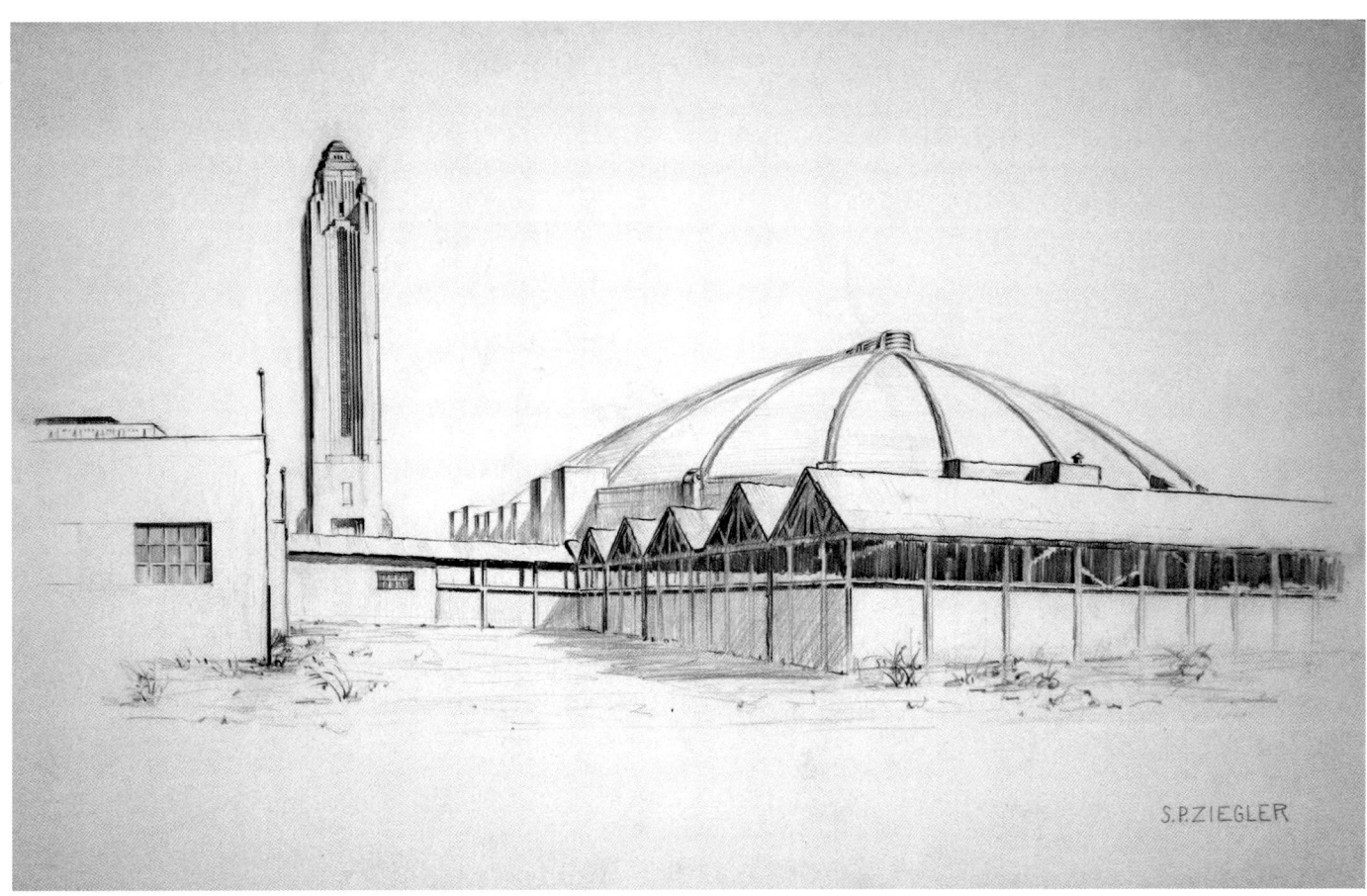

Will Rogers Coliseum and Pioneer Tower from the South, ca. 1944. Graphite on paper.

Few local buildings are more recognizable to residents of Fort Worth than Will Rogers Memorial Coliseum, the Will Rogers Auditorium, and the soaring Pioneer Tower. Their allure was evident from the time the coliseum, civic auditorium, and landmark tower, known collectively as the Will Rogers Memorial Center, first opened. Built to serve as focal points of local participation in the Texas Centennial celebration, the buildings were shepherded to completion in 1936 by a committee headed by Amon Carter Sr. and named for Carter's close friend, the late humorist Will Rogers. Fort Worth's annual Feeders and Breeders livestock show was permanently moved from the Northside Coliseum to the Will Rogers Memorial Coliseum in 1944. In this drawing, Ziegler depicted the Pioneer Tower and self-supporting dome of the coliseum as seen from the south. Rows of temporary livestock shelters, each shelter featuring ample ventilation, were situated behind the coliseum. These temporary shelters were used from 1944 until 1948.

William G. Newby Memorial Hall, n.d. (early 1930s).

Here Ziegler selected the Newby Memorial Hall from among the several buildings that made up the Woman's Club compound as the motif for this finished pencil drawing. The Woman's Club of Fort Worth received a generous gift in 1923 when Mrs. William G. (Etta) Newby donated a large private residence to the club for use as a permanent clubhouse. The former home of a German cotton merchant, the donated residence was located at 1316 Pennsylvania Avenue. As a condition of the gift, the residence was named William G. Newby Memorial Hall in honor of Mrs. Newby's late husband. In the 1930s and 1940s Ziegler made many appearances at the Woman's Club of Fort Worth as a cellist with the Pro Arte String Quartet.

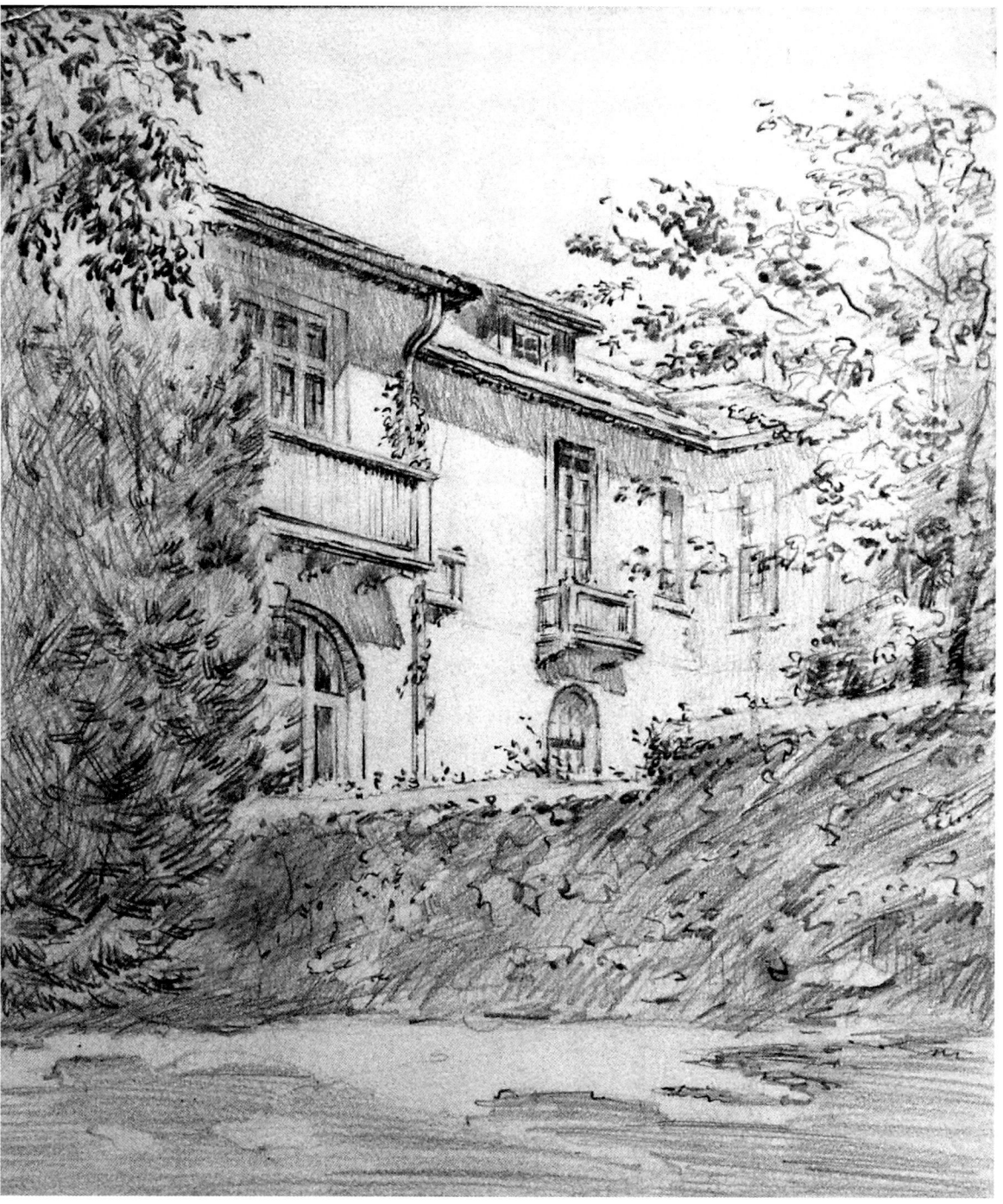

***Entrance to Fort Worth Public Market,
n.d. (early 1930s). Graphite on paper.***

The stepped entrance tower of the new Fort Worth
Public Market drew Ziegler's attention in this nicely
rendered pencil sketch. The public market at 1400
Henderson Street provided retail space for dozens
of fruit and vegetable vendors and local farmers.
The building opened in 1930 and remains standing
over ninety years later, its heyday as an outlet for
locally-grown agricultural products long past.

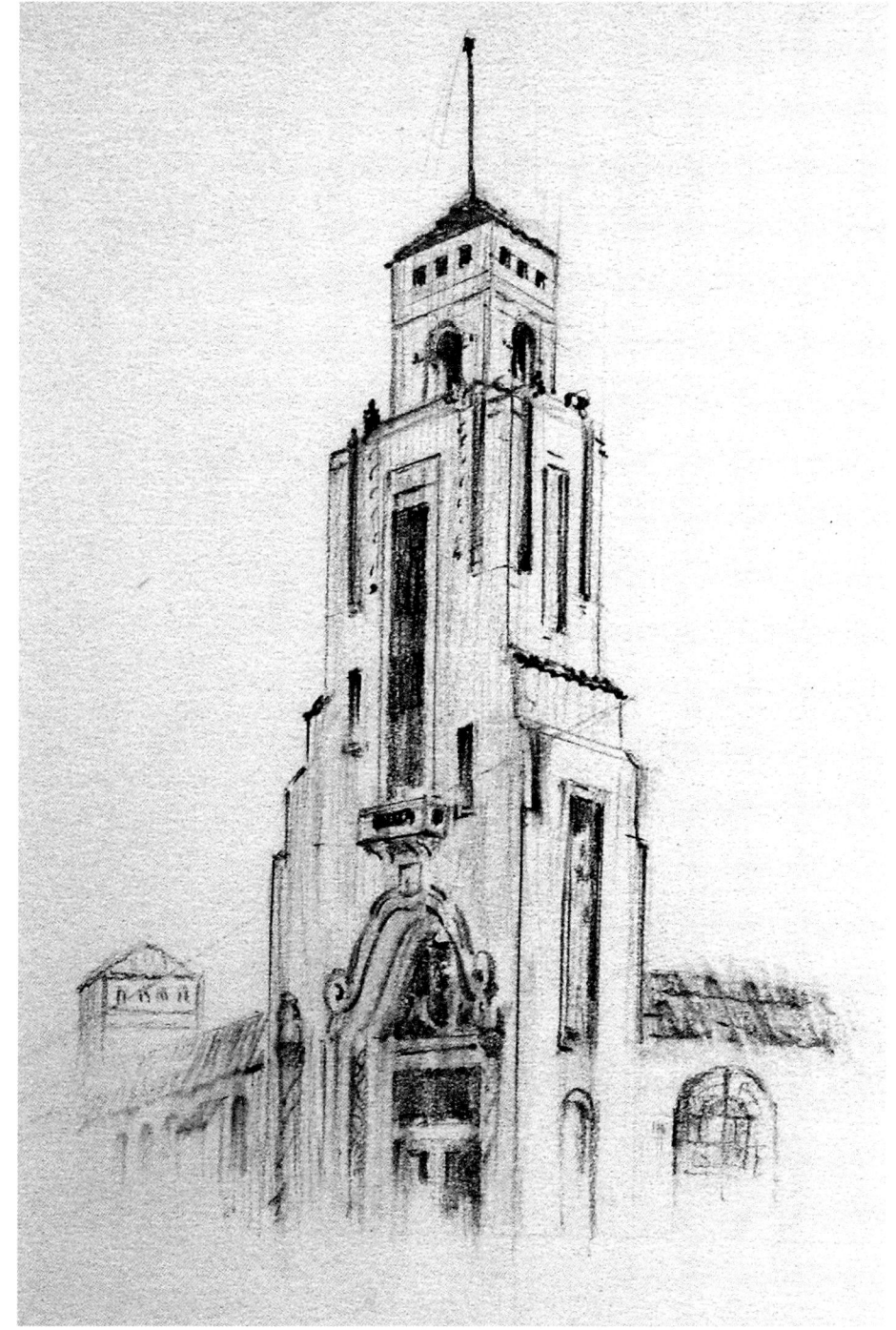

**Study of Purina Mills,
n.d. (early 1930s). Graphite
on paper.**

In the 1930s, locally owned grain mills serving a regional customer base were major components of the Fort Worth economy. Their impact was such that Fort Worth was said to be "the largest terminal grain market in the South." Purina Mills, located on the eastern edge of Fort Worth's central business district, was one of the city's large feed milling operations. This pencil study of Purina Mills served as the preparatory drawing for a related etching (opposite).

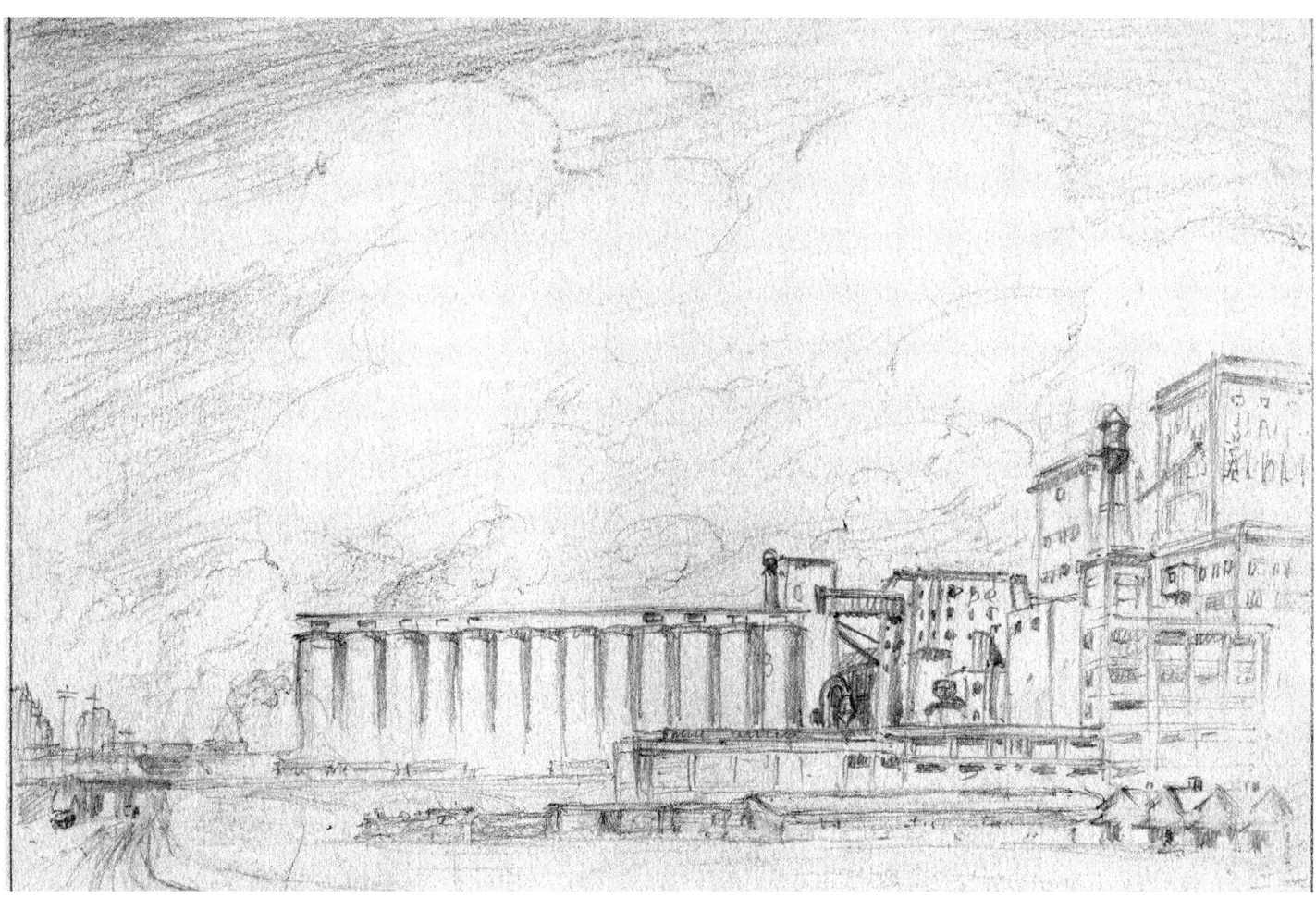

Purina Mills,
n.d. (early 1930s). Etching.

Built in 1917-18, Fort Worth's
Purina Mills was the newest addition
to a chain of grain mills owned by
the Ralston Purina Company of Saint
Louis, Missouri. The Fort Worth mill
was designed to bring the company's
presence into close proximity with the
burgeoning Texas livestock and poul-
try industries. The Fort Worth location
produced a variety of scientifically
formulated animal feeds that were
marketed throughout the southwest
in distinctive red and white checker-
board bags. Popular Purina feed products included Purina Cattle Checkers,
Purina Chick Startena with Buttermilk,
and Purina Hen Chow. The Fort Worth
mill also made feeds for horses,
mules, hogs, and sheep.

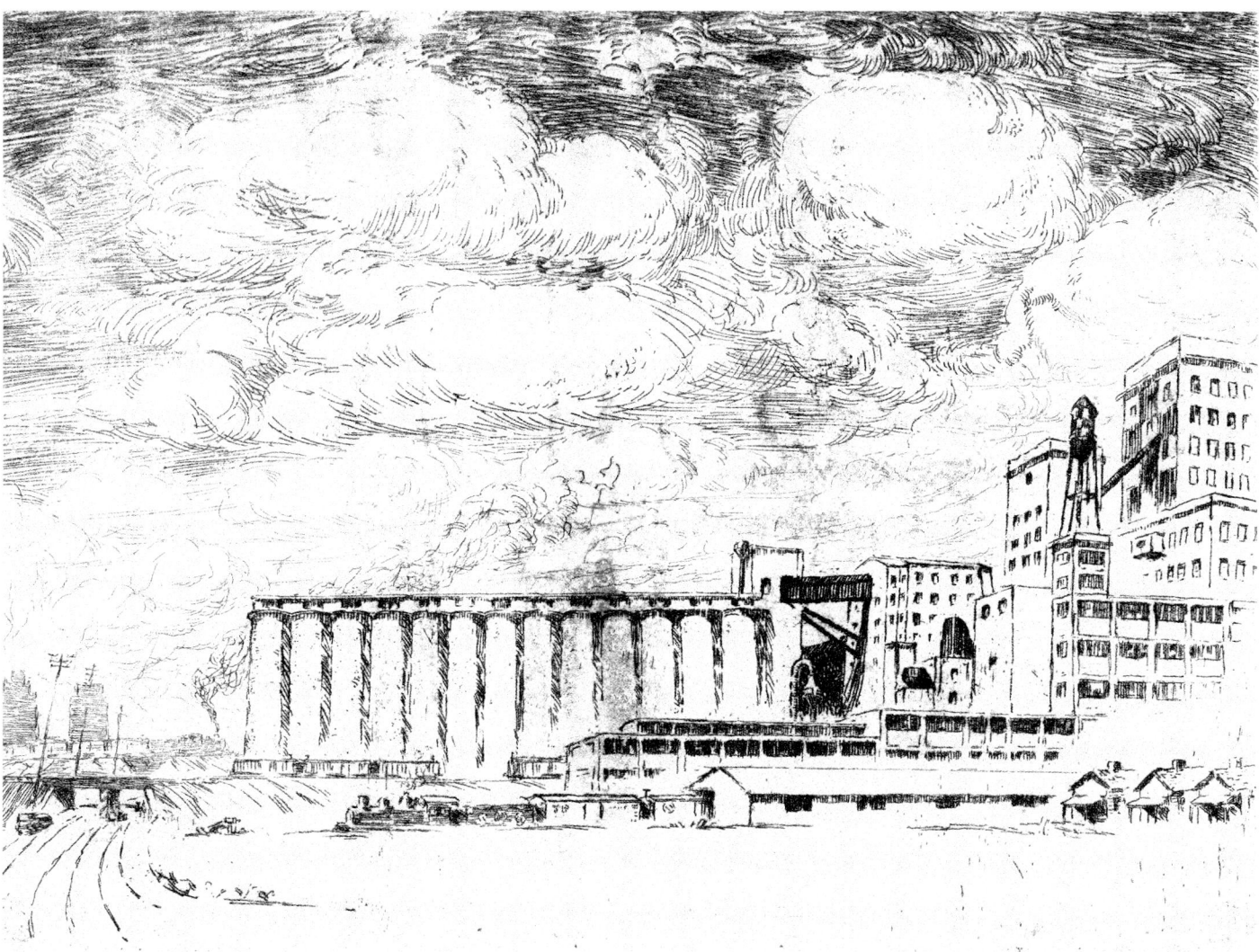

***Study of the Katy Elevator,
June 26, 1931.*** **Graphite
on paper.**

The Katy Elevator of Fort Worth
Elevators and Warehousing Company,
3700 Alice Street, was the subject of
this 1931 Ziegler pencil study. The
Katy Elevator was one of two large
storage elevators operated by the
Fort Worth Elevators and Warehousing
Company. The Katy Elevator was
named for the Missouri-Kansas-Texas
(M-K-T) Railroad that provided transportation services to the site. The Katy
Elevator's sister operation was located
on East First Street and known as
the Rock Island Elevator.

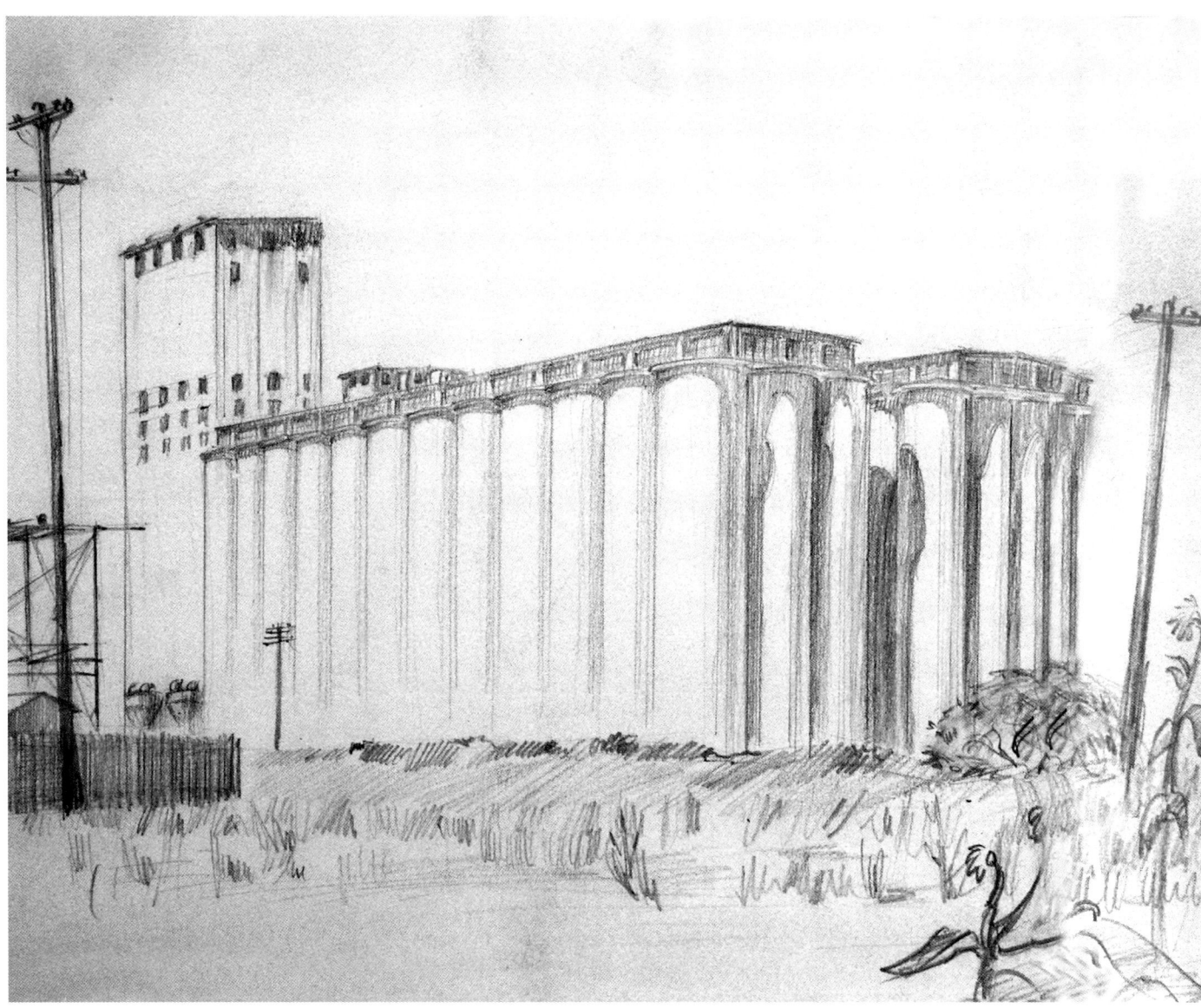

Bain Peanut Company Elevator, ca. 1930. Lithograph.

About 1930, Ziegler produced this lithograph of the storage elevator operated by Bain Peanut Company of Texas. The Bain Peanut Company wholesaled Texas-grown peanuts of the Spanish and Virginia varieties from its elevator located west of downtown Fort Worth. The elevator sat two blocks south of West Seventh Street, just west of the Clear Fork of the Trinity River, along tracks operated by the Frisco Railway. A factory building that had once served as a Chevrolet automobile assembly plant and later as a temporary home for Montgomery Ward was situated between the elevator property and West Seventh Street. The nineteen silos that made up the elevator complex made national news in 1989 when they withstood repeated efforts to topple them with dynamite.

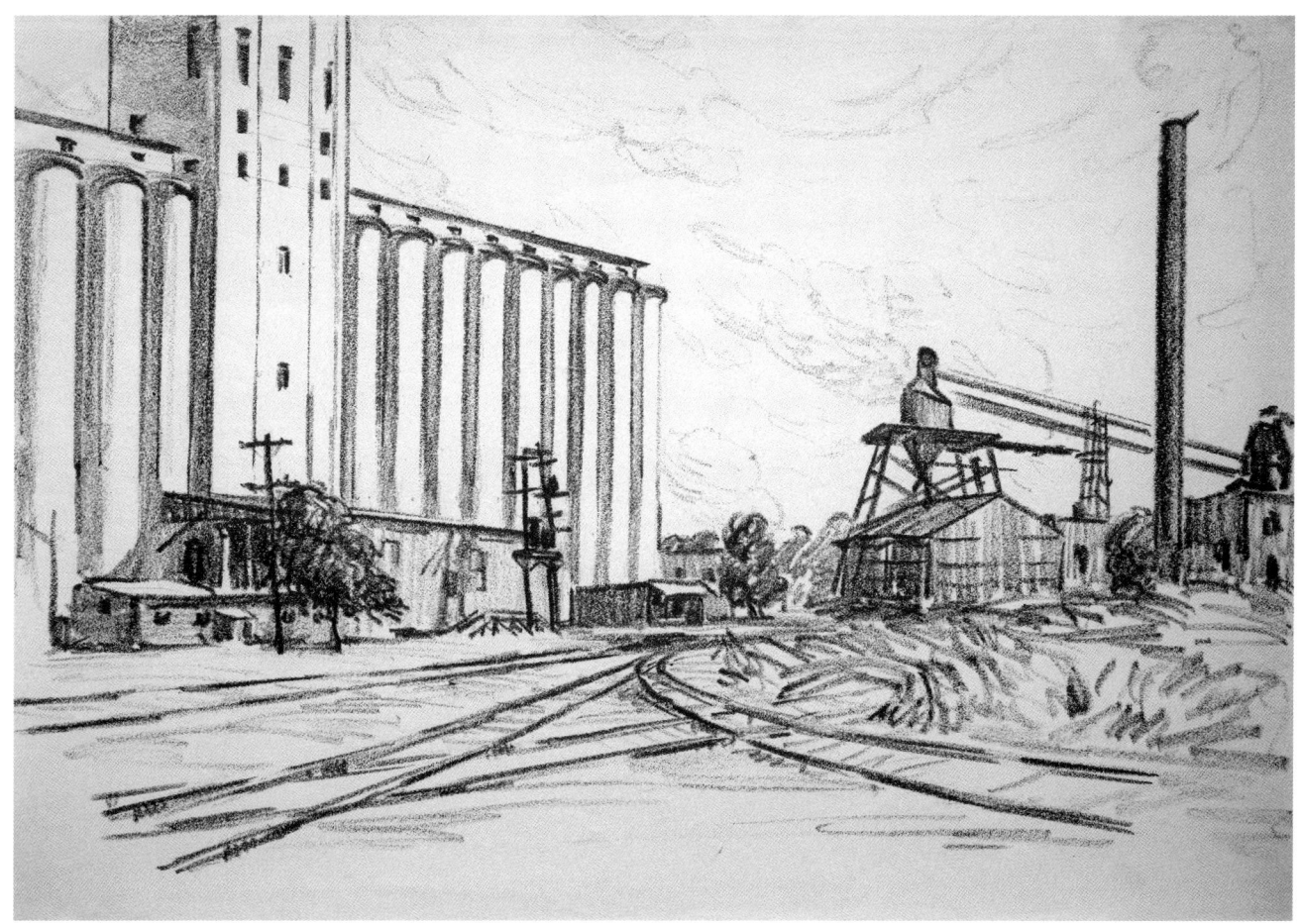

Bewley Mills, ca. 1930.
Lithograph.

At the time Ziegler produced this lithograph, Bewley Mills was Fort Worth's oldest and perhaps best-established milling operation. The company's signature flour, Bewley's Best, enjoyed wide regional distribution, as did its line of Anchor-brand animal feeds. The mill was founded in 1883 as the Anchor Roller Mill by Murray P. Bewley Sr., a former riverboat captain from Ohio. The mill was first located at Front and Cherry Streets on the western edge of town. Around 1910 a much larger mill opened on E. Ninth Street, at the eastern edge of the downtown area. As the facility grew, distinctive signage carrying the Bewley name became a familiar sight to commuters entering and leaving the downtown area via the eastern corridor.

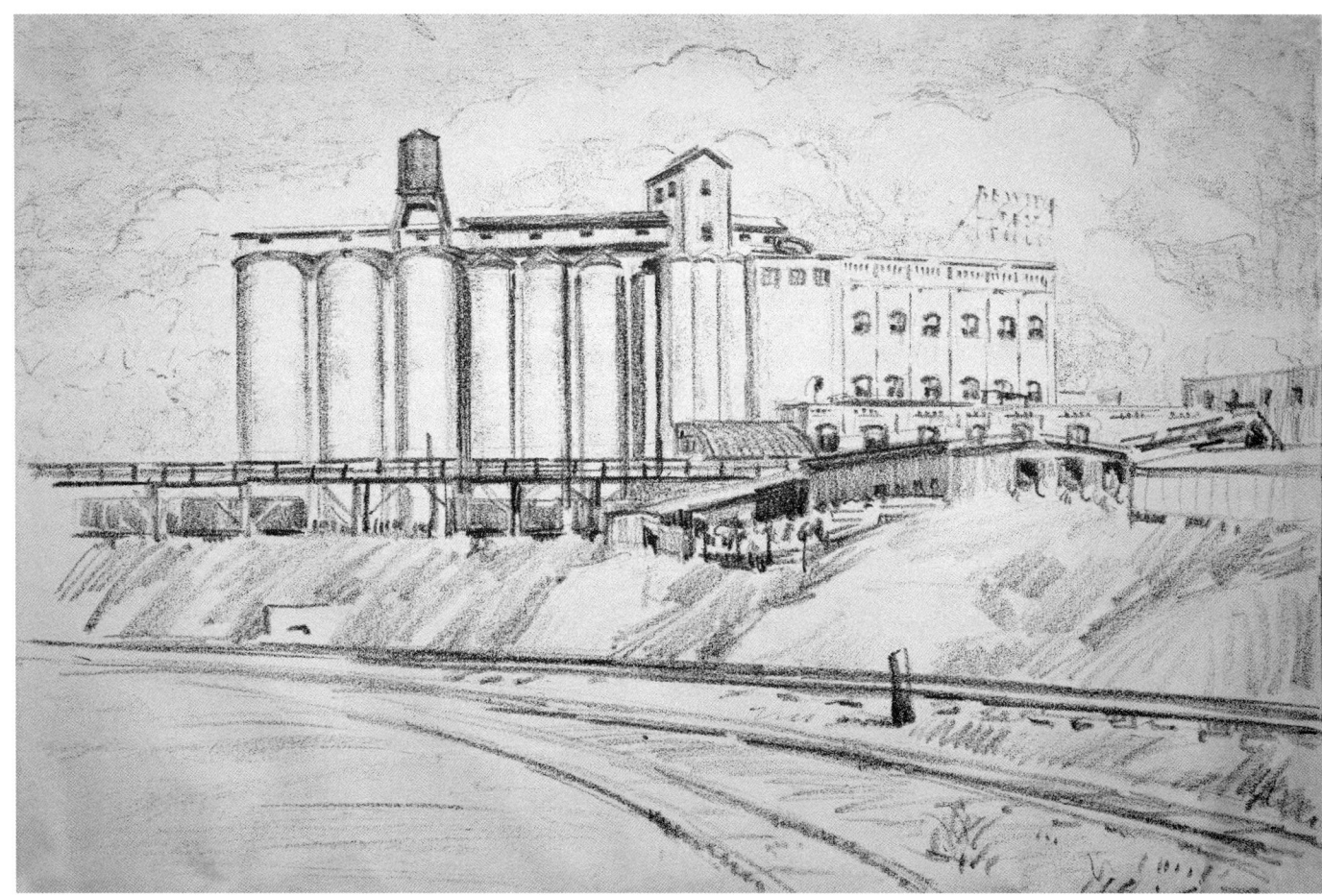

The S. P. Ziegler House,
1931. Etching.

This etching from 1931 depicted the home of
the Ziegler family at 2908 West Cassell Blvd.
The street name later changed to West Lowden.
The house sat directly across the street from
the Mary Couts Burnett Library. Samuel Ziegler
and his wife raised four sons, a daughter, and
an adopted daughter here. Ziegler appropriat-
ed space in a bedroom to operate his etching
press and store still-life props and painting
equipment. Ziegler turned sketches of his family and everyday household objects into scores
of paintings.

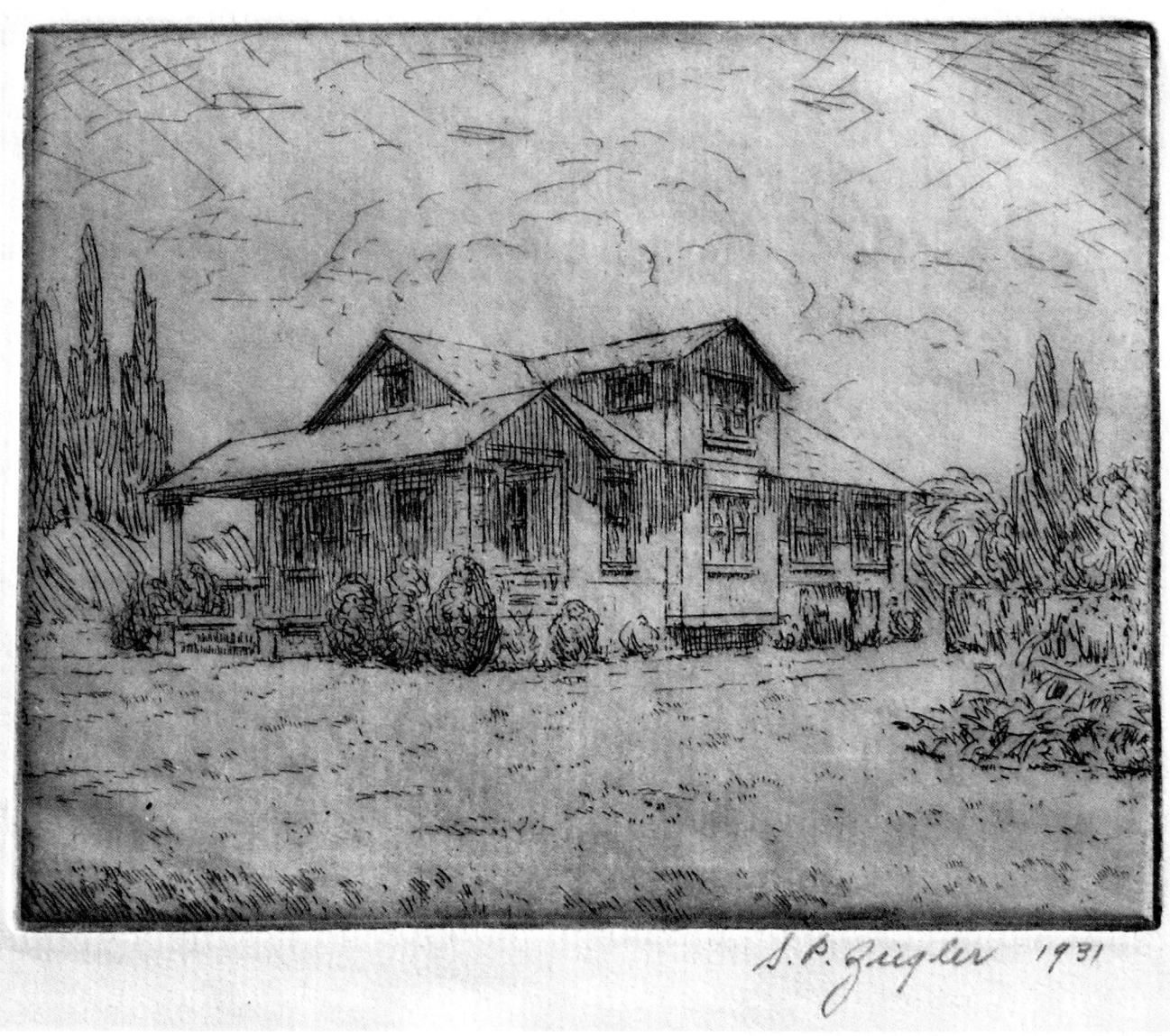

Untitled (Entrance to Trinity Park), ca. 1930. Etching.

Although the title to this image is lost, the procession of automobiles and canopy of trees over the roadway suggest an entrance to Trinity Park. Ziegler was known to frequently sketch and paint along the park's winding drives.

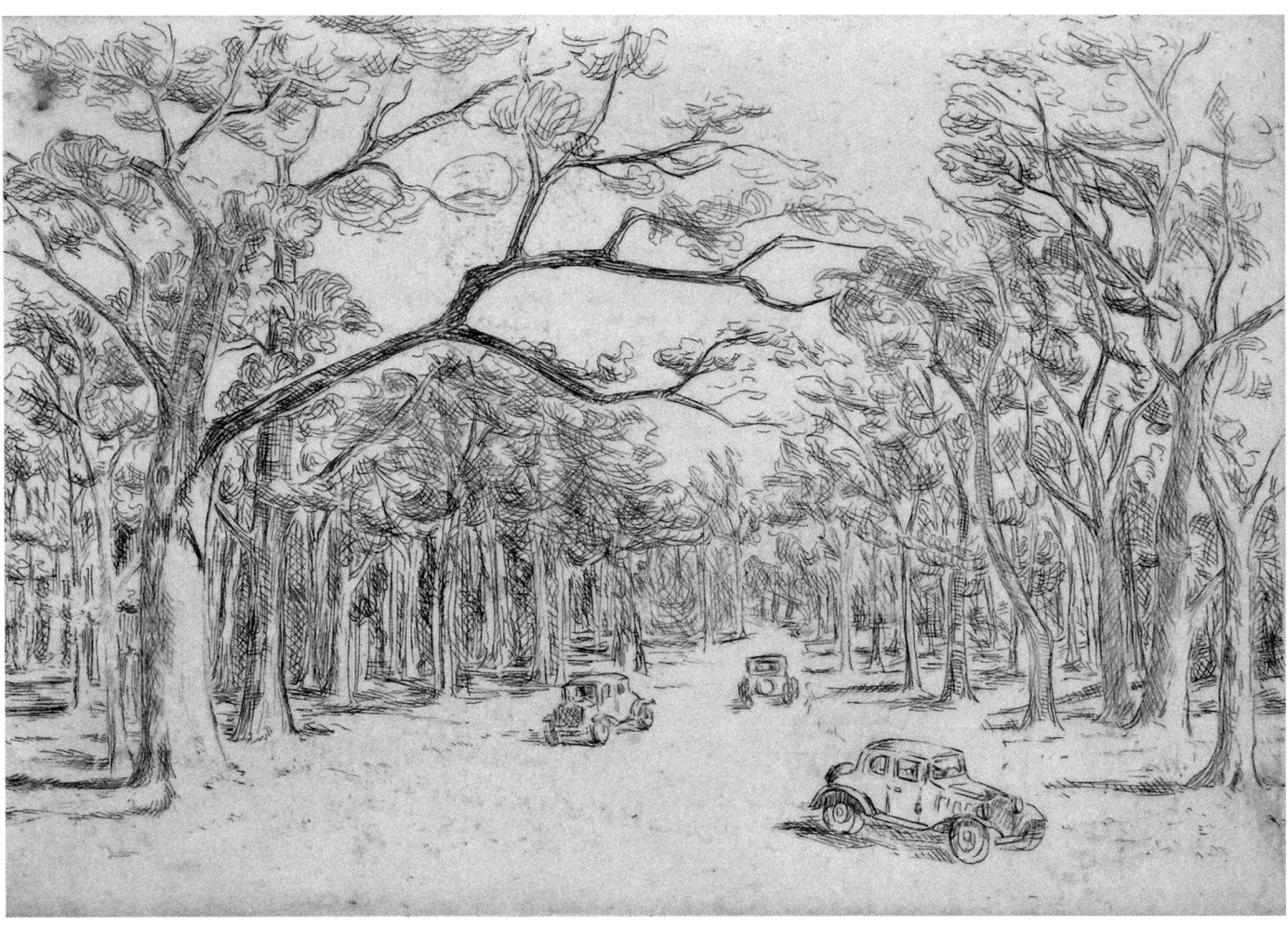

Depression: Aug 1933.
Graphite on paper.

The visual record of the effects
of the Great Depression on the
people of Fort Worth is surprisingly
sparse. During the decade of the
1930s, hardships caused by the
great economic downturn seem
to have had little impact on the
viewpoint of local artists or on the
content of their art. This pencil
drawing by Ziegler was an exception.
According to notes left by the artist,
the men shown in the drawing were
waiting in line for food at a downtown
soup kitchen. The architectural
design over the doorway suggests
a church as the gathering place.

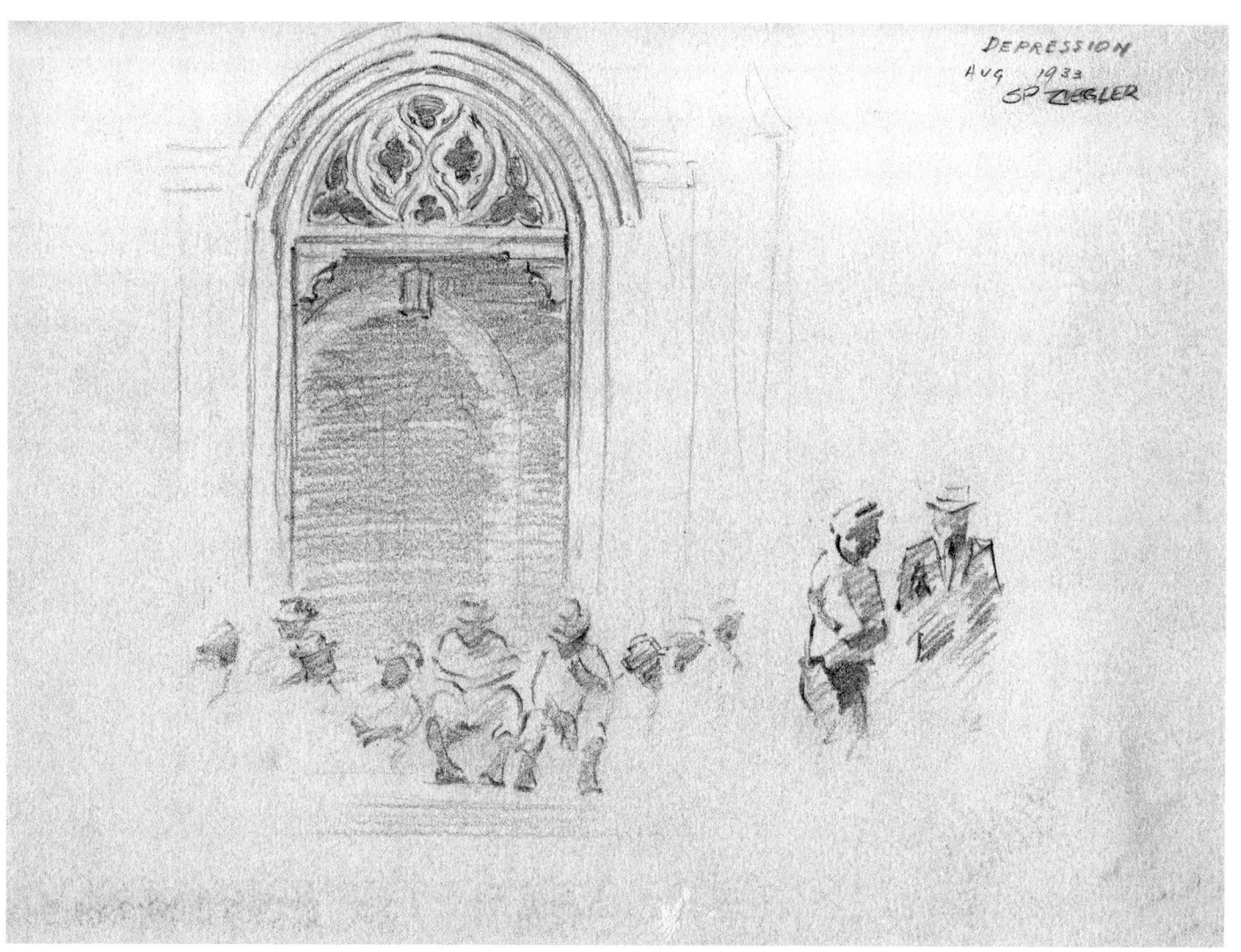

The Tamale Man's House, ca. 1930. Lithograph.

In the 1930s, a Mexican street vendor working from a pushcart carved his niche in Fort Worth by selling homemade tamales to downtown workers. Around 5:00 p.m. each day, the Tamale Man moved his cart to the corner of Summit Avenue and West Seventh Street, where he sold the remaining tamales to hungry commuters on their way home. Late one afternoon, Ziegler followed the enterprising food vendor in order to discover where he lived. The result was this lithograph called *The Tamale Man's House*. Ziegler also produced an oil painting of this scene.

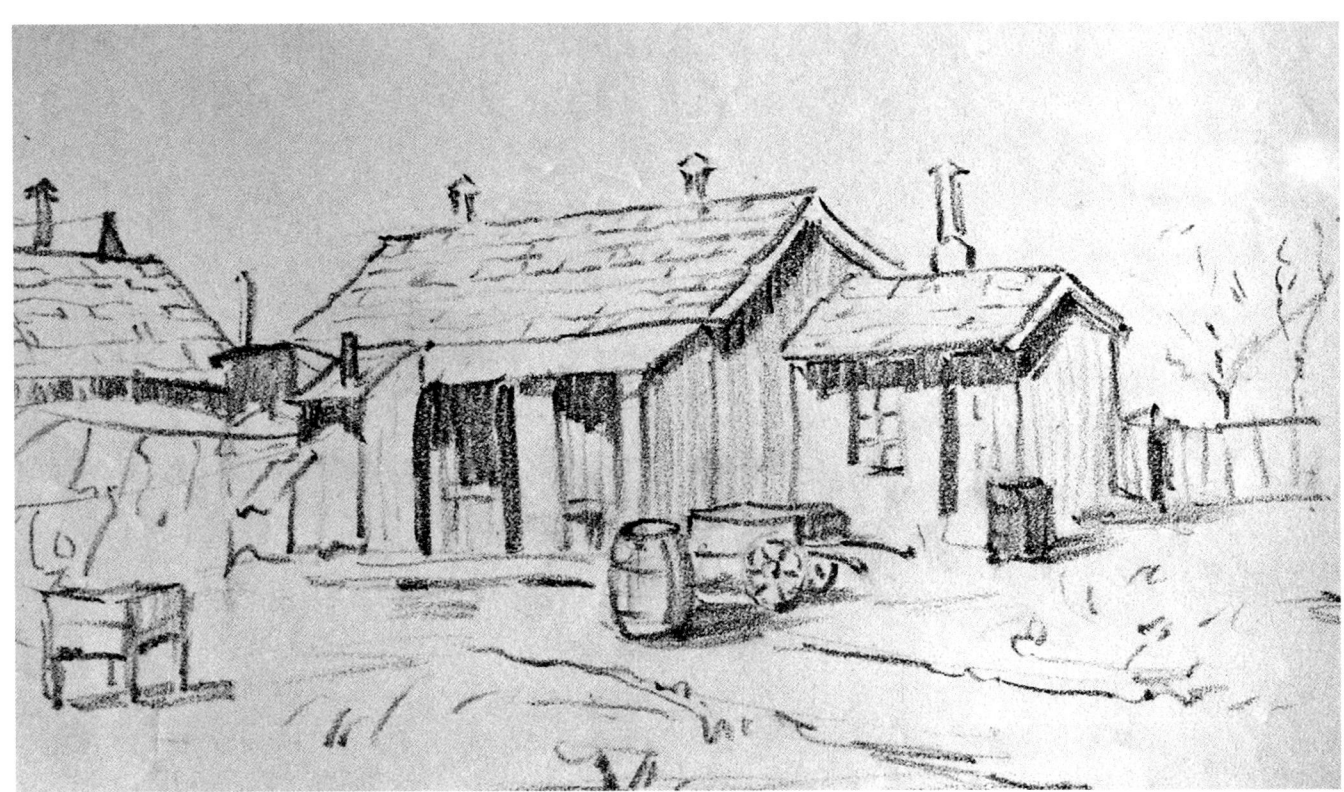

Forest Park in Winter,
ca. 1928. Etching.

Texas Oil Industry

Perkins Gusher, Eastland, Texas, 1931. Etching.

The Perkins Gusher was drilled in the spring of 1919 by the partnership of Root, Hupp, and Duff. The discovery well was located three and a half miles northeast of Eastland on an eighty-acre farm owned by Eli Perkins. Perkins had leased his land for 25 cents an acre prior to joining the U. S. Navy and was at sea when oil was struck. The Perkins Gusher produced at a rate of nine thousand barrels a day, reportedly earning Perkins $40,000 a month while he served out his enlistment as a coal stoker on the transport ship USS *Imperator*. The discovery of oil on the Perkins tract triggered an explosion of drilling activity on land bordering the Perkins Farm and helped cement Eastland County as a center of oil-drilling activity. Professor Ziegler's depiction of the Perkins gusher was a tip of the hat to Eastland's significance in the history of Texas oil exploration and Fort Worth's economic development.

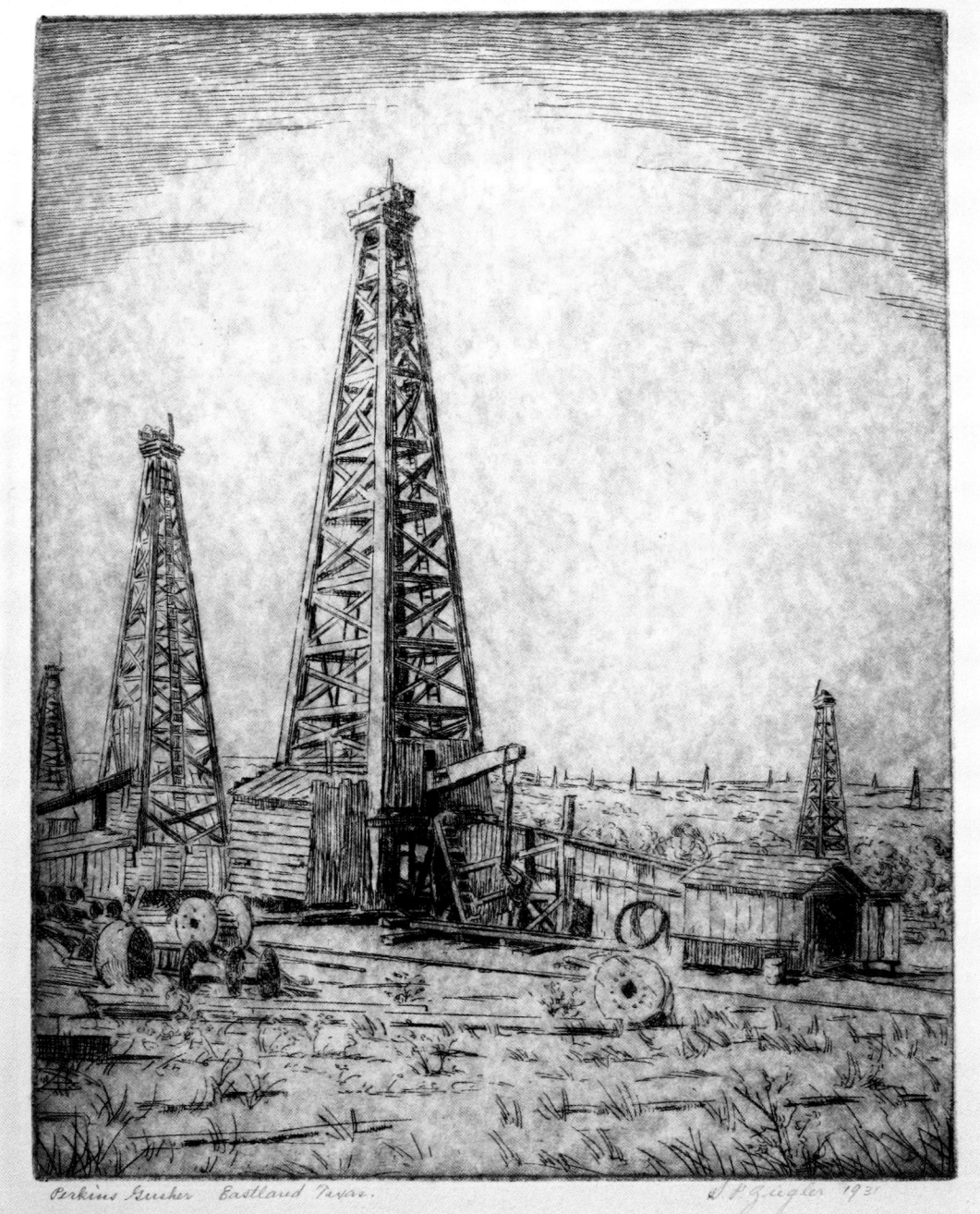

Untitled (oil well coming in), 1930. Etching.

A letter from the Eastland Chamber of Commerce, sent in 1927, prompted Ziegler to schedule the first of several summer trips to the West Texas oil fields. In the letter he was invited by the president of the chamber of commerce to "come among them and paint the very interesting oil activities thereabouts." Ziegler's forays resulted in a series of lithographs, etchings, and paintings that formed a visual record of the sights and techniques in use in the Texas oil industry at the time. The discovery of oil in Eastland County in 1917 triggered an economic boom that within a few years, transformed Fort Worth and the entire West Texas region.

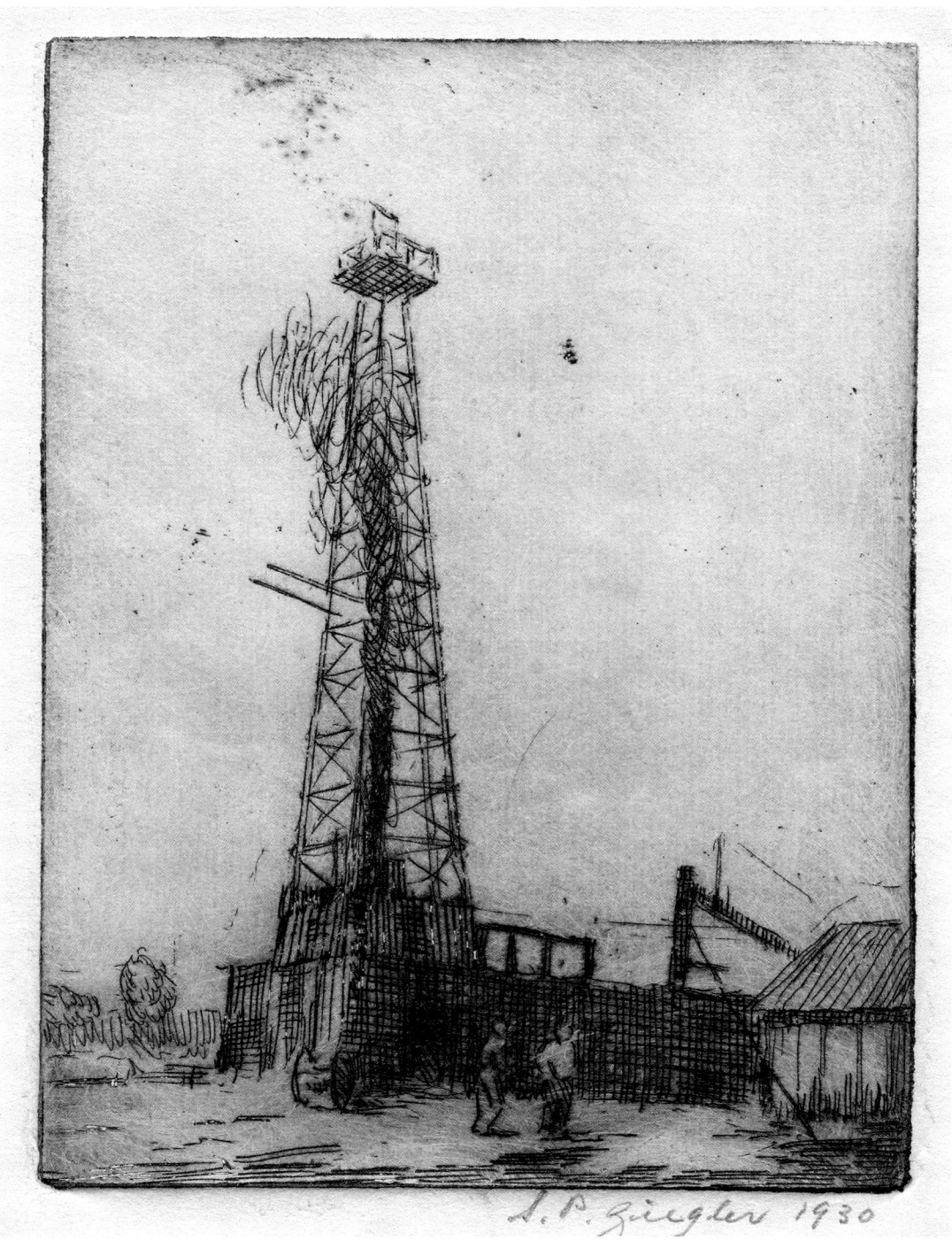

McCloud No. 1 – No. Central Texas, 1931. Etching.

The McCloud No. 1 was drilled in April 1930 in southern Young County, east of Graham. The well struck oil on April 10 and, prior to its flow being restricted, produced at an unheard-of rate of twenty-five thousand barrels a day. The _Fort Worth Star-Telegram_, on April 20, described the McCloud No. 1 as "the district's sensation" and "without doubt, the greatest high grade producer ever brought in in North Central Texas." A pencil notation in the bottom left margin of this etching suggests that Ziegler printed this image from a plate etched by Lucille Richhart, one of his printmaking protégés.

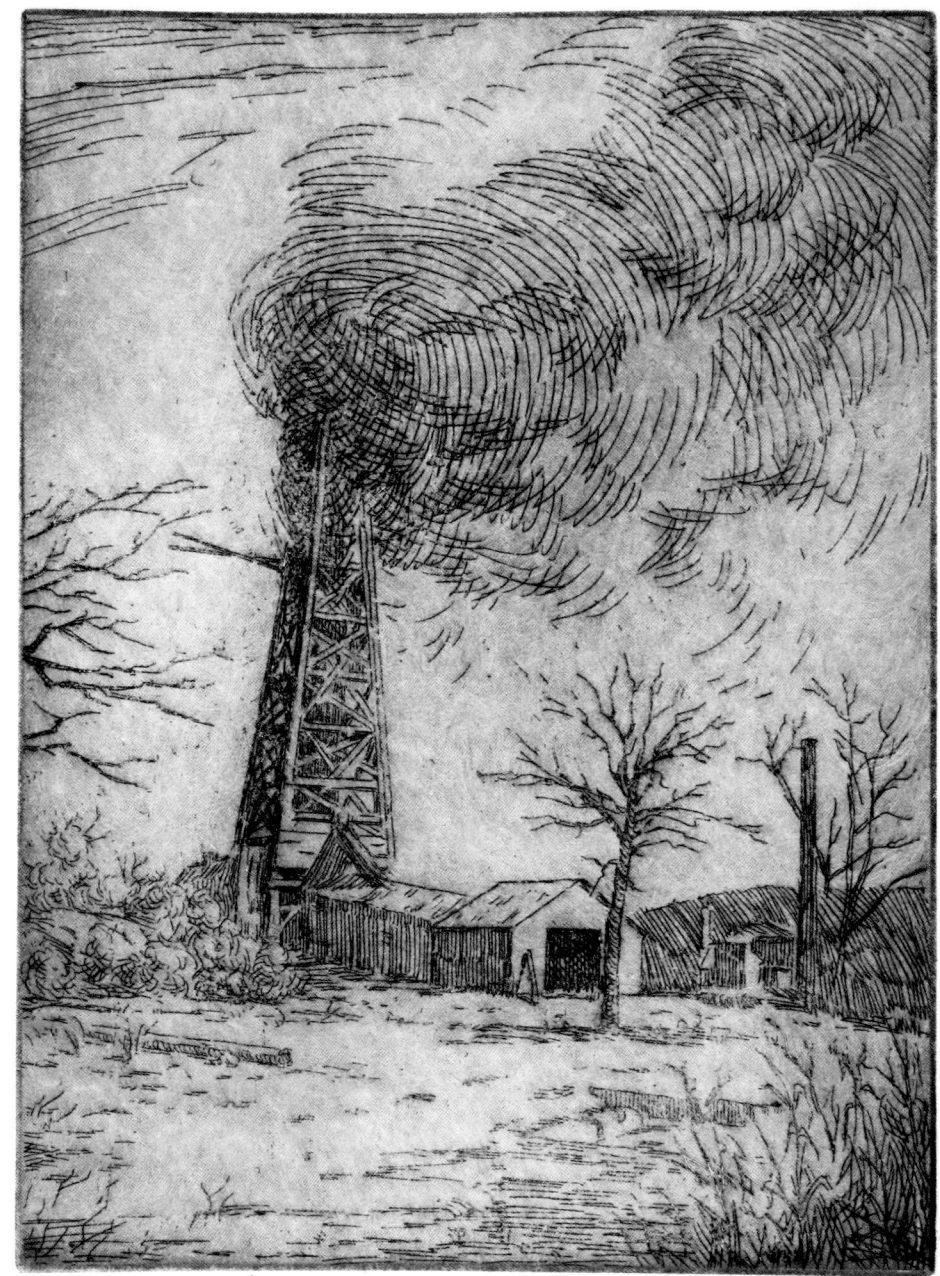

Lucille Richhart print   S.P. Ziegler 1931

***Contrary Mary – Oklahoma,* 1931. Etching.**

On the morning of March 26, 1930, residents of Oklahoma City were threatened by clouds of gaseous oily mist filling the sky in the southern part of the city. With wind out of the north, oil-saturated air drifted as far south as Norman. The environmental disaster would last eleven days and repeatedly frighten residents with every wind shift. The entire country was riveted by twice-daily reports on the emergency over national radio. The source of the unwanted pollution was a blowout of the Mary Sudik No. 1, a newly drilled oil well located on the farm of Vince and Mary Sudik, just south of the OKC Center. The gusher, which spewed oil four hundred feet into the air, was finally capped after three attempts, but not before hundreds of thousands of barrels of oil had been wasted. In his etching, Ziegler depicted the presence of pollution in every crevice of the oil-soaked ground surrounding the stricken well.

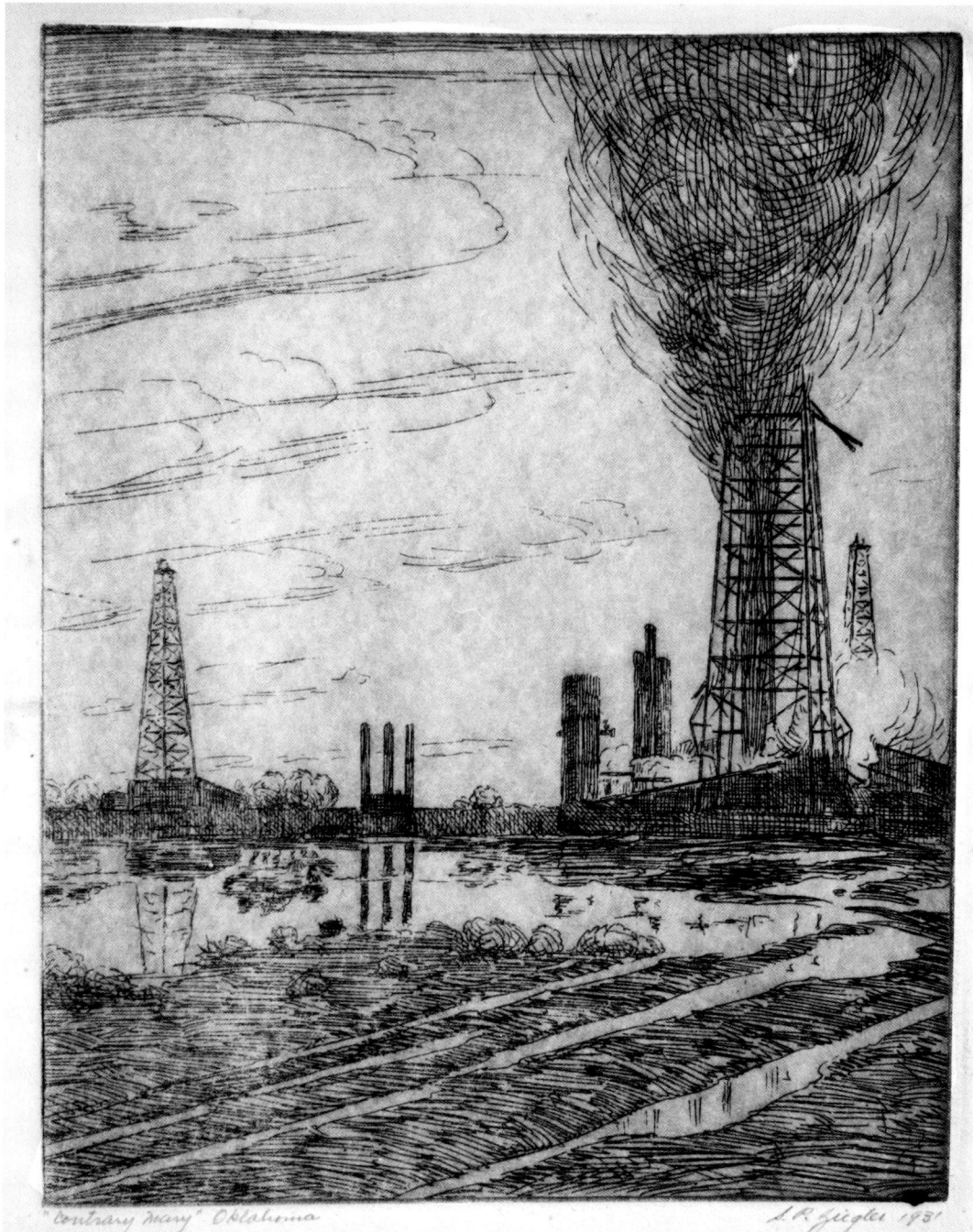

"Contrary Mary" Oklahoma   L.R. Ziegler 1931

Untitled (Discovery Field, Lake Eastland), late 1920s. Lithograph.

The original drawing for this lithograph was made near Eastland, Texas, in the summer of 1927 from the artist's direct observations. Ziegler sent the drawing to Ketterlinus Lithographic Manufacturing Company in Philadelphia afterwards and obtained a proof copy of the image. The same year Ziegler produced an impressive oil painting of this scene that measured 28 x 40 inches.

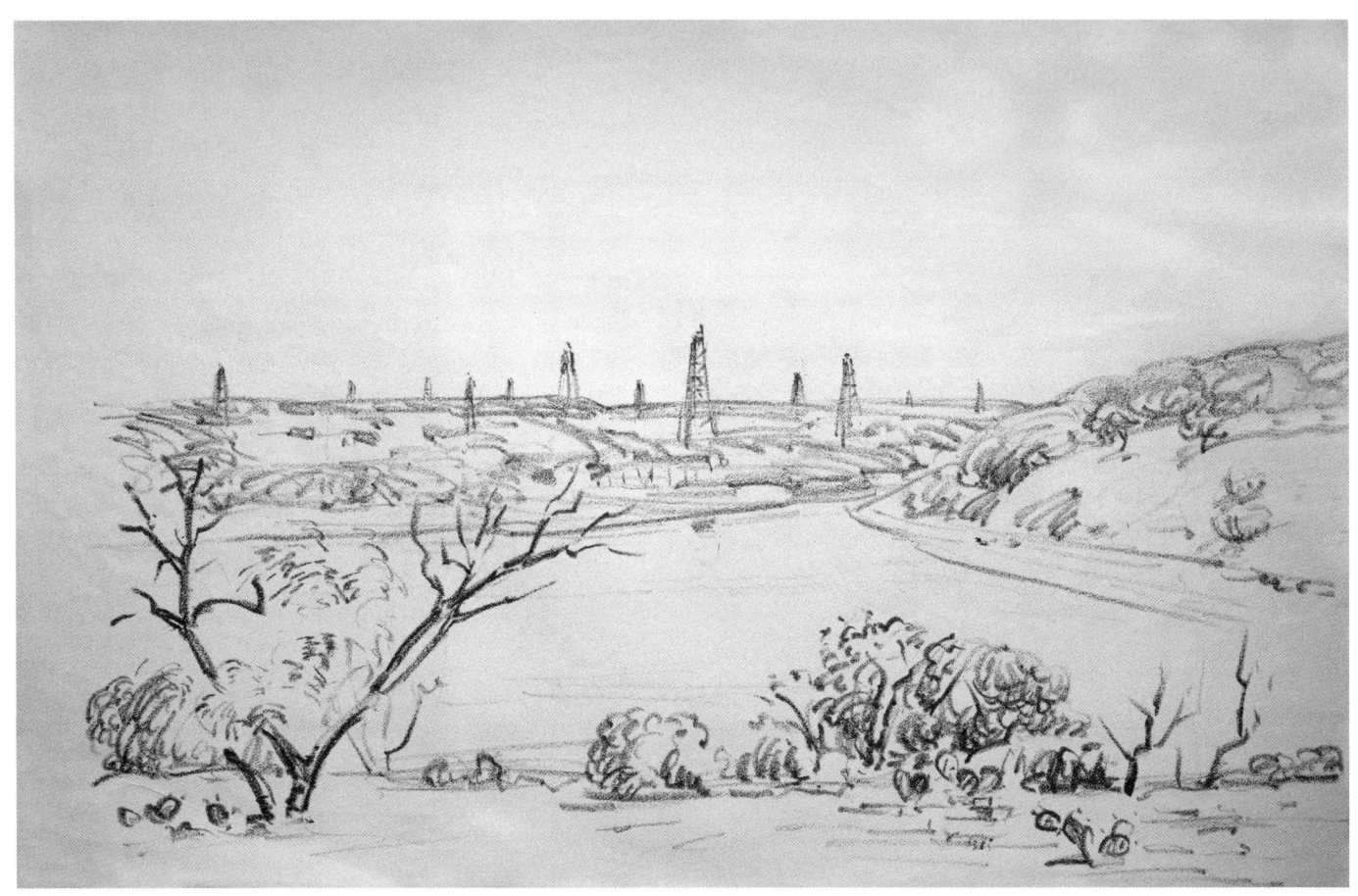

**Untitled (Discovery Field,
Lake Eastland), ca. 1930. Etching.**

This etching of the Eastland discovery
field was made one or two years after
the related lithograph (opposite) and
depicted the identical scene.

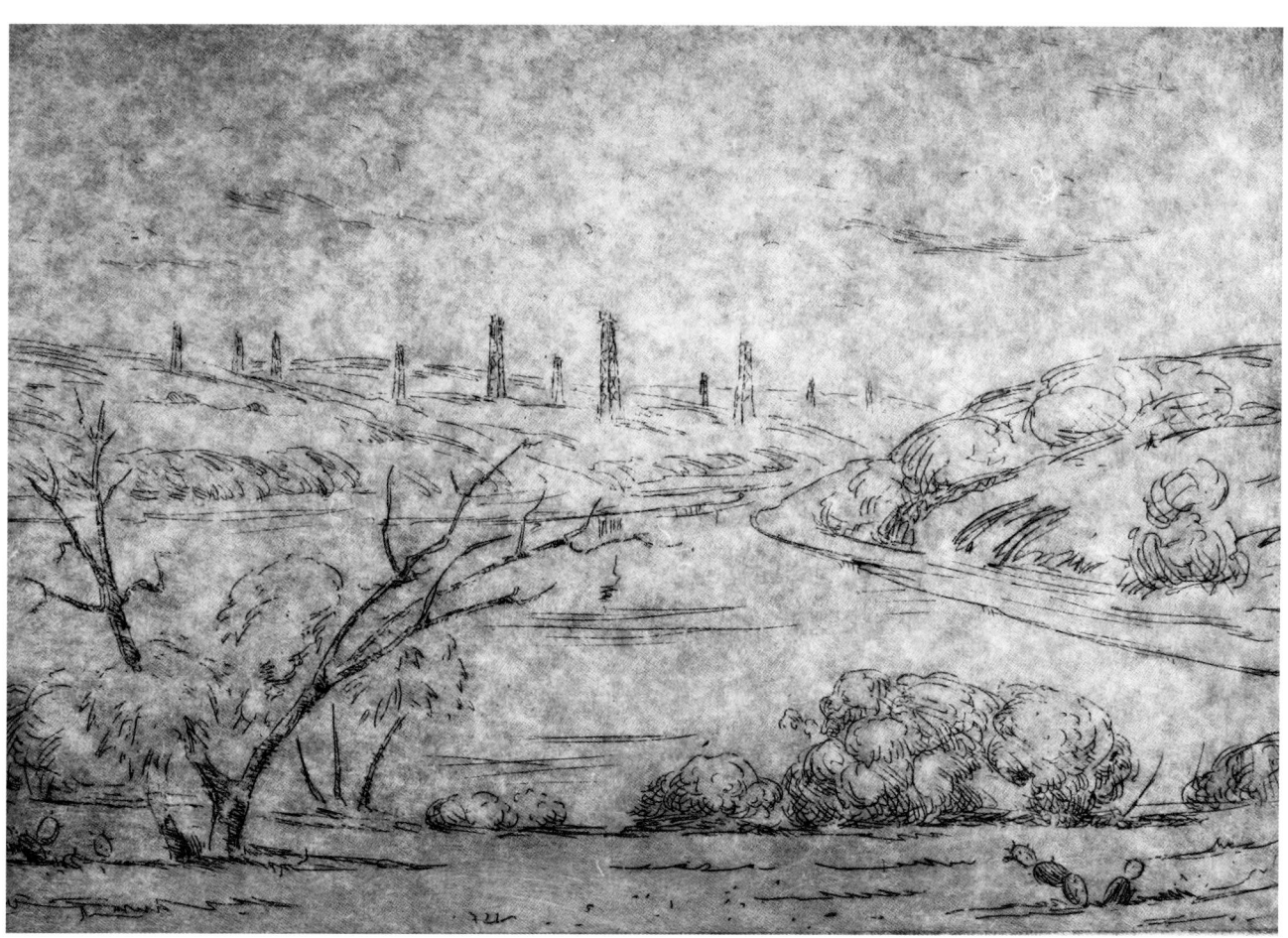

Untitled (West Texas discovery field), n.d. (late 1920s). Lithograph.

The exact location of the scene depicted in this lithograph is no longer known.

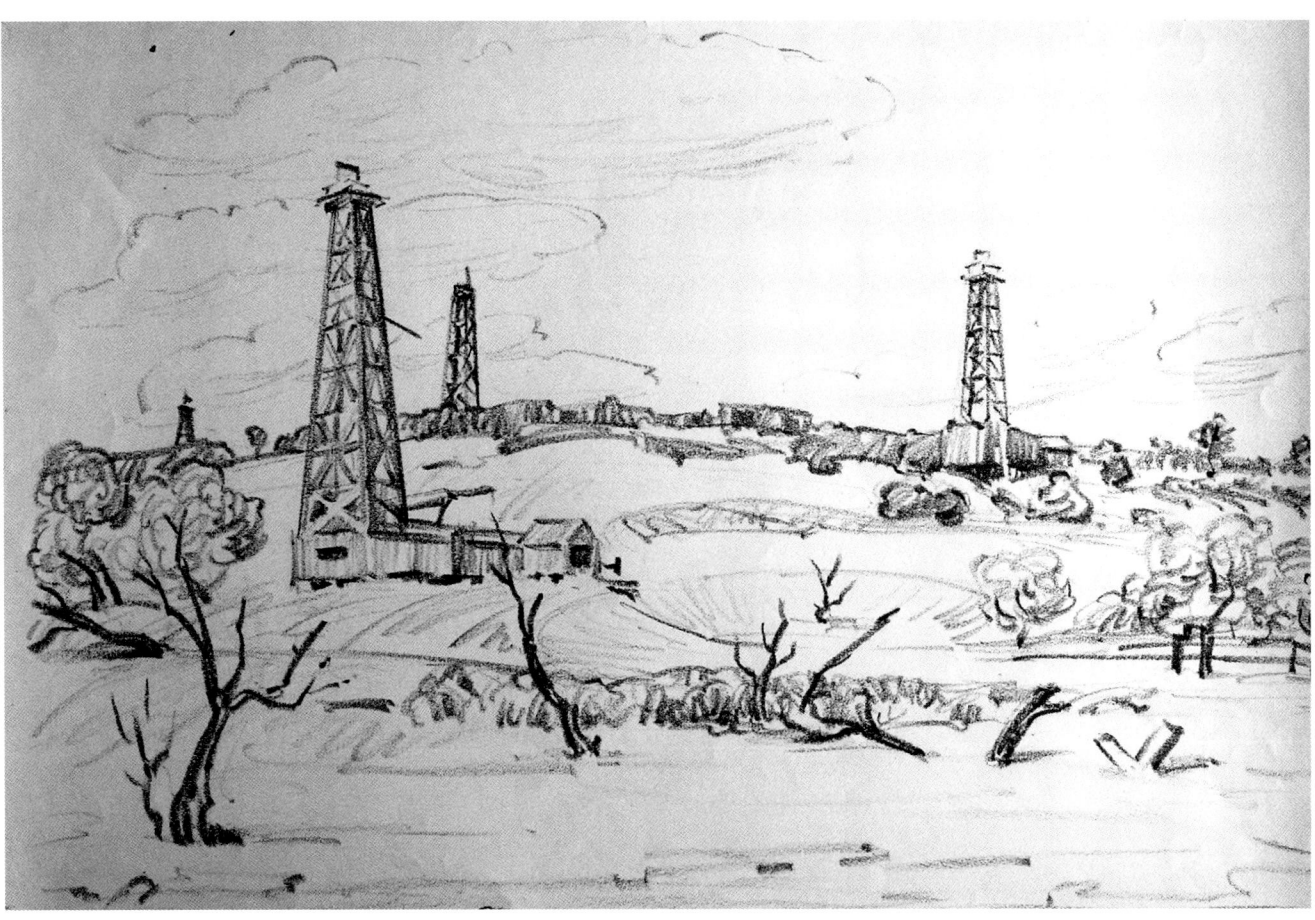

Untitled (West Texas discovery field), ca. 1930. Etching.

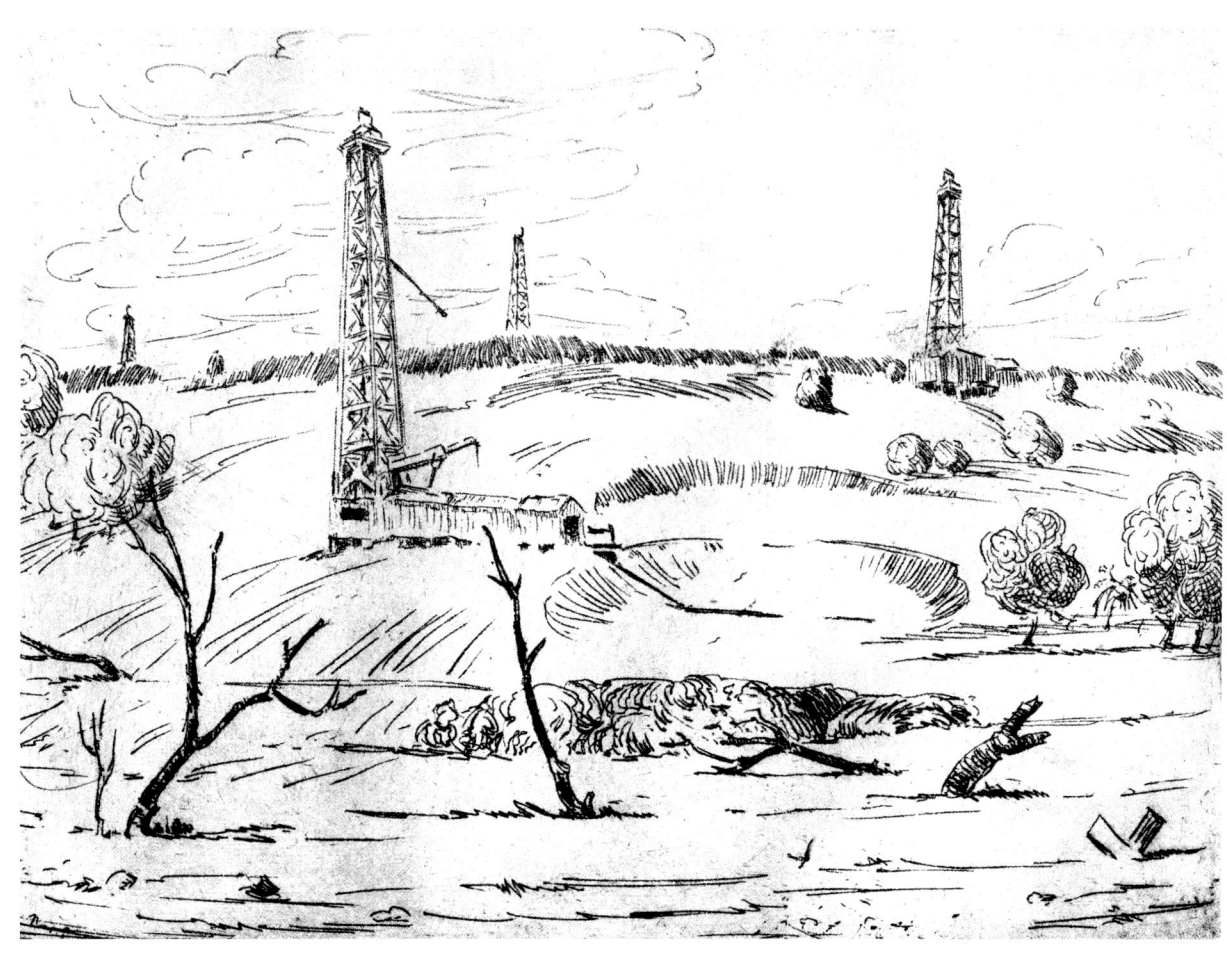

Untitled (West Texas oil derricks), n.d. (late 1920s). Lithograph.

Ziegler's earliest lithographs were inspired by the sights and sounds of oil production in Eastland County. It is likely that this scene was one of the first that he recorded.

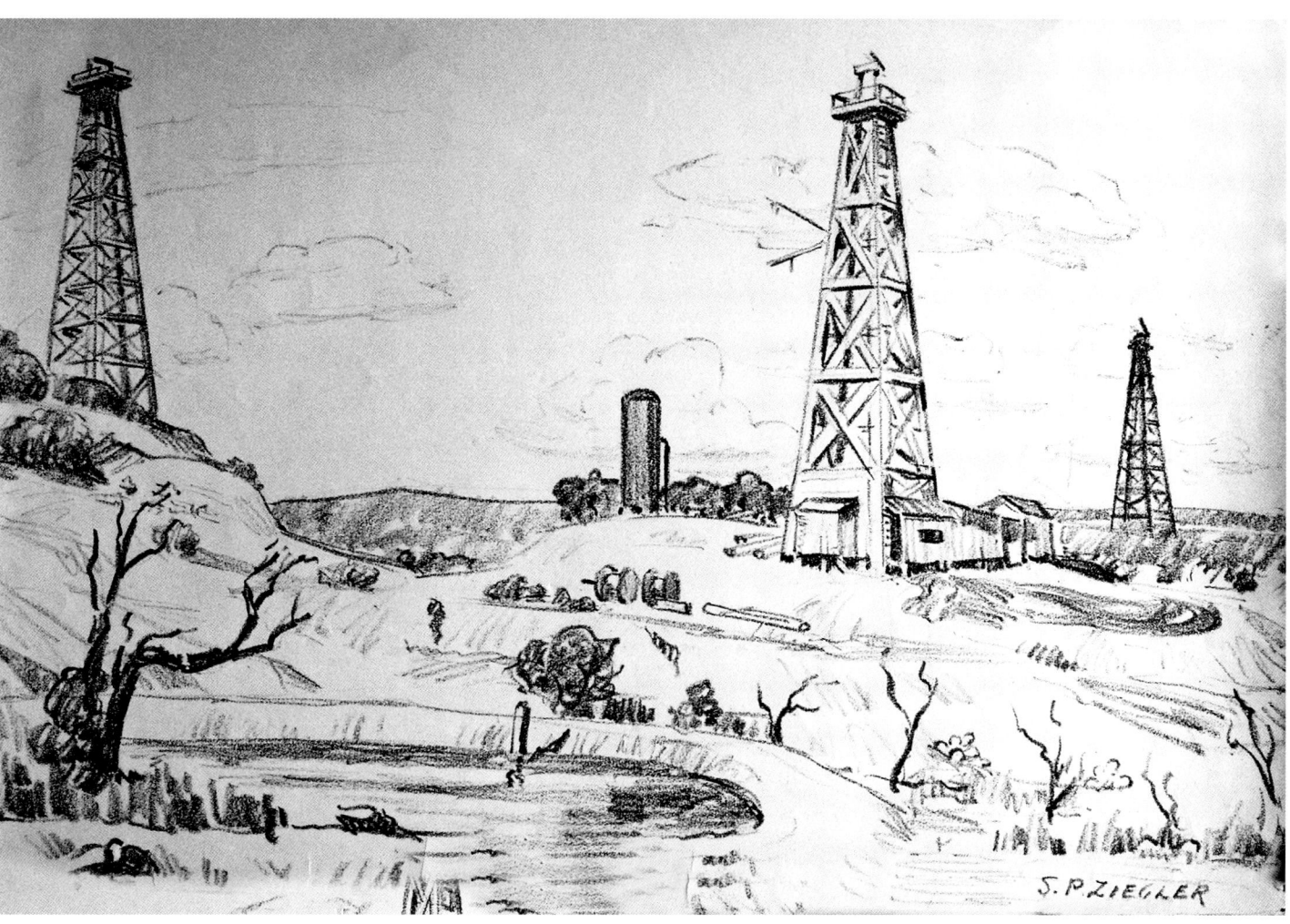

Burning the Slush Pit,
ca. 1930. Etching.

One of Ziegler's most dramatic oil
field images. Ziegler also produced
an oil painting of a similar scene.

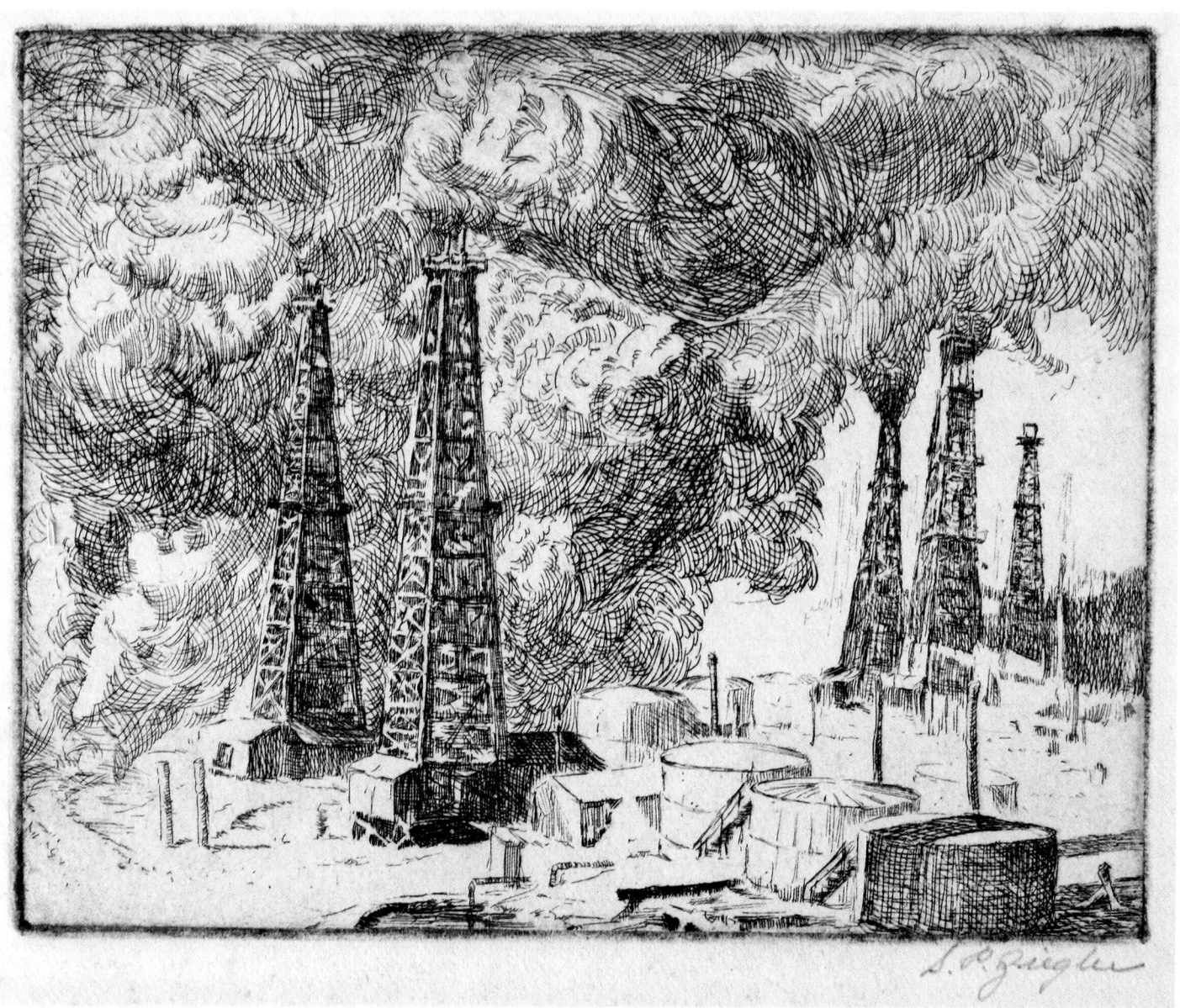

Oil Well Afire – Night*,*
ca. 1930. Etching.

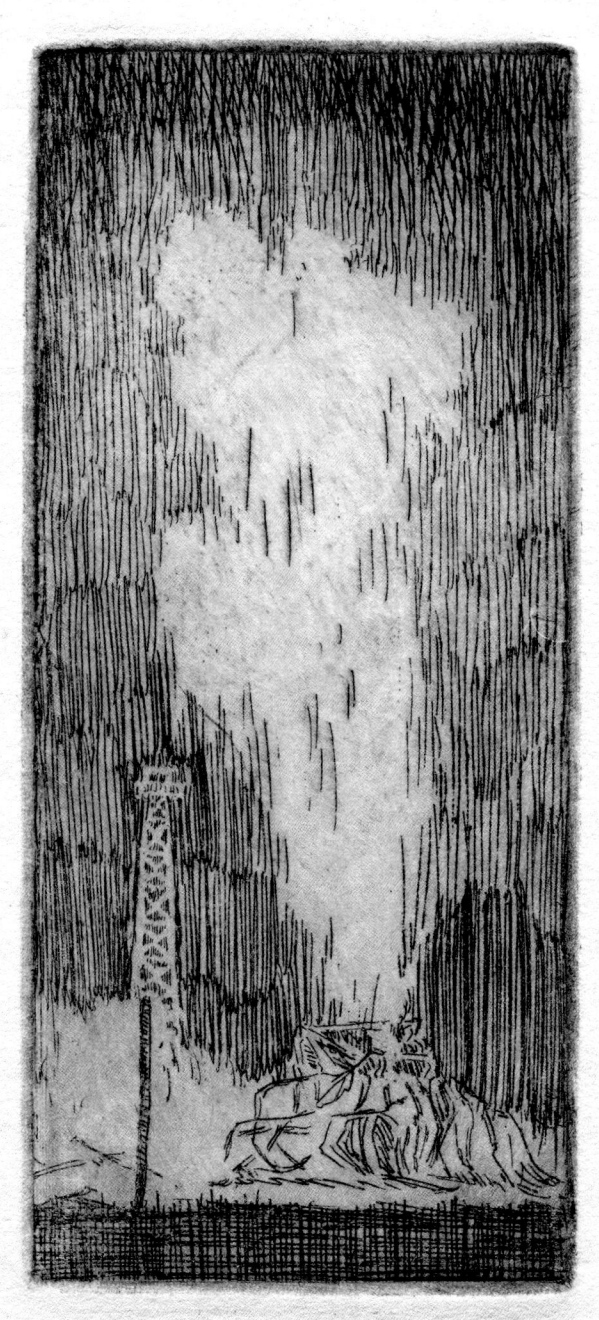

Setting the Casing, 1931.
 Etching.

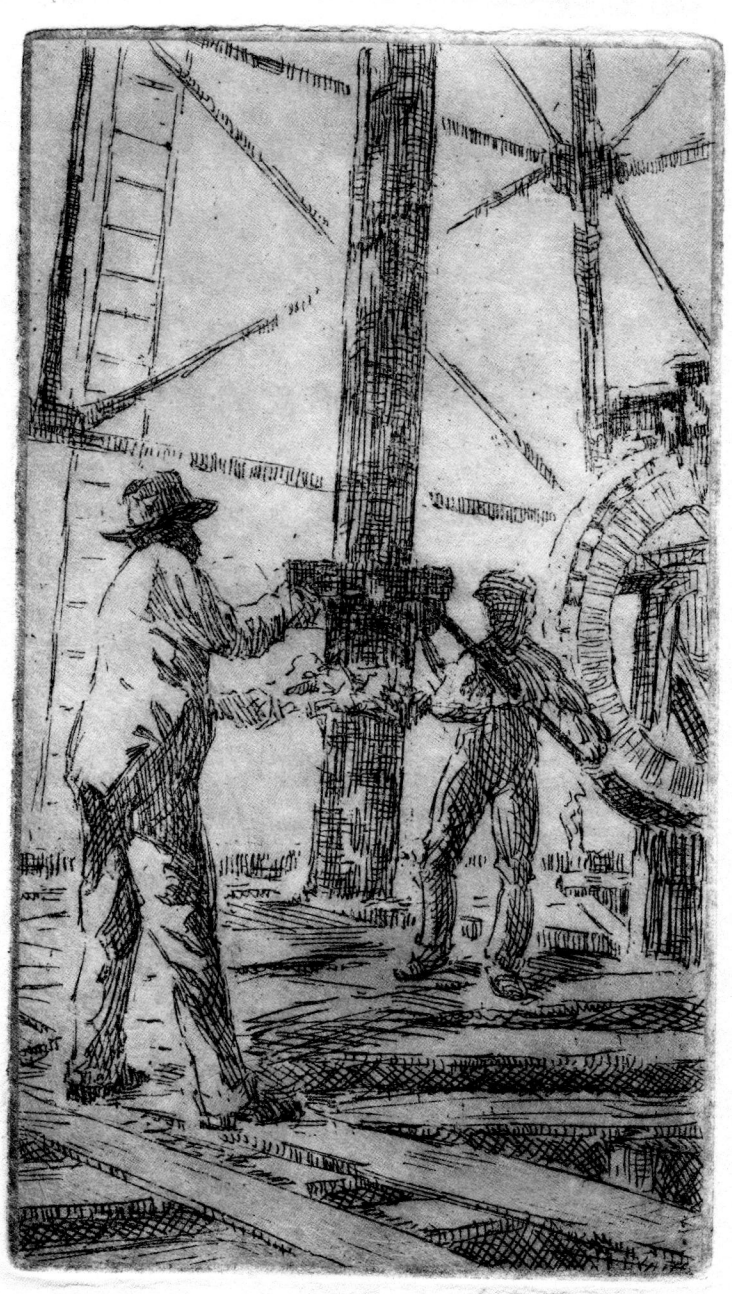

Inside the Derrick, 1930.
Etching.

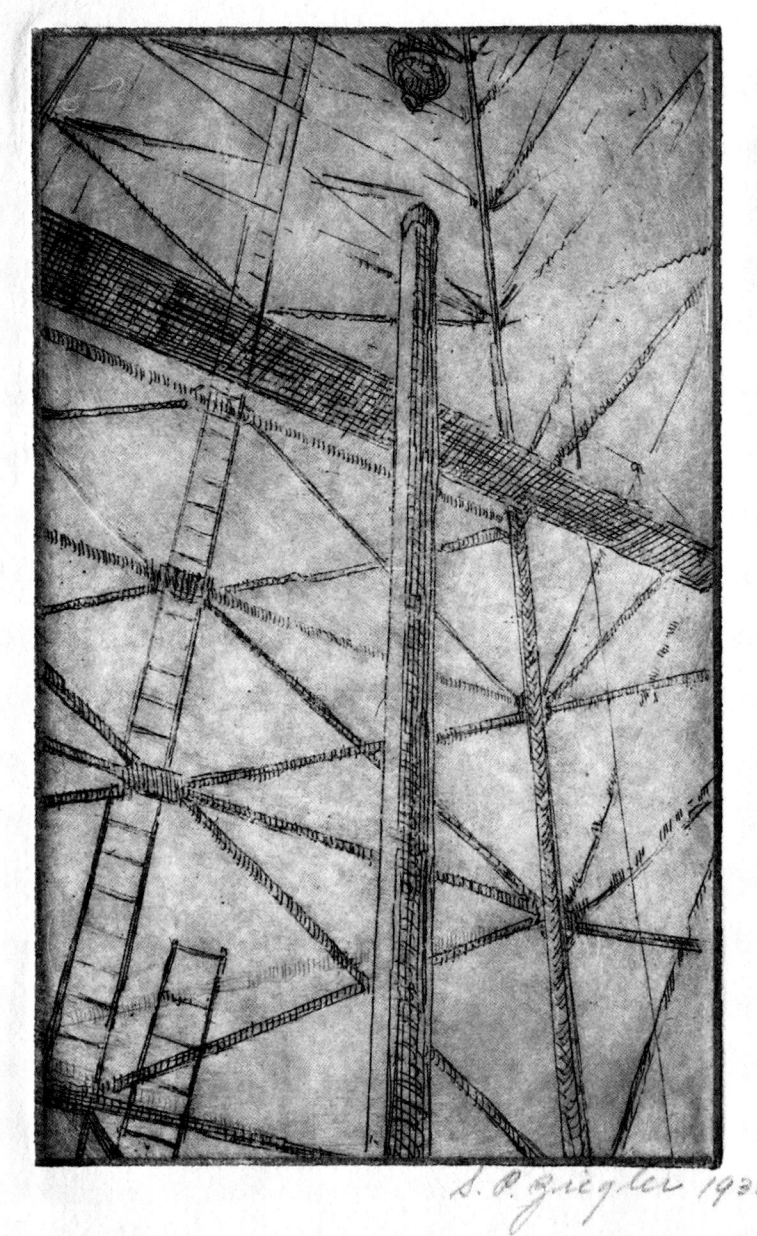

**A Shallow Willow, ca. 1930.
Etching.**

A fountain of crude oil spraying into the air evidently reminded Ziegler of the shape of a shallow-rooted willow tree growing along a riverbank, a sight he may have seen in his native Pennsylvania.

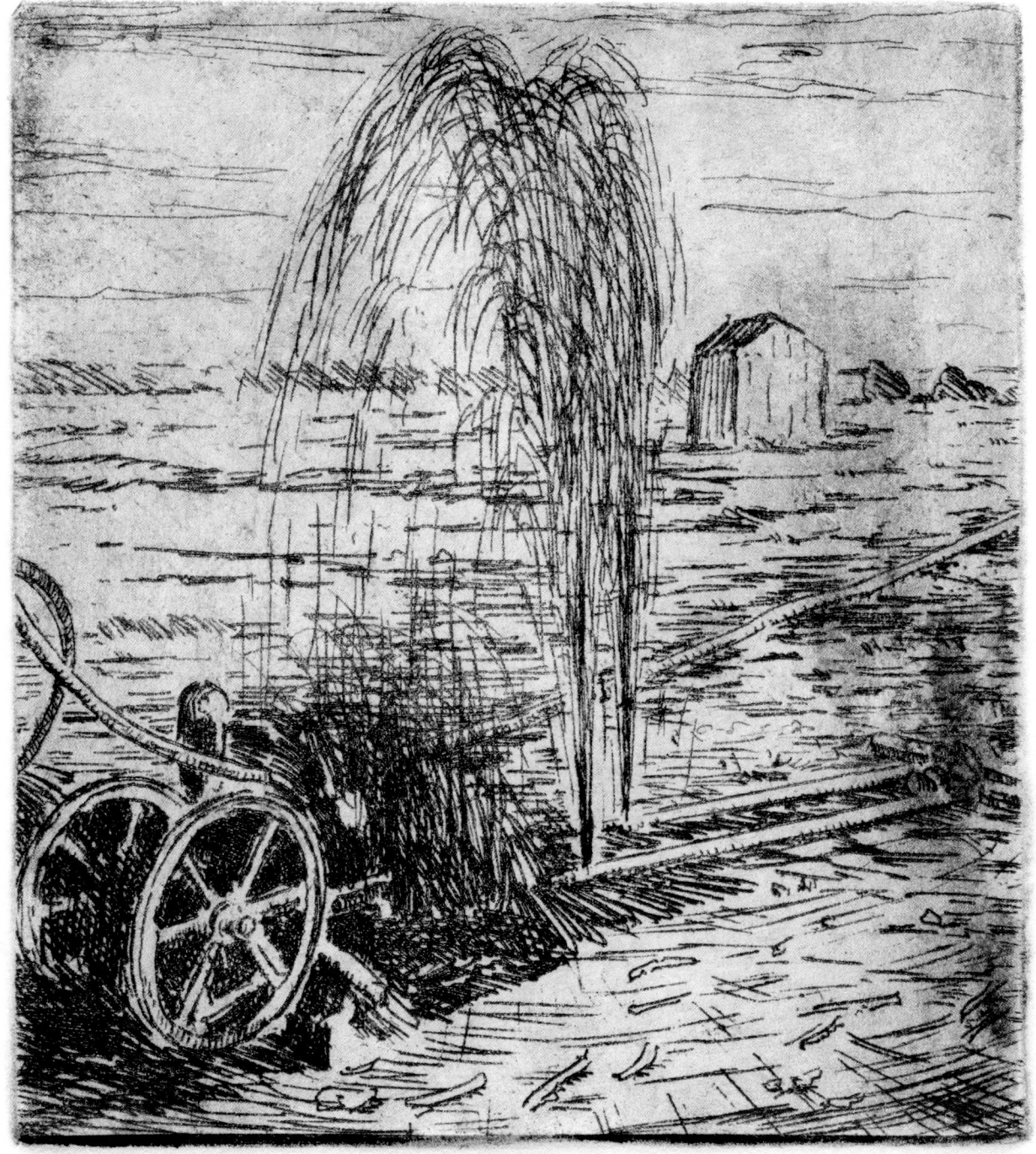

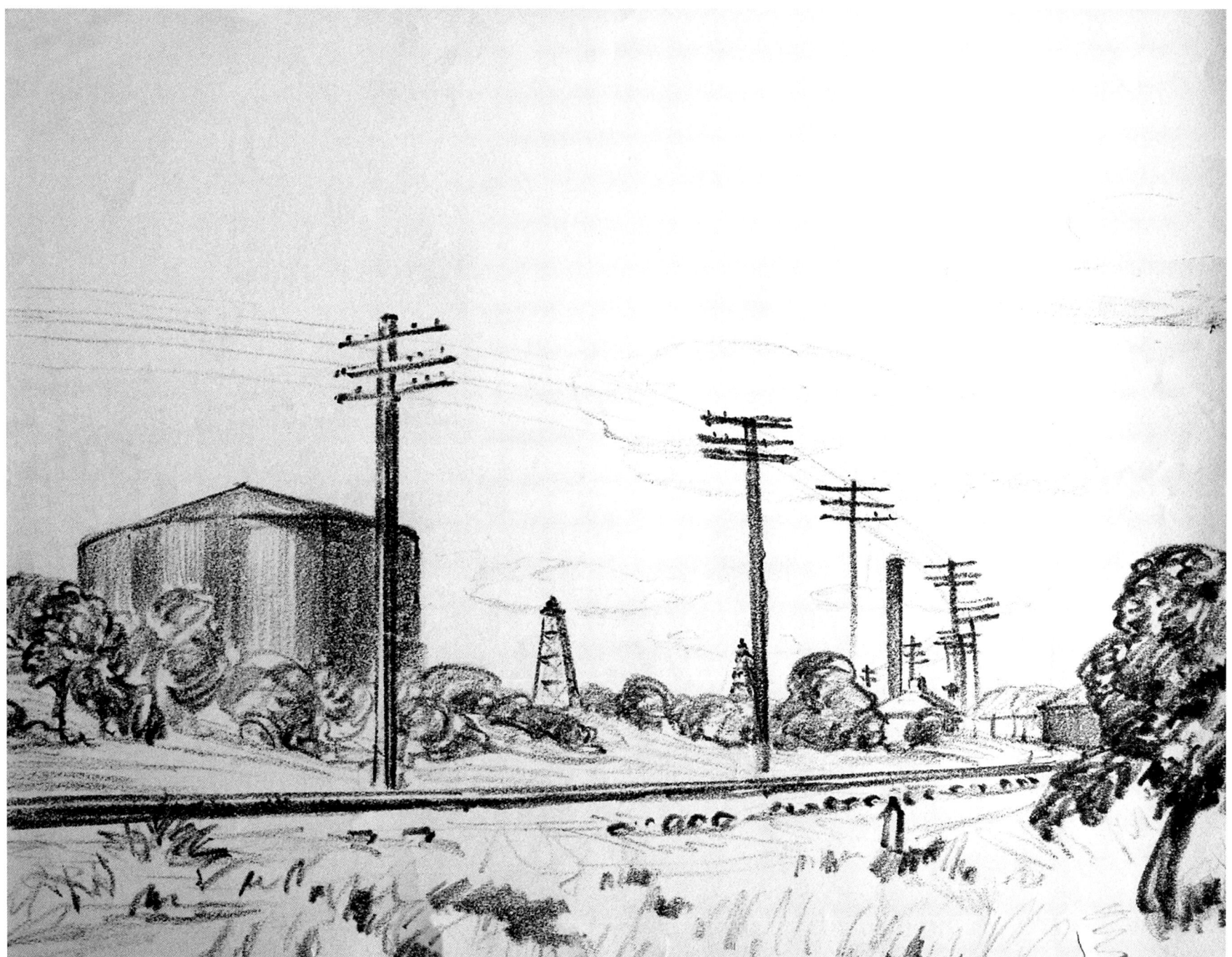

**Untitled (railroad tracks and storage tank),
n.d. (late 1920s). Lithograph.**

West Texas and New Mexico

Last of the Herd, n.d.
(early 1930s). Etching.

Seen on one of his West Texas sketching
trips, this small herd of American bison
represented for Ziegler the last chance to
study and admire this once-plentiful species.
Between 1875 and 1880, almost the entire
West Texas buffalo population fell victim
to hunters seeking hides for tanning.

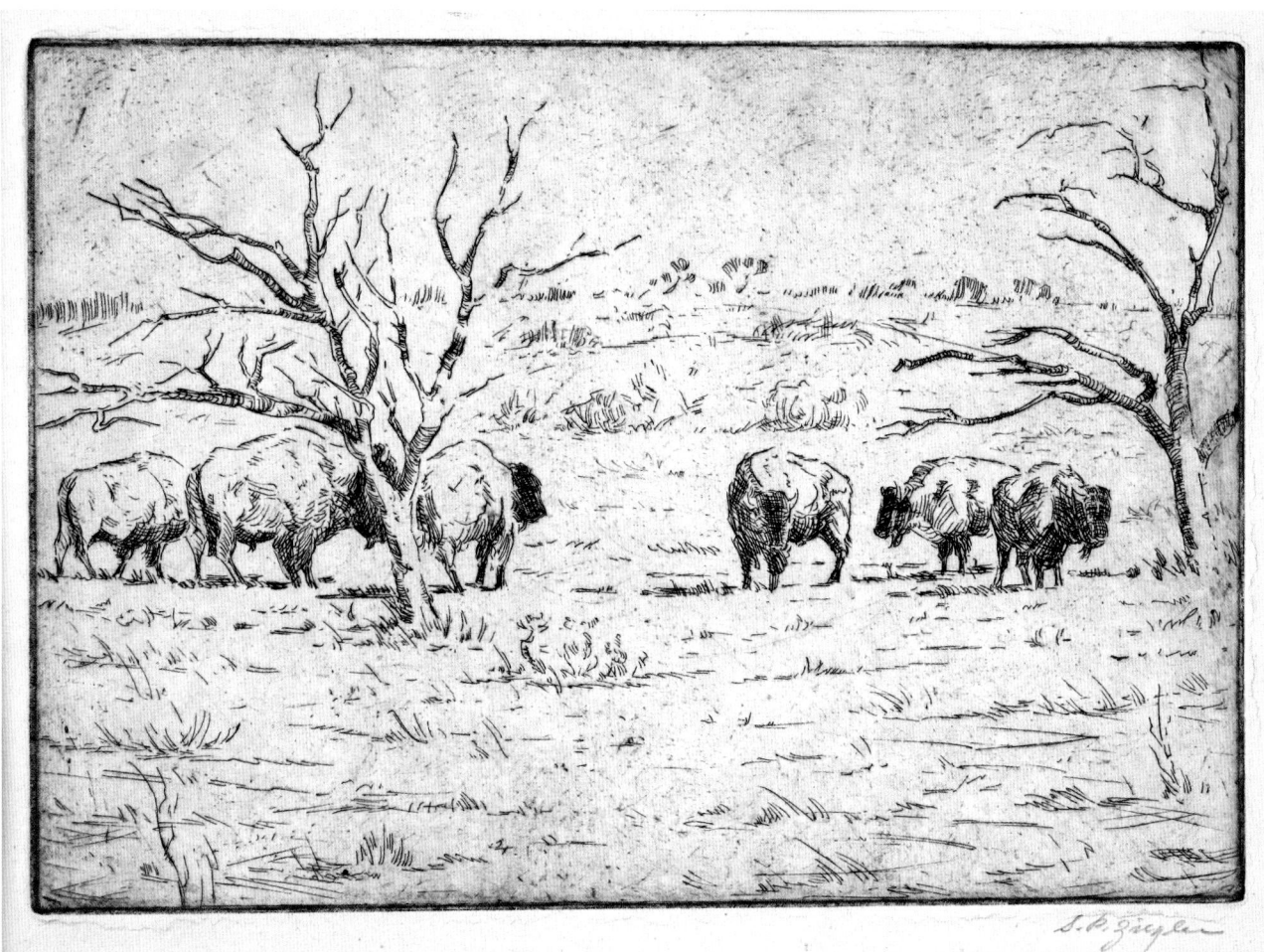

West Texas Ranch, 1932. Etching.

In 1927 Ziegler made the first of several summer pilgrimages into West Texas to study the oil industry and soon became interested in the landscape and lifestyles of people living in the rural areas. This print of a ranch house, windmill, and outbuildings was probably based on a sketch made during one such trip.

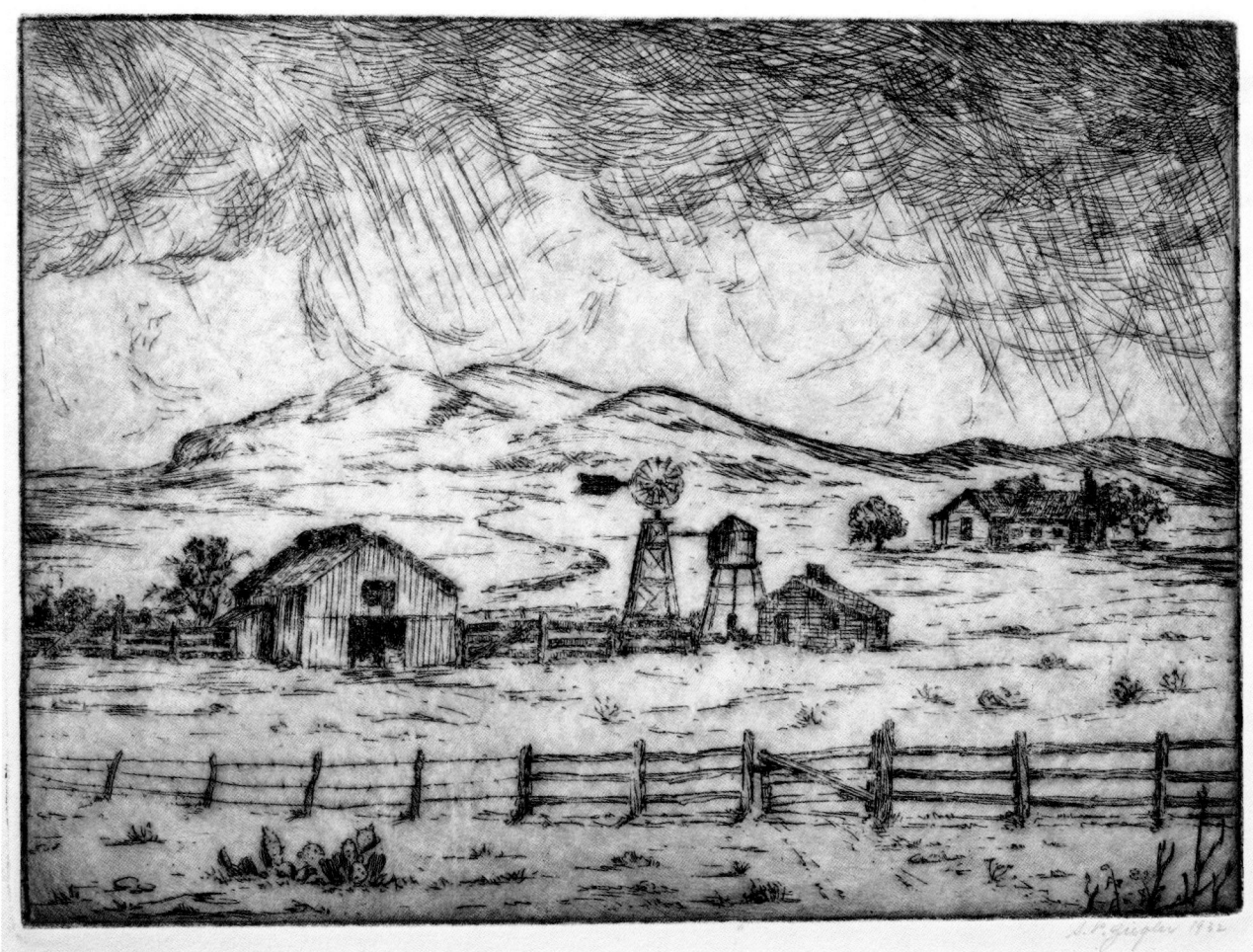

Bronco Buster, 1930. Etching.

In addition to this intaglio print, Ziegler produced at least one oil painting of a similar Texas scene, the iconic ritual of breaking a horse to the saddle. While studying ranch life he also observed cattle-branding scenes and captured them in etchings and oil paintings. His interest in ranching was a natural offshoot of his fascination with Texas.

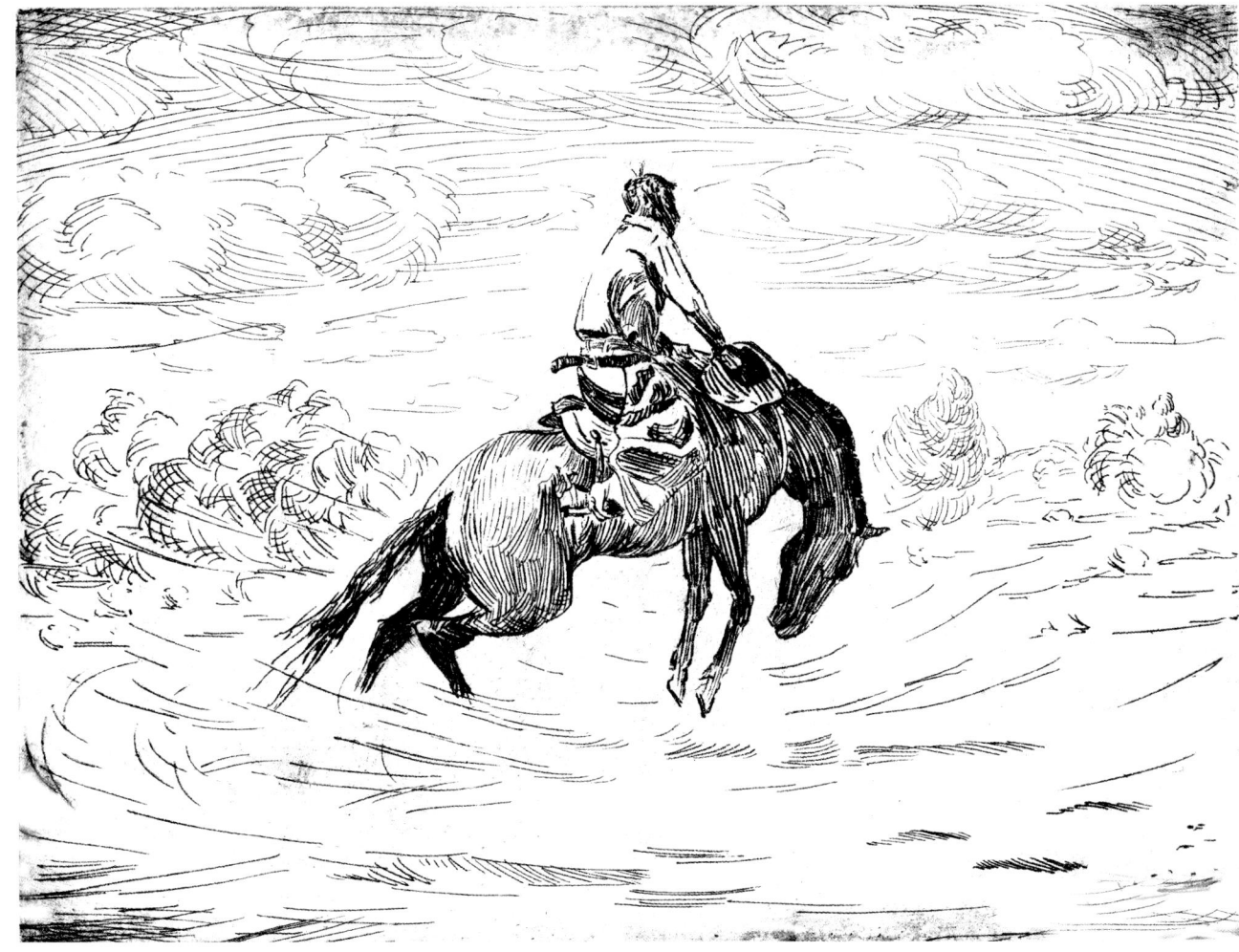

Cattle Grazing, 1931. Etching.

Untitled (branding the calves), ca. 1934. Etching.

Ziegler also produced an oil painting of this scene, signed and dated 1934.

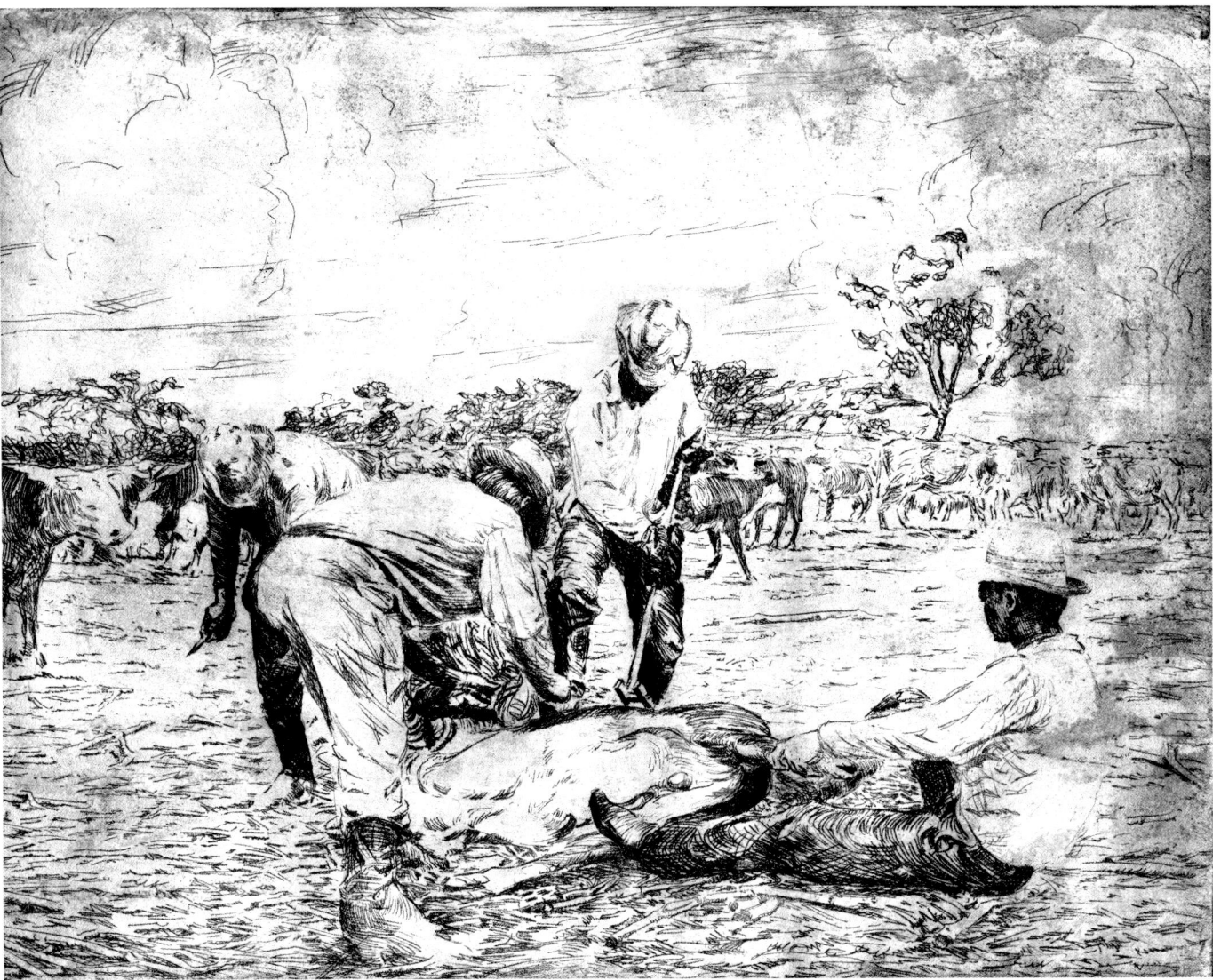

Four Gallon Hat, **n.d. (early 1930s). Etching.**

This etching's title refers to the official hat design chosen to celebrate the Fort Worth Golden Jubilee. The Jubilee event, held in November 1923, celebrated the fiftieth anniversary of Fort Worth's incorporation as a city and the seventy-fifth anniversary of Fort Worth's founding as a United States Army outpost. All male residents of Fort Worth were encouraged to buy these hats at Washer Brothers Clothiers and wear them during the four-day Golden Jubilee celebration. Using a friend for a model, Ziegler composed and painted a prize-winning painting of a cowboy wearing the Jubilee hat while rolling a cigarette. He originally called the painting *Rolling His Own*. Ziegler replicated the image in an intaglio print about 1930, when etchings became an important focus of his art.

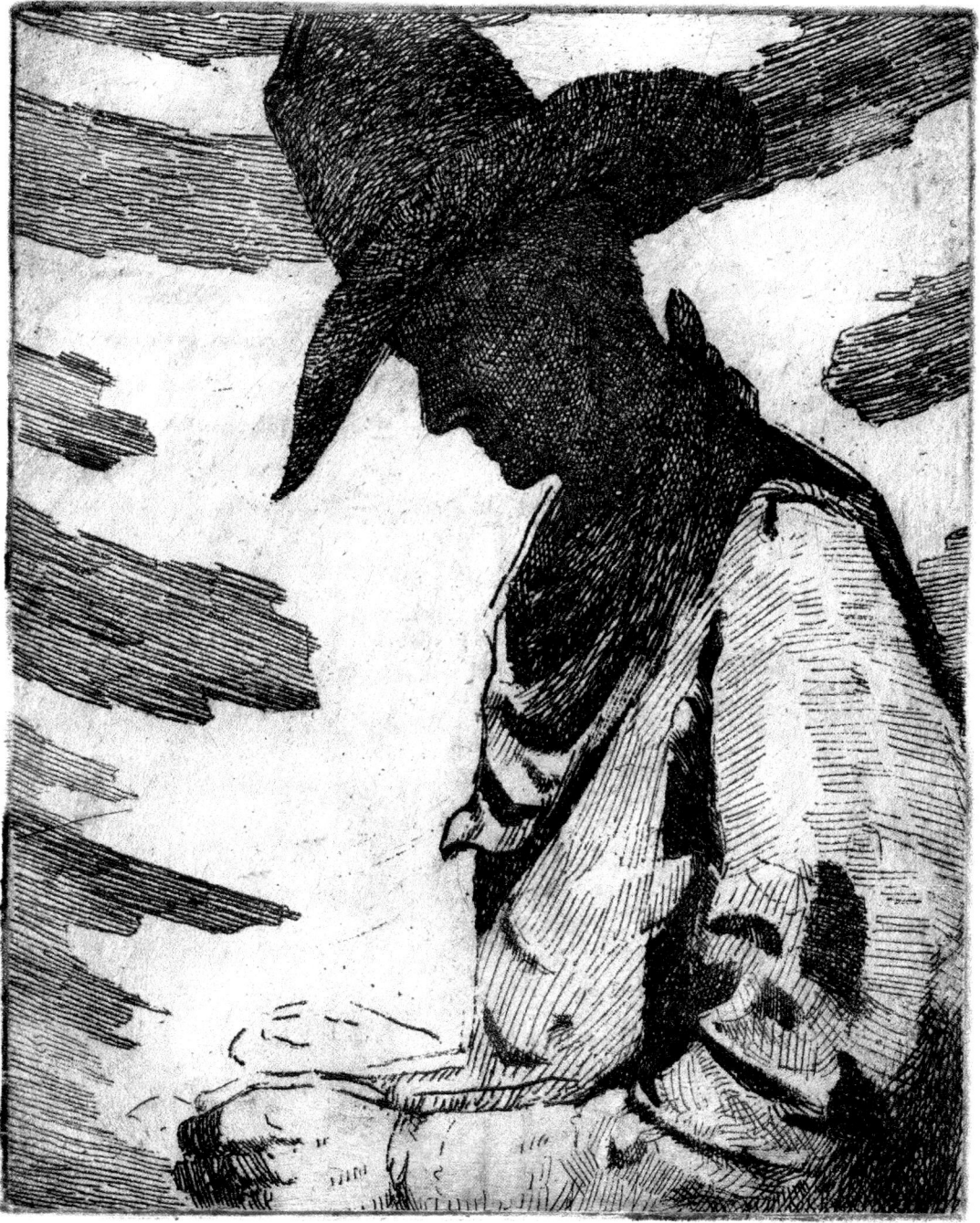

Sky – Lake Worth, n.d.
(early 1930s). Etching.

In the 1920s and 1930s, Lake Worth served as a popular painting and sketching spot for local artists who were attracted to interesting or secluded locations along the shoreline. Some of those locations had names like Inspiration Point, Mosque Point, and Casino Beach. In Ziegler's day the lake functioned as both a recreational reservoir and water supply for the city of Fort Worth.

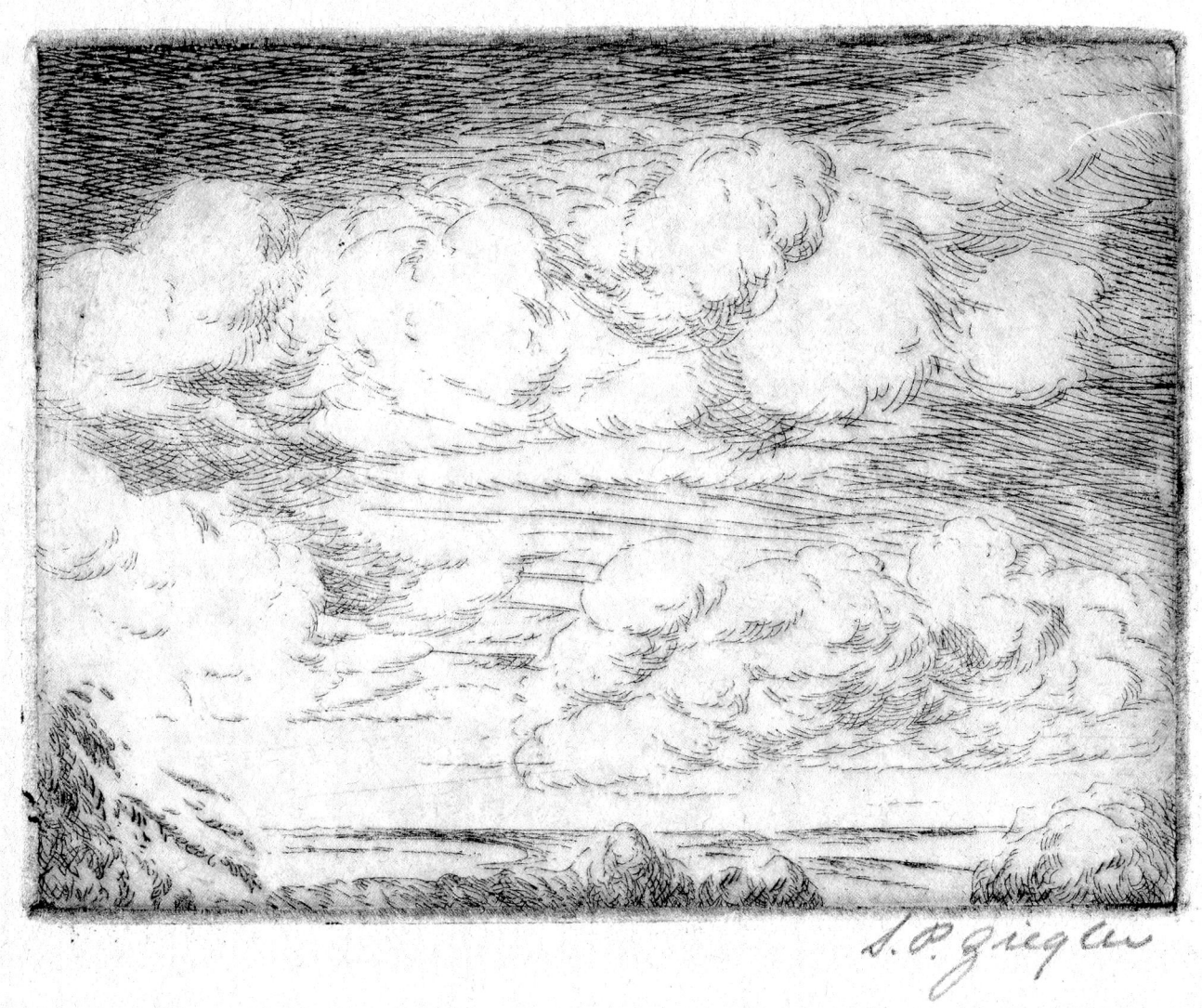

West Texas Sky, n.d. (early 1930s).
Etching.

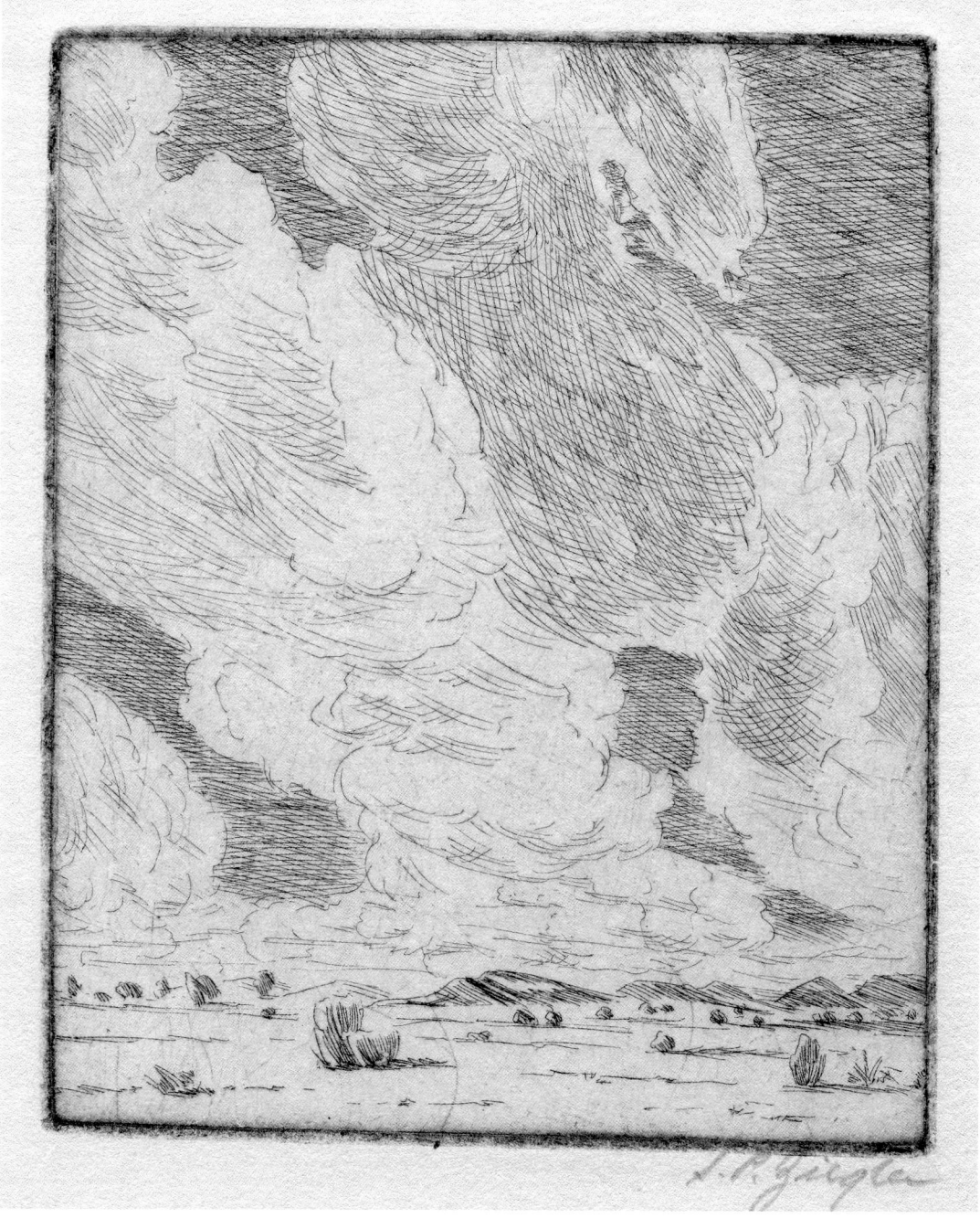

West Texas Yucca, n.d.
(early 1930s). Etching.

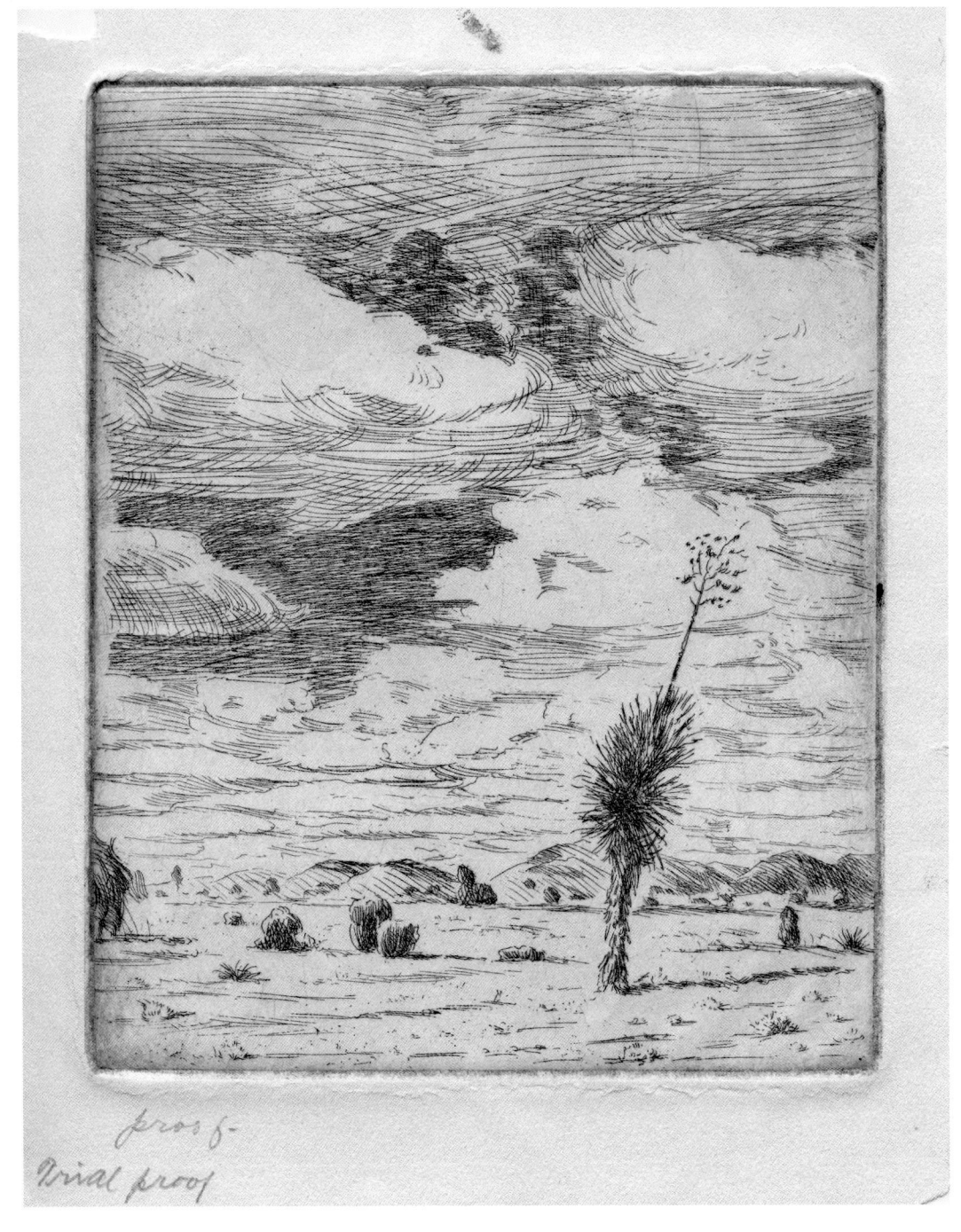

proof-
Trial proof

Untitled (mountains near Taos, New Mexico), n.d. (early 1930s). Etching.

Ziegler paid his first visit to Taos, New Mexico in 1925. He returned there once or twice more in succeeding years. Along with a number of sketches, several Ziegler oil paintings of the Taos area survive into the present day. Several of these paintings depict views of mountain ranges to the north and east of the town. The oldest of his known Taos paintings is dated 1925 and depicts an adobe house on a dirt street.

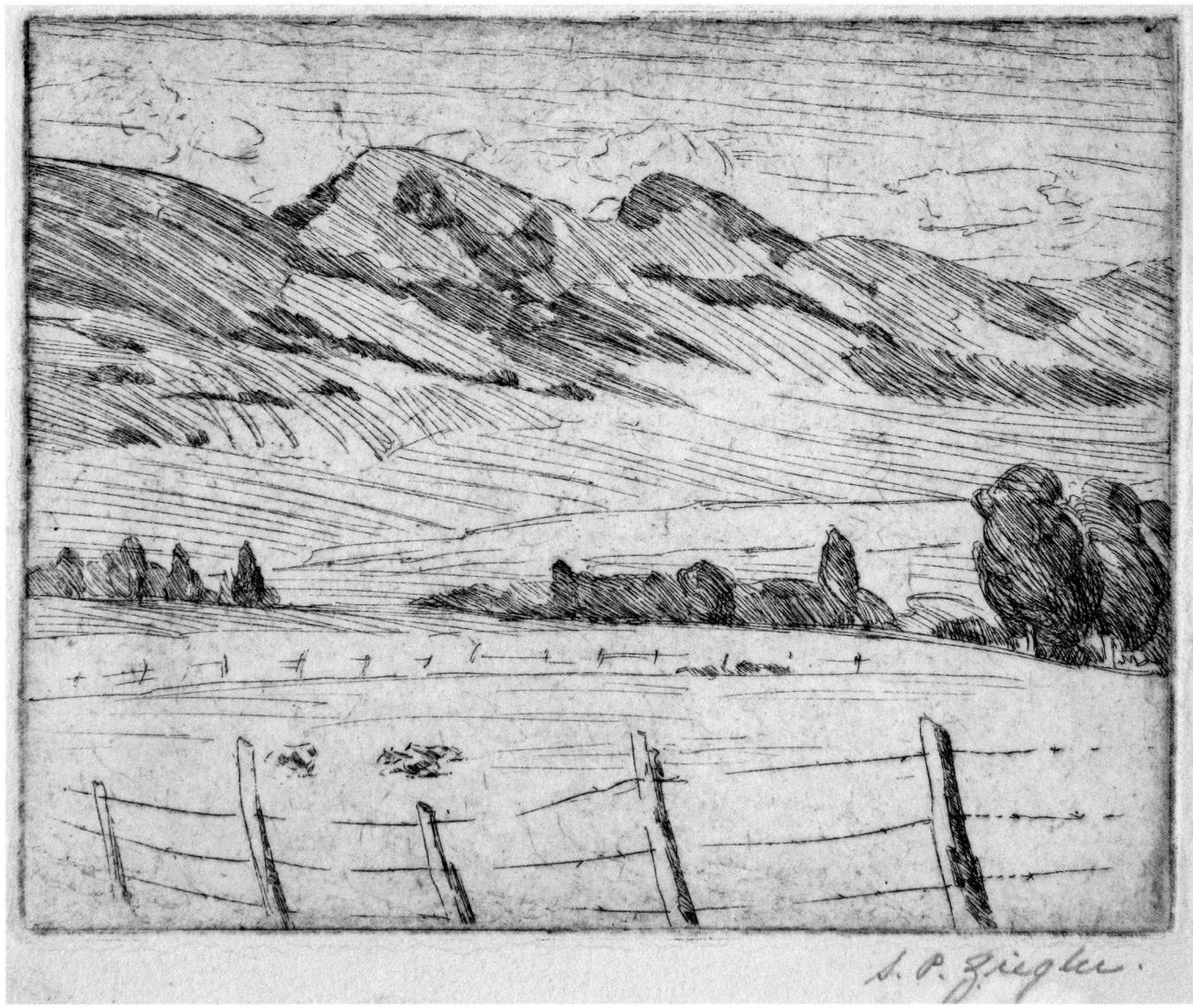

Bishop's Palace (Monterrey, Mexico), 1931. Etching.

In this print Ziegler depicted one of Monterrey, Mexico's most distinctive landmarks. Known as the Bishop's Palace, the stone building was constructed in 1789 and once served as the official residence of the regional Catholic bishop. During the Mexican-American War, the capture of the palace by American forces in September 1846 was a major step in the battle for control of Monterrey. In Ziegler's print the distinctive summit of Saddleback Mountain (Cerro de la Silla) is visible in the distance. It is not known whether Ziegler's print was based on firsthand observation or on some other source.

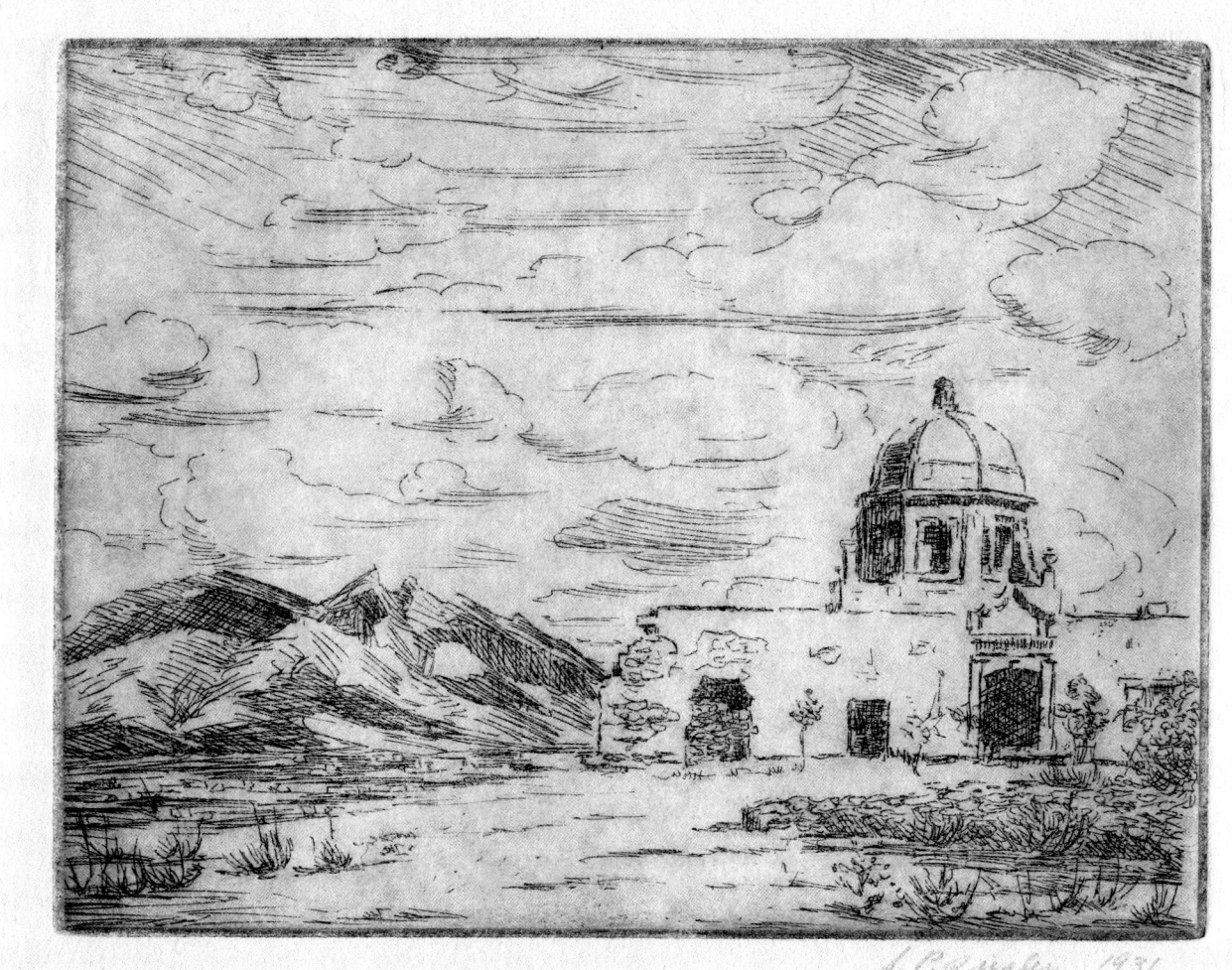

Untitled (Taos Pueblo), n.d. Etching.

This image of Taos Pueblo may be based on sketches produced as early as 1925, the year of Ziegler's first visit to New Mexico.

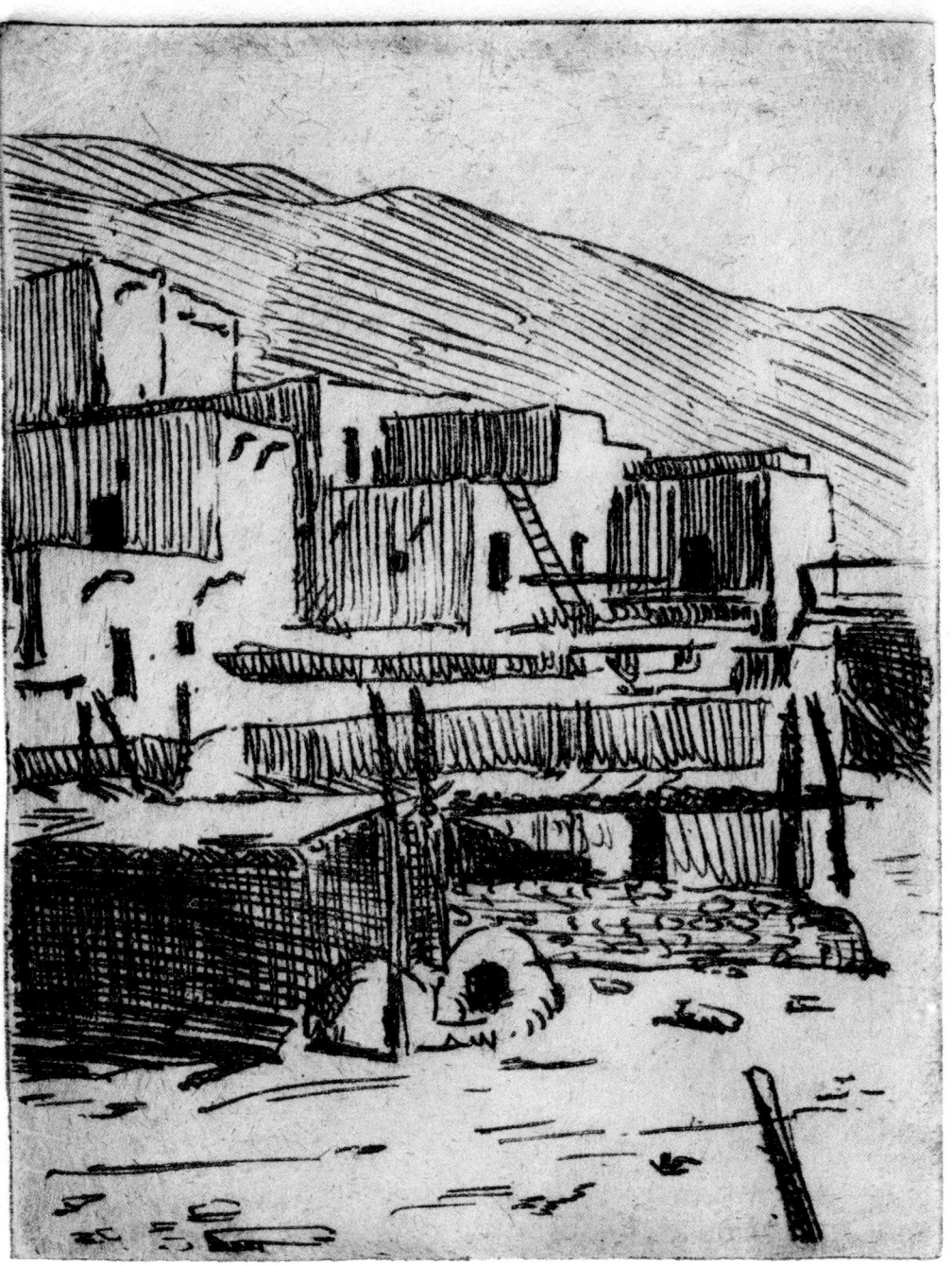

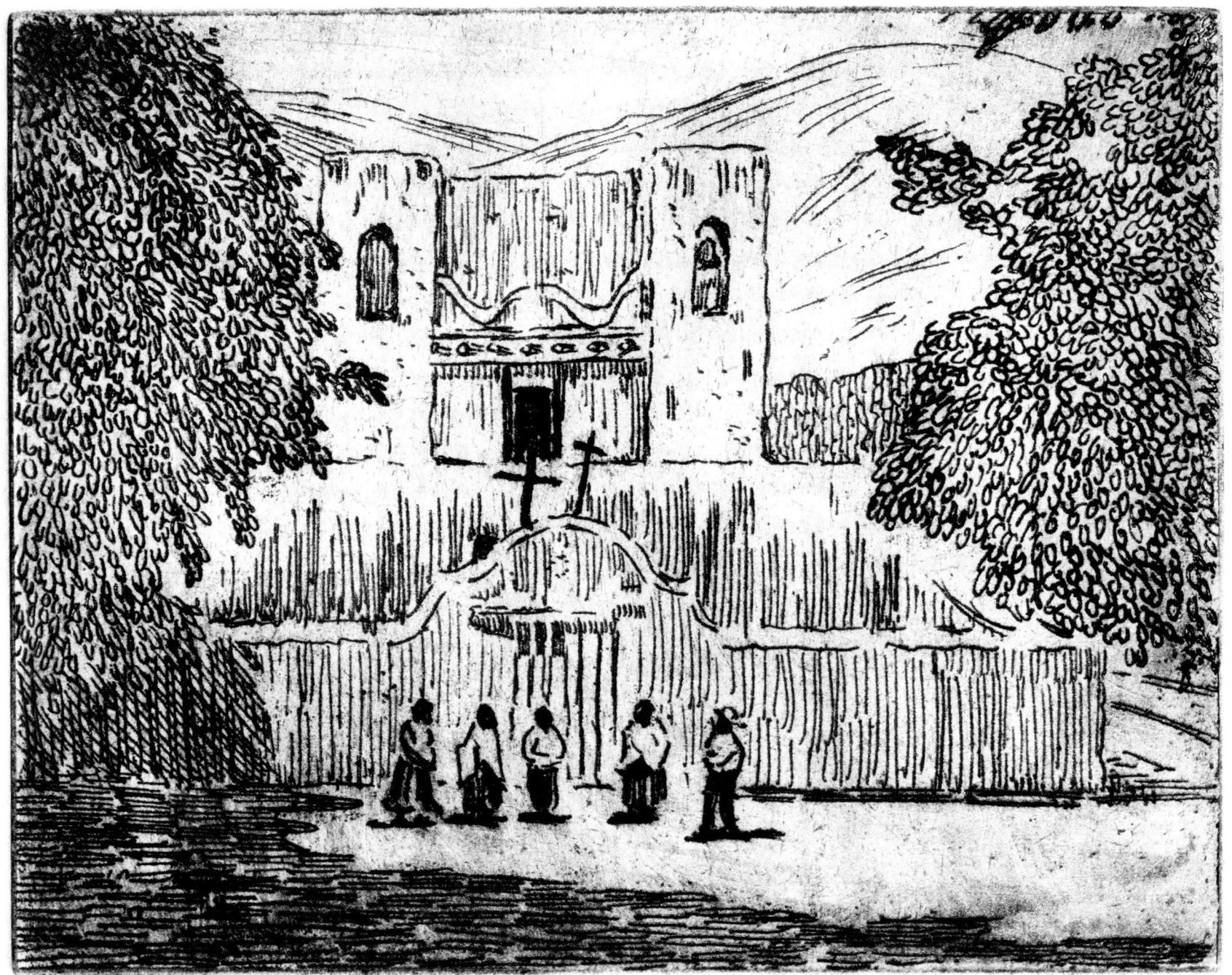

***El Santuario de Chimayó*, n.d. Etching.**

This etching of the adobe Catholic church in Chimayó, New Mexico, may be based on sketches produced as early as 1925, the year of Ziegler's first visit to the Santa Fe and Taos area. His print depicts the church's bell towers in their original configuration, prior to the addition of pitched metal roofing

Artwork Index

Subject Index